Contemporary
Social Welfare

WINIFRED BELL
EMERITUS, CLEVELAND STATE UNIVERSITY

Contemporary Social Welfare

MACMILLAN PUBLISHING COMPANY
NEW YORK
COLLIER MACMILLAN PUBLISHERS
LONDON

To the memory of my parents,
RUPERT AUGUSTUS BELL and ELIZABETH MARY BELL,
for their sense of fair play, inquiring minds,
and good humor.

Macmillan Publishing Company
866 Third Avenue, New York, New York 10022

Collier Macmillan Canada, Inc.

Library of Congress Cataloging-in-Publication Data

Bell, Winifred.
  Contemporary social welfare.

  Includes bibliographies and index.
    1. Public welfare — United States.   2. United States —
Social policy.   I. Title.
HV95.B44   1987   361'.973   86–14716
ISBN 0-02-307941-X

Printing: 1 2 3 4 5 6 7   Year: 7 8 9 0 1 2 3

ISBN 0-02-307941-X

Preface to the Second Edition

Although the format and central themes of this text are unchanged, statistical and program data are updated throughout, discussions are sometimes compressed to allow space for new and emerging issues, and specific federal policy changes are incorporated in appropriate chapters.

I greatly appreciate the several hundred communications from students and faculty members in response to the first edition. A few asked that certain subjects be clarified or expanded, and I have tried to do so. Many more expressed the wish for my recommendations for reform. Although I have included in the final chapter a few changes in income maintenance and social service programs that I have long favored, what I wish to convey most are my new reasons for hope that we can move together as a society to reverse the long decline in the U.S. economy, which has contributed so significantly to the current polarization, tensions, and loss of a sense of community. In recent years some very thoughtful, progressive, and highly regarded economists have been busily developing reform proposals aimed at helping us to recapture the American dream. I hope that my brief sketch of their message will stimulate more careful study of their ideas and that these ideas will prove as cheering and clarifying as they have for me.

A few suggestions made by readers of the first edition, I found, did not fit my concept of the book or my judgment regarding priorities. In such instances, far more people who communicated with me agreed with my decisions. The result is that Owen's theories are still discussed, and Marxian theory and various "schools" or perspectives on social work practice are not. However, although I could not comply with all suggestions, I greatly appreciate the thoughtful responses to the first edition.

Columbia, Maryland   WINIFRED BELL

Preface to the First Edition

This book has been written out of a deep and long-standing conviction that very stormy weather is ahead for social welfare unless both citizens and future social welfare professionals better understand its role and significance in modern societies and become better prepared to sort out the ideological, political, and economic issues that threaten to control its destiny. Although a considerable hiatus has probably separated social welfare decision makers from average citizens for years, since the early 1970s I have been certain that until the gap is bridged there can be no genuine, lasting social welfare reform.

Two experiences dramatized this for me. In the summer of 1968, I was urged to work with the Model Cities staff in Gary, Indiana, in designing the nation's first family allowance experiment. I was assured by Washington officials that the groundwork was all laid, that Gary residents and leaders were eager to launch the experiment as quickly as possible, and that my role was simply to commit their ideas to paper in the form of an approvable proposal. But during my first weeks in Gary, I found only two people — a social work professor and a graduate student from the University of Chicago — who gave clear evidence of knowing what a family allowance was. Importantly placed leaders did not even realize that what Washington had in mind was a three-year experiment, not a long-term program, and that if the schedule was kept the experiment would end just before the next mayoralty election. As for Gary's target area residents in that decade of "maximum feasible participation," they had not been consulted, had never heard of family allowances, and were outspokenly resentful of their "rubber stamp" role.

My decision to spend the summer educating the various interest groups so that they could make informed decisions was not well received in some

Washington circles, although it later occasioned enthusiastic applause in others. But at least there was the satisfaction, two and a half months later, of realizing that not only local leaders but some target area residents, including a nice sprinkling of former and current AFDC* mothers, could probably surpass some professional social workers in differentiating among income strategies and weighing the issues involved in choosing among them.

Then in the early 1970s the Nixon Administration tried to promote a negative income tax, and later Senator George McGovern proposed a yearly subsidy of $1,000 for every American. And for several years, policy experts debated such esoteric matters as "notch" problems, "break-even points," income disregards, marginal tax rates, refundable tax credits, boundary problems between positive and negative taxes, and work incentives that somehow boomeranged to become strong work disincentives, while average citizens wondered what on earth politicians were trying to sell them and why hard-working people would be expected to support even larger "giveaway" programs. The two parties, the policy makers and the public, might as well have been on different planets for all the meaningful communication they achieved in those years.

Believing by then that citizen education was a mission of overriding importance for social work educators, I decided to shift from graduate to undergraduate teaching and from the liberal Northeast to a more conservative region. Cleveland State University, with an attractive undergraduate social services program and a course in contemporary social welfare that attracted thousands of students yearly, provided the opportunity I was seeking. But when I began teaching, I could find no textbook that met my needs. I was looking for a book that satisfied the following criteria:

- Because I felt a comparative approach held the greatest promise of expanding student horizons and developing a critical faculty, I wanted a text that would set American social welfare in international perspective, and then would compare contrasting theories, organizing principles, ideologies, social welfare strategies, financing methods, and impacts.
- Because social welfare issues are never decided in a vacuum, I wanted a text that would make connections between current issues and ideological, historical, economic, and political forces that inevitably determine the outcome at any given time.
- Because modern scholars are so aware of the dual functions of social welfare — control and assistance — and of the societal ambivalence that pervades public policy in this area, I wanted a text that would sensitize students to both manifest and latent consequences, would call attention

*Aid to Families with Dependent Children.

to unanticipated consequences, and would possibly help them to cope better with their own ambivalence.

- Because many widespread misconceptions about poverty and social welfare provisions reflect the scarcity of sound, factual, systematic public education in this highly politicized area, I wanted a text that would analyze at least major research findings and programs in reasonable depth. In the process, I believed that a text should guide students to the best literature on the subject, whether in the domain of economics, political science, sociology, anthropology, demography, or social welfare.
- Because the cost of social welfare had become *the* issue by the late 1970s, I wanted a text that would directly discuss mushrooming social welfare costs, place them in realistic and comprehensible perspective, and deal explicitly with contrasting views on the subject.
- Because work is so central to life and the inability to find steady, decently paid jobs has such profound and lasting impact on personal well-being, family stability, and the cost of social welfare, I wanted a text that would highlight this problem and keep reform priorities in reasonable perspective, rather than focusing solely on more traditional social welfare or social work problems and programs. This is especially important because I believe that the harm done successive generations of youth by failing to provide enough jobs to go around is the single greatest tragedy and danger in the American scene. I also believe that all professions, but especially social work, must adapt their services to provide more and better help to the unemployed and underemployed.
- Finally, because so many Americans seem to believe that ending poverty is a hopeless mission, I wanted a text that proposed solutions but left the options open for readers to think about and discuss.

In this book I have attempted to meet these criteria. I believe that it is appropriate for introductory courses at both the undergraduate and graduate levels. This text is policy-oriented, not practice-oriented, and makes no pretence of covering the subject of contemporary social welfare exhaustively. In fact, concentrating on issues, societal context, and comparative analysis seemed more important than "covering the waterfront." This book aims instead to instill systematic habits of analysis and inquiry, to increase the readers' awareness of their own biases and misconceptions, and to train them to ground their analysis on hard facts or the best informed judgments available. This last point should be emphasized. My teaching experience has led me to believe that students are hungry for facts when facts are organized conceptually. Also, for the teacher, laying an analytic, theoretical, and factual foundation has the virtue of raising the level of classroom discourse above that usually achieved by relying on descriptive or anecdotal texts.

I am indebted to a host of people who have contributed directly or indirectly to this effort, including generous colleagues from my early days in social work to the present and a legion of fine scholars whom I have come to know personally or through their insightful writings. Many current colleagues and hundreds of students at Cleveland State University have read and commented on early drafts. A few deserve special acknowledgment, including Paul and Sonia Abels, Sarah Austin, William Barker, Richard Cloward, Marian Wright Edelman, Margaret Emery, Helen Ginsburg, Vicki Knight, Edward McKinney, Robert Morris, James Peterson, Sam Richmond, Dorothy Thorne, and Borge Varmer. Finally, I wish to thank Ira Arlook, originally scheduled to co-author this book, whose commitment to the Ohio Public Interest Campaign eventually had to take precedence. He left a valuable legacy of ideas and information that eased my work on Chapter 5.

Shaker Heights, Ohio   WINIFRED BELL

Contents

List of Tables

CHAPTER 1

An Overview of Social Welfare

Social welfare is steeped in controversy and contradiction. People disagree about its goals, methods, and consequences. What some perceive as a bloated "welfare state," others view as disgracefully inadequate compensation for continuing social and economic injustice. Programs that impress some citizens as reflections of the finest humanitarian values, others dismiss as cop outs or thinly disguised agents of social control. Services that some groups believe hold promise of curing, restoring, and rehabilitating, others see as warehouses of misery, the graveyard of hope.

Endless contradictions within the social welfare system add fuel to the fire. Services to protect children from parental neglect all too often come to symbolize community neglect. Financial support is provided for some but not all poor households, and is rarely sufficient for any. While we claim to honor senior citizens, large numbers of them are consigned to nursing homes where even elementary physical care is wanting. We build huge housing complexes with little, if any, protection for life or limb. We tie many benefits to the willingness to work, but never provide enough jobs, let alone sufficient supportive services for working parents. We subscribe to democratic values but seldom permit service users to share in planning or evaluating service programs.

These contradictions are not unique to social welfare. Nor are they mere accidents or oversights inherited from a less logical past. They are predictable, patterned responses to the value conflicts in American society. Our social welfare system is blinded by the same hidden assumptions and influenced by the same conflicting ideologies that touch us every day of our lives. It is firmly grounded in our economic, political, and social context and can be understood only in that context.

The important question is: Should social welfare simply reflect or at best somewhat compensate for societal imperfections? Or does it have a responsibility for striving toward social justice and equity? If the former role is sufficient, the mere existence of a network of benefits and services, however inadequate, irrational, or maldistributed, may bring a sense of accomplishment. But if the latter is paramount, then social welfare must be judged against standards of equity and social justice and by its success in translating humanitarian values into living realities.

What Is Social Welfare? _____

One of the more frequently cited definitions of social welfare was developed by Elizabeth Wickenden after she reviewed worldwide literature on the subject:

> Social welfare includes those laws, programs, benefits, and services which assure or strengthen provisions for meeting social needs recognized as basic to the well-being of the population and the better functioning of the social order. (47)

This embraces a long list of income maintenance benefits and educational, developmental, medical, rehabilitative, urban renewal, housing, vocational, recreational, protective, and counseling services.

Social welfare programs provide direct services to individuals, groups, and neighborhoods. They serve people of all ages. They are organized by all levels of government and under voluntary auspices. They are administered by many federal, state, and local agencies. They include community-based and institutional services. Some are national and regional in scope; many are concentrated in large cities. Directly and indirectly, they affect every citizen in the nation.

Social Welfare Serves All Income Classes _____

Perhaps the most frequent misconception about social welfare is that it serves only the poor. Nothing could be further from the truth. Around the world, as nations grow in complexity, people have recognized that collective efforts are necessary to satisfy social needs and to resolve social problems. In preindustrialized societies, the initial focus is often on public health measures and education. Income maintenance programs tend to appear early on the agenda, too. By 1983, 130 nations had social security systems to assure minimum income when workers retire, become disabled, or die, while 136 had workers' compensation plans providing medical care and cash benefits for work-related illnesses or accidents. Eighty-five nations had short-term sickness and maternity insurance, and forty insured workers in the event of involuntary unemployment (39).

When provisions spread benefits over all income classes, they are known as *universal* programs. When they are designed solely for the poor they are called *selective* programs. Contrary to a widespread assumption, far more is spent worldwide and in the U.S. on universal measures than on programs limited to the poor. By 1982, one sixth of public social welfare expenditures in the U.S. were for selective measures like Aid to Families with Dependent

Children (AFDC, sometimes called ADC), Supplemental Security Income (SSI), food stamps, Medicaid, and public housing. The other five sixths were spent on universal programs like public education, social insurances, most veterans' benefits, and Medicare (7).

Whether five sixths for universal programs and one sixth for selective programs constitutes a reasonable balance in the U.S. has been hotly debated for years. But the overriding point is that knowing this ratio certainly casts doubt on the frequent charge that "welfare" programs — our collection of selective measures — are "bankrupting" the nation or adding significantly to the federal budget deficit. We are investing five times as much in social welfare programs that provide benefits for all income classes.

The Evolution of Modern Social Welfare Systems _____

In western, industrialized nations, the impetus for modern social welfare programs came from reformers who were appalled at the personal and social cost of industrialization and urbanization (1, 44). The subservience of men to machines, the exploitation of women and children, the disease-ridden, overcrowded slums, the breakdown in social controls in the wake of urbanization all set fire to reform movements that swept over northern Europe, England, and the U.S. in the late nineteenth and early twentieth centuries (8, 14, 30). Liberals, like the Fabian Socialists of England and the Progressives in the U.S., who often dominated these efforts, sometimes began with unbounded faith that once leaders became aware of the enormous loss of human potential and the degradations of poverty, the essential rationality of man would assure a better world and reasonable constraints on greed.

Few early reformers were egalitarians (21). Nor were they persuaded that all poor people could be salvaged (12). Whenever they surveyed the slums, however, they found striving, promising, "worthy" families who they felt deserved help (5). Reformers saw their task as twofold: to secure new laws to end the worst forms of exploitation and to try with encouragement and advice to assuage the harshness of life for the "worthy poor." In the early twentieth century in the U.S., reform efforts resulted in child labor laws, shorter work days for women and youth, and scattered Mothers' Pension programs for carefully selected fatherless families (2). Unfortunately, however helpful such measures were to some groups, they did little to improve conditions for most poor families.

This reform movement coincided with another more promising development: the growth of trade unions, determined to secure better work conditions and higher wages (9). As this effort blazed the way for modern social security systems, a new anti-poverty approach was set in motion. In the nineteenth century, most leaders of society were convinced that poverty was a sign of personal weakness. The trade unions and socialists refused to buy that idea, and they launched a series of investigations to learn exactly why hard-working people were so often poor (27). Soon facts were collected pointing to external circumstances over which workers had little if any control. Of these, miserly wages, work accidents and illnesses, forced retirement, and the death of wage earners were the most compelling (45). Later, when labor scholars and labor leaders became convinced that industry and business could stabilize production rather than practice wholesale, uncontrolled hiring and firing, involuntary unemployment was added to the list of culprits. With this new definition of the situation, preventive measures like old age pensions, minimum wages, unemployment insurance, and workers' compensation for industrial accidents and illness became favored solutions.

In most western industrialized countries, around World War II these various reform movements joined hands, as trade unions (or Labor Parties) and liberals collaborated in efforts to extend benefits to *all* citizens who experienced any of the common, predictable risks of poverty. The resulting national policies set an income floor below everyone. In the process, periods were identified when people should not work (e.g., around the birth of a baby, during school years, old age, or severe illness or disability), and cash allowances were made available to encourage and enable them to stop working. They equalized the distribution of medical services and socialized their cost (6, 36). They made heavy government commitments to assure better and reasonably priced housing for low-income families and to rebuild cities devastated by war (13, 20), and to a great extent they eliminated the financial barriers to higher education (32, 33).

In the U.S. the liberal reform movement and the trade unions rarely joined forces in behalf of the entire population, although they often united to press for measures to protect members of the labor force from poverty. Achieving even this limited goal has been an uphill struggle (24). Far more often than in other western nations, economic goals took precedence over social goals, and reform proposals were set aside because of possible adverse effects on profits or price stability. Even the idea that economic development might depend on social development or go hand in hand with it was often interpreted as an unpatriotic attack on the free enterprise system or simply as the loose and irresponsible talk of visionaries (36). Over the years there was enough citizen pressure to push the U.S. toward better income protection and more community services, but there were still egregious gaps and inadequacies when Wilensky (48) observed in 1975, "We move toward the welfare state, but we do it with ill grace, carping and complaining all the way." Ten years later, the shortfalls are even more noticeable, especially in programs for children and low-income families.

Three Cornerstones of Social Welfare in Other Developed Nations

The U.S. social welfare system is known as a *risk-by-risk approach* as distinguished from the comprehensive *cradle-to-grave* programs in other industrialized nations. Our system has grown by fits and starts so that the parts are often not logically related to one another, and gaps abound. Also, some programs and policies regarded as vital underpinning elsewhere are entirely lacking here.

1. National Health Care. Other industrialized nations provide two types of sickness benefits: (a) cash benefits during periods of illness that prevent work, and (b) medical, dental, and hospital services for all residents or citizens. Where coverage is not compulsory, most people enroll voluntarily.*

Systems of health care are financed in several ways. The most common sources are general government revenues, employee and employer insurance premiums, and a combination of the two. Users must often meet modest out-of-pocket expenses, an arrangement intended to discourage frivolous demands on the system. In some nations services are organized under government auspices. Others rely on national or decentralized insurance schemes with government supervision of the organization and delivery of services. The important point is that the cost is socialized so that no family has the exorbitant expense of serious or prolonged illness or injury, and no one has to go without medical care for financial reasons alone (37); Senator Kennedy (22) has amply documented this predicament of many American families. When nations invest in universal health care systems, they reap another advantage: the focus shifts from treating sickness to maintaining good health.

The worldwide recession of the early 1980s put severe strains on health care systems everywhere, primarily because their cost inflated more rapidly than other items consumers purchase. Several European nations made financial adjustments by either increasing revenues or curtailing expenditures, but in doing so they carefully protected the "right" of their people to health care (39), while in the U.S., with similar inflating health care costs, many unemployed and other poor families lost their coverage.

2. Family Allowances. Sixty-seven nations pay allowances in behalf of some or all children. Programs of this nature began in the late eighteenth century, but most national programs were not enacted until around World

---

*As an example of the rates of coverage for comprehensive health care in other countries, all Swedes, Norwegians, Danes, Czechoslovakians, New Zealanders, and Japanese were covered by 1975, as were 98 per cent of French and Canadian citizens and over 90 per cent of the residents of Israel, Ireland, and Australia (39, 40). By way of contrast, only about one third of adults between twenty and sixty-four years of age in the U.S. had comprehensive coverage that year.

War II. There are two types of systems. One provides allowances to all resident families with a specified number of children. The other is limited to children of employed and occasionally self-employed workers.* Usually allowances are paid from birth through compulsory school age. Their size varies with the major purpose. When the intent is to stimulate birth rates, as in France, they are more generous than when the goal is to reduce the income deficit of families with children to bring them to more nearly equal footing with childless couples. But even when allowances are reinforced by measures like maternity benefits, housing allowances for new parents, and extensive child day care, they still have not succeeded in affecting birth rates. In recent years these have been consistently lower in Europe than in the U.S. (35, 38, 42, 46).

Some nations tax the allowances, thereby recovering part of the cost from well-off families. One of the virtues of family allowances is their very low administrative cost — due to the ease of confirming eligibility and the fact that standard allowances are paid. No other income support program yet devised equals their record in this regard. All that is needed usually is proof of birth, age, and address.

3. Full Employment Policies. As European nations adopted comprehensive social welfare programs, they also made a commitment to maintain full employment. In doing so, they reflected a conviction that everyone should have the right and opportunity to work. Productive work was not only important to the nation, it was held, but it gives meaning to life and self-respect, and so whether jobs were available could not be left to the vagaries of business cycles, corporate mobility, trade unions, or styles of architecture (which in the U.S. prevent some handicapped persons from working). Accordingly, governments accepted responsibility for assuring sufficient jobs for everyone who wanted and needed to work, including the disabled. As they strove toward this goal, they created networks of training and resettlement programs, and established national labor exchanges. Far more often than in the U.S., the workplace was adapted to workers rather than forcing workers to adapt to the workplace. In electing the goal of full employment, other industrialized nations recognized that it would both reduce the cost of social welfare programs and generate the tax revenues needed to support them.

The result of their efforts was that until the mid-seventies, most postwar European governments managed economies with unemployment rates between two and three per cent (3). Sweden's rate rarely reached even that level (16). Worldwide recessions in the seventies and early eighties finally jeopardized this record, but despite the fact that the recent economic recovery occurred earlier in the U.S. than in Europe, during the first

---

*A handful of nations focus their programs on children of poor unemployed or nonemployed parents.

quarter of 1985, when 7.3 per cent of our labor force was jobless, unemployment rates in Japan, Italy, and Sweden were only 2.6, 5.4, and 3.0 per cent, respectively (29).

Although we claim to be deeply committed to the work ethic, as Ginsburg (15) has pointed out, since World War II the economy has never provided enough jobs to keep pace with the growth in population and the rising number of women seeking paid work. When recessions occur, the new decrease in jobs simply piles on top of the normal job shortage. The way unemployment is measured in the U.S. often misleads citizens about the gravity of the problem. Official rates only include people actively and recently seeking work, but in a long, deep recession like the one in the early 1980s, disheartened men and women eventually stop searching for nonexistent jobs, whereupon they are dropped from the labor force and the unemployment count. Also, underemployment is not reflected in our official data, although millions of people wanting to work full time had to settle for part-time jobs. The difference these two shortfalls make is substantial. When an average of 8.5 million workers were officially unemployed during each quarter of 1984, there were another 500,000 "discouraged" workers who had stopped searching for jobs, and 5.7 million people who were involuntarily in part-time jobs—for a total of 14.7 million unemployed and underemployed workers (29). It should be emphasized, too, that these are averages of rates at given periods of time. Over a year, millions more than these data suggest lost their jobs, had work hours reduced, or found only part-time jobs.

Social Welfare as a Response to Social Needs, not Social Problems

Wickenden refers to social welfare as a response to social needs, not social problems. What is the significance of this distinction? It reminds us that over the world people share many social needs, and that ideally social welfare's business is to make certain that they are satisfied promptly for all citizens. A decent income, housing, education, health care, personal safety, and the ability to participate in community affairs are among the most basic needs. To assure effective, equitable, and updated services requires orderly planning mechanisms, good social accounting, prompt feedback, and close coordination of economic and social policies (41). But some or all of these ingredients are often missing in the U.S. One reason is that many Americans still regard social planning as something that communist or socialist nations indulge in and as totally irrelevant in a free enterprise system (19). The result is that not even Congress centralizes responsibility in the social arena. Nor is there a Council of Social Advisors to balance the

Council of Economic Advisors, and the latter rarely consults with social welfare experts even though everyone knows that economic policy often has grave and sometimes catastrophic social consequences.

Typically, the American way is to postpone action until there is consensus that a critical social problem exists. The process by which an accumulation of unmet needs becomes defined as a social problem that suddenly requires large-scale intervention is often obscure until well after millions of dollars have gone down the drain without solving the problem. One difficulty is that social problems are inherently so complex that people often perceive them very differently, depending on their relationship to the situation and their own self-interests; what is one group's problem may be another's solution. Unless all relevant groups confront each other from the outset and join in a search for solutions, this divergence may not surface for years. In European nations, ubiquitous trade unions are heavily involved in citizen education and assure lively participation in public affairs. But in the U.S., what with the dearth of social planning mechanisms, an increasing concentration of economic and political power, declining union membership, voter apathy, and the habit of professionals to regard themselves as problem-solving experts, average citizens — let alone families victimized by so-called social problems — rarely get a hearing. If they do, there is no assurance that their perception of what is needed will influence program or funding decisions. This helps to explain why after billions of dollars were invested in urban renewal, our inner cities are still decaying and their residents are still among our most neglected citizens. A brief review of what happened in urban renewal programs over the past few decades will clarify the issue.

Urban Renewal: A Case in Point.   Although inner cities had been deteriorating for years, urban blight came into sudden prominence around World War II when people became preoccupied with slums as eyesores, trouble spots, and non-revenue-producing oases in cities with rising land values and dwindling stocks of land (18). Soon a package emerged from Washington consisting of vast urban renewal projects that would first clear away the slums (4). New inner cities would then be built through an intricate combination of private and public sponsors and financial arrangements. This package was to be supplemented by increased appropriations for public housing and the rehabilitation of old housing. Large sums were provided for acquiring land and demolishing buildings. Only picayune amounts were earmarked to assist displaced residents and small businessmen with the problems this plan predictably created for them.

Soon bulldozers were razing the slums. Before long it was painfully clear that the neighborhoods of the poor had been destroyed and with them their sense of community and network of supportive relationships (43). The fact that most displaced families were black was not lost on civil rights leaders or slum dwellers, who caustically proposed that urban renewal be renamed Negro Removal. For the most part, the homes of the poor were replaced by shining condominiums sold primarily to middle- and upper-income white families, by fine office buildings and universities, and by expressways to help white suburbanites drive to and from work. The whole process expedited the middle-class flight to the suburbs, thereby increasing the fiscal squeeze on cities. Years later, some inner-city land still lay fallow because funds had dried up or complex negotiations with private developers had collapsed (11, 17).

Ironically, urban renewal also forced the poor to shoulder a good share of the cost of subsidies to land developers, new better-off users of the land, and their creditors. Sawers and Wachtel (34) explain this phenomenon. The government announced plans to clear the land well in advance, and residents stopped improving their property. Months later, exercising its right of eminent domain for the first time in history to force one group of citizens to move so that others could replace them, the government bought the land at a "fair market price," usually well below what might have tempted families to sell had they had a choice or had they maintained the property in its earlier condition. Small businesses were reimbursed only for the value of physical assets lost in the move; and received so little that few could afford to reopen. Over three fifths never did so. In the end the cost to government of acquiring, clearing, and improving the land was considerably higher than what private developers paid for it.

As for the poor, they crowded into nearby neighborhoods with rising rents — because the dwindling supply of housing made what was left more expensive — but no more services. Public housing never materialized in sufficient supply. By 1963 urban renewal had removed over 177,000 family units and 66,000 individual units from the market, and replaced them with 68,000 units of which only 20,000 were for low-income people (28). In 1970 about 8.5 million Americans still lived in substandard housing. Today the inner cities, which once housed both blacks and whites and a mixture of income classes, are almost solely black and poor. Given American racism and widespread contempt for the poor, this enormously complicates efforts to resolve urban problems.

Why, instead of forcing the wholesale removal of the poor, were their neighborhoods not provided with amenities and services that other citizens expect and enjoy? Why were inner-city residents not encouraged to rebuild and refurbish their dwellings, and given technical and other necessary assistance to do so? Why did years pass before measures were taken to streamline the transfer of titles to abandoned buildings so that people prepared to invest some "sweat equity" could renew them for personal use? One important reason is that the inner-city residents and small business owners were rarely consulted by planners, and urban blight was not perceived from their point of view. Thus, it was rarely viewed as a problem of "normal" people with overcrowded, inadequate housing, unsafe streets, too few jobs, and far less than their share of civic services (23, 26). On the contrary; in the view of many decision makers, poor people themselves, rather than civic neglect, a discriminatory social structure, private greed, and poor planning, created urban blight.

One way to avoid fiascoes of this scale is to shift the focus from social problems to social needs. If citizens are encouraged to organize and set priorities for improving their own communities and neighborhoods, and given vital roles in all stages of the renewal process, then plans can proceed methodically to fill the gaps in services and to equalize their distribution, as resources permit. Urban renewal is only one part of a reform strategy that must involve new jobs, improved housing, safer streets, and better municipal services. But it starts with people and their vision of a more livable, just, and fulfilling environment. In defining both the needs and solutions, residents are the experts since they know best what they need and want.

It is axiomatic in the U.S. that powerful economic interests will try to gain control of decision making whenever costly federal interventions are in the offing. Atomizing solutions by giving essential control to neighborhood and community residents will help to counterbalance this known danger. This approach removes corporations, politicians, and professionals from the driver's seat. It also requires more time, patience, and effort. But widespread citizen alienation will only be reduced by giving citizens mastery over their own fate and enlisting their talents and resources in setting their lives aright.

It gradually became an American habit to rely on the federal government for large-scale reform. The past five decades suggest that it is one thing to pledge federal resources to the cause of creative revitalization of the cities and to protect equity; it is quite another to lose or relinquish control over the shape and direction of reform that intimately affects our daily lives. An involved citizenry can reverse these trends and shape a more congenial, livable society on the human scale.

Individual and Societal Functions of Social Welfare

In her definition of social welfare, Wickenden (47) refers to its dual purpose: (a) to meet the social needs of the population and (b) to promote the better functioning of the social order. In her text she emphasizes that social welfare serves societal as well as individual goals. This is worth examining since many citizens seem to believe that social welfare is a one-way street for conveying their hard-earned dollars to the poor and hapless, with no hope of return except the glow of good deeds or the feeling of superiority that often distinguishes the giver from the receiver. But over the last several decades it has become clear that social welfare is not just a bundle of goodies or a reflection of altruism. Instead, programs of this nature are just as vital to the host society as to individual recipients, and often in serving the former they do great disservice to the latter.

For example, schools do not simply prepare youngsters to pursue careers of their choice or to become better parents and citizens. They instill the values around which given societies are organized, and in the process they teach children to accept very different lots in life, largely reflecting their parents' status in society. They train children to subdue their own needs and desires in the interest of keeping schedules and maintaining productivity levels. They teach what not to think about or question as often as they do the opposite. They serve as gatekeepers, effectively closing doors on some children while keeping them wide open for others. Attendance records, tuition, and competency testing are only some of the many tools at hand. So, like other social institutions, far from being single-minded allies of progress, schools often serve to perpetuate the traditional social order, however unjust or wasteful of human resources it may be.

Similarly, while all income maintenance programs provide necessary funds to families, they also buttress capitalist economies by reinforcing the work ethic, instilling admiration for the captains of industry, and helping to maintain law and order. Piven and Cloward (31) have shown that when great civic unrest erupts, public welfare caseloads tend to rise, and soon the poor are "cooled off" by their new or more generous grants. When order is restored, welfare payments begin lagging behind prices, rigorous work requirements are reinstituted, and caseloads soon fall. The result has been the persistence of a fairly steady segment of easily exploited, relatively docile, cheap workers to perform the dirty, menial jobs. From this perspective, far from being programs whose function is to end poverty, public welfare has served to prolong it.

Even the referral systems in social welfare are class and race conscious, as Cumming (10) showed in her study of agency networks some years back. Other evidence of class and race bias abounds. The rich still get the best schooling, health care, legal advice, and housing. The inner cities get the worst. Whites fare better than blacks. Too often under the guise of "helping people accept reality," counseling services press their clients to accept their "lot in life," however miserable it may be (25). AFCD has been known to reject unmarried mothers *en masse* without referring one to prenatal services (5).

Because the U.S. is a more diversified society than other modern democracies, perversities of this type have been more compelling and troublesome on this side of the Atlantic — although storm clouds have gathered in Europe as more dark-skinned members of former Commonwealth nations migrated to England and foreign laborers found themselves cut off from citizenship privileges on the Continent and were sometimes forced to return home as unemployment rates rose. But nowhere among other developed nations does the immigrant flow equal the number of fairly recent arrivals in the U.S. from Vietnam, Mexico, Cuba, Jamaica, Haiti, and elsewhere. Nor does any other western nation subject such large groups of long-standing citizens to the persistent discrimination that blacks, native Americans, and Hispanics encounter in the U.S. Frustrations and injustices of this scope create the particular mandate for social welfare.

References

1. Abbott, Edith. *The Tenements of Chicago, 1908–1935.* Chicago: University of Chicago Press, 1936.
2. Abbott, Grace. *The Child and the State.* Chicago: University of Chicago Press, 1938, Vol. 1, pp. 259–269; Vol. 2, pp. 229–247.
3. Alperovitz, Gar and Jeff Faux. *Rebuilding America.* New York: Pantheon Books, 1984, pp. 107–109.
4. Anderson, Martin. *The Federal Bulldozer.* Cambridge: MIT Press, 1964, Ch. 1.
5. Bell, Winifred. *Aid to Dependent Children.* New York: Columbia University Press, 1965, pp. 3–19, 174–198.
6. Beveridge, Sir William. *Social Insurance and Allied Services.* New York: Macmillan Publishing Co., Inc., 1942.
7. Bixby, Ann Kallman. "Social Welfare Expenditures, 1981 and 1982." *Social Security Bulletin,* **47** (December 1984), pp. 14–22.
8. Bremner, Robert H. *From the Depths: The Discovery of Poverty in the United States.* New York: New York University Press, 1956, pp. 67–85.
9. Bruce, Maurice. *The Coming of the Welfare State.* London: B. T. Batsford, 1961, pp. 44–73, 137–149.
10. Cumming, Elaine. *Systems of Social Regulation.* New York: Atherton Press, 1968.
11. Edel, Matthew. "Urban Renewal and Land Use Conflicts." In David M. Gordon, Ed., *Problems in Political Economy: The Urban Perspective,* 2d ed., rev. Lexington, Mass.: D. C. Heath & Co., 1977, pp. 519–526.
12. Fried, Alfred and Richard M. Elman. Eds. *Charles Booth's London.* New York: Pantheon Books, 1968, pp. xi–xxxix.
13. Fuerst, J. S. Ed. *Public Housing in Europe and America.* New York: John Wiley & Sons, Inc., 1974, Foreword, p. 7.
14. Garraty, John A. *Unemployment in History: Economic Thought and Public Policy.* New York: Harper & Row, Publishers, 1978, pp. 103–129.
15. Ginsburg, Helen. "Needed: A National Commitment to Full Employment." *Current History,* **65** (August 1973), pp. 71–75.
16. ————. *Full Employment and Public Policy: The United States and Sweden.* Lexington, Mass.: D. C. Heath & Co., 1983, p. 113.

17. Glazer, Nathan. "Renewal of Cities." In *Cities: A Scientific American Book.* New York: Alfred A. Knopf, Inc., 1966, pp. 175–191.
18. Grier, Scott. "Urban Renewal and American Cities." In Jewel Bellush and Murray Hausknecht, Eds., *Urban Renewal: People, Politics and Planning.* Garden City: Doubleday & Co., Inc., 1967, pp. 81–89.
19. Harrington, Michael. *The Accidental Century.* New York: Macmillan Publishing Co., Inc., 1965, Ch. 1.
20. Headey, Bruce. *Housing Policy in the Developed Economy: The United Kingdom, Sweden, and the United States.* New York: St. Martin's Press, Inc., 1978.
21. Hofstadter, Richard. *The Progressive Movement, 1900–1915.* Englewood Cliffs, N.J.: Prentice-Hall, Inc., 1963, pp. 1–15.
22. Kennedy, Edward M. *In Critical Condition: The Crisis in America's Health Care.* New York: Simon and Schuster, Inc., 1972.
23. Liebow, Elliot. *Tally's Corner.* Boston: Little, Brown & Co., 1967.
24. Lubove, Roy. *The Struggle for Social Security.* Cambridge: Harvard University Press, 1968, pp. 25–44.
25. Mandell, Betty Reid. "Whose Welfare? An Introduction." In Betty Reid Mandell, Ed., *Welfare in America: Controlling the "Dangerous Classes."* Englewood Cliffs, N.J.: Prentice-Hall, Inc., 1975, pp. 1–22.
26. Marris, Peter. "A Report on Urban Renewal in the United States." In Leonard J. Duhl, Ed., *The Urban Condition: People and Policy in the Metropolis.* New York: Basic Books, Inc., Publishers, 1963, pp. 113–134.
27. Mencher, Samuel. *Poor Law to Poverty Program.* Pittsburgh: University of Pittsburgh Press, 1968, pp. 235–236, 273–277.
28. Morris, Robert. *Social Policy of the American Welfare State.* New York: Harper & Row, Publishers, 1979, p. 101.
29. Moy, Joanna. "Recent Trends in Unemployment and the Labor Force, 10 Countries." *Monthly Labor Review,* **108** (August 1985), pp. 9–17.
30. Muggeridge, Kitty and Ruth Adams. *Beatrice Webb: A Life, 1858–1943.* New York: Alfred A. Knopf, Inc., 1968, pp. 101–117, 130–142.
31. Piven, Frances Fox and Richard A. Cloward. *Regulating The Poor: The Functions of Public Welfare.* New York: Vintage Books, Inc., 1971.
32. Poignant, Raymond. *Education and Development in Western Europe, the United States, and the U.S.S.R.* New York: Columbia University Teachers College Press, 1969.
33. Sauvy, Alfred. *Access to Education: New Possibilities.* The Hague: Martinus Nijhoff, 1973.
34. Sawers, Larry and Howard N. Wachtel. "Who Benefits from Public Housing Policies?" In David M. Gordon (11), pp. 501–506.
35. Schorr, Alvin L. *Poor Kids.* New York: Basic Books, Inc., Publishers, 1965, Ch.5.
36. Schottland, Charles I. Ed. *The Welfare State.* New York: Harper & Row, Publishers, 1967.
37. Titmuss, Richard M. *Essays on "The Welfare State."* London: George Allen & Unwin, Ltd., 1959, pp. 133–202.
38. U.S. Bureau of the Census. *Statistical Abstract of the United States, 1982–83.* Washington, D.C.: U.S. Government Printing Office, 1982, p. 861.

39. U.S. Department of Health and Human Services. *Social Security Programs throughout the World 1983.* Washington, D.C.: U.S. Government Printing Office, pp. x, xii–xiii, xxv–xxvi.

40. ———. *National Health Care Systems in Eight Countries.* Washington, D.C.: U.S. Government Printing Office, 1975.

41. ———. *Toward a Social Report.* Washington, D.C.: U.S. Government Printing Office, 1969.

42. Vadakin, James. *Children, Poverty, and Family Allowances.* New York: Basic Books, Inc., Publishers, 1968, pp. 4–8, 95–101.

43. Weaver, Robert. "The Urban Complex." In Jewel Bellush and Murray Hausknecht (18), pp. 90–101.

44. Webb, Beatrice. *My Apprenticeship.* London: Longmans Green, 1926.

45. ———. *Prevention of Destitution.* London: Longmans Green, 1911.

46. Whitney, Vincent H. "Fertility Trends and Children's Allowances." In Eveline M. Burns, Ed., *Children's Allowances and the Economic Welfare of Children.* New York: Citizens' Committee for Children of New York, 1968, pp. 123–139.

47. Wickenden, Elizabeth. *Social Welfare in a Changing World.* U.S. Department of Health, Education, and Welfare, Welfare Administration. Washington, D.C.: U.S. Government Printing Office, 1965, p. 1.

48. Wilensky, Harold. *The Welfare State and Equality.* Berkeley: University of California Press, 1975, p. 32.

CHAPTER 2

Perspectives on American Social Welfare

American and European social welfare systems have many specific programs in common. Yet the total systems add up to something very different. Why should this be true? Quite simply because like other major social institutions, social welfare reflects its host society. Nations have different historical experiences, attitudes toward government, economic systems, and cultural values. Their populations may be homogeneous or heterogeneous, relatively stable for generations or constantly replenished by newcomers who arrive with varied backgrounds, ideologies, and expectations.

The U.S. has been described as the "contrapuntal civilization . . ., a land of polarity and paradox" (27), "high ideals and catchpenny realities . . ., piety and advertisement" (15), diversity and conformity. In the same vein, Americans are known for their godly materialism, conservative liberalism, and pragmatic idealism. In contrast to other western peoples, they are said to be more preoccupied with personal and private values than social and political ones, and hence to be more competitive. While many European nations also have capitalist economies, the U.S. is proud of its quintessential capitalism.

Furthermore, the migration to the U.S. and westward was selective. The journey, the struggle, and the challenge appealed to some more than others, and not all stayed. Those who did shaped the new society in their own diverse images.

The hallmarks of the American experience and their influence on social welfare are examined in the following discussion of (a) economic individualism and social welfare, (b) universal and selective organizing principles, and (c) the role of government in redistributing income.

Economic Individualism and Social Welfare

The folk heroes of America were pioneers, cowboys, and captains of industry. They are honored for their rugged individualism and resourcefulness in wresting the land from the original inhabitants, opening up the west to European immigrants and their descendants, and building unparalleled industrial empires. They left to generations of young Americans a legacy of romance, fabulous fortunes, and violence that obscured the drab harshness of frontier poverty and the fear and misery of disease-infected, teeming, lawless eastern slums (5, 21). Steeped in economic individualism, American youth were imbued with a zest for competition and the optimistic belief that strength of character, self-reliance, hard work, and noninterference by government were the keys to their heroes' success. If a great deal of luck in being in the right place at the right time, generously larded with more than their share of greed and ruthlessness, also played a role, such faults were soon turned into virtues.

Economic individualism had a profound influence on how social welfare was viewed and organized. Not until the great Depression of the 1930s did a rival ideology seriously challenge our traditional assumptions about poverty and the role of social welfare. The result was still another polarity — residual versus institutional conceptions of social welfare (25, 48).

The Residual role of Social Welfare. The centuries-old conception of the residual role of social welfare reflects belief in the economic logic of free enterprise and unbounded faith that American capitalism will thrive to the benefit of all so long as it remains sufficiently unfettered by government and undiluted by social welfare benefits to keep the spirit of competition alive. In this conception, the economic market and the family system are viewed as the primary structures of support. Together, they are all that most people need to prosper and succeed. Only when these basic structures break down does social welfare have a "residual" role to play in human affairs. When economic recessions put people out of work or wage earners die, short-term reliance on public aid may be necessary. But long-term dependence is an anathema except for vulnerable groups like orphaned children, the aged, or the severely disabled.

Residualists view poverty in individualistic terms as due to personal weakness, improvidence, immorality, and indolence (6). The worst sin is to discourage incentives to work, an ever-present threat, it is claimed, when social welfare enters the scene. Adversity, far from breaking the human spirit, is believed to strengthen character and stimulate heightened efforts toward self-support. Proponents of this view chronically mistrust the poor. They are always trying, it is said, to "get something for nothing," but if they are in want they have "no one to blame but themselves." In this climate, when cash or services are provided, programs are overrun with controls to prevent fraud and abuse.

Wherever the residual view holds sway, social welfare programs tend to be scarce and mean. Not only is poverty stigmatizing, so is the mere act of asking for help.

The Institutional Role of Social Welfare. This school of thought believes that social welfare plays a major role, equal in importance to the economic market and the family system, in meeting normal, everyday needs of average citizens, as well as helping vulnerable populations (24, 26). In fact, the two so-called primary institutions cannot hope to satisfy all human needs; nor do they succeed in doing so. In a wage economy when full-time, year-round workers earn too little to support families decently, and the economic market generates too few jobs to go around even in good times, people cannot fairly be blamed for their poverty. Nor can they be expected to resolve independently the problems it creates. Furthermore, if the family system is to thrive in complex, rapidly changing, urban societies, a wide range of services is essential. And sharing their cost so that everyone can use them is often the most sensible solution.

In addition, while many services are provided in the economic market and the voluntary nonprofit market, as well as the public social welfare market, some services like education are regarded as too vital to the general welfare or, as with child care institutions and nursing homes for the aged, too risk-laden to operate without the restraining influence of state standards and inspection to protect access, safety, and quality. State licensing of professions, foster homes, and day-care centers, are an endorsement of this principle.

To institutionalists, providing and using community services are intelligent responses to commonly encountered needs. Services should be readily accessible, it is emphasized, and offered in ways that protect self-esteem and promote self-mastery; also, citizens should be closely involved in their planning, delivery, and evaluation (45).* Frankel (18) believed that this attitude accounted for much of the resistance to the institutional view. "The policy of helping others while allowing them to retain their self-respect," he wrote, "has not been . . . usual in human affairs."

Background of the Residual Institutional Conflict. The residual view has been strongly entrenched in the U.S., and has persisted much longer here than in Europe, where it originated. It existed in its purest form in the old Poor Laws of England, which were codified in 1601 and soon exported to the colonies. They marked the first acceptance of public responsibility for the relief of poverty. But they were very much the product of a propertied class. For the law also marked the first time in Anglo-Saxon law that primary responsibility for support was placed squarely on the family system. If families proved incapable of support, only the most vulnerable members — the aged, disabled, and blind — were eligible for public aid. Alternative arrangements like indenture of children and provision of work materials for adults in times of extreme hardship were also provided.

*The Task Force for the Reorganization of the Social Services, appointed by the U.S. Department of Health, Education and Welfare in late 1967, brought together a number of proponents of this view. The final report, submitted just before Administrations changed in Washington in 1969, was never published. A brief summary and appraisal appeared in *Social Work* (9).

Thus, for the able-bodied, work and welfare were inseparable, but even these conditional public responsibilities were extended only to town residents (43). Centuries were to pass before nations broadened the scope of responsibility or recognized that industrial societies required an educated, skilled, mobile labor force and an institutional structure designed to accommodate these needs.

In colonial America if fathers died prematurely or were killed, widows and children might be lodged temporarily with neighbors at public expense, if necessary. Occasionally, intact families were given temporary aid in their own homes. But if after a few months they still had no plans for self-support, they could be indentured, auctioned off to the lowest bidder, or let out on contract to the town (3, 16). Town fathers zealously protected their private fortunes as well as the public till. Even if strangers arrived with money and possessions, they were often required to post bond. Deutsch (17) reports on the frequent practice of spiriting away mentally ill paupers and abandoning them in distant towns in order to avoid the burden of support.

The belief that poverty is due to personal weakness, and the willingness to help neighbors but not strangers, have shown remarkable staying power in the U.S. For centuries marked by wars, frontier tragedies, epidemics, repeated crop failures, economic panics, and depressions, these views neatly rationalized decisions to share little with the poor and hapless. In the process, waves of immigrants and black and native Americans were victimized (13, 21). Why was reform so long in coming? Why was the labor movement that pressed European nations toward an institutional role for social welfare still so minuscule and faltering in the U.S.? Thernstrom (39) explains part of the lag by the selective pattern of migration to the U.S. and westward. Those immigrants who suffered the most extreme hardships and had the greatest reason to feel outrageously exploited — the Irish in the 1840s and 1850s, the French Canadians in the 1870s, and the Italians and various East Europeans in later years — came from peasant societies. American tenements might be deathtraps, the work brutal and underpaid, but what they found was a "damn sight better" than what they left behind. Under the best of circumstances, organizing collectivist movements was difficult when people spoke so many different languages and rarely knew any but their own. But having escaped famine and persecution, thousands of immigrants became fanatically loyal Americans, resentful of any criticism of their adopted land, and inevitably an important source of conservatism. In this climate, even investigating and exposing visible shortcomings in economic and social arrangements became "unpatriotic." They invested their energies in improving their personal lot, settled among others of similar ethnic origin, religion, and perspectives, and too often constituted themselves as "super-patriots," impervious to the man-made misery around them, oblivious to the lessons of history, insistent on a static society. All of which added up to something very different from the insights, personal qualities, and public conscience required to organize an effective labor movement in those harsh and unwelcoming years. Different, too, from the resilience, compassion, aspirations, courage, and deep involvement that with all its imperfections had caused America to be perceived as the "promised land" by millions of immigrants.

Then too, Thernstrom adds, those who pressed on toward the West were disproportionately failures in the East. But while horizons beckoned and free land was in the offing, they served as both safety valve and promise. And if nothing else had impeded their development, strong labor unions were not likely in such a highly mobile society. Finally, unlike the politicized labor movements spreading over Europe, protest and organization died aborning when "returning home" in failure was so intolerable to proud people.

It has been observed that in the excessively competitive, success-oriented climate in the U.S., as poor immigrants "made it" into the mainstream, they, too, joined the pecking order and perceived the next arrivals as outsiders threatening the purses, lives, and customs of "good, hardworking Americans." The Chinese Exclusion Act of 1882 was an extreme example. The Chinese were lured to America to build our railroads, but when the hardest work was done chauvinistic alarms about the Yellow Peril spread across the land. The result was a series of laws that greatly reduced the influx from China and finally halted it entirely for a generation after 1924 (30). Another illustration is the discriminatory treatment of recent immigrants and blacks in the small Mothers' Pension programs organized in the first quarter of the twentieth century. Blacks were rarely admitted to this elite program for fatherless families, and as late as 1922 social workers reported that "low-type" families like Mexicans, Italians, and Czechoslovakians were seldom helped. If they were, they usually received lower grants than "high-type" Anglo-Saxons (47).

By far the greatest damage was done to black and native Americans who, except for the stream of immigrants, might well have received a warmer welcome in the industrial labor force. Exploited by southern landowners until they were pushed aside by the mechanization of agriculture, and neglected and harassed when they migrated to cities, blacks were poorly educated, often denied the right to vote, and were virtually always consigned to decaying urban and rural slums and dead-end jobs (33, 34). As for native Americans, they became the poorest Americans whether the index used is health, education, income, a sense of belonging, or mastery over their own destiny and culture.*

Virulent racism and the arrogance, indifference, and greed that have

---

*In recent years the reorganization and improvement of medical care have brought about significant reductions in infant mortality rates among native Americans.

characterized our relationships with minorities have all played a key role in keeping the residual conception of social welfare alive. Some progress toward an institutional role has been made in the U.S., but mainly in behalf of workers with a long, steady attachment to the labor force. The great breakthrough came with the Depression of the 1930s, which put enough citizens out of work to assure passage of the Social Security Act in 1935. Two decades later, well after European nations launched comprehensive "cradle-to-grave" programs covering entire populations, the civil rights movement finally forced Americans to confront the issues of unequal rights and maldistributed services. Dr. Martin Luther King, Jr., gave his life attempting to unite his people and all poor Americans in efforts to achieve social justice. Poverty lawyers in the 1960s challenged discrimination on many fronts and won impressive victories. Walter Reuther, before his death in 1970, struggled with indifferent success to persuade unions to join in a genuine war on poverty. In their various ways, all endorsed a broader institutional role for social welfare, and all were keenly aware of the many forces beyond individual control that determined whether people are poor or rich, employed or unemployed, sick or well.

Organizing Principles — Universal or Selective _____

Social welfare programs are either universal or selective. The key distinction is that the former provide benefits irrespective of income while selective measures are designed solely for the poor (40).

Their relative merits have been debated almost unceasingly for the past two decades. While all industrialized nations rely more heavily on universal measures, few people question that a small selective program is essential to help households with extraordinary or emergency needs and to bring the poorest of the poor up to an acceptable income floor. But the problems seemingly inherent in the selective approach are widely felt to make it inappropriate for large-scale programs. There is no question that universal measures have been far more popular with users, program administrators, and the general public. As differences are reviewed in the following pages, it would be well to keep an open mind about feasible ways of neutralizing or correcting weaknesses so that both approaches might become better social policy instruments.

The Eligibility Determination Process. Eligibility is generally much easier, simpler, and less costly to determine in universal than selective measures. Universal programs provide benefits to certain statuses or groups of people, like retired, disabled, or unemployed workers, survivors of deceased workers, veterans, children under sixteen years of age, workers injured on the job, or miners with black lung disease. For the most part, so long as beneficiary groups can be defined precisely in the parent legislation, verifying membership in the group is a fairly straightforward task. Age, of course, is the simplest criterion. This is one reason why family allowances cost so little to administer. But death of a wage earner, loss of a job, and retirement as criteria are usually close seconds. Even if people retire from regular jobs and work elsewhere for a while, "retirement tests" can prescribe earnings levels or maximum hours of work that distinguish the "truly retired" (7). In the U.S., determining occupational disability often causes headaches, primarily because so many actors become involved, including doctors, state vocational rehabilitation agencies, lawyers, and program administrators. But this difficulty cuts across both selective and universal measures and has no bearing on programmatic differences between the two.

Conversely, determining eligibility for selective benefits is complex, time-consuming, abrasive, error-prone, and expensive. First, poverty must be defined. Then methods must be devised for separating the poor from the nonpoor. Together, these steps are often referred to as the "means test."

Defining poverty may sound like a simple task, but it rarely proves to be, since it always involves politically sensitive and emotionally laden judgments about the relative needs of poor families and public treasuries. The first step in the process is to set upper limits on household assets and current income. Historically, these have usually been set as low as possible to make certain that families who qualify are indeed impoverished.

Few subjects are more vexatious than assets tests. Traditionally, welfare investigators were required to search for every conceivable resource. In fixing the value of resources, arguments proliferated over whether the proper reference was the original price, current value, or equity (28, 29, 32). After settling this issue, appraisers often had to be consulted to fix the exact value. As time passed, some assets like homegrown produce, small savings accounts for a child's education, burial lots, and owner-occupied homes were partly or wholly disregarded. In 1981, in addition to settling on equity value as the appropriate measure, the list of exempt assets was narrowed in AFDC to include only an owner-occupied home, burial lots and funeral arrangements up to $1,500, essential personal belongings and household furnishings of "limited value," and an automobile with an equity value no higher than $1,500. Simultaneously, the family ceiling for nonexempt assets was dropped from $1,500 to $1,000 — or less if states preferred. In some situations a grace period was allowed for the sale of excess property like livestock for farm families or a reliable car for working mothers with no access to public transportation. Otherwise, when limits were exceeded, applications were summarily denied, even though disposing of the property often greatly increased the risk of long-term dependency.

The same process must be repeated in sorting out whether family income is within bounds. Most AFDC families have very little, but for those who have other income, the most likely sources are earnings and child support payments from absent fathers. During the 1960s, when ending poverty was a national objective, federal law was amended to require states to exempt a share of earnings sufficient to cover work expenses, including child day care, and a cash work incentive amounting to about a third of earnings. Also, states were required to disregard the earnings of children who were full-time students, on the theory that their money was essential for current and future school expenses. This package of disregards made work affordable for more welfare families and resulted in more consistent work patterns (8). Child support payments were treated in a similar spirit. When only one of several children in a family, for instance, received support money, it could be disregarded so long as the child was not included in the AFDC application. Still another pitfall for poor families was outlawed in the 1960s: assumed income policies, which permitted welfare agencies to assume that all *expected* income actually arrived, as with child support, or later during the 1970s the low-wage earner's tax credit.

When the Reagan Administration took office, it soon became apparent that the liberalized policies of the 1960s were slated for repeal or retrenchment. Although some of the resulting cutbacks were modified in 1984, the main thrust survives. Now all children in the home must be included in the AFDC application, and only fifty dollars of child support a month can be disregarded. As for earnings and smaller disregards, some were eliminated, others were reduced, and a few crucial ones were redefined as temporary, not permanent, exemptions.* In the process, a gross income ceiling representing a percentage of the state's welfare standard was set so low as to disqualify most families with a full-time worker, and "assumed income" policies were reinstated.

Other complications face welfare applicants who live with relatives defined as "liable" or "responsible" for family support by welfare law (38). In this situation, *all* household assets and household income must fall below welfare ceilings in order for any member or members to qualify for public aid. Both are subject to the usual disregards, but everything left over is assumed to be available to the entire household — at welfare standards. Whole kinship networks have been impoverished by provisions of this kind over the centuries. Young, ambitious, striving members are particularly vulnerable. Money set aside for college is suddenly confiscated, in effect, by welfare agencies for family support. To some Americans, this is as it should be: it is better for entire families to be poor than for family bonds and

---

*For current information regarding federal regulations, state plans, standards of need, maximum money payments, and federal reimbursement rates, see the federal government's yearly publication, *Characteristics of State Plans for Aid to Families with Dependent Children* (46).

responsibilities to be overlooked or "spurned." In the 1960s, a consensus of citizens disagreed with the proposition that this was good anti-poverty policy, let alone good family policy. But the Reagan Administration would have us believe the mood has changed. In this connection, it is significant that *welfare* concepts of liability do not necessarily coincide with those in the General Statutes of the various states. When the two are not congruent, welfare may be denied on the assumption that a "responsible" relative will support the children; but the relative in question may not be sued for nonsupport.

Since World War II at least, most modern nations, including belatedly the U.S., progressively narrowed the list of liable relatives to include only (1) natural and adoptive parents for their minor children—unless the latter were "emancipated"—and (2) spouses for each other. In 1981, federal law reversed its direction. Now when AFDC applications are made in behalf of children, their stepparents, "blood-related" siblings (including half siblings), and grandparents are liable when they share a home with the young family. This means in the first instance that welfare agencies must hold these relatives liable, even if the states in which they reside do not. By the same token, such policies also expand the income pool that must fall below welfare ceilings. The inclusion of half siblings has the anomalous result of diverting court-ordered support from the intended child to the entire household. The inclusion of grandparents is the Administration's answer, apparently, to teenage pregnancy. Introducing this new social control means that young mothers may no longer apply for aid in behalf of themselves and their children; only the teenagers' parents may do so. Nor may teenagers move from home in order to qualify for AFDC. Infusing selective measures with social controls is an old habit, which sociologists usually find is more successful at spreading poverty than changing behavior.

Finally, another Administration cost-saving device was to lower the upper age limit of eligibility for AFDC. Raised from eighteen to twenty-one during the 1960s when older children were full-time students, it was cut back to eighteen unless school children were confidently expected to complete a course of study by their nineteenth birthday. Since many poor children are two years behind normal grade placement by their high school years, this means that more will leave before graduating. This is one reason for the surge in school dropout rates in many large cities.

While the Reagan policy shifts have been illustrated by referring to AFDC, they have been extended, whenever relevant, to all selective programs, including higher educational grants and loans to low-income students, food stamps, school lunches, and so forth.

Finally, pervading the administration of selective programs is a ubiquitous fear of fraud, which generates horrendously detailed procedures for verifying everything. The paper work itself is staggering, and the procedural labyrinth invites high error rates.* But while Americans continue to distrust the poor, the price will have to be paid, both in errors and in hard cash. Unfortunately, human nature being what it is, no measures yet devised succeed in totally eliminating fraud—in welfare, tax systems, or private business.† In welfare, the typical pattern involves many charges of fraud for very small sums and a fair number of dismissals for want of evidence. A case in point occurred in 1977 when former Secretary of the U.S. Department of Health, Education, and Welfare (HEW), Joseph Califano, proclaimed a "crackdown on welfare cheats." Ten months later he happily announced the names of fifteen current or former HEW employees who had been indicted on felony charges. After another ten months it was revealed—but not by the Secretary or HEW—that five cases had been dismissed and in four the charges were reduced to misdemeanors. Federal judges were unimpressed with government cases against the remaining six women who pled guilty to felonies. Only $2,000 repayment was ordered for the entire group (23). As usual in situations of this kind, the cost incurred in the process was not made public. Often it is never computed. But it would certainly far exceed $2,000 if investigative, administrative, and court costs are taken into account.

Benefit Structures. Universal programs pay standardized benefits that are spelled out precisely in the parent legislation. This means that in social security, for instance, everyone earning the same amount, working the same number of years, and retiring at the same time receives the same benefits. If programs pay dependents' allowances, these, too, are standardized. This means that benefits are calculated by computers in seconds.

Selective benefits are less standardized and far less predictable. In SSI and food stamps, "standards of need" (as income ceilings are usually called in public aid) are set and updated by the federal government. For AFDC this is a state prerogative. Standards supposedly reflect what officials regard as the cost of essential maintenance items for different-sized families. Paradoxically, having set standards, about three fifths of the states appropriate too little money to meet them. This, in turn, gives rise to "maximum money payments," which become the effective income ceiling.

In 1985 maximum AFDC payments for a mother with two children varied from $96 in Mississippi (25 per cent of the state standard) to $555 in California. Thirteen states paid less than $250; five paid over $500. But no

---

*By far the most accurate account of the process is found in Edgar May's Pulitzer prize–winning book (31) on public welfare.

†The IRS estimates that in 1981, $82 billion was lost in tax revenues because of the underreporting of income. By 1985 it was expected the figure would exceed $100 billion (14). Employees are reported to steal about $3 billion of their employers' property yearly (20). The rising flood of evidence of corporate crime—against stockholders, consumers, and government—also confirms that the inclination to commit fraud is no respecter of income levels.

one can predict how long payment levels will remain constant, a fact of life that makes family budgeting very difficult for the poor.

A special problem plagues working mothers of AFDC today — "retrospective budgeting." First mandated in 1981,* this budgeting method requires welfare agencies to base money grants on family needs and financial circumstances during the *previous* month, not the *current* month. Inevitably, this makes for a very slow response to family crises, which abound in the lives of the poor. A case illustration will show how this budgeting approach works.

> Mrs. Brown, with two elementary school children, earned enough to meet two thirds of the family's needs. Their AFDC check made up the balance. She was laid off, with no advance notice, in early January, and called the welfare agency the next day. But her welfare check could not be increased to reflect this midwinter crisis until the family had survived on her current AFDC check and a few days' pay for a full month. Only then did the loss of earnings signal the need for a higher AFDC grant.

Incidentally, like all families with earnings, Mrs. Brown must file a monthly report with the welfare agency; if she forgets to do so, her grant will be discontinued.

Treatment of Beneficiaries. Universal programs like social security and public employee pensions have earned a far better reputation for courteous, fair, and thoughtful treatment of recipients and the general public. In part this reflects the greater respect for "earned" benefits than for the "dole," a distinction that was vigorously reinforced by social security enthusiasts.†

But there is apparently a great deal more to be said for programs that serve all income classes. With a mix of recipients, sheer numbers tend to be larger which makes for a larger concerned public, including a fair proportion with well-developed instrumental skills that help them negotiate successfully with government bureaucracies. Often, too, recipients represent natural groups that organize around common interests — like the countless organizations of retired people or the labor unions, which play such strategic roles in bringing about legislative and administrative reforms in social security. The mere fact that when recipients represent a broad population spectrum, a higher share will have long-established reading habits or be more likely to read, speak, and comprehend English, gives them added power. Between having more complex programs to master and

---

*It applied to the entire caseload until late 1984.

†Ozawa (35) and widespread informal reports suggest that since the Social Security Administration became responsible for the means-tested SSI program, the favorable image is becoming somewhat tarnished.

having less education, the poor are signally handicapped in confronting government bureaucracies. All of these factors contribute to the dismal conclusion, well documented over the years, that programs for the poor soon become poor programs.

Economic Efficiency. Many economists prefer the selective approach because of its greater *economic efficiency.* This term refers to the share of program costs that goes directly to poor households (10). Unless administrative expenses are exorbitant, as was sometimes true in earlier years when welfare agencies hired special investigators to "stake out" the homes of suspect families for weeks on end, programs designed exclusively for the poor are always more economically efficient than those extending over all income classes.

Yet universal measures have had far more impact on poverty rates in the U.S. than selective programs. One reason is that, thriving better, they can afford higher benefits, thereby lifting more households out of poverty and preventing millions of others from sinking below poverty levels. In this connection, it should be kept in mind that in choosing groups to be targeted by universal cash transfers, planners have concentrated on poverty-prone segments like retired, disabled, or unemployed workers, and widows and orphans, whose median incomes tend to be very modest. Certainly, the very wealthy are few and far between. All of this means that if the goal is to reduce poverty rates, doubts have to be raised about measuring economic efficiency solely in terms of the share of program expenditures going yearly into the pockets of the poor. At least as important is the proportion of eligible people who move or stay out of poverty over one, five, or ten years *because of each program.* It is fairly clear by now that less "economically efficient" universal programs that consistently prosper and win friends have far more impact on both the level and distribution of poverty than highly "efficient" but constantly threatened selective measures that do little but help some of the poor become somewhat less poor. For this and many other reasons, the search continues for universal solutions to the "welfare mess" (19).

The Role of Government in Redistributing Income _____

Many people seem to believe that the only direction in which government redistributes income is downward, from the rich and middle class to the poor. Some years back, Titmuss (42) of England tried to correct this misconception. His efforts resulted in a tripartite analysis of social policy, designed to demonstrate how governments actually affect the distribution and redistribution of household income. He identified three types of "welfare": fiscal, occupational, and public. Each is financed in different ways, which greatly affects their relative visibility; and their primary beneficiaries come from different income classes.

Fiscal Welfare. This package consists of tax exemptions, deductions, and credits as well as special tax treatment of certain types of income like capital gains, all of which are particularly helpful to upper-income households. Titmuss points out that whether income redistribution is achieved by tax policy — commonly referred to as "tax expenditures" in this context — or by "public expenditures" is simply a matter of national style. If $1,000 is conserved by one family through tax policy while $1,000 is received by another family from AFDC, both families are equally beneficiaries of government policy. They both have $1,000 more to spend and they both cause the public treasury to be $1,000 poorer (1, 37). Despite their equivalence in this regard, families receiving "welfare" through the tax system get the better bargain by far since tax shelters are relatively invisible as compared with AFDC grants, and exploiting all possible tax loopholes elicits very different responses from those elicited by being on welfare. Then, too, once incorporated into tax law, loopholes may remain forever; but public expenditures are reviewed and appropriated yearly (4).

Identifying the fiscal welfare package soon led others to point out a host of government policies that redistribute income, although not necessarily or ostensibly as a primary objective (12, 36). Futurist Henderson (22) observes that both government action and government inaction affect the distribution of pretax household income. Her list includes government subsidies to the sugar and tobacco industries, farmers, airlines, and so on, and the failure of our government (unlike its European counterparts) to curb the propensity of large corporations for deploying facilities and resources to cheaper labor markets and lower-taxing jurisdictions. Governments also have a marked effect, she notes, on employment and unemployment patterns that determine both initial distribution and redistribution of income. Government purchasing decisions, the habit of "bailing out" some but not all hard-pressed industries, defense contracts, subsidized research, and protective tariffs are other cases in point. The current trend to cut back civil service employees by contracting with private firms to carry out long-standing government functions is another example.*

While the total redistributional impact of all such policies has never been determined, there is no disagreement that they funnel money primarily toward the well-to-do. A 1975 study of federal subsidies, which then totalled some $96.1 billion, concluded that "they redistribute money to the

---

*The most conspicuous losers in this instance may well be blacks since they have been more heavily represented in the government labor force than in the reasonably well paid commercial labor force.

affluent and in too many cases their costs far exceed their benefit to society as a whole" (44). Using an equivalent definition, the 1984 federal budget listed "tax expenditures" of $388.4 billion, $100 billion of which represented tax loopholes, which could be "closed to good advantage," as Joseph Pechman (4), well-known economist at the Brookings Institution commented, "if there were a will to do so." Instead, they have remained intact or increased yearly — although lawmakers are now determined to reform the tax code.

Occupational Welfare. This second part of Titmuss's tripartite scheme includes a long list of fringe benefits workers qualify for as a result of their occupational status. These comprise the largest share of income distributed through social welfare programs. The chief beneficiaries are not the chronically poor or the occasionally employed but regularly employed workers and their families. In the "occupational welfare" system, benefits rise with earnings. Employed millionaires pile up infinitely larger pensions than average workers. The list of benefits will sound familiar:

- social security (cash benefits and Medicare).
- unemployment compensation.
- workers' compensation (cash benefits and medical care).
- public and private employee pensions and health insurance.
- veterans' pensions and other benefits.
- railroad retirement benefits.
- sick and vacation pay.
- low-cost meals in employer's cafeteria.
- credit unions.
- group life insurance.
- dental and vision insurance.
- related benefits like entertainment expenses, use of company automobiles and airplanes, free tuition at some universities for professors and their families, sabbatical leaves, and free or low-cost employer-sponsored cultural and athletic events.*

This generous group of fringe benefits underscores the importance of steady work and the hardship of unemployment. Pensions grow in value with the length of employment, whereas unemployment causes many benefits to stop entirely and interrupt "coverage" in others, thus ending health insurance and reducing delayed benefits like retirement pensions. In nations where full employment is the goal and is usually achieved, attaching so many benefits to the workplace may make good sense and reflect widely shared views of social justice. But in the U.S., where millions of workers

---

*Only part of this group is reflected in social welfare expenditures, but all are financed or subsidized by public funds.

have been unemployed every year since World War II, deploying resources so heavily in this direction can only enhance the poverty and alienation of groups who cannot work, cannot find work, or are always among the "first fired and last hired." One obvious way to correct the skewed impact of government measures that redistribute income, intentionally or not, is to include in the social welfare package some universal, non-work-related cash benefits, like children's and youth allowances or flat old age pensions as in Canada.

Public Welfare. Finally, the third sector of Titmuss's scheme consists of the bundle of selective programs providing cash grants and in-kind benefits like food stamps and social services to the poor. For years they have commanded less than one fifth of social welfare expenditures in the U.S. and a much smaller share of the total cost of government policies that redistribute income. In the interest of equity and social justice, this fact deserves far more attention than it receives.

References

1. Aaron, Henry J. "Tax Exemptions — the Artful Dodge." *Trans-action,* **6** (March 1969), pp. 4–6.
2. ———. *Why is Welfare So Hard to Reform?* Washington, D.C.: Brookings Institution, 1973.
3. Abbott, Grace. *The Child and the State.* Chicago: University of Chicago Press, 1938, Vol. 1, Pt. 3.
4. Alperovitz, Gar and Jeff Faux. *Rebuilding America.* New York: Pantheon Books, 1984, p. 123.
5. Asbury, Herbert. *The Gangs of New York: an Informal History of the Underworld.* New York: Alfred A. Knopf, Inc., 1927, pp. 1–20.
6. Axinn, June and Herman Levin. *Social Welfare: A History of the American Response to Need.* New York: Harper & Row, Publishers, 1975, pp. 39–45.
7. Ball, Robert M. *Social Security Today and Tomorrow.* New York: Columbia University Press, 1978, p. 269.
8. Bell, Winifred. "Relatives' Responsibility: A Problem in Social Policy." *Social Work,* **12** (January 1967), pp. 32–39.
9. ———. "Services to People: Appraisal of the Task Force on Reorganizing the Social Services." *Social Work,* **15** (July 1970), pp. 5–12.
10. ——— and Dennis M. Bushe. "The Economic Efficiency of AFDC." *Social Service Review,* **49** (June 1975), pp. 175–190.
11. ——— and Dennis M. Bushe. *Neglecting the Many, Helping the Few: The Impact of the 1967 AFDC Work Incentives.* New York University, Center for Studies in Income Maintenance Policy, 1975.
12. ———, Robert Lekachman, and Alvin L. Schorr. *Public Policy and Income Distribution.* New York: New York University, Center for Studies in Income Maintenance Policy, 1974.

13. Billingsley, Andrew and Jeanne M. Giovannoni. *Children of the Storm: Black Children and American Child Welfare.* New York: Harcourt Brace Jovanovich, Inc., 1972, passim.

14. Bradley, Bill. *The Fair Tax.* New York: Pocket Books, 1984, pp. 12–13.

15. Brooks, Van Wyck. *America's Coming of Age.* New York: B. W. Huebsch, 1915, pp. 7, 9.

16. Coll, Blanche D. "Public Assistance in the United States: Colonial Times to 1860." In E. W. Martin, Ed., *Comparative Development in Social Welfare.* London: George Allen & Unwin, Ltd., 1972, pp. 128–158.

17. Deutsch, Albert. *The Mentally Ill in America.* Garden City, N.J.: Doubleday, Doran & Co., 1938, pp. 44–45.

18. Frankel, Charles. "The Welfare State: Postscripts and Prelude." In Charles I. Schottland, Ed., *The Welfare State.* New York: Harper & Row, Publishers, 1967, pp. 207–214.

19. Garfinkel, Irwin. "What's Wrong with Welfare?" *Social Work,* **23** (May 1978), pp. 185–191.

20. Goode, William J. *The Celebration of Heroes — Prestige as a Control System.* Berkeley: University of California Press, 1978, p. 250.

21. Handlin, Oscar. *The Uprooted.* Boston: Little, Brown & Co., 1951.

22. Henderson, Hazel. *Creating Alternative Futures: The End of Economics.* New York: Berkley Publishing Co., 1978, pp. 93–105.

23. Hendricks, Evan. "How Not to Catch Welfare Cheats." *Washington Post,* July 8, 1979.

24. Kahn, Alfred J. *Social Policy and Social Services,* 2d ed. New York: Random House, Inc., 1978, pp. 11–32.

25. ——— . Ed. *Issues in American Social Work.* New York: Columbia University Press, 1959, Ch. 1.

26. ——— and Sheila B. Kamerman. *Not for the Poor Alone: European Social Services.* New York: Harper & Row, Publishers, 1977, pp. 171–179.

27. Kammen, Michael. Ed. *The Contrapuntal Civilization: Essays Toward a New Understanding of the American Experience.* New York: Thomas Y. Crowell Co., 1971, pp. 3–30.

28. Lurie, Irene. "Income, Asset and Work Tests in Transfer Programs for Able-Bodied, Nonaged Individuals." In Institute for Research on Poverty, *The Treatment of Assets and Income from Assets in Income Conditioned Government Benefit Programs.* Washington, D.C.: Federal Council on the Aging, 1977, pp. 52–90.

29. MacDonald, Maurice. *Food, Stamps, and Income Maintenance.* New York: Academic Press, Inc., 1977, pp. 27–38.

30. Marden, Charles F. and Gladys Meyer. *Minorities in American Society,* 5th ed. New York: D. Van Nostrand Co., 1978, p. 280.

31. May, Edgar. *The Wasted Americans.* New York: Harper & Row, Publishers, 1965, Ch. 6.

32. Moon, Marilyn. "The Treatment of Assets in Cash Benefit Programs for the Aged and Disabled." In Institute for Research on Poverty. *The Treatment of Assets and Income from Assets in Income-Conditioned Government Benefit Programs.* Washington, D.C.: Federal Council on the Aging, 1977, pp. 15–51.

33. Myrdal, Gunnar. *An American Dilemma: The Negro Problem and Modern Democracy,* rev. ed. New York: Harper & Row, Publishers, 1962, pp. 205–219.

34. Newman, Dorothy, et al. *Protest, Politics, and Prosperity: Black Americans and White Institutions, 1940–1975.* New York: Pantheon Books, 1978.

35. Ozawa, Martha. "SSI: Progress or Retreat?" *Public Welfare,* **32** (Spring 1974), pp. 33–40.

36. Rein, Martin. "Equality and Social Policy." *Social Service Review,* **51** (December 1977), pp. 565–587.

37. Surrey, Stanley S. "Federal Income Tax Reform: The Varied Approaches Necessary to Replace Tax Expenditures with Direct Government Assistance." *Harvard Law Review,* **84** (1970), pp. 352–408.

38. tenBroek, Jacobus. "California's Dual System of Family Law: Its Origin, Development, and Present Status." *Stanford Law Review,* **16** (January, July 1970), passim.

39. Thernstrom, Stephan. "Urbanization, Migration, and Social Mobility." In Barton J. Bernstein, Ed., *Towards a New Past: Dissenting Essays in American History.* New York: Random House, Inc., 1978, pp. 158–175.

40. Titmuss, Richard M. *Commitment to Welfare,* 2d ed. London: George Allen & Unwin, Ltd., 1976, pp. 113–123, 188–199.

41. ———. *Essays on "the Welfare State,"* 2d ed. London: George Allen & Unwin, Ltd., 1963, pp. 215–243.

42. ———. "The Role of Redistribution in Social Policy." *Social Security Bulletin,* **28** (June 1965), pp. 14–32.

43. Trattner, Walter I. *From Poor Law to Welfare State,* 2d ed. New York: The Free Press, 1979, pp. 18–19.

44. U.S. Congress, Joint Economic Committee. *Federal Subsidy Programs.* Staff Study prepared for the use of the Subcommittee on Priorities and Economy in Government. Washington, D.C.: U.S. Government Printing Office, 1974, pp. 1–5.

45. U.S. Department of Health, Education, and Welfare. "Services for People." Report of the Task Force on the Reorganization of the Social Services. Mimeographed. Washington, D.C.: Office of the Secretary, 1978.

46. U.S. Department of Health and Human Services. *Characteristics of State Plans for Aid to Families With Dependent Children.* Washington, D.C.: U.S. Government Printing Office, 1985.

47. U.S. Department of Labor. *Proceedings of Conference on Mothers' Pensions,* Providence, Rhode Island, June 28, 1922. Children's Bureau Publication #109. Washington, D.C.: U.S. Government Printing Office, 1922, p. 2.

48. Wilensky, Harold L. and Charles N. Lebeaux. "Conceptions of Social Welfare." In Paul E. Weinberger, Ed., *Perspectives on Social Welfare,* 2d. ed. New York: Macmillan Publishing Co., Inc., 1974, pp. 23–30.

CHAPTER 3

The Cost of Social Welfare: Too High or Too Low?

Modern social welfare systems are expensive. In 1978, the most recent year for which comparable analyses are available, public and private social welfare together cost $548.9 billion (20). Both sectors grew remarkably after 1950, with the public somewhat outpacing the private and ending with responsibility for about three quarters of the total cost.*

The severe recessions in the 1970s and soaring inflation pushed public expenditures up sharply by 1980. But when the effect of inflation is subtracted it becomes apparent that the annual rate of growth actually peaked in 1975 at 21.2 per cent. In the next six years the real growth rate never went above 4 per cent (5).

The late 1970s witnessed widespread protests over rising government costs, and specifically the mounting social welfare bill. But there was little evidence that citizens wanted fewer services or less income protection. Every season found Congress and state legislatures beseiged by special interest groups pressing their particular claim on the public treasury.

In the following pages, the trends and distribution of public social welfare costs since 1950 are examined, and the broad picture is compared with that of other industrialized nations. Then the central issues in the debate over the cost of social welfare are explored.

Public Social Welfare Expenditures

Scope and Trends

Public social welfare includes cash and in-kind benefits† and services provided by federal, state, and local governments to civilians, members of

---

*About two fifths of the public cost is financed from taxes earmarked for specific programs like social security and unemployment insurance. The balance comes from general revenues, derived mainly from individual and corporate income taxes and sales and property taxes. Private social welfare is financed by employee and employer contributions to private pensions, individual charitable contributions, gifts from foundations and corporations, bequests, user fees, and government contracts, the last providing about 35 per cent of the total until the 1980s (13, 25).

†In-kind benefits are cash equivalents like food stamps.

the armed forces, and refugees. The services may be provided directly or be purchased from nonprofit or profit-making organizations or independent professionals. Summaries of yearly expenditures are published in the *Social Security Bulletin.*

In 1950 public social welfare programs cost $23.5 billion. By 1983 the total was twenty-seven times higher, $640.0 billion. Does this mean that citizens received twenty-seven times more services and benefits? Not at all. In these thirty-three years, population growth and inflation pushed up all government costs, while economic growth whetted American appetites for more and better services and provided the wherewithal to finance them. The important question is what share of the increase was due to each factor? Only when this is sorted out can cost trends be understood.

The Influence of Inflation. Table 3–1 shows total expenditures for 1950 and 1983 in current and constant dollars. Current dollars are the sums spent each year. Constant dollars correct for inflation by holding the real value of money constant, in this case at its 1983 level. This exercise shows how much the benefits and services provided in 1952 would cost in 1983. When the increased cost that was solely due to inflation is subtracted (by shifting from current to constant dollars), expenditures increased only sevenfold. Like citizens, government had to pay higher construction and repair costs and steeper prices for utilities, supplies, furnishings, food, and salaries. Also a great deal of social welfare is distributed in the form of cash payments to help families meet daily living costs, and the same inflationary pressures that plagued other American households plagued those receiving cash transfers.

The Influence of Population Growth. In 1950 the total U.S. population numbered about 152 million.* By 1983 it had grown by 54 per cent to about 234.5 million. With more people to serve, the 1950 range and level of services would be more costly. The effect of this increase can be weighed by shifting to per capita cost. As Table 3–1 shows, when the cost is averaged over the population, the 1950 share per person was about $153. By 1982 it was $2,699, reflecting an eighteenfold rise. But if both population growth and inflation are discounted, costs rose only fivefold.

The Influence of Economic Growth and Rising Expectations. Despite the series of recessions since World War II, the long-term economic growth trend caused expectations to rise. As compared with 1950, most people now have a more varied diet, newer housing, more telephones, television sets, air conditioners, and clothes requiring far less

*Total population includes the *resident* population plus the armed forces and federal civilian employees and their dependents overseas, and the civilian population in U.S. territories and possessions.

care because of some welcome technological breakthroughs. They are better educated, travel more, and live longer. In constant 1983 dollars, median family income rose by 79 per cent over the past thirty-three years — moving from $13,736 to $24,580. And because family size declined, the gain was even greater than appears on the surface.

In an atmosphere of rising expectations and rising income, it was natural that citizens also wanted more and better health care, education, and other community amenities. To measure the change in cost in this context, the Social Security Administration compares the share of gross national product (GNP) devoted to social welfare each year. The GNP is the total yearly national output of goods and services valued at market price. It can be viewed as the value of all purchases of goods and services by consumers and government plus gross private domestic investment and the net exports of goods and services. The index is used to measure economic growth from one year to the next and also to facilitate international comparisons.*

As Table 3–1 shows, in fiscal 1950 the GNP was $286.5 billion as compared with $3,304.8 billion in 1983. In the earlier year social welfare costs represented 8.2 per cent of the total. By 1983 the share had more than doubled, reaching 19.4 per cent. This is another way of saying that as citizens balanced their rising needs and desires against their growing but finite resources, and decided what to purchase, they chose to double the share committed to social welfare.

What does this tell us? Simply that, when kept in perspective, a twenty-seven-fold increase in social welfare turns out in the real world of rising prices, growing populations, and expanding expectations to be a twofold increase.

The Relative Cost of Various Programs

What programs were chiefly responsible for the increase, and how were funds allocated among programs?† Table 3–2 provides the answers. The giant in both original size and growth, not unexpectedly, is the collection of social insurances which, in addition to social security, includes railroad retirement, unemployment compensation, public employees' benefits, workers' compensation, military pensions, and cash benefits provided

---

*GNP is a seriously faulted, rather primitive measure. Among its worst features is the exclusion of the social costs of production. Thus, the cost of environmental pollution or health hazards is not subtracted from the value of goods produced. Nor is any distinction made between a given dollar value of cigarettes, oranges, soft drinks, milk, bombs or vitamins. In short, in "value-free" economics, everything with a price tag is created equal. GNP is also criticized for not assigning a value to unpaid work performed in the home or in a volunteer capacity in the community, although clearly any society is enriched by both (11, 15).

†The federal budget uses another method of classifying social welfare benefits and services that calls particular attention to those making "payments to individuals," as distinguished from community development or education. In 1983 the federal cost of payments to individuals represented 11.8 per cent of GNP.

Table 3-1. **Public Social Welfare Expenditures, Fiscal Years 1950 and 1983**[a]

	1950	1983	1950:1983
Total expenditures (billions)			
Current dollars	$ 23.4	$ 640.0	1:27
Constant (1983) dollars	87.9	640.0	1:7
Per capita expenditures			
Current dollars	$152.56	$2,698.72	1:18
Constant (1983) dollars	572.70	2,698.72	1:5
Gross National Product (billions)[b]	286.5	3,304.8	1:12
Social Welfare expenditures as per cent of GNP	8.2	19.4	1:2

[a]Excludes 0.2 per cent of total which was expended in foreign countries.
[b]Revised in 1981 by the Bureau of Economic Analysis, Department of Commerce.

Source: Ann Kallman Bixby. "Social Welfare Expenditures, 1981 and 1982." *Social Security Bulletin,* **47** (December 1984), Tables 3 and 4; and Ann Kallman Bixby. "Social Welfare Expenditures, 1963–83." *Social Security Bulletin,* **49** (February 1986), Tables 3 and 4.

through a few state temporary disability insurance schemes. A substantial part of the growth was due to the maturing of the social security system, an evolutionary process that was anticipated when the Social Security Act was passed in 1935. The program began in a small way, but the goal was total coverage of the working population, realistic benefits, and extension of the insurance principle to more of the predictable risks of poverty (1, 8). The result is that while slightly under two thirds of 60 million persons in

Table 3-2. **Public Social Welfare Expenditures, by Function,[a] as Per cent of GNP, Fiscal Years 1950, 1976, 1980, and 1983**

	% of GNP			
	1950	1976	1980	1982[b]
Total expenditures	8.2[c]	19.3[c]	18.7[c]	19.4[c]
Social insurance	1.7	7.3	7.3	8.1
Education	3.3	5.4	4.7	4.3
Health & medical	1.1	3.4	3.8	4.4
Public aid	0.9	1.9	1.7	1.5
Other social welfare	0.1	0.5	0.5	0.4
Veterans' programs	1.2	0.6	0.5	0.5
Housing	—[d]	0.2	0.3	0.3

[a]The official expenditures series, arranged by program, has been rearranged by function in order to include all educational programs under education, and all health and medical programs under health and medical. When items were shifted, the share of GNP was recalculated for each category.
[b]Preliminary data.
[c]Items may not add to total because of rounding.
[d]Less than 0.1 per cent.

Source: Ann Kallman Bixby. "Social Welfare Expenditures, 1981 and 1982." *Social Security Bulletin,* **47** (December 1984), Tables 2 and 4; and Ann Kallman Bixby. "Social Welfare Expenditures, 1963–83." *Social Security Bulletin,* **49** (February 1986), Table 2.

paid employment were covered in 1950, by 1983 the program embraced over nine tenths of the nation's 112 million paid workers. During this period the number of monthly beneficiaries grew more than tenfold from 3.5 to 36.1 million.

For years the second largest item was education, which is the major social welfare expenditure of state and local government. But it slipped to third place in 1983. In constant dollars, the nation's investment in public education declined every year between 1975 and 1982 and rose only slightly in 1983. This is one reason for the current teacher shortage and the widely reported decline in the quality of education.

Conversely, health care costs continue to grow. By 1983 they constituted the second largest item, having advanced beyond education for the first time. They include such varied programs as Medicare, Medicaid, veterans' medical and hospital care, and medical care paid through vocational rehabilitation, workers' compensation, state temporary disability programs, and the Department of Defense. Then there are school health services, maternal and child health care, medical facilities/construction costs, medical research, and public health. Since 1965, when Medicare and Medicaid were enacted, medical and hospital expenses have inflated more rapidly than any other item in the household budget.

In the functional classification used in Table 3–2,* public aid ranks fourth. It includes AFDC, SSI, state–local general assistance, repatriate and refugee assistance, emergency aid, food stamps, surplus foods for the needy, work relief, work experience training, and, since 1981, low-income energy assistance. Perhaps the most common misconception about "welfare" is that it is the most costly social welfare program. But this has not been true since World War II brought about recovery from the Depression of the 1930s and the Works Progress Administration, which supported millions of people in useful work, came to an end. In 1983 public aid expenditures amounted to only 1.5 per cent of GNP and less than 8 per cent of public social welfare costs. Despite significant growth in the poverty population between 1980 and 1983, it should also be noted, the money allocated to public aid declined in both relative and absolute terms.

Expenditures for veterans' programs, in fourth place, have been declining in constant dollars since 1950. It is sometimes charged that the downward trend demonstrates a "turning away" from Vietnam veterans. While many were treated very shabbily, the giant share of the decline in expenditures reflects the fact that in 1950 the largest active armed force in U.S.

*In the official social welfare expenditures series, the Social Security Administration organizes items by program, not function. This results in such anomalies as having Medicaid appear in the public aid column simply because in 1965 Congress found the public assistance grants-in-aid the most feasible channel for financing medical care for low-income individuals. Similarly, a good share of the cost of community social services, some of which are available to persons of any income level, are subsumed under public aid in the government's programmatic classification.

history was just a few years past demobilization. Hundreds of thousands of veterans still claimed educational benefits and still received medical and hospital care.*

"Other social welfare" is in fifth place in our functional classification. This category covers vocational rehabilitation, special Office of Economic Opportunity programs, and many personal and community services in behalf of people of all ages and income levels. A substantially higher investment was made in such services in 1983 than in 1950, but they still cost considerably less than 1 per cent of GNP. Between 1980 and 1983 they suffered an absolute decline of $1.6 billion, about 12 per cent of their 1980 budget.

Housing programs trail the rest. From a relatively small start in 1950, expenditures constituted 0.3 per cent of GNP in 1983 — a very modest investment in housing for the poor and aged, considering the expensive, tight housing market and the generous tax breaks for homeowners.

International Comparisons

All industrialized nations have been called "welfare states" at one time or another. But conceptual clarity is better served by reserving the term for those countries that assure government-protected minimum standards of income, nutrition, health care, and education to all citizens as a matter of legally enforceable right. So defined, the U.S. does not yet qualify and most other industrialized nations do.

In a preliminary report of his long-range study of social welfare expenditures, Wilensky (34) classified nations as "big spenders," "mid-range spenders," and "laggards" according to the share of GNP devoted to social welfare, excluding education and housing. In 1966 the U.S. ended second from the bottom among "laggards" in company with such contrasting nations as U.S.S.R., Switzerland, Israel, and Japan. Among the "big spenders" were West Germany, Sweden, France, Czechoslovakia, and East Germany. With this mix, whatever else can be said about modern "welfare states," they are obviously not as a group communistic, totalitarian, or radical.

More recent comparisons show the U.S. still trailing well behind. Table 3–3 tells the story. Europeans tax themselves more heavily, and devote a higher share of GDP† to social welfare (19). These facts reflect their greater commitment to universalism — which means, for example, income protection and comprehensive health care for everyone. From 1960 to 1982, they also achieved greater yearly growth in manufacturing productivity than the U.S., and in seven nations in this group GNP grew at a

---

*During World War II, over 16.1 million men and women served in the armed forces as compared with 3.3 million in the Vietnam conflict.
†GDP equals GNP minus the share of GNP originating outside the country.

Table 3–3. Intercountry Comparisons of Taxes, Social Welfare Expenditures, and Growth in Manufacturing Productivity

	Taxes as Percentage of GDP^a 1980	Social Welfare Expenditures^b as Percentage of GDP^a, 1981	Per Capita GNP 1981	Annual Growth in Manufacturing Productivity, 1960–1982
Belgium	44.7	30.2	9,655	7.2
Canada	32.9		11,318	3.6
Denmark	45.7	29.3	10,957	5.9
France	42.6	27.2	10,619	5.8
West Germany	37.4	29.5	11,132	5.1
Italy	32.4	24.7	6,122	5.7
Japan	26.1		9,578	9.2
Netherlands	46.2	31.7	9,740	7.0
Norway	47.3		13,463	3.7
Sweden	49.6		13,233	4.8
United Kingdom	36.1	23.5	8,941	3.6
United States	30.7	14.4^c	12,783	2.6

^aGross domestic product
^bExcludes housing and education
^cEstimated by removing housing and education from total

Sources: Donato Alvarez and Brian Cooper. "Productivity Trends in Manufacturing in the U.S. and 11 Other Countries." *Monthly Labor Review,* **107** (January 1984), p. 53; Lillian Liu. "Social Security Problems in Western European Countries." *Social Security Bulletin,* **47** (February 1984), p. 20; U.S. Bureau of the Census. *Statistical Abstract of the United States.* Washington, D.C.: U.S. Government Printing Office, 1982, Tables 1526 and 1530.

faster rate than in the U.S. Norway and Sweden, long considered quintessential welfare states, won the prizes for per capita income, with the U.S. coming in third, followed fairly closely by Canada, West Germany, and Denmark.

Too Much or Too Little?

People in all walks of life differ about whether too much or too little is spent on social welfare. In doing so, they reflect different values, perspectives, degrees of self-interest, and levels of knowledge. Unfortunately, the public debate is often rife with misconceptions, distortions, and omissions, and it can be exceptionally difficult for citizens to separate the wheat from the chaff.

In the balance of the chapter, important trade offs that should be kept in mind are first examined. Then the most frequent arguments about investing in social welfare are explored and evaluated.

Important Trade Offs

Social welfare does not exist in a vacuum. Economic and social policies constantly interact, with savings in one area increasing costs in others. One glaring example involved decisions in Washington during the 1970s and early 1980s to reduce inflationary pressures by putting the economy into recession, which soon led to the layoff of millions of workers. This caused revenues from income, sales, and payroll taxes to drop while costs were rising for unemployment compensation, social security, public assistance, food stamps, Medicare, Medicaid, and a host of less visible community services (31). Eventually, state unemployment compensation reserves neared exhaustion, and the federal government had to lend the states money to pay insurance claims. When high unemployment persisted, the federal government financed extended benefits. Simultaneously, lost revenues and higher costs brought about a sharp decline in social security reserves. To protect the system, in 1977 Congress enacted a series of steep tax increases. But this was not all. Rising social welfare expenditures helped to push the federal deficit in the mid-1970s to the highest levels ever recorded in American history, much to the embarrassment of two Republican Presidents. This paved the way for a backlash that led to demands for a constitutional ceiling on the deficit, as if the primary problem was unlicensed deficit spending rather than the initial decision that pushed millions of taxpayers out of jobs. Why anyone was surprised, let alone outraged, is hard to see. Government economists had warned the White House and Congress that every 1 per cent rise in unemployment rates would add

$17 billion to the federal deficit (32). By 1980, with much higher inflation, the cost of a 1 per cent rise had shot up to $25 billion; and then to $35 billion by the time the scenario was repeated in 1982 and 1983. But this time, with the federal deficit already climbing, unemployment rates rose to over 10 per cent, where they remained for ten long months. Even during 1984 an average of 900,000 more persons were jobless each month than during the Reagan Administration's first year in office. By then most citizens felt some degree of panic over the huge federal deficit and the crushing public debt it was creating. But they cannot be faulted for inconsistency: instead of concentrating on ways to move toward full employment, which would automatically generate the needed tax revenues, demands for a balanced budget resurfaced again.

Another important trade off was brought home by the decision during the late 1960s to press AFDC mothers into paid work or job-training. This followed the "discovery" by White House officials that what all families most need is a wage earner. Soon the old slogan "from welfare rolls to payrolls" was dusted off and preached across the land as federal spokesmen tried to sell their work-welfare "reform" as sound family policy and a fine tax-saving measure.

What they overlooked is that AFDC families abound with preschool children, disabled fathers, and mothers with little education, limited work skills or experience, and less earning power. If the mother is forced out of her home into paid work, substitute child and invalid care often becomes essential. As poor parents and social workers have reason to know, the cost of good day care runs well above the cost of maintaining families at home on AFDC. Financially, the policy could spell disaster for states since they had to put up their share of the cost. To add to the problem, jobs and training slots were too scarce to accommodate the AFDC caseload. Day-care facilities have always been in too short supply to absorb children of even those mothers who wish to work and for whom using day care might be a paying proposition. Also, child development experts and child psychiatrists were horrified that government officials would presume to know better than mothers what children needed at any given time. Extending the big arm of a male-dominated Congress and welfare officialdom into the delicate mother–child bond impressed child specialists as foolhardy and shortsighted in the extreme (9). But however one views such a government stance, it makes no sense as a tax-saving device. Poor women simply do not earn enough on the average to offset the cost of expensive day-care subsidies.

Other trade offs that should be kept in mind proliferate these days, as AFDC, school lunches, the Special Supplemental Food Programs for Women, Infants, and Children (WIC), food stamps, and Medicaid are funded at levels that severely limit coverage of needy families. One consequence is that as we underfinance less costly preventive measures, we incur very costly corrective and emergency care. The Children's Defense Fund (7) spells out a few such trade offs:

- It costs an average of $1,500 to provide complete prenatal and delivery services to a poor pregnant woman; it costs about $1,500 a day to provide intensive hospital care to a premature baby and total hospital costs can easily range from $20,000 to $40,000.
- It costs $35 a month to provide a complete WIC nutritional package to an infant; it costs about $1,400 per week to hospitalize an infant for treatment of malnutrition.
- It costs an average of $380 annually to care for a child who receives regular preventive care; without such care, the annual cost averages $640.
- It costs about $20 for an office visit to a doctor to have a child's strep throat treated; it costs about $3,500 to hospitalize a child whose untreated strep infection develops into rheumatic fever.

In other words, when policy options are weighed, their consequences for the human beings involved and for long- as well as short-term costs should be taken into account.

Public Versus Private Sectors

As prices and unemployment rose during the 1970s, and taxes took an ever larger bite from American households, citizens became angry and alarmed. Perhaps the most dismaying lesson learned in those years was that economic diagnoses and prescriptions differed so dramatically from one school of thought to another that the national economy seemed virtually rudderless. In this atmosphere, battle lines were soon drawn between groups with very different perceptions of the proper role of government and of the relative efficiency of public and private sectors of the economy. Where citizens stood on these issues significantly affected their willingness to support social welfare services.

The Role of Government. For centuries people have disagreed about the respective roles and optimum balance between the public and private sectors. During the nineteenth century many influential Americans subscribed to the laissez-faire philosophy of no governmental interference in economic affairs. They saw a very limited role for government except in protecting private property and defending national boundaries. "That government is best which governs least" was the prevailing sentiment. But this view was never without critics, and gradually courts upheld modest legislative restraints on the excesses of private entrepreneurs.

The Depression of the 1930s represented a quantum jump in the public sector, especially in the federal government's role in assuring more equal access to the basic necessities of life for all citizens. Two decades later the exposure of widespread economic and social discrimination against minorities confirmed for many people their belief that the problem would never yield if left solely to the private sector and state and local governments. And soon the pendulum swung toward greater federal involvement. Even though rumbles of discontent were heard in the early 1970s, groups of citizens still persisted in pressing for more service and more active federal oversight of the private sector. They were enraged at mining companies for their continued indifference to lifesaving safety measures; at companies that blithely dumped dangerous wastes at Love Canal and elsewhere; at DC-10s crashing without survivors because of what appeared to be careless maintenance. The crisis of confidence climaxed in March, 1979 at Three Mile Island when the nation waited breathlessly for the expulsion of deadly gases that never materialized. Each tragedy and near-tragedy has generated new demands for more rigorous and effective government inspection and controls.

But old and new conservatives were on the offensive. Suddenly the liberal agenda — national health care, better services for the aged, better protection for abused and exploited children, equal access to education at all levels, more citizen involvement, far more attention to cities, and a genuine full employment policy — were being widely discredited as decadent and old hat. Liberals, critics complained, were bankrupt for new ideas. They excelled only in spending other people's money. As for their handmaiden, the federal bureaucracy, it was bloated with inefficient, overpaid, meddlesome, and self-serving civil servants who would be unemployable elsewhere in the economy.

Libertarian Robert Ringer (22), William Simon, Nixon's Secretary of the Treasury (30), Nobel laureate Milton Friedman, a conservative economist from the University of Chicago (10), and George Gilder, an evangelistic defender of capitalism who is close to Reagan's advisors (12), all wrote best sellers on the subject. All were critical of the growth of the federal government and the proliferation of government regulations that "strangled" private enterprise.

Taxing citizens in order to redistribute money and services to the poor is abhorrent to this group of conservatives and their followers. Ringer spells out the case against taxing for any purpose except national defense and protection of property, the old nineteenth-century laissez-faire notion. Men, he explains, own their own lives and their property is an intimate extension of themselves. Unless they forcibly interfere with another man's life, they should be absolutely free to live as they choose and dispose of their property as they wish. This freedom, Ringer wrote in a book endorsed by Simon, transcends all others and is totally incompatible with public sector intervention to increase equality. Simon applauded, insisting in turn that not only men but corporations must be free to do whatever they feel is best without Congressional interference.

All of these conservatives view the growth of social welfare since the 1930s as symbolic of the success of liberals in undermining the confidence of citizens in themselves and private enterprise. The Depression and ensuing economic troubles were not the fault of business, but of government, they insist. America can only regain supremacy and courage as Americans turn back to the old-fashioned virtues of economic individualism, unfettered private enterprise, and a very limited role for government. Capitalism, Ringer holds, is not the enemy of the poor but their savior. Instead of one chicken in every pot, as in communist nations, everyone has the chance in capitalist America to end with a dozen chickens — if they only turn their backs on government mollycoddling and rely on their own resources, ingenuity, and drive.

The social security system, unemployment compensation, public welfare, government intercession in the health care system, food stamps, public education, and the "explosion" of new community services are vigorously attacked for their overwhelming cost, depressing effect on savings and private investments, and as ill-conceived liberal efforts to equalize the distribution of goods and services. Offering only questionable evidence, critics nonetheless insist that income redistribution has advanced relentlessly in recent decades (18).

Ringer is convinced that poverty no longer exists in the U.S., which, in turn, makes the liberal platform no longer tenable. Simon (30) is particularly incensed by what he perceives as a major deceit of liberals: they sell social welfare for the poor and then design programs chiefly for the middle class.

A common theme running through many conservative attacks on social welfare is outrage over its role in stimulating the growth of the federal government. Is it possible to sort out the facts? First, just how much has the federal government grown in recent decades? Federal civilian employees comprised 3.4 per cent of the labor force in 1955, 3.3 per cent during the 1960s and 1970s, and 2.7 per cent in 1980.* The two largest clusters, consistently accounting for almost three fifths or more of federal civilian employees, *worked in the Defense Department or the Post Office.* It is true that total government employees represented a larger share of the labor force by 1980, but the growth was at the state and local levels. Similarly, so far as revenues collected, expenditures, and outstanding debt are concerned, the federal share of the total declined while state and local shares rose. Looking specifically at the federal budget, between 1953 and 1973, it was a fairly consistent 20 per cent of GNP (32). In the late 1970s, after a recession and sharp rise in prices, the budget hovered around 22 per cent.

---

*The Bureau of Labor Statistics in the U.S. Department of Labor adjusts labor force statistics periodically. The data cited were published in the September 1985 issue of the *Monthly Labor Review.* Because of a readjustment a few months earlier, they do not coincide precisely with data published prior to June 1985.

By 1983, after the conservatives who opposed big government had been in office for three years, it had climbed to 24.7 per cent.

What about the public debt? At the end of World War II, it amounted to 129.4 per cent of GNP. By 1960 it had declined to 47.6 per cent, and by 1980 it was a "mere" 27.8 per cent of GNP (23). During recent decades it was not public but private debt that skyrocketed. Between 1950 and 1979 corporate and consumer debt each rose fourteenfold, mortgage debt sixteenfold, and state and local debt thirteenfold (14). By 1984, the nation's public debt was following suit. If current spending policies and tax rates are continued, wrote Alice Rivlin (23), former director of the Congressional Budget Office, in 1984, "the cumulative effect" of budget deficits will be reflected "in a nearly fourfold rise in the public debt . . . to 49 per cent of GNP in 1989."

What about *federal* social welfare expenditures — the major target for reduction during and since the 1980 Presidential campaign? After doubling as a percentage of GNP in the decade following the enactment of Medicare and Medicaid in 1965, federal social welfare expenditures stabilized at between 11 and 12 per cent of GNP. They declined slightly from 1976 through 1979, and then rose slightly with the recession in the early 1980s, reaching their highest point ever — 12.1 per cent of GNP — in 1983, the last year for which reports are available. None of this increase was in programs designed for the poor.

Finally, what about the so-called "exponential growth" in federal regulations during the 1970s, and their impact on productivity? Proponents of deregulation often sound a bit hysterical on this subject, but perhaps anyone who has examined volumes of regulations can understand why. Sale (26), for example, points out that new laws in 1975 alone spawned 60,000 pages of regulations in the *Federal Register* and covered a shelf fifteen feet long. In recent years, he reported in 1980, Congress created some 200 new laws yearly, and federal agencies added about 7,000 new regulations with the force of law. But Nobel laureate Paul Samuelson (28) claims the notion that government regulations accelerated significantly in the 1970s is an illusion. As compared with the 1960s, no notable change occurred. Nor has it under the deregulators: in 1984, over 50,000 pages of rules were published by the federal government — enough in bound volumes to fill a shelf thirteen feet long. Nonetheless, while Sale argued for decentralization, the conservatives' desire was to get rid of all regulations, which they blamed almost solely for America's declining productivity. Jewell G. Westerman (33), vice president of a management–consultant firm, takes issue. He was quoted in *Fortune* to the effect that in over 200 studies his firm made of large corporations, he could not recall a "single company in which coping with government regulations raised a significant opportunity for lowering labor costs." What he criticized far more vigorously was the inept bureaucracies in private business and the increasing share of costs devoted to management at the expense of production.

The Efficiency Issue. People also disagree about the relative efficiency of the private and public sectors. Whatever government does, business does better, one group asserts. Opponents counter with stories of faulty appliances, incendiary baby clothes, dangerous, cost-saving automobile parts, contaminated cheese, useless warranties, and greedy, incompetent auto repairmen.*

One version of this argument is that big government is always bad government, a theme reminiscent of Schumacher's *Small is Beautiful* (29). But Schumacher was as vehemently critical of big industry as big government, as a fair number of economists are today (21). Huge organizations, whatever their auspices, Schumacher charged, soon generate inefficiency, inflexibility, insensitivity, impersonality, resource exploitation, and a lust for ever more profits and power. What is urgently needed is a return to the "human scale" — neighborhood or community control, small business, and small farms.

Is there any hard evidence about the relative efficiency of public and private sectors? Reliable comparisons are difficult to make. The jobs performed by the two sectors differ substantially, with government increasingly responsible for human services where efficiency is only one of several relevant measures. Also, as Rivlin (24) has pointed out, measuring efficiency or effectiveness in the human services is fraught with pitfalls. The parent legislation often contains many goals, some contradictory and others ambiguous. Or programs with ambitious goals are funded at poverty levels. In such circumstances, against what expectations are programs to be measured?

In 1977 the Institute for Social Research at the University of Michigan used an opinion survey to secure citizen views of the two sectors and their performance (16). Respondents were asked to rate government offices and business along six variables — promptness of service, "really taking care of the problem," considerate treatment, fairness, and avoidance and correction of errors. Business scored well ahead of government on all counts. But this did not mean that citizens favored transferring government functions to the private sector. When given a list of eight problems or services and asked which sector could better handle them, respondents overwhelmingly voted for public agencies rather than private enterprise. The list included job training, unemployment compensation, relief for needy children, crime control, prevention of environmental pollution, enforcement of safety standards for automobiles, retirement benefits, and screening or payment for medical care. Quite outside of other considerations, it is difficult to think how these services could return a profit or that most citizens would consider this appropriate.

---

*Fantastic overcharges by defense industries which were approved and paid by the Defense Department — $9,600 for an allen wrench and $2,034 for a nut, available at the corner hardware for 25¢ and 13¢ respectively, for instance — suggest a good bit of inefficiency and/or fraud in both sectors.

Another question further muddied the water. When asked "By and large, do most government offices do a good job?", "yes" was the response of 61 per cent. The reaction was even more favorable from citizens with direct experience with government agencies. About 72 per cent were satisfied with how their problems were handled, 77 per cent felt public personnel made "about the right amount" or "more effort than required," and 80 per cent felt they were treated fairly. Fully 88 per cent of respondents who had direct contact with social security offices expressed satisfaction. This was also true for over 60 per cent of former welfare clients. All of which raises questions about whether the initial vote in favor of private business was a thoughtful response or a reflex Americanism.

Certainly, on the other side of the ledger, private business inefficiencies practically spawned the consumer movement and are often held responsible for the surge of foreign cars on U.S. highways. Also, best seller lists and business journals seem to have one book and article after another in which businessmen exhort their colleagues to improve their performance — to listen more closely to consumers and employees, to lead in ways that free, not stultify, creativity, and to pay more attention to the quality of their products and less to the growth of their profits. Raising at least as serious questions about the private sector is the recent rash of corporate crimes and fines, and the many verified overcharges on defense contracts.

The one inescapable conclusion seems to be that for all their inventiveness, Americans have yet to succeed in imbuing most large organizations, whether public or private, with the human and ethical qualities that make for continuing vitality and excellence.

The Priority Issue

Since the mid-1960s the debate over whether "guns or butter" should have top priority in the federal budget has been almost nonstop. First came the War on Poverty, which soon lost out to the War in Vietnam. Then the pendulum swung back: in the early 1970s defense investments lagged while social welfare thrived. But a bit later the Carter Administration convinced Congress to support major modernization of both nuclear and conventional armed forces (6, 17), and within a few years internationalist Norman Cousins (2) wrote "1979 was the first year in human history when spending for destructive purposes exceeded $1 billion a day. . . . As long as the world's resources are being squandered in this manner, any talk of making the planet more congenial to the human species is academic."

Notwithstanding the Carter buildup, the Reagan Administration promoted the idea that national security had been dangerously neglected, thereby permitting the Soviet Union to gain supremacy. In an excess of mortified pride, citizens supported a greatly accelerated arms race, essentially modelled on the Carter strategy, and eventually expanded to embrace

"Star Wars." What makes this plan different from its predecessors is the Administration's insistence on heightening the arms race while reducing and indexing taxes.

At this stage most householders are wondering how the bills are to be paid? At the outset the options seemed to be to scuttle or emasculate domestic programs immediately or to go heavily into debt. As it turned out (some think to the vast surprise of the Administration), citizen support for social welfare was too strong to rely solely on the first option. In fact, after some brief skirmishes, social security, the only program that could offset the huge defense bills, was soon declared out of bounds. This left only programs financed from the General Fund, which, unlike social security, relies on nonearmarked revenues like income taxes. In addition to defense and interest on the public debt, the General Fund pays for a collection of domestic programs, including a share of Medicare, the major means-tested programs, the federal contribution to government pensions, social services, education, and the space, science, energy, natural resources, environment, transportation, agricultural, and community and regional development programs. A good portion of this list is notable for being supported by highly committed interest groups who feel deeply about the relevance of their goals for the quality of life. They also tend to attract scientists and finance experts capable of pinpointing every mistaken assumption, overcharge, duplication, and irrelevance in the defense budget. And they are keenly aware that reductions in their budgets in the early 1980s are just harbingers of future cuts unless the Administration veers from its present course. As Alice Rivlin (23), former director of the Congressional Budget Office, pointed out in 1984, their fears were well-founded. Table 3–4 shows actual and projected shifts in General Fund expenditure patterns from 1980 to 1989. As a share of GNP, defense rises from 5.2 to 7.6 per cent, and

Table 3–4. General Fund Revenues and Outlays as Percentage of GNP, Fiscal Years 1980 and 1989

Budget Component	% of Gross National Product	
	Actual 1980	Projected 1989
General Fund		
Receipts	14.8	12.3
Expenditures	16.5	17.9
Defense	5.2	7.6
Net Interest	2.0	4.0
Nondefense	9.3	6.3
Surplus/Deficit	−1.6	−5.6

Source: Alice M. Rivlin. Ed. *Economic Choices 1984.* Washington, D.C.: The Brookings Institution, 1984, p. 28. (Calculated from data in Congressional Budget Office, *Baseline Budget Projections for Fiscal Years 1985–1989.* Washington, D.C.: Government Printing Office, 1984, as revised by the CBO.)

nondefense programs drop by an equivalent share. Because of high deficits and high interest rates, interest on the public debt rises a full 2 per cent, and the yearly General Fund deficit claims double its 1980 share of GNP. Finally, with tax reductions and indexing, General Fund revenues will cover only two thirds of expenditures by 1989. If the scenario is played out, a good share of the defense bill will be a charge against our children and grandchildren. At the very least, critics suggest, the generations that support an arms race should pay for it.

The basic assumptions of the Administration's defense policy are also challenged. The U.S. was building up, not neglecting, the armed forces in the late 1970s, and according to the CIA's best estimates, it is pointed out, the Soviet Union has considerably moderated its defense budget (23). Also, despite the huge cost, there is no real assurance of greater security in 1989 than in 1980 (4). It is not just faulty defense strategy, large-scale duplication among branches of the armed services, or undisciplined planning and purchasing that trouble some observers. They are deeply persuaded that peace and real security are not likely consequences of nuclear stockpiles and mighty shows of force, and in concentrating on the goal of world supremacy, they believe underlying problems creating world tensions are neglected both at home and abroad. The glaring inequities within and between nations pose far greater threats to our security, it is felt, than any presumed disadvantage in nuclear power. Almost thirty years ago, Galbraith (11) warned of the imbalance between private plenty and public penury in our affluent society. Today, Barnet observes, the debate over guns and butter somehow misses the point.

> Excessive military spending now produces some of the same consequences as military defeat. . . . Increasingly, national power comes out of innovative minds rather than . . . barrels of guns. The nation best able to confront the unprecedented problems of advanced civilizations, to recognize the limits of national power in an interdependent world, and to create a legitimate social order within the confines of a slow-growth economy is the one that is likely to emerge as No. 1. (3)

References

1. Altmeyer, Arthur. *The Formative Years of Social Security.* Madison: University of Wisconsin Press, 1966, pp. 3–42.
2. Associated Press News Release: Stockholm. "Arms Outlays $1 Million a Minute." *New York Times,* June 5, 1981.
3. Barnet, Richard J. "A Reporter at Large: The Search for National Security." *The New Yorker,* **57** (April 27, 1981), p. 140.
4. ———. *Real Security: Restoring American Power in a Dangerous Decade.* New York: Simon and Schuster, Inc., 1981.

5. Bixby, Ann Kallman. "Social Welfare Expenditures, 1981–1982." *Social Security Bulletin,* **47** (December 1984), pp. 12–22.
6. Boston Study Group. *The Price of Defense.* New York: A New York Times Book, 1979.
7. Children's Defense Fund. *A Children's Defense Budget: An Analysis of the President's FY 1986 Budget and Children.* Washington, D.C.: Children's Defense Fund, 1985, p. 39.
8. Douglas, Paul. *Social Security in the United States.* New York: Whittlesey House, McGraw-Hill Book Co., 1936, pp. 292–305.
9. Fraiberg, Selma. *Every Child's Birthright: In Defense of Mothering.* New York: Basic Books, Inc., Publishers, 1977.
10. Friedman, Milton and Rose Friedman. *Free to Choose: A Personal Statement.* New York: Harcourt Brace Jovanovich, Inc., 1980.
11. Galbraith, John Kenneth. *The Affluent Society.* Boston: Houghton Mifflin Co., 1958, pp. 251–269.
12. Gilder, George. *Wealth and Poverty.* New York: Basic Books, Inc., Publishers, 1981.
13. *Giving — USA.* New York: American Association of Fund-Raising Councils, 1978.
14. Harrington, Michael. *Decade of Decision: The Crisis of the American System.* New York: Simon and Schuster, Inc., 1980, p. 61.
15. Henderson, Hazel. *Creating Alternative Futures: The End of Economics.* New York: Berkley Publishing Corp., 1978, pp. 21–22 and Pt. 2, passim.
16. Katz, Daniel, Barbara Guteck, Robert L. Kahn, and Eugenia Barton. *Bureaucratic Encounters: A Pilot Study in the Evaluation of Government Services.* Ann Arbor: University of Michigan, Institute for Social Research, 1975, Chs. 3 and 4.
17. Kistiakowsky, George B. "Weaponry: The Folly of the Neutron Bomb." *The Atlantic,* **241** (June 1978), p. 14.
18. Kuttner, Robert. *The Economic Illusion: False Choices Between Prosperity and Social Justice.* Boston: Houghton Mifflin Co., 1984, p. 1–49.
19. Liu, Lillian. "Social Security Problems in Western European Countries." *Social Security Bulletin,* **47** (February 1984), pp. 17–22.
20. McMillan, Alma W. and Ann Kallman Bixby. "Social Welfare Expenditures, Fiscal Year 1978." *Social Security Bulletin,* **43** (May 1980), pp. 3–17.
21. Piori, Michael J. and Charles F. Sabel. *The Second Industrial Divide: Possibilities for Prosperity.* New York: Basic Books, Inc., Publishers, 1984.
22. Ringer, Robert J. *Restoring the American Dream.* New York: QED, distributed by Harper & Row, Publishers, 1979, p. 103.
23. Rivlin, Alice M. Ed. *Economics Choices 1984.* Washington, D.C.: The Brookings Institution, 1984, pp. 26, 27, 28–29.
24. ———. *Systematic Thinking for Social Action.* Washington, D.C.: The Brookings Institution, 1971.
25. Salamon, Lester M. and Alan J. Abramson. *The Federal Budget and the Nonprofit Sector.* Washington, D.C.: The Urban Institute Press, 1982.
26. Sale, Kirkpatrick. *Human Scale.* New York: Coward, McCann & Geoghegan, Inc., 1980, p. 100.
27. Samuelson, Paul A. *Economics,* 11th ed., rev. New York: McGraw-Hill Book Co., 1980, pp. 143–145.

28. —————. Quoted in "Productivity: Two Experts Cross Swords." *Newsweek,* **96** (September 8, 1980), p. 68.

29. Schumacher, E. F. *Small is Beautiful.* New York: Harper & Row, Publishers, 1973.

30. Simon, William E. *A Time for Truth.* New York: Berkley Publishing Corp., 1979.

31. *The Social Costs of National Economic Policy.* New York: Community Council of Greater New York, 1977.

32. U.S. Congress, Joint Economic Committee. *1976 Joint Economic Report.* Washington, D.C.: Government Printing Office, 1976, pp. 9–10.

33. Westerman, Jewell. "A Difference of Opinion." *Fortune,* **103** (May 4, 1981), pp. 357–362.

34. Wilensky, Harold L. *The Welfare State and Equality.* Berkeley: University of California Press, 1975, pp. 31–32.

CHAPTER 4

The Distribution of Income and Wealth

Introduction

Despite hopes and fears to the contrary, the distribution of income and wealth has remained remarkably stable since the end of World War II. This is not what economic seers foresaw thirty years ago. Distinguished economist Simon Kuznetz (29), writing shortly after the war, predicted that the income-equalizing trend characteristic of the first half of the century would continue. If a strong growth economy could be sustained, many Keynesian economists argued, in a tight labor market with jobs opening up on a broad front, even inexperienced, unskilled workers would be in demand. Wages at all levels would be pushed up, thereby causing the growth factor to "trickle down" to even the poorest paid workers.

In 1958 Galbraith (16) wrote about America's unparalleled affluence and the economic security it assured the vast majority of citizens. But he also issued warnings. An affluent society, preoccupied with private production and consumption, he wrote, ran many risks including producing for the sake of producing irrespective of quality or kind, and embracing an ethos of bloated private consumption without regard to its public cost. It was too easy to forget that a car or two for every household requires highways, street maintenance, bridges, parking space, protective police services, traffic control, license bureaus, and snow removal. On all sides he saw grave imbalance — private opulence and public starvation — which spelled disaster for already decaying, underserviced cities. He urged greater commitment to the public sector.

Two remarkable books carried the argument further. Michael Harrington's (24) *The Other America* was published in 1962. Little noticed at first, sales soared after Dwight MacDonald's (34) stunning review, "Our Invisible Poor," appeared in the *New Yorker*. Suddenly poverty was rediscovered as millions of people became aware of the vast material differences separating Americans. Plans for a war on poverty were barely outlined when Gunnar Myrdal's (35) *Challenge to Affluence* was published. Swedish economist Myrdal had already earned a place of affection and respect in the U.S. for his incomparable study of race relations (36). In his new book he called attention to our lagging production. Four of the seven recessions between 1949 and 1980 had already occurred, and each was deeper and longer than its European counterpart. Despite relatively higher defense expenditures than in Europe where unemployment rates were substantially lower, the U.S. economy failed to absorb the labor force even in good times. Unless greater economic stability could be achieved and production increased, Myrdal foresaw difficulties on both foreign and domestic fronts. He felt that great inequality of income and opportunity threatened democratic ideals and posed a high risk of creating a permanent underclass of deprived, often jobless citizens. One thing a nation striving to expand and sustain productivity gains did not need, he insisted, was a large group of households with very limited purchasing power. Correcting the maldistribution of income was the obvious first step toward achieving national economic and social goals.

With the advent of the War on Poverty, daily newspapers were filled with facts about discrimination against blacks, Hispanic Americans, and native Americans. People everywhere began hearing about the time bomb of "felt relative deprivation" among the poor. This thesis held that whether they were better off in the U.S. than in the Third World was irrelevant. What mattered was the anger and alienation aroused by being poor, often jobless, and dark-skinned in a highly materialistic, success-oriented, white society where huge advertising budgets whetted consumer appetites, and racism and contempt for the poor pervaded most social institutions. Americans were told that, as Tawney (47) had observed years earlier, it was one thing to recognize that ability, motivation, and career objectives varied among individuals and in turn influenced income distribution, and quite another to erect institutional barriers which discriminated against whole groups of citizens. What was needed was a significant shift in attitudes on the part of the white majority so that the man-made odds against the rest could be neutralized at long last.

Before this lesson was absorbed ghettos burned, and a highly regarded middle-of-the-road Commission on Civil Disorders issued a surprisingly stinging and sobering report (37). In summarizing the causes of civil disorders, it referred to persistent and pervasive inequalities of income, opportunity, schooling, housing, and neighborhood services. It was as though rich and poor, whites and blacks lived in different societies, and the nation was rapidly turning into fortress America.

By the 1970s, even middle-income white Americans began to realize how fragile their hold on economic security was. Middle-class status, it was turning out, was often not the protection many had been led to expect (39). In a large sample of families monitored since 1967, during a ten-year period less than 1 per cent of the individuals involved were poor every year, but 24 per cent fell in the poverty population for at least one year (13). As the

1973-to-1975 recession advanced, poverty rates rose for the first time in years, real median family income dropped, and *stagflation*, the simultaneous rise of prices and unemployment rates, became the new nightmare of economists.

With these developments, economists like Thurow (48), Galbraith (17), Lekachman (32), Harrington (23), Comanor and Smiley (9), and Barnet and Müller (3) renewed their warnings that great disparities of income and wealth were dangerous in a democratic society, and that the economic system could not be relied on to solve the problem. Furthermore, new prescriptions were necessary to cure stagflation, especially in an economy characterized by increasingly concentrated, monopolistic power that gave large corporations and professions license to protect profits and raise prices even during a recession. As for the "trickle-down" thesis, it held little water when prices and wages competed to see which could outstrip the other. Even with the progressive income tax system and cash transfers, the poor were losing out. Tobin (49) proposed that at least *the basic necessities of life should be guaranteed, and removed from the assortment of prizes in the income race. Let the rewards of free enterprise,* he urged, *be limited to luxuries.*

But a conservative tide was sweeping the land, and the offensive was soon taken by another group of economists who happily accepted the challenge of proving that the nation had already progressed too far toward income equality (6, 15). As for poverty, most of this group were sure that it was little more than an artifact created by the Census Bureau's definition of income. The trouble lay, they believed, with the fact that mushrooming in-kind benefits and services provided by government were not taken into account. At worst, if any poor people were still around, they were very young, with the future ahead of them, or very old, with easy access to social security, SSI, food stamps, public housing subsidies, senior citizen centers, low-cost transportation, special tax concessions, and medical care. Who in his right mind could regard poverty as a serious problem under these circumstances?

In the following pages conflicting evidence about the distribution of income and wealth is examined. No one questions that they are very unevenly divided. What is at issue is the magnitude of the disparity and, by implication, whether there is any longer reason to worry about the standard of living of America's poor. To understand the argument requires examination of conceptual and methodological problems that specialists must resolve in order to arrive at any conclusion. Usually details of this sort are buried in professional journals, which means that most people have little choice but to rely on the accuracy of whatever they read. One objective in the following pages is to provide some tools needed to make an independent judgment.

The Distribution of Income —————————————————

Definitions and Sources

The U.S. Bureau of the Census publishes yearly and decennial reports on consumer income.* While the work of the Census Bureau is admired over the world, no one doubts that population is undercounted and income underreported. If all citizens cooperated fully with government and were honest and accurate in doing so, there would be far fewer problems. As it is, the Census Bureau must go to elaborate lengths to estimate both population and income. The 1983 estimates suggest about a 10 per cent income shortfall, but the proportion varies from 1 per cent of earnings to 55 per cent of interest, dividends, and rental income (51).† As for the number of citizens who are missed, it represents a very small fraction of the total, and in general consists of inner-city residents and young black males — obviously overlapping groups which mainly fall in the low-income population.

Census reports refer to "total money income," but this term should not be confused with actual total income or purchasing power. The first fallout occurs because the Census Bureau deals with pretax, not posttax, income.** The second comes about by the exclusion of various types of income. Among the income exclusions are capital gains and losses, tax refunds, gifts, lump sum inheritances and insurance payments, and non-money items like undistributed corporate profits, employer-paid fringe benefits, imputed rent from owner-occupied housing, consumer durables, food produced and consumed on farms, and government noncash (in-kind) benefits and services like food stamps, public housing subsidies, medical care, and education. All other types of income are included — earnings from employment and self-employment, cash transfers, dividends, royal-

*Detailed yearly reports are published in Series P – 60 of the Current Population Reports on consumer income. See, e.g., U.S. Bureau of the Census. *Current Population Reports, Consumer Income 1983,* Series P – 60, no. 146.

†For 1981 federal tax returns, the Internal Revenue Service estimates that $250 billion of legal income was underreported, for a loss in tax revenues of $82 billion (5). The problem is increasing. In 1984 lost tax revenue because of underreporting of income and overstatement of deductions was estimated at $100 billion. Chief offenders are well-off persons with income from sales of real estate or collectibles and exchanges of various types of property. Since brokerages were required by 1982 tax amendments to report to IRS on dividends and stock and commodity sales, there is now more compliance with tax law in this area (20).

**By mid-1985 the Bureau had published four special studies, using simulated models, to estimate posttax income (including only federal and state income taxes, property taxes on owner-occupied housing, federal retirement and social security taxes), but so far no attempt has been made to collect information from households on the taxes they actually paid. See U.S. Bureau of the Census. *Current Population Reports, Special Studies,* Series P – 23, no. 143. Washington, D.C.: U.S. Government Printing Office, June 1985. It should also be noted that data collection and verification would be more complex for government and burdensome to citizens if posttax income were the goal. One reason is the wide and frequent variation of state and local tax rates (21).

ties, rents, child support payments, alimony, annuities, pensions, and other intrafamilial transfers. Just how much household income drops from sight is unknown. Estimates for the rich go as high as $200 billion yearly (26). But more fuss is generally made about omitting to count in-kind benefits and services for low- or average-income households.

Another complication should be noted. The Census Bureau reports annual income of persons aged 14 years and over, unrelated individuals, families, and households. The degree of income inequality varies with the unit and time period selected for analysis. Arguments are made for using longer time periods, even lifetime income (4, 33). As for reporting units, the most exhaustive reports are on families, but some people object to this unit since family size has not only declined over the years but varies by income level. Also, family income is distributed somewhat more equally than income of other units (11). However, since this is the consumer unit of central interest, we focus on families to the extent possible in the following analysis.

Patterns of Distribution

For years, in successive editions of his famous, widely studied *Economics,* Harvard's Paul Samuelson (43) has provided a vivid picture of income distribution in the U.S. by observing that "If we made an income pyramid out of a child's blocks, with each layer portraying $1,000 of income, the peak would be far higher than the Eiffel Tower, but most of us would be within a yard of the ground." What are the facts behind this generalization?

1. Pretax Income Shares. Each year census reports order all families by income from the poorest to the richest, divide them into quintiles, add up the total income received by each quintile, and then calculate the share of aggregate family income received by each fifth. The results for selected years between 1950 and 1984, as well as the upper-income levels for the first four quintiles, are shown in Table 4–1. Even though upper-income limits (in current dollars) rose steadily over the years — for instance, from $1,661 in 1950 to $12,489 by 1984 for the bottom quintile — the proportion of aggregate income changed little. In every year, the income share of the highest fifth of families is from seven to nine times larger than the bottom fifth's share. In 1984 the richest 5 per cent had a higher share than the two bottom fifths, evidence that income distribution is becoming more concentrated. In the late 1960s a zestful economy with the help of rising transfer payments pushed up the share of the lowest fifth to 5.6 per cent, but since the mid-1970s, and especially during the early 1980s, the two richest quintiles have gained at the expense of the three lowest fifths — the poor, near-poor and middle-income families.

This suggests that even in economic recessions the well-to-do manage to

TABLE 4–1. Percentage Share of Aggregate Pretax Family Income Received by Each Fifth of Families and Family Income at Selected Levels, Various Years 1950–1984

	Percent of Aggregate Income Received by					
	Lowest Fifth	Second Fifth	Middle Fifth	Fourth Fifth	Highest Fifth	Top 5%
1984	4.7	11.0	17.0	24.4	42.9	16.0
1980	5.1	11.6	17.5	24.3	41.6	15.3
1975	5.4	11.8	17.6	24.1	41.1	15.5
1970	5.4	12.2	17.6	23.8	40.9	15.6
1965	5.2	12.2	17.8	23.9	40.9	15.5
1960	4.8	12.2	17.8	24.0	41.3	15.9
1955	4.8	12.3	17.8	23.7	41.3	16.4
1950	4.5	12.0	17.4	23.4	42.7	17.3

Income at Selected Positions (Current Dollars)

	Mean Income All Families	Upper Limit of Each Fifth				Lower Limit of Top 5%
		Lowest Fifth	Second Fifth	Middle Fifth	Fourth Fifth	
1984	$31,052	$12,489	$21,709	$31,500	$45,300	$73,230
1980	23,974	10,286	17,390	24,630	34,534	54,060
1975	15,546	6,914	11,465	16,000	22,037	34,144
1970	11,106	5,100	8,320	11,299	15,531	24,250
1965	7,704	3,500	5,863	7,910	10,800	16,695
1960	6,227	2,784	4,800	6,364	8,800	13,536
1955	4,962	2,221	3,780	5,082	6,883	10,605
1950	3,815	1,661	2,856	3,801	5,283	8,615

Source: U.S. Bureau of the Census. *Current Population Reports, Consumer Income 1984.* Series P–60, no. 151, Table 12.

keep their high-paying jobs and lucrative professional practices, and continue to realize some return on investments. Even if they suffered earlier losses in the market, they probably recovered more quickly than other families. The "turnabout" in the stock market, for instance, is often one of its most profitable periods.

Economists disagree sharply about whether great income disparities are needed to maintain incentives. One test is to look at other nations. While the ratio between the pretax income of the richest and poorest quintiles in the U.S. is now 9 : 1, in Japan and West Germany, where productivity accelerated more rapidly than in the U.S. during the 1970s, the ratios are 5 : 1 and 7 : 1, respectively (2). Far from being an economic necessity, Harrington (23) regards incentives on the U.S. scale as a "fairy tale" to justify gross maldistribution of riches. While they may be less sweeping, many other economists take exception to the notion that sheer money rewards explain efforts of the very rich to stay on top. Gaining and holding power and enjoying the prestige and privileges great wealth commands are more their meat.*

2. Posttax Adjusted Income Shares. As mentioned earlier, a number of social scientists regard the Census Bureau's definition of "total money income" as anachronistic. During the 1970s economists responded to the challenge by estimating income shares using extended definitions of income after taxes. Using such an approach, Browning (6, 7), Kuznetz (28), Paglin (38), and Smeeding (45) were among the group that reported a decrease in income inequality during the past thirty years or so. Browning made by far the most extreme claims: he found such a marked trend toward equality that he doubted the nation could let it continue. Still other economists, including Budd (8), Gatsworth (19), Henle (25), and Reynolds and Smolensky (42), found little change or even more of an income gap than in earlier years.

Working with the Figures. Why do the results differ so greatly? It is usually because researchers made different assumptions and used different concepts, methodologies, or data sources. Some with less time than others may have taken shortcuts. But in research, as in all human activities, some decisions are better than others, and both the validity and the reliability of results may be at stake. Since income redistribution promises to be an important issue for years to come, it is worth examining published claims of the progress made to date in some detail.

Smeeding (44), who found only a modest equalizing trend, examined Browning's widely publicized articles to learn why their estimates differed so drastically. Table 4–2 shows their results. According to Browning, the

---

*A brief, insightful discussion of these issues can be found in an article by Robert J. Lampman (30), University of Wisconsin's great expert on income and wealth distribution.

TABLE 4-2. Net Adjusted Income Share of Lowest Income Quintile, 1952, 1962, and 1972

	Browning		Smeeding	
	% of Sum of Per Capita Income for Each Quintile	% Gain 1952–1972	% of Aggregate Net Income	% Gain 1952–1972
1952	7.8		5.5	
1962	9.0		5.7	
1972	12.6ᵃ	61.5	6.5	18.1

ᵃIf Browning's results are recalculated to obtain the lowest income quintile's share of net aggregate income, it would be 10.7% not 12.6%.

Source: Edgar K. Browning. "The Trend Toward Equality in the Distribution of Net Income." *Southern Economic Journal,* **43** (June 1976), p. 919; Timothy M. Smeeding. "On the Distribution of Net Income: Comment." *Southern Economic Journal,* **45** (January 1979), pp. 938 and 942.

lowest quintile's share of adjusted net income rose from 7.8 to 12.6 per cent between 1952 and 1972, for a gain of 61.5 per cent. Smeeding found only an 18.2 per cent gain, from 5.5 to 6.5 per cent.

Both economists started with 1972 census data which they adjusted for income underreporting. Then they added capital gains and a cash value for in-kind benefits. Smeeding's list of benefits was more inclusive, but both took major programs into account. They also both deducted taxes to arrive at net income for each quintile. But looking below the surface reveals some striking differences at every stage.

1. Income Underreporting. Specialists in this field usually rely on census microdata, which gives them direct access to the crucial details they need. This was Smeeding's source. But Browning, oddly enough, relied on published census reports for both the extent of underreporting by broad income category* and the distribution of each type of income among families at different income levels (which do not fit income cutoff points for the quintiles at all precisely). Browning's problem was that census reports come in summary form, which makes it impossible to recapture details needed in this type of adjustment. His less reliable approach resulted in his assigning $1.2 billion more than Smeeding to the two bottom quintiles.

2. In-kind Benefits. Browning added $15.8 billion more in in-kind benefits than Smeeding and assigned a higher share to the bottom quintile. He made some odd assumptions and a few fatal shortcuts.

Starting with total expenditures for his chosen in-kind programs, he should have subtracted the share distributed to the institutional popula-

---

*E.g., property income is a broad category that covers dividends, rents, royalties, and the like. Census microdata enabled Smeeding to distribute underreported dividends, rents, and royalties separately, while all Browning could do was to distribute property income as a lump.

tion* and to American families living outside of the fifty states, who are not included in yearly census reports. (Puerto Rico has the largest per capita food stamp program of any jurisdiction.) Browning apparently forgot these two steps. Then in subtracting the share of in-kind benefits going to unrelated individuals, he "guessed" that they received 13 per cent of the total. Smeeding not only subtracted the share for the first two groups noted above, but — again using microdata reports of the largest programs, Medicare, Medicaid, food stamps, and public housing subsidies — he learned that the share distributed to unrelated individuals was nearer 28 per cent. (The group includes many poor aged persons living alone in cities.)

In assigning a money value to in-kind benefits, Browning repeated the same error that government economists have made for years. He simply distributed the *total cost* of his selected in-kind programs among income quintiles as if the object were to arrive at a per-quintile cost figure. For instance, he included *all* public health expenditures, like the Food and Drug Administration budget and such capital expenditures as construction costs for medical facilities and libraries. But the goal of this exercise was to measure the effect of in-kind benefits on family income. As has been pointed out repeatedly in the literature, at the very least researchers should limit themselves to counting those benefits that are directly distributed to individuals and families. This was Smeeding's approach. He first subtracted extraneous costs, and then, using the best work done in the field as his guide, he placed a value on the benefits to recipients. This value is something less than 100 per cent of the cost, most specialists agree. If one thinks of Medicaid "mills" that rake in profits by giving unnecessary examinations, medication, and "shots," the logic of deducting some share of the cost becomes apparent when the object is to estimate the value to families.

Finally, in distributing these benefits among quintiles, Browning assumed that all of the poor were in the lowest quintile, and that all families in that quintile received the same in-kind benefits per capita as poor families do. These are tempting shortcuts, but he was wrong on both counts. Only 91 per cent of the poor were in the lowest quintile in 1972, and only about 42.5 per cent of that quintile were officially classified as poor. This paradox occurs for several reasons. First, as is explained in detail in Chapter 6, the poverty threshold varies with the size of the family, the age of householders, and until 1981, with the sex and residence of householders. None of these variables are considered in dividing families into quintiles. Second, a glance at Table 4–1 shows that the income cutoff for the bottom quintile in 1975, for example, was $6,914; the poverty threshold for average-size families that year was only $5,550. Putting these two facts

---

*This includes everyone in nursing homes, prisons, child care institutions, state hospitals, institutions for the mentally retarded, the deaf, and the blind, students living in dormitories, and persons in homes for the aged, foster homes, and boarding homes.

together, it should be clear that many small families may fall in the bottom income quintile but not be counted among the poor, while many large families may be poor but be well over the income limit for the bottom quintile. Smeeding, with better command of the facts, assigned the lowest quintile 49 per cent of in-kind benefits in contrast to Browning's 58 per cent.

3. Education Transfers. In handling the cost of public education, Browning failed to subtract the share received by unrelated individuals. He distributed elementary and secondary school expenditures over all families with children under eighteen years of age. Smeeding excluded the cost of school construction, the share for unrelated individuals, and assigned nothing to preschoolers. This resulted in lower shares for the bottom quintiles. He also gave somewhat more weight to research showing an inverse relationship between income and college attendance (22), which also decreased the share assigned to the lower quintiles.

4. Capital Gains. Since capital gains are not included in the census definition of income, both researchers had to estimate the total and its distribution over family quintiles. Browning, using research based on income tax distributions of households by *adjusted gross income,* applied the findings by some unspecified method to published census distributions of *money income.* This is not a simple, straightforward exercise. First, the two concepts of income differ remarkably. In 1972, the lowest quintile of families had 5.4 per cent of census money income and only 1.3 per cent of adjusted gross income. Second, income classes are not the same in the two sets of published data. Given these problems, at the very least he should have spelled out his distribution formula. But he simply states his result — he allocated 8.7 per cent of capital gains to the lowest quintile.

Smeeding relied heavily on detailed work carried out at the Brookings Institution with the use of the great MERGE file. This computer file is the result of skillful, laborious efforts to reconcile income tax returns and census data, in the process correcting for the undercount of people and underreporting of income. It is widely accepted as the best estimate available of household income. Smeeding's method resulted in assigning only 3.5 per cent of capital gains to the lowest quintile.

5. Other Nonmoney Income. Browning added an item worth $121.4 billion which he called "potential additional earnings," over a third of which was allocated to the lowest quintile. Knowing how he calculated its money value provides clues to what he had in mind. He multiplied the number of adults in each quintile who were not earners by the average earnings per worker in each quintile, and added the product to the income of each quintile. What was his logic? He was tapping a favorite myth of classical economics — that anyone who is not working has voluntarily elected leisure. While it is everyman's choice, so the myth goes, to idle the days away, doing so carries a price tag which must be added to income. Otherwise, "voluntary" poverty — the self-willed consequence of preferring to "do nothing" — might be defined as a problem. Browning's reasoning assumes that all unemployed persons are out of work by choice, including the aged forced out of the labor market by mandatory retirement policies, the sick and disabled, and mothers with young children at home.

Smeeding questioned whether this reasoning would appeal to most economists and, rejecting it out-of-hand, substituted the employer's share of fringe benefits, an item which tax experts have long recommended be subject to income tax, and which he estimated was worth $79 billion, about 3 per cent of which he allocated to the bottom quintile.

Their different reasoning at this stage accounted for most of the variance in final results.

6. Taxes. After making the above additions to income, Browning subtracted only federal payroll and income taxes while Smeeding subtracted all taxes.

Most researchers would agree that the next logical step was to reorder families to reflect the new net income concept since some households gained and others lost income in the process, and certainly many could have shifted to new quintiles. Browning omitted this step; Smeeding carried it out.

Then, preparatory to estimating the progress toward equality between 1952 and 1972, Browning made a very odd decision. He decided there was no way to allocate capital gains among quintiles of families in 1952 and 1962, or to estimate underreported income. So, for the sake of consistency, he dropped both items from his 1972 calculations. Smeeding, relying on prior published research in the field — which Browning, too, should have known about — kept his methodology intact for all three years.

Browning took a final step. Instead of using his new net income totals to calculate quintile shares of aggregate net income, which is the commonly accepted practice followed by Smeeding, Browning decided at this late stage to correct for the difference in family size among quintiles. He did so by shifting to per capita income. After working out the per capita income for each quintile, he added the five figures, calculated the percentage each represented of the total, and reported the result as the "income shares" of each quintile of families. This series of maneuvers raises logical and technical issues that boggle the mind. Suffice it to say that however desirable it may be to take the different size of families in each quintile into account, the decision must be made at the beginning, not the end, of the exercise. Both money income as reported to the Census Bureau and each new income component would have to be allocated to individuals, not families. Smeeding and others believe the results would be very different.* Had

*Browning's approach at this stage also assumes that a seven person family needs seven times what a one person household needs, thereby assigning no weight to economies of size.

Browning calculated his quintile shares in the usual way, his bottom quintile would have ended with 10.6 per cent of aggregate net income rather than 12.6 per cent.

This has been a long review of an involved process. But Browning's estimates are much admired and touted by conservatives who are bent on proving that low-income families are much better off than Census reports suggest. From all appearances, many people accept them at face value. Unless we look below the surface, the nation stands a very good chance of prematurely closing the door on the poor and losing all the gains so far made on their behalf. The evidence strongly suggests that Smeeding was right when he concluded that ". . . we have *not* made a great deal of progress toward income equalization . . ."*

The Distribution of Wealth

Definitions and Data Sources

What is meant by *wealth?* Wealth consists of the total economic assets possessed by people. These assets include such property as stocks, bonds, real estate, notes and mortgages, cash deposits, family-owned businesses and professional practices, equity in cars, homes, and insurance policies, the value of farm animals and equipment, trusts, art objects, and jewelry. Since assets can be converted into cash they go a long distance in determining the relative access families have to other scarce resources like quiet, well-guarded neighborhoods, the finest medical care, power, and prestige. Income and wealth are closely interrelated. Turner and Starnes (50) suggest that it helps to think of income as the *flow* of money and goods and wealth as a *store* of the same. the possession of wealth, in other words, determines the capacity to generate income. Most often, income is compensation for something — 85 per cent typically represents earnings; while wealth may produce income, it also connotes power and control.

Until recently information about wealth was much harder to come by than income data. Estate tax returns were the usual source (53), but their usefulness was severely limited by the Tax Reform Act of 1976, which reduced by 90 per cent the number of individuals required to file such returns (12). When the need for more complete and current information became apparent, the Federal Reserve Board contracted with the Institute for Social Research (ISR) at the University of Michigan for a special 1983

---

*We can expect to hear much more about the presumed value of in-kind benefits, especially to the poor. It might be well to keep in mind that in 1970 the estimated value of all in-kind benefits and services was $559 for families with incomes under $1,000, while they averaged $1,965 for families with incomes of $25,000. In 1976 the weighting toward the nonpoor was still in evidence (1). See Chapter 6 for further discussion of this issue.

survey. Shortly thereafter the Bureau of the Census decided to initiate a new series of periodic surveys on the distribution of wealth. The first was carried out in 1984.*

Patterns of Distribution

1. The Share of the Top 1 Per Cent of Wealth-holders. Wealth is largely created by the cumulative impact of income inequities, and so it is not surprising to find it far more concentrated than income. This has been true since colonial days, but systematic studies cover only the last 170 years. In 1972 (52) the richest 1 per cent of adults held about the same share of household wealth as the top 1 per cent of families in 1810 (18), 20.7 and 21.0 per cent, respectively. Over the years the share rose gradually to 36.3 per cent in boom-and-bust 1929, dropped to 20.8 per cent by the end of equalizing World War II (31), rose to 29.2 per cent in zesty 1965 (46), dropped to 20.7 per cent in 1972, and rose to 26.9 by 1983.

But even this gives a picture of more dispersion than exists. In 1972 more than three quarters of the wealth held by the top 1 per cent was actually controlled by the top .5 per cent.

The relationship between income and wealth is well illustrated by analyzing the kinds of property great wealth holders own. In 1972 the top 1 per cent held the following shares of the aggregate value of various assets:

- 15.5 per cent of real estate.
- 56.5 per cent of corporate stock.
- 60.0 per cent of bonds.
- 13.5 per cent of cash deposits.
- 52.7 per cent of debt instruments like notes and mortgages.
- 7.0 per cent of life insurance (cash surrender value).
- 89.9 per cent of all trusts.
- 9.8 per cent of miscellaneous assets.

By 1984 the top 2 per cent owned 70 per cent of tax-exempt bonds, 50 per cent of corporate stock (which is one source of wealth that has become somewhat more widely dispersed), and 20 per cent of all real estate (40). Obviously, a high percentage of their holdings are income-producing, which in turn bolsters their position at the top of the income pyramid. Unlike wage earners, though, they manage to hold on to a large share of this wealth-generated income. Senator Bradley (5), in advancing his "Fair

*The census survey will eventually be published under the title, "Household Wealth and Asset Distribution: 1984." Major findings of both studies were released to the press in July 1986. See, e.g., Spencer Rich, "Wealth Disparity Surveyed," *Washington Post,* July 19, 1986; John M. Berry, "U.S. Wealth Becomes More Concentrated," *Washington Post,* July 26, 1986. A month later an error was found in the ISR study which invalidated its major conclusion. Hence most recent data in these pages are from the census report.

Tax" proposal, noted that families reporting $1 million or more in income during 1981 paid, on the average, an effective tax rate of 17.7 per cent, and they did so legally through the canny use of tax "loopholes." Their real estate alone saved the richest 2 per cent $7 billion in tax breaks on the home mortgage interest deduction — one quarter of the total cost to the U.S. Treasury of this particular "tax expenditure" (40). Finally, their stock holdings ensure substantial ownership and control of our key economic institutions, the major corporations (9).

Some economists insist wealth is really more widely dispersed because one form of wealth — social security — is never included in the total. This is the major form of wealth of most households, they insist. Martin S. Feldstein (14), former chairman of President Reagan's Council of Economic Advisors, claimed that including such assets reduces the share of the top 1 per cent of wealth holders by almost a third. Other specialists in this area vigorously object. Wealth, they hold, carries with it the freedom and potential of maneuver, control over decisions, and the right to convey that wealth to whomever one wishes. Social security "wealth" meets none of these tests. It cannot be cashed in, borrowed on, or conveyed prior to retirement, and if and when it arrives, it comes in small monthly dribbles fixed by law, not determined by individual preference. Also, if contributors to the social security system die leaving no dependents, the estate receives nothing, nor is the "legacy" distributed to widows after they remarry. Nonetheless earned credits in both social security and employer-based pensions are worth something. The unresolved issue is how they should be valued during the individual's working life.

2. Distribution of Wealth by Race, Type of Household, Education, and Age. Median household net wealth (assets minus liabilities) is not much higher than median yearly income. This is scarcely unexpected since the U.S. is a nation of spenders, not savers. But there is a vast difference in the wealth accumulated by different population groups.

Median white net wealth, $39,135 in 1984, was almost twelve times greater than that of black households, $3,397. In other words, wealth (and the power and prestige it bestows) is far more concentrated than income. Over three tenths of black households had no assets at all or were in debt as compared with only one twelfth of white households. The recent census releases did not include any analysis of the distribution by quintiles. Nor did the Bureau of the Census plan to report on the "super rich" specifically. But it did classify households by broad levels of net wealth. Although 22.4 per cent of white families had accumulated less than $5,000 in assets, this was true for over half of all black and Hispanic households. At the other extreme, almost one in every four white households was worth $100,000 or more as compared with only one in every twenty-five black and one in every ten Hispanic households.

As with income, it is far easier for married couples to accumulate wealth than it is for lone female or male householders. In 1984 the median net worth of the 51 million married couple households was $50,116, as compared with only $13,885 for female householders and $9,883 for lone male householders. (The difference between the last two groups probably reflects the number of relatively affluent widows among female householders.)

Education also made for substantial differences in wealth. Households headed by college graduates were twice as wealthy as those less well educated. Median net worth reached $60,417 for college graduates, dropped to $31,892 for high school graduates and $23,447 for those with less than twelve years of schooling. If present labor market trends continue, the gap could become wider as well-paid manufacturing jobs and the unions that protected their wage scales decline and low-paid, nonunionized service jobs increase.

Back in 1962, when Dorothy Projector and Gertrude Weiss (41) studied the distribution of wealth, the oldest age cohort, those sixty-five years or older, ranked as the top wealth-holders, followed closely by the group between fifty-five and sixty-four years of age. By 1984 the two groups had changed places. The younger had a median net worth of $73,664 as compared with $60,266 for the oldsters. This suggests that although relative wealth is a function of age, it also reflects earning capacity. Both groups contrasted sharply with young householders (under thirty-five years of age), whose net worth was only $5,764.

While recent studies suggest that making the first million dollars or two reflects hard work, long hours, good intelligence, and careful planning, Thurow (48) points to a different set of variables to explain the great wealth-holders who are so widely admired in the U.S.

"Large fortunes," he writes, "are passed from generation to generation and great fortunes occur suddenly," primarily because when investments were made, the market kindly behaved in the "right" way. "*Fortune* biographies that accompany lists of the most wealthy" describe "the winners . . . as brighter than bright, smarter than smart, quicker than quick," he observes. But having looked behind the climas, he finds Lady Luck in the star role. Great wealth is accumulated too rapidly to be the result of patient savings and skillful planning. Nor does extraordinary investment talent play much part thereafter. "The typical pattern is for a man to make a great fortune and then to settle down and earn the market rate of return on his existing portfolio."

3. The Wealth Ladder. Turner and Starnes (50) describe a ladder of wealth with different types of assets at each ascending rung. Few approaches so well illuminate the contrast between the very wealthy and other Americans. Although they drew their evidence from the 1962 study mentioned earlier, the types and relative levels of assets are much the same today.

Households with assets worth under $1,000 were on the bottom rung. About three quarters "owned" automobiles and almost four fifths had some liquid assets — cash in a checking account to pay utilities, perhaps. But how much in all? Only an average equity of $190 in their old, beat-up cars and $134 to meet the bill collector. These two items constituted four fifths of their "wealth."

Moving up to the second rung, with $1,000 to $4,999 in assets, homeownership became possible for more than half of the group. But even in 1962 dollars, their small equity, $1,298, probably gave them a hold on little more than the latchkey. The American dream of a home of one's own, a car to drive to work and perhaps another for errands, and stand-by checking and savings accounts continued to explain most household wealth until assets totalled $50,000 or more. But several things began happening at the $25,000 to $49,999 rung. The average value of assets doubled, and people began thinking in terms of family-owned businesses and professional firms, as well as investing in stocks and bonds. Their equity or portfolios were still modest, on the average worth only $6,644 and $7,518, respectively. But as total worth and diversification increased, homes, cars, and cash deposits became less significant parts of the whole.

When assets reached the $50,000 to $99,999 rung, wealth again doubled, and people turned in all directions to put it to work. This was the first rung on the wealth ladder where investments dominated the whole, with fully 36 per cent committed to the cause. On the next rung, where wealth ranged from $100,000 to $199,999, and averaged $132,790, investments in stocks and bonds accounted for almost half of the total. For the 1 per cent of households that managed to climb to the second highest rung, where wealth ranged from $200,000 to $500,000, equity in family-owned businesses and professional firms more than tripled, investments almost tripled, and total assets averaged $300,355.

Then the dizzy heights were scaled and everything exploded. Total wealth quadrupled, averaging $1,260,667. The value of homes doubled, the value of business and professional firms quadrupled, liquid assets more than doubled, and average investments soared to $628,271. But the unique feature was the appearance of the beneficial trust, a device that permits the rich to place sizeable portions of their wealth into generation-skipping trusts in order to escape or reduce estate and inheritance taxes. Virtually all such trusts are in the control of the super-rich. On the second highest rung, the average value of trusts was $5,393 in 1962. On the top rung, it jumped to $222,600.

Among industrialized nations, the U.S. is not only notable for its benign neglect of accumulating wealth, but for its gentle treatment of inherited wealth. Hereditary concentration of riches creates an economic and political aristocracy in theoretically democratic America. Is this wise or necessary? From an economic point of view, the wish to accumulate wealth may be a powerful work incentive, but the expectation of inheriting great wealth can only be a work disincentive. In 1972, the richest 1 per cent of the population had assets worth five times more than the cost of all public social welfare programs that year. Nonetheless, although large inheritances could be taxed at the nominal rate of 77 per cent, Columbia University law professor, George Cooper (10) after studying the tax avoidance methods of the rich, concluded it was simple for their lawyers and accountants to reduce the effective tax rate to 5 to 10 per cent. But in fact less than 2 per cent of estates paid any taxes at all in 1979. Nevertheless, in 1981, the Reagan Administration pressed Congress to liberalize estate and gift taxes. Robert Kuttner (27) tells how this welfare for the rich was sold to Congress:

> In a well-orchestrated lobbying stunt (by the capital formation lobby), a legitimate concern of small family businesses and farms was made the stalking horse for a larger assault on the inheritance tax. For the proprietor of a small family farm, there was real worry that inheritance taxes levelled against the inflated cash value of a farm might be so burdensome that the farm would have to be sold to pay the taxes. . . . Out of solicitude for the family farmer, Congress eventually rent a much broader hole in the large inheritance tax. . . . Besides giving special treatment to small family businesses and farms, Congress raised the exemption and lowered tax rates on *all* inheritances.

When the law became fully effective in 1986, only 0.3 per cent of estates were subject to any tax. By then the loss in revenues from estate taxes alone was estimated at $9.7 billion — more than enough to offset the Administration's planned cutbacks in federal child nutrition funds in those years.

References

1. Aaron, Henry J. *Politics and the Professors*. Washington, D.C.: Brookings Institution, 1978, p. 12.
2. Alperovitz, Gar and Jeff Faux. *Rebuilding America*. New York: Pantheon Books, 1984, p. 230.
3. Barnet, Richard J. and Ronald E. Müller. *Global Reach: The Power of the Multinational Corporations*. New York: Simon and Schuster, Inc., 1974, pp. 290–302.
4. Benus, Jacob and James N. Morgan. "Time Period, Unit of Analysis, and Income Concept in the Analysis of Income Distribution." In James D. Smith, Ed., *The Distribution of Personal Income and Wealth*. National Bureau of Economic Research Studies in Income and Wealth, Vol. 39. New York: Columbia University Press, 1975, pp. 209–224.
5. Bradley, Bill. *The Fair Tax*. New York: Pocket Books, 1984, pp. 12, 13.

6. Browning, Edgar K. "The Trend Toward Equality in the Distribution of Net Income." *Southern Economic Journal,* **43** (June 1976), pp. 912–923.

7. ———. "How Much Equality Can We Afford?" *Public Interest,* **43** (Spring 1976), pp. 90–110.

8. Budd, Edward. "Postwar Changes in the Size Distribution of Income in the United States." *American Economic Review,* **60** (May 1970), pp. 247–260.

9. Comanor, William S. and Robert H. Smiley. "Monopoly and the Distribution of Wealth." *Quarterly Journal of Economics,* **89** (May 1975), p. 184.

10. Cooper, George. *A Voluntary Tax?* Washington, D.C.: Brookings Institution, 1978, p. 2.

11. Danziger, Sheldon and Michael K. Taussig. "The Income Unit and the Anatomy of Income Distribution." Discussion Paper #516–78. Mimeographed. Madison: University of Wisconsin, Institute for Research on Poverty, 1978.

12. David, Martin. *Wealth and Public Policy: The Relevance of SIPP and a Program for Future Research.* Reprint 310. Madison: University of Wisconsin, Institute for Research on Poverty, 1979, unpaged.

13. Duncan, Greg J., Richard D. Coe, and Martha S. Hill. "The Dynamics of Poverty." In Greg J. Duncan, Ed., *Years of Poverty, Years of Plenty.* Ann Arbor: University of Michigan, Institute for Social Research, 1984, pp. 40–42.

14. Feldstein, Martin. "Social Security and the Distribution of Wealth." *Journal of the American Statistical Association,* **71** (December 1976), pp. 800–807.

15. Friedman, Milton and Rose Friedman. *Free to Choose: A Personal Statement.* New York: Harcourt Brace Jovanovich, Inc., 1980, pp. 128–149.

16. Galbraith, John Kenneth. *The Affluent Society.* Boston: Houghton Mifflin Co., 1958.

17. ———. *Economics and the Public Purpose: How We Can Head Off the Mounting Economic Crisis.* Boston: Houghton Mifflin Co., 1973, pp. 193–198.

18. Gallman, Robert E. "Trends in the Size Distribution of Wealth in the Nineteenth Century." In Lee Soltow, Ed., *Six Papers on the Size Distribution of Wealth and Income.* New York: National Bureau of Economic Research, 1969, p. 6.

19. Gatswirth, J. L. "The Estimate of the Lorenz Curve and Gini Index." *Review of Economics and Statistics,* **54** (August 1972), p. 306–316.

20. Graetz, Michael J. "Can the Income Tax Continue to Be the Major Revenue Source?" In Joseph A. Pechman, Ed., *Options for Tax Reform.* Washington, D.C.: Brookings Institution, 1984, pp. 56–65.

21. Halstead, D. Kent. *Tax Wealth in Fifty States.* Washington, D.C.: U.S. Government Printing Office, 1978.

22. Hansen, W. Lee and Burton Weisbrod. "The Distribution of Costs and Direct Benefits of Public Higher Education: The Case of California." *Journal of Human Resources,* **4** (Spring 1969), pp. 176–191.

23. Harrington, Michael. *The Decade of Decision: The Crisis of the American System.* New York: Simon and Schuster, Inc., 1980, pp. 148–177, 166.

24. ———. *The Other America: Poverty in the United States.* New York: Macmillan Publishing Co., Inc., 1962.

25. Henle, Peter. "Exploring the Distribution of Earned Income." *Monthly Labor Review,* **95** (December 1972), pp. 16–27.

26. Herriot, Roger A. and Herman P. Miller. *The Taxes We Pay*. Washington, D.C.: The Conference Board, May 1971.
27. Kuttner, Robert. *The Economic Illusion: False Choices Between Prosperity and Social Justice*. Boston: Houghton Mifflin Co., 1984, pp. 205–206.
28. Kuznets, Simon. "Demographic Aspects of the Distribution of Income Among Families: Recent Trends in the United States." In Willy Sellekaerts, Ed., *Econometrics and Economic Theory: Essays in Honor of Jan Tinbergen*. London: Macmillan Publishers, Ltd., 1974, pp. 233–245.
29. ———. "Shares of Upper Income Groups in Income and Savings." Occasional Paper 35. New York: National Bureau of Economic Research, 1950.
30. Lampman, Robert J. "Measured Inequality of Income: What Does It Mean and What Can It Tell Us?" *The Annals of the American Academy of Political and Social Science*, **409** (September 1973), pp. 81–91.
31. ———. *The Share of Top Wealth Holders in National Wealth, 1922–1956*. New York: National Bureau of Economic Research, 1962, p. 204.
32. Lekachman, Robert. *Economists at Bay: Why the Experts Will Never Solve Your Problems*. New York: McGraw-Hill Book Co., 1976, pp. 39–93.
33. Lillard, Lee. "Inequality: Earnings vs. Human Wealth." *American Economic Review*, **67** (March 1977), pp. 42–53.
34. MacDonald, Dwight. "Our Invisible Poor." *The New Yorker*, **38** (January 19, 1963), pp. 82 ff.
35. Myrdal, Gunnar. *Challenge to Affluence*. New York: Pantheon Books, Inc., 1962, pp. 3–67.
36. ———. *The American Dilemma*. New York: Harper and Bros., 1944.
37. National Advisory Commission on Civil Disorders. *Report of the National Commission on Civil Disorders*. New York: Bantam Books, Inc., 1968, pp. 236–281.
38. Paglin, Martin. "The Measurement and Trend in Inequality: A Basic Revision." *American Economic Review*, **65** (September 1975), pp. 598–609.
39. Parker, Richard. *The Myth of the Middle Class*. New York: Harper & Row, Publishers, 1972, p. 167.
40. Pascall, Glenn. *The Trillion Dollar Budget: How to Stop the Bankrupting of America*. Seattle: University of Washington Press, 1985, p. 36.
41. Projector, Dorothy S. and Gertrude S. Weiss. *Survey of Financial Characteristics of Consumers*. Washington, D.C.: Board of Governors of the Federal Reserve System, August 1966.
42. Reynolds, Morgan and Eugene Smolensky, "The Fading Effect of Government on Inequality." *Challenge*, **21** (July–August 1978), pp. 32–37.
43. Samuelson, Paul A. *Economics*, 11th ed., rev. New York: McGraw-Hill Book Co., 1980, p. 80.
44. Smeeding, Timothy M. "On the Distribution of Net Income: Comment." *Southern Economic Journal*, **45** (June 1979), pp. 932–944.
45. ———. "The Trend Toward Equality in the Distribution of Net Income: A Re-examination of Data and Methodology." Discussion Paper #470–77. Mimeograph. Madison: University of Wisconsin, Institute for Research on Poverty, 1977.
46. Smith, James D. and Stephen D. Franklin. "The Concentration of Personal

Wealth, 1922–1969." *American Economic Review,* **64** (May 1974), pp. 162–180.

47. Tawney, R. H. *Equality,* rev., with an introduction by Richard M. Titmuss. London: George Allen & Unwin, Ltd., 1964, p. 55.

48. Thurow, Lester. *Generating Inequality: Mechanisms of Distribution in the U.S. Economy.* New York: Basic Books, Inc., Publishers, 1975, pp. 129, 153.

49. Tobin, James. "On Limiting the Domain of Inequality." *Journal of Law and Economics,* **13** (October 1970), pp. 263–277.

50. Turner, Jonathan H. and Charles E. Starnes. *Inequality, Privilege and Power in America.* Santa Monica, California: Goodyear Publishing Co., 1976, pp. 11, 29–48.

51. U.S. Bureau of the Census. *Current Population Reports, Consumer Income 1983,* Series P–23, no. 143, p. 53.

52. ———. *Statistical Abstract of the United States 1979.* Washington, D.C.: U.S. Government Printing Office, 1979, p. 464.

53. U.S. Department of the Treasury, Internal Revenue Service. *Statistics on Income: Estate Tax Returns 1976.* Washington, D.C.: U.S. Government Printing Office, 1978.

CHAPTER 5

The Concentration of Economic and Political Power

The large corporation, usually American-based and global in scope, is the dominant social invention of the twentieth century. The corporation occupies a place as important in our time as that of the Holy Roman Church in medieval Europe or of the monarch who ruled by reason of divine right during the sixteenth- and seventeenth-century heyday of mercantilism.

Robert Lekachman (43)

The role of the planetary enterprise is producing an organizational revolution as profound in its implications for modern man as the Industrial Revolution and the rise of the nation-state itself.

Richard J. Barnet and Ronald E. Müller (6)

When the nation was founded, four fifths of the labor force were independent farmers. Independent handicraftsmen and tradesmen dominated the other fifth. Today less than one in every thirty workers is a farmer, and less than one twelfth of the nonagricultural labor force is self-employed. Virtually the entire balance consists of wage and salary workers.

Many of them work on assembly lines and in the offices of large corporations. Between 1980 and 1984, the 500 largest industrial corporations in the U.S. reduced their work force by almost two million men and women; and still the number employed by only eight of these firms outnumbered the federal work force (48, 81). In 1983, when more than ten million workers were jobless during each of the first nine months, the profits of the twenty-three U.S.-based firms included in the stellar group of the world's largest corporations, climbed by 30 per cent (22). Their profits were often used not to improve operations and to create more jobs, but to buy — and frequently soon sell — other companies, as "merger mania" swept through corporate boardrooms. These facts alone give large corporations a transcendent role in the national economy and make their internal decisions a matter of vital domestic concern.

The Free Market? ─────────────────────────────

Economic theory, as presented in most texts and classrooms, primarily explains an economic market made up of myriads of firms competing for a share of resources and consumers (30, 44). Gigantism changes the rules of the game and is not easily accommodated in discussions of free (unfettered, competitive) markets where consumers are sovereign and their free and rational decisions determine the relative supply and quality of goods and services. One fact overlooked in this model is the enormous concentration of economic power in the hands of a relatively few huge corporations that dominate national and world economies (64). About the only systematic deviation from perfect competition that is recognized by all economists is *oligopoly* — the dominance of particular markets (like steel, copper, automobiles) by a few firms. The more concentrated the market, the more monopolistic power firms have to set limits on production and to fix prices. "Administered pricing" is the term used to describe this new "nonmarket" process of price setting. It results in rigid prices, prices that do not respond to economic conditions. Instead of going down during economic slumps, they often rise. In 1950, only 40 per cent of the manufacturing sector showed rigid prices in the face of falling demand. Because of increasing economic concentration, by 1974 an estimated 70 per cent did so (54). This explains in part why traditional anti-inflation measures designed for free competitive markets no longer work.

But the distortion of prices brought about by oligopolies is just part of the story. When large corporations make huge investments in new products, they do not leave the sale of these products to chance. They "develop" markets by underwriting dazzling advertising campaigns, which over time have transformed America into the quintessential consumer society — with an unparalleled consumer debt (61). In the process, they have created previously unheard-of needs, deified obsolescence and the throw-away syndrome, and promised easy credit to finance the splurge. Critics suggest that in these circumstances a leap of imagination is required to describe consumers as any longer "sovereign." At some stage the power of the brainwashers over the brainwashed must be taken into account in economic theory.

On the other side of the coin, when large corporations abound with interlocking directorates, and large banks collaborate daily in decisions to finance or cut off funds for ventures riskier or larger than any one firm wishes or is able to handle alone, oligopoly becomes just one of several reasons why "competition" no longer describes their relationship.

Decisions of corporate leaders about where and how to conduct business, what and how much to produce, and how to produce it, play a key role in mediating basic societal issues of equity and survival — who will work, what workers will earn, who will receive credit, insurance, or mortgages, which neighborhoods, regions, and nations will prosper or decline, how rapidly the world's nonrenewable resources will be exhausted, whether the environment will be noxious or healthful, and what resources will be needed by social welfare to protect living standards and provide essential community services.

In a booming economy most people are winners, and they probably worry very little about how or where distributive decisions are made. But when declining productivity becomes the norm, as has been true for some years in the U.S., citizens begin to realize that sharing losses is very different from sharing spoils. In a situation of scarcity, as Thurow (72) warned in 1980, who determines the winners and losers, and how openly and fairly decisions are made, become matters of great importance to everyone. So does the question of what can be done to revitalize America so there are enough jobs to go around and the divisive tears in the social fabric can be mended.

The Concentration of Economic Power _____

Remnants of the Free Market

At last count (in the late 1970s) there were 14.7 million business units in the U.S. Most — 11.3 million — were very small, with no or very few employees. These minuscule firms tend to be here today and gone tomorrow. Less than half survive longer than three years; but births usually exceed deaths. The millions of small and medium-sized firms comprise what is left of the "free market." Referred to as the "second economy" by insightful economic historian Bert Cochran (17), it is "labor intensive, competitive, subject to violent oscillations, and prone to bankruptcy or being swallowed up through purchase by big corporations." In 1979 the free market was responsible for 30 per cent of all private economic activity, 15 per cent of GNP, half of all nongovernment jobs, and two thirds of all newly created jobs (56). Whether there has been a net gain in the number of small firms in the 1980s is not clear. The long recession convinced many displaced workers to go into business for themselves. In 1983 alone just under 600,000 new businesses started up, more than double the number in 1970. But, of course, the recession forced an unusual number into bankruptcy, too.

Small firms are the backbone of their communities. Many are family-owned, sometimes over several generations. Both owners and workers have been shaped by community values and share a concern about the quality of life for themselves and their children. Their network of relationships and their mutual striving for a good and secure life are important sources of community vitality. But small firms are far more vulnerable than corporate giants to inflation, high interest rates, rising payroll taxes, plant closings, and sudden shifts in national economic policy. Also, the way executive departments (especially Defense) in Washington handle procurement creates almost insurmountable obstacles for small businesses wishing to bid on government contracts (78, 71). To deal more effectively with such difficulties, nuclei of small companies are appearing in industrial parks around the nation to facilitate collaboration in research and production. This phenomenon is heralded by some economists as one of the promising models for a more productive and smoothly functioning economy that builds and sustains a sense of community rather than destroying it (58).

The Planning System in a Postmarket World

Then there is what Galbraith (30) calls the planning system, consisting of about 800 large manufacturing, merchandizing, transportation, power, communication, and financial corporations that produce upwards of 70 per cent of all goods and services provided by the private sector. Cochran (17) suggests that to understand our economic situation two truisms about huge corporations must be kept in mind. First, there is a concentration of enormous capital accumulations in large corporations. Second, the corporate "leviathans are getting bigger and fatter at a faster rate than ever before. . . . They are genetically programmed for expansion." The goad is excess capacity, which keeps them seeking ever larger markets — and higher profits. They are the most profligate users of nonrenewable resources (18), and they find capital-intensive technologies, not human labor, one of the surest ways to increase profits. These facts help to explain why the agricultural work force continues to decline, and why so many jobs disappeared in the manufacturing sector during recent decades.

Despite economies of size, increasing evidence confirms that there are limits to growth. Moderate-sized firms often surpass the giants in efficiency, and individuals working alone or in small laboratories are credited with most of the important product innovations during this century (63). The transactional costs of gigantism apparently make for the difference — long and complex communication lines, endless committee meetings, mountains of paper work, too many people alienated by being "mere cogs in the machine," too much underused talent, and too little regard for the human cost of corporate mobility (35, 82).

The enormous gap between the widespread *perception* of the political economy and its *reality* is a major problem today. The former, based in our traditional free enterprise ideology and reinforced by outdated economic theory, leads to the impression of remarkable self-sufficiency on the part of large corporations; in reality they could not have survived, let alone thrived, without ubiquitous government assistance and services. Galbraith (30) is just one of many economists who have explored the scope of corporate dependence on government. At the core are huge government expenditures for the purchase of goods and services, especially weapons. But the shopping list also includes such items as office supplies, equipment and furnishings, transportation, textbooks and teaching aids, and elaborate communications systems. The planning system also relies primarily on government to provide qualified and educated manpower and it expects government to sustain community purchasing power during economic slumps by providing cash transfers. If the planning system is to sell and transport its goods, government must build and maintain roads, bridges, and airports, control traffic, and dredge harbors.

From another perspective, government is of enormous help to the planning system because it reinforces the ideology of the dominant corporations. It helped to make family cars essential by letting central cities rot, starving mass transportation, and underwriting low-cost loans for suburban housing. It boosted the trucking industry and airlines by neglecting railroads.

For years, development of high technologies has been openly socialized. In this connection, Galbraith writes,

> The planning system needs support, either directly or indirectly through military expenditures, for technical development, much of it too expensive for the firm itself. Atomic power, computers, all modern air transports, satellite communication, numerous other products and services have their origins in such socialized technology. The government also supplies capital to the industries for which it is also the market; the large weapons firms use much plant and equipment belonging to government and get their working capital in the form of progress payments. (30)

Finally, government literally prevents failure, which lies at the heart of capitalism, by becoming the lender of last resort for large corporations threatened by insufficient revenue or capital, as with Lockheed, several stock exchange houses, railroads, and more recently Chrysler Corporation. And if foreign competition poses problems, businessmen rush to Washington demanding and receiving protection through import duties, quotas on foreign imports, and the like. "The modern economy," Galbraith concludes, "features socialism for large corporations, free enterprise for the small." Turner and Starnes (75) echo this sentiment: "wealthfare for the rich, welfare for the poor." A few rigorous free enterprisers wish capitalism were better served by capitalists. William Simon (70) scolds businessmen for going to Washington with hat in hand. But more realistic Milton Friedman (36) observes "the businessman is all in favor of free enterprise and free markets — for everybody . . . but himself." As a matter of fact, the dependence of big business on government spans capitalist and socialist nations alike. The difference between U.S. and other industrialized nations is not that our corporations are not subsidized, as in other nations, but that our subsidies are hit-and-miss while theirs are carefully planned and open.

The Elites and Oligopoly. The planning system is a stratified society. Even in lackluster 1984, when the soaring dollar depressed sales of U.S. exports and invited a cascade of foreign-made imports, the sales of the 500 largest industrial corporations in the U.S. totalled $1.76 trillion — almost half of the GNP. The top twenty firms made two fifths of the sales and reaped a higher share of the profits (48).

Oligopoly is rife in American markets. By 1963, twenty-nine of forty-two different industries were already highly concentrated oligopolies (17). Today, steel, copper, and aluminum are each dominated by a handful of companies (5). Three companies produce most American cars, with the giant's share, 55 per cent, coming from one. Thanks in part to quotas on their Japanese competitors, the three enjoyed $9.8 billion in profits in 1984 (12), at a cost of $8.5 billion to U.S. consumers (19). In the same year, four of the seventeen largest airlines earned 94 per cent of the group's profits (48). As for the "micro business," Utall (77) observes, "the barriers to entry are staggering." The designs made by two firms command 90 per cent of industry sales.

One per cent of our farms sell about a quarter of all food products (40). Four giants make over 90 per cent of our breakfast food, while Campbell makes about the same share of our soup (67). Two companies produce 70 per cent of all candy (41). McDonald's sells 40 per cent of all fast-food hamburgers (80). Canned and frozen food, fast-food restaurants, many farms, food research groups, and even seeds are controlled by a handful of huge corporations. Their combined impact on the national diet overwhelms the warnings of dentists and nutritionists. Americans reduced their milk consumption by 30 per cent between 1960 and 1980. Tooth-decaying soft drinks are now the number-one beverage.* In the meantime thousands of small operators have been crowded out or gobbled up. The number of food companies was halved between 1947 and 1972, and is still declining.

The same trend toward concentrated ownership and control, and the squeezing out of the little man, is found among financial institutions. In 1984 among the 100 largest commercial banking companies, the top four held 46 per cent of the assets. Among the fifty largest insurance firms,

*The story of how Coca Cola was introduced as the answer for the Temperance Movement, only to be charged with being addictive, is recounted in *The Cola Wars* (47).

seven now control 57 per cent of the assets (49). AT&T's share of the telecommunications market shrivelled to a mere 35 per cent in 1984, down from 70 per cent in 1980 (15).

What are the consequences of this concentration? "With few exceptions," Cochran (17) notes,

> the major markets are under the authority of three, four, half a dozen, sometimes up to a dozen, giant corporations. They make the decisions for the entire industry, with one or two of them assigned the role of price leaders. The firms may compete fiercely, but the competition is in advertising, image creation, name-brand inculcation, not *in prices on goods and services of comparable quality.*

Our traditional free market ideology, in other words, has no relevance in an economy of concentrated corporate power; perpetuation of the myth only delays resolution of our grave economic problems.

Interlocking directorates among corporations in the planning system further increase their power. Back in 1969 thirty-two large banks had a total of 514 interlocking directorates with the 220 largest industrial corporations. In 1980 directors of the top eight oil companies were heavily represented on the boards of six large banks, which meant that every time the boards met, from about three to five oil company executives could visit with each other (14). By 1985 among the 100 largest corporations four out of five chief executives had an average of three outside directorships. This was one reason, Patton (55) surmised, for the stunning escalation of corporate executive salaries to $1 million per year or more. "You scratch my back, and I'll scratch yours" was the notion. But as emoluments of this magnitude spread during 1984, even editors of business journals became uneasy. With millions of jobless workers and many more reluctantly accepting wage constraints, common sense, it was felt, suggested the wisdom of self-discipline on the part of corporate executives.

Antitrust laws were designed to prevent occasions — like board meetings — that might lend themselves to collusion or conspiracy. But the laws were written years ago before the emergence of the planning system with its "old boy" network and administered pricing. In a postmarket world, many economists agree, our antitrust laws are anachronistic. Certainly they have not prevented monopoly, nor do many economists believe doing so would serve any useful purpose at this stage (72). The Reagan Administration essentially agrees. While frowning on collusion and price fixing, bigness and oligopoly are not viewed as problems (60). Nonetheless, it is obvious that the concentration of investment capital and numerous interlocking directorates result in a handful of corporate leaders controlling untold numbers of decisions bearing on the public good, and doing so largely out of sight. One result is increasing demand for public representation on corporate boards, but the token response has not diluted the power of corporate executives or apparently widened their perspective. So a younger generation of economists and entrepreneurs are exploring ways to decentralize and democratize the economic structure.

Mergers and Conglomerates. The trend toward concentrated economic power received a remarkable boost with the first wave of corporate mergers around the turn of the century. This step reflected the desire to control the firm's environment by dominating sources of supply as well as markets. This led to vertical integration — control over all stages of production from acquisition of raw materials to distribution of finished products. After World War II, the largest and most technologically advanced industries led the way to a second stage focused on diversification. In time most large corporations became conglomerates, offering a variety of products and services. Cochran (17) writes that tax shelters, the wish to spread the risk, "stock market vagaries, and fast killings for brokers" all played a role in the "continuing conglomerate merger boom." Between 1979 and 1982 corporations spent $170 billion to acquire new companies, and still the pace accelerates. The number of mergers doubled between 1983 and 1984. People of all persuasions take exception to this trend. Too many "predatory" firms spend their spare cash, it is held, acquiring new companies instead of updating their own plants or improving technologies and creating new jobs (3). Conservative George Gilder (32) blames the phenomenon on tax laws and government spending patterns which "distort business decisions and undermine American entrepreneurship." Reich (59), a favorite of Democratic Party leaders, blames "merger mania" for the decline of the U.S. in world markets. Burck (13), a prominent securities lawyer who has handled hundreds of corporate acquisitions, regards mergers as indispensable to the functioning of capitalism, but insists "the nation would be better served if the buyer were a group of private investors or a medium-sized company, not a giant." Too often in his experience, takeovers by the giants damage companies that once were "star performers," and in the process communities, too, are harmed, as employees and advisors with roots in the community are displaced by strangers who take orders from distant headquarters, where they would prefer to be. The rash of divestitures — in this instance, selling recently acquired companies — is accepted as proof by others that the ability to build a business producing one type of product or service is not necessarily transferable to all types of companies. This point focuses attention on the frequency with which companies are bought with no intention of building on their past success, but rather to take hefty tax losses or even to use their cash reserves to buy up still more companies. In either case the bottom line is not enhanced productivity, but enhanced profits.

The Multinationals. Almost all of America's largest corporations have become multinational in scope over the last twenty-five years. While ownership and control remain within the borders of the U.S., manufacturing and service operations span the globe, giving the nation an imperial corporate presence in many foreign countries. "Increasingly," writes Richard Barnet,

> global resource systems are being managed by multinational corporations. The mining, melting, refining, and mixing of animal, vegetable, mineral, and human resources into products for sale is an integrated operation on a planetary scale. Viewed from space, the Global Factory suggests a human organism. The brain is housed in steel- and glass-slabs located in or near a few crowded cities — New York, London, Frankfurt, Zurich, and Tokyo. The blood is capital, and it is pumped through the system by global banks assisted by a few governments. The financial centers . . . and their fictional extensions in such tax havens as Panama and the Bahamas, function as the heart. The hands are steadily moving to the outer rims of civilization. More and more goods are now made in the poor countries of the southern periphery under direction from headquarters in the north, and most are destined to be consumed in the industrial heartland . . . (5)

The U.S. led in the development of multinationals. By 1959 American firms were the largest in the world in eleven of the thirteen major industries: aerospace, automotive, chemical, electrical equipment, food products, general machinery, metal products, paper, petroleum, textiles, and commercial banking. In the late 1960s, Europeans were cautioned that American-based firms were rapidly becoming the dominant economic force in the world (68). The result was a vigorous counteroffensive by western nations and Japan that succeeded so well that soon American newspapers were carrying headlines about declining U.S. power. By 1976 American firms dominated only seven of the thirteen industries, and in all but aerospace the number of American companies listed among the world's top dozen corporations had declined. But this did not mean that American multinationals had been toppled from their leadership position. They had simply been forced to share the spoils more equitably with firms headquartered in other nations. By 1984, of the world's fifty largest corporations, twenty-two were headquartered in the U.S. Japan and West Germany, with six each among the leaders, tied for second place (46). But once other industrialized nations recover from the recession,* few people feel very sanguine about the ability of U.S. corporations to hold on to their lead.

---

*Because the baby boom peaked several years later in Europe than in the U.S., the worldwide recession coincided with relatively larger numbers of young people arriving at working age. This was one reason for the higher than usual unemployment rates and more prolonged emergence from recession in European nations.

The Overseas Flight of Investment and Profits. The growth of multinationals has meant that increasingly U.S. firms invest abroad, hire abroad, and profit abroad. In 1960 their foreign dollar deposits were less than 10 per cent of their domestic holdings; by 1980, they exceeded 65 per cent. During the intervening years, our largest banks were often accused of "redlining" needful parts of the U.S. economy in favor of investing in Japan and other foreign nations. A case in point occurred when Lykes Corporation closed its steel subsidiary, the Youngstown (Ohio) Sheet and Tube Works, in 1977 after U.S. banks reduced or withdrew their financial support. As this was occurring, two of the banks increased their loans to the Japanese steel industry, and within a year a third followed suit. Altogether, the loans jumped from $133 million to $516 million in those few years (8), while Youngstown was suffering with some of the worst unemployment ever experienced in that area.

As U.S. firms move their physical operations abroad, comparative wages, tariffs, transportation costs, tax rates, antitrust laws, environmental pollution controls, consumer activism, and political and labor conditions are among the factors weighed by corporate leaders. They are often offered generous tax abatements or reductions and promised a long list of investments in factories, roads, and manpower training by hopeful governments in the same kind of auctioning process so familiar to American cities and states (65).

In the absence of coordinated policies among nations, the scope of multinationals gives them extraordinary facility in evading or minimizing taxes, escaping the effect of unfavorable political and economic events, and manipulating foreign currency exchanges (16). They may obey antitrust laws in their own country and violate them elsewhere, in the process paralyzing international markets with cartels (73). Much of their power to reduce taxes and minimize profits derives from "transfer pricing," a Treasury Department term referring to transactions among subsidiaries owned by the same parent corporation. With "transfer pricing" a multinational may direct its subsidiaries in low-tax countries to sell goods at grossly inflated prices to its subsidiaries in high-tax countries, thereby taking most of its profits where minimum taxes prevail. Or, high customs duties may be minimized by underpricing imports (10).

Manipulations of this sort help to explain why corporate income taxes in the U.S. declined from 30 per cent of federal revenues in the mid-1950s to 16 per cent by 1978, leaving middle-income households with an increasing share of the tax bill. But multinationals have other tax loopholes. They may defer payment of U.S. taxes on foreign earnings until profits are brought home, and they receive dollar-for-dollar tax credits on any foreign taxes they pay. Between 1960 and 1976 the foreign tax credit of American corporations jumped from $1 billion to $24 billion. Most of the increase came during the Ford Administration. The credit rose in value from $10 billion in 1973 to $21 billion in 1974 (76), years of gathering recession, rising layoffs, and mounting government deficits. In 1981 the tax laws were amended to reduce corporate income taxes to near zero within a few years. By 1985 the corporation income tax produced about 10 per cent of federal receipts (57). So generous had the tax shelters become that eighteen of America's largest corporations with profits between $1.1 billion and $9.6 billion received tax refunds or owed no taxes at all. By then, too, newspaper headlines were increasingly focused on the "world banking crisis," as one nation after another seemed about to default on their debts. The Federal Reserve Board reported that in June 1983 public and private foreign borrowers owed U.S. banks $356 billion, and speculation was rife over whether the U.S. Treasury would bale out the banks, as happens so often when big corporations get themselves into trouble. Events like this brought home again the urgent need for the tax reform underway in Congress and for the public sector to have a voice and some control over major capital investment decisions.

The Overseas Flight of Jobs. For many years U.S. corporations were shutting down domestic mills and factories in the snowbelt and migrating to the sunbelt, leaving faltering economies, ghost towns, and redundant workers behind in the Northeast and North Central regions. In time, the overseas flight of jobs affected both the South and the North. By the end of the 1970s, Bluestone and Harrison (8) report, overseas profits accounted for a third or more of the total profits of our hundred largest multinational producers and banks. In 1979, for example, the Ford Motor Company derived 94 per cent of its profit from overseas operations, and Coca Cola 63 per cent. In 1977, Citicorp earned 83 per cent of its banking profits from foreign operations.

Industry and labor proponents argue hotly over the number of U.S. jobs lost through resettlement abroad. On the one hand, the multinationals generally claim that these were defensive moves — if they had not resettled where wages were lower, corporations based in other nations would capture new markets in the developing nations. Labor proponents counter by pointing to the 29 per cent of imports in 1976, for example, which were manufactured in overseas plants and subsidiaries of U.S. multinational corporations. After reviewing the controversy over numbers, Bluestone and Harrison (8) comment that, numbers aside, what workers feel is a deepening *sense of insecurity* resulting from

> collapse all around them of the traditional economic base of their communities. . . . Counting only those effects that are presently "countable" — plant closings, relocations, and estimated physical contractions — a sizeable fraction of all the private sector jobs that existed at the beginning of the . . . 1970s had been destroyed by the end of the decade through private disinvestment in the productive capacity of the American economy.

By the mid-1980s the overseas movement was abating somewhat. With worldwide recession, profits were disappointing in the industrialized nations, while in the debt-ridden developing nations, political and financial instability persuaded some multinationals that withdrawal was the wisest alternative (39).

The majority of overseas operations have been in other industrialized nations where people could afford to buy the products of U.S. multinationals. But when the purpose of resettlement was to find steady, low-paid, productive labor, multinationals usually had a penchant for locating in developing nations where arbitrary governments eagerly collaborate to assure a docile labor force. Barnet's exhaustive research leaves little doubt that the prosperity of multinationals is partly due to their willingness to exploit "slave-labor cultures." Long hours of work are endemic, and strong-arm and other oppressive controls keep militants in line. If a courageous few protest, the presence of large pools of unemployed men and women soon has a very sobering effect.

Under these conditions it is little wonder that foreign workers often surpass their American counterparts in productivity. To cite only a few of Barnet's (5) examples, in Singapore, McGraw-Hill produces in one year an encyclopedia that American workers take five years to produce. Mexican metal workers are 40 per cent more productive than U.S. workers, electronic workers 10 to 15 per cent more productive, and seamstresses about 30 per cent more. While wages are rising in the Third World, they are still very low in many places. In 1975 the Banco Central de Nicaragua advertised for semiskilled workers to assemble electronic computers at 25 cents an hour. In an area of the Dominican Republic controlled by the U.S. conglomerate Gulf & Western, the average hourly wage in 1978 was 34 cents.* In 1975, unskilled female workers in Mauritius were paid 70 cents per day. General Electric, Samsonite, RCA, Rockwell, and other firms are doing a booming business in Mexico along the U.S. border; workers receive a fifth to a third of U.S. wage rates. In South Korea, 44 per cent of unionized textile workers earn less than $62 monthly, $30 below their country's poverty level. One study showed that after a year's work in South Korea's textile factories, where only women with perfect eyesight are hired, 88 per cent had chronic conjunctivitis and 44 per cent had become nearsighted. Container Corporation of America and B. F. Goodrich have used prison labor at substantially less than prevailing wage rates in Colombia. This form of exploitation was outlawed in the U.S. early in the 20th century.

The Balance Sheet for Developing Nations. Spokesmen for U.S. multinationals are often euphoric about their accomplishments. They

---

*In December 1984, it was reported that Gulf & Western was withdrawing from the Dominican Republic because of "difficulties over foreign exchange."

claim to use world resources with maximum efficiency and minimum waste. By introducing modern technologies in developing nations and upgrading work skills, they assure an industrial base for future growth. By locating operations overseas, they help to "spread the wealth" and improve worldwide standards of living.

More objective witnesses suggest otherwise. British economist Barbara Ward (79) reports that at the end of World War II, over 80 per cent of the world's wealth, trade, and skills were controlled by the population of industrialized nations. The share was unchanged as the 1970s began. A United Nations report in 1973 showed that the inflow of direct investments from 1965 to 1970 in a sample of developing nations was only 68 per cent of the income outflow (47). In 1977 the U.S. sold developing nations $29.5 billion in manufactured products and bought goods from them at a cost of $18 billion (79). To add to the disparity, every year sees a brain drain of doctors and scientists from developing to developed nations. Most were educated at their government's expense with the expectation that they would help with the process of development.

Multinationals appear to have added to, not allayed, the world's hunger problems (6). Agribusiness has gained control of considerable arable land, often complicating the task of food distribution. City factories in developing nations have provided far fewer jobs than were destroyed in the countryside. Corporate advertising sometimes plays havoc with the health and budgets of the poor. Multinationals huckster their consumer ideology, pushing the sale of nonessential items in nations where few people yet have the essentials. Coca Cola's displacement of fruit and vegetable juices may be the most egregious example. But whole grains are also neglected in favor of "store-bought" white bread.

For years corporate advertising campaigns in developing countries involved hiring women to dress up as nurses in order to visit new mothers to promote the sale of prepared infant formula. They extolled its superiority over cow's milk or breast milk and distributed samples, but they failed to clarify that without pure water and sanitary cooking equipment and facilities, which few mothers had, the product could become lethal to their infants. Alan Berg (7), in studying the situation, concluded that the effect of such high pressure advertising on the budgets of the poor was as serious as the nutritional loss. In 1981 the Reagan Administration caused the U.S. to be the only nation in the world refusing to support the U.N. code calling upon all nations to ban such practices. Lobbyists representing Bristol–Myers, Abbott Laboratories, and American Home Products, which control 15 per cent of the world infant formula market, all argued against the code. They were joined by Heinz, Gerber's, and the Grocery Manufacturers of America because of their fear that the ban might cover all baby foods. The upshot was that two high officials in our Agency for International Development resigned in protest and Third World countries were quick to charge that Americans were hard on babies but soft on big business. Private citizens in the U.S. were not willing to support the Administration's stance. Instead, they supported the efforts of the Infant Formula Action Coalition, based in Minnesota, to boycott the products of the largest distributor of commercial infant formula in the developing nations, Nestlé. This boycott was remarkably effective. On January 25, 1984 Nestlé not only agreed to stop providing free supplies that discouraged breast feeding, but to provide only enough for those few babies in clear need of bottle feeding. The corporation also agreed to include warnings of the hazards in all literature to mothers and health professionals, to end all promotional gifts to health workers and officials, and to include effective warnings on all their product labels. Having been pressured to make these concessions, Nestlé could be counted on, it was felt, to see that its competitors followed suit (38).*

Corporate claims about "spreading the wealth" are further challenged by World Bank reports showing that where multinationals have been most active, the income gap between rich and poor nations has become wider, and within developing nations income is now even more maldistributed (5).

The Concentration of Political Power _____

Huge corporations are systems of power, and when they spread around the world they have an almost infinite capacity to control national and world economies. Within the U.S. many thinkers believe that big multinationals hold government and consumers alike hostage. "Evidence of corporate clout is overwhelming," Lekachman (43) writes. "Their interests set the national agenda." "Large corporations," Sale (63) comments, "are beyond the influence of both the traditional supply and demand market and regulatory government." "Corporate leaders," Silk and Vogel (69) add, "constitute America's upper class" and are treated as such. They have easy access to presidents, cabinet members, congressmen, and regulatory commissions when it serves their purpose, as it often does.

Theories of Political Power

Debates over the source and distribution of power are unending. Theorists classify their models in different ways, but currently two points of view command most attention. Both recognize the proliferation of special inter-

*Susan George's exhaustive investigation of the causes of world hunger, *How the Other Half Dies: The Real Reasons for World Hunger* (31), links both the rich nations and multinational corporations to the problem.

est groups intent on influencing public policy. Most proponents of both viewpoints accept the existence of broad consensus among citizens on ideal values, but they part company sharply on the real meaning of these values and the extent to which they are reflected in our daily lives. They also tend to differ on the importance they attach to democratic participation (34, 51).

Pluralism. The enormous growth and heightened visibility of interest groups since World War II have brought pluralist theories into particular prominence. Rooted in James Madison's writings in the *Federalist Papers,* numerous versions of pluralism have emerged in modern times. Huntington (37) identifies two principal ones, the process version and the organization version. The former perceives the political scene as consisting of a large number of small interest groups; the latter perceives a small number of large interest groups. Running through both is the idea that all citizens have equal opportunities to join interest groups of their choice, and that all groups have an equal chance to be heard. Free and open competition among these groups, it is held, eventually results in public policies that reflect the "public will." Some pluralists assert that a degree of citizen apathy is required for the efficient operation of democratic political systems. Far from being bothered by low electoral participation rates, they are regarded as a virtue (34).

Pluralism has received the most detailed attention from two political scientists, Robert Dahl (20) and David Truman (74). Validation of the theory rests primarily on studies of local decision making. Both Dahl and Truman argue that the upper class is no longer a ruling class, as it was at the birth of the nation. The sheer size and complexity of our society have resulted in a diffusion of power among interest groups like corporate managers, consumers, technical–intellectual elites, organized farmers, organized labor, and environmentalists. Their struggle for an ever-increasing share of resources constitutes our political process.

At times, it is claimed, special interest groups join together to influence public policy (21). But such coalitions are inherently fragile, rarely lasting for long. Each group or coalition may be influential in one area and weak in others, but their veto power is usually more apparent than their ability to assure positive action. In the end, no one group or coalition regularly prevails in key political decisions.

Nor does government succeed in doing so. One reason is that it never speaks with one voice. Pluralists find many centers of power in government, reflecting the many different interests and their relative strength in society. When policy finally emerges, it represents a compromise among conflicting forces.

Power Elite and Governing Class Theories. In the late 1970s, Yale University's distinguished Charles Lindblom, long a highly respected mainstream political scientist, deserted the pluralists. In his study of *Politics and Markets,* he wrote:

> It has long been a curious feature of democratic thought that it has not faced up to the private corporation as a peculiar organization in an ostensible democracy. Enormously large, rich in resources, the big corporations . . . command more resources than do most government units. They can also, over a broad range, insist that government meet their demands, even if these demands run counter to those of citizens. . . . Moreover, they do not disqualify themselves from playing the partisan role of a citizen — for the corporation is legally a person. And they exercise unusual veto powers. The huge corporation fits oddly into democratic theory and vision. Indeed, it does not fit. (45)

Something akin to this view was advanced long ago by sociologist C. Wright Mills of Columbia University. In 1956 he wrote:

> The powers of ordinary men are circumscribed by the everyday world in which they live. . . . But not all men are in this sense ordinary. . . . The power elite is composed of men whose positions enable them to transcend the ordinary environments of ordinary men and women; they are in positions to make decisions having major consequences. . . . For they are in command of the major hierarchies and organizations of modern society. They rule the big corporations. They run the machinery of state and claim its prerogatives. They direct the military establishments. They occupy the strategic command posts of the social structure, in which are now centered the effective means of power and the wealth and celebrity which they enjoy. (52)

Vietnam, Watergate, and the recent remarkable arms buildup have each won considerable support for this view. Among the more seminal "governing class" theorists is G. William Domhoff. He argues that there is a governing class drawn from the nation's upper class, which receives a disporportionate share of the nation's wealth and contributes a disproportionate number of its members to the controlling institutions and key decision-making groups in the nation (24). Domhoff does not question that leaders emerge from other classes, but after studying their backgrounds he finds that most were selected, trained, and employed in insitutions that benefit and are controlled by members of the upper class. To the argument that an upper-middle-class of well-educated specialists — the meritocracy — has replaced property owners as wielders of power, he points out that advising decision makers is not tantamount to making decisions. Also, he insists it is erroneous to downgrade the expertise of the upper class, which includes many hard-working, competent, and very well-educated men from the best universities in the land.

Domhoff does not claim that upper-class dominance is either malevolent or beneficent in its effect. He is simply interested in identifying the source of power in America. Nor does he claim that the citizenry has lost ultimate control or sovereignty. But he points out that citizens are hopelessly fragmented among income classes and religious, ethnic, and racial groups, and hence have far less potential for acting in unison than the governing class.

In 1978, with the publication of *The Powers That Be* (23), he focused on four processes that the governing class controls — the special interest process, the policy-formulation process, the candidate-selection process, and the ideological process — by which citizens' beliefs, attitudes, and opinions are shaped. In addition to a great deal of other evidence, he notes that among twenty-nine men who served as heads of the three most powerful executive departments — State, Treasury, and Defense — between 1932 and 1964, only three were not members of his governing class. He also advances evidence showing that this class now succeeds in dominating a variety of special interest groups, in nominating and electing key candidates, and in controlling regulatory and other strategic commissions and councils.

Critics have asked why, if wealthy corporate leaders dominate government, do they criticize it so vigorously? Domhoff points out that American institutions were born in revolt against a strong central government, and this hostility continues to be prominent in American thought. Other ruling class theorists speculate that the adversarial relationship may be more apparent than real, and that any other public stance might mobilize citizen opposition and is therefore avoided. They also point out that not all businessmen oppose a strong government. Some view New Deal measures as stabilizing forces. And some industries have actively sought government regulation — the radio industry, airlines, railroads and trucking, the oil companies.

Corporate Lobbyists. Few people any longer doubt that large corporations bring rich and talented resources to the cause of protecting their own interests. Elizabeth Drew's (25) lively account of one of Washington's quintessential corporate tax lobbyists, Charls Walker, bears on this point. During Nixon's Administration, Walker served as Deputy Secretary of Treasury. Earlier, he was Executive Vice President of the American Bankers Association. His income as lobbyist easily places him among the top 1 per cent in the income distribution. When Drew interviewed him, he was wheeling and dealing with the principals in Congress over the energy bill, especially those parts affecting corporate taxes. He and Senator Russell Long, then Chairman of the Senate Finance Committee, were interested in securing a "refundable" investment tax credit that would be payable whether or not corporations paid any income taxes, and this seems to be one reason for introducing the principle first in the low-wage earner's tax credit. This and other tax issues were of particular concern to the "Group of Ten," all large corporations that Walker represents.

He has countless other irons in the fire. To list just a few, he represents the high-powered Business Roundtable, composed of the chief executives of 180 of America's largest corporations. He helped organize this group in 1972 to give them "more of a political presence" in Washington. In their behalf he worked to kill President Carter's industrial use tax proposal which would have levied a tax on industries that continued to use oil or gas in order to encourage conversion to coal or other fuels. In the end, he told Drew, the Senate Finance Committee substituted an amendment that would virtually have no effect on corporate income. He represents the Committee of the Present Danger, dedicated to assuring a conservative stance on arms control.* The Senate Finance Committee, he confided, "will not approve" a SALT agreement opposed by this group. (Within a few years, the group was also influential in convincing Congress to enact a huge reduction in estate taxes.) He chairs the American Council on Capital Formation and is an important voice in the Joint Council on Economic Education, chaired by a senior vice president of DuPont. This national organization is intent on "improving economic understanding" among citizens. "We're going to try to get economics taught better, starting in kindergarten, all the way up." (25)

Corporate PACs.   In his insightful book, *The New Politics of Inequality,* Thomas Edsall (28) writes about the network of corporate Political Action Committees (PACs), trade associations, and industry groups in the mid-1970s that "saw their political mission as the partisan and ideological conversion of Congress." In practical terms, Edsall notes, this meant that "a significant segment of industry became a de facto arm of the Republican Party." In 1978 there were 764 corporate PACs (9). By 1984 they numbered 1,536. By then many groups had joined the bandwagon. Altogether, 3,525 PACs were registered, representing every type of corporation and association. But they commanded very different levels of power to raise money. How much was spent in 1984 on political campaigns is not known since much of it need not be reported, but Senate and House candidates alone spent $374 million (62). On the average, senators who won raised more than $3 million, while successful House members averaged $334,000. Typically, winners far outspent losers. Estimates of the share of the total contributed by corporations vary from about one third to over one half (1). In her remarkably thorough investigation of campaign financing, Elizabeth Drew (26) documents both the inordinate cost of elections these days and the contaminating influence of money on lawmakers and the laws they enact. Raising money, rather than passing wise laws, has too often become

---

*Barnet (4) directly links this group's propaganda with the mounting fear in America that the U.S.S.R. has greatly outstripped us in military strength. One method of doing so was to use CIA estimates of the defense buildup in the Soviet Union and to calculate the cost in terms of American prices. Barnet refers to the whole idea as "the great illusion."

the major preoccupation of politicians in Washington, she claims. Republicans have been far more successful in this effort than Democrats. In 1982, Republican National Party and Senate and House fund-raising committees had seven times more money to distribute to Republican candidates than their Democratic counterparts. Drew concludes that the constant scramble for money is demeaning, diverting, time-consuming, and most of all corrupting.

> We are paying in the declining quality of politicians and of the legislative product, and in the rising public cynicism. . . . Until the problem of money is dealt with, the system will not get better. We have allowed the basic idea of our democratic process — representative government — to slip away. The only question is whether we are serious about trying to retrieve it. (26)

With this type of evidence, it is difficult to regard the corporate-dominated coalition of conservative interest groups that contributed the majority of money to the winners as the fragile, ephemeral coalition posited in mainstream pluralist theory.

Implications for Social Welfare

These are confusing times. Books extolling the glories of free enterprise and American capitalism tumble over each other in the scramble toward best-seller lists. Small business gets short shrift in these books. But their authors worry about the national character and the decline in excellence. The fault, they often insist, lies in social welfare benefits and services and the welter of federal regulations. Together they are destroying the work ethic, strangling business, taking the joy and sense of achievement out of work, and constitute a deadly peril for capitalism. Yet other economists and a mountain of facts suggest that corporate leaders are often capitalism's worst foes.

What is the significance of the concentration of economic and political power for social welfare? Why is it important to understand modern economic and political dynamics, and to take them into account in efforts to achieve a more democratic and just society?

The Impact of Job Loss and Corporate Mobility

We have reviewed how the quest for higher profits has led to an almost exclusive emphasis on labor-saving technologies, unrestrained corporate mobility, and tax laws that force displaced farm workers into underserviced cities, discriminate against the small firms that actually create the bulk of jobs, and facilitate the overseas flight of jobs and capital. It is not necessary to subscribe to the notion that bigness is bad in either the private or public sector to realize that these facts have enormously important implications for workers and their families, the health of communities, and social cohesion.

Many studies have shown the high price families pay for our boom-and-bust economy and for the habit of corporations of moving at will, withdrawing their entire investment in communities in one fell swoop. The studies tell of disrupted school years, disturbed children, broken marriages, alcoholic wives, and unfulfilled men — often earning good money but with their personal lives in shambles — as families follow the corporate trek (66).

But most families are left behind, and whole communities feel the impact. The Northeast is spotted with ghost towns — once proud textile and shoe manufacturing centers. The closing of the Youngstown Sheet and Tube Works during the late 1970s by its parent, the Lykes Corporation, shows what happened to the North Central region. When the plant closed, 4,100 workers immediately lost their jobs. But another 12,000 to 13,000 jobs disappeared through "ripple" effect as small businesses in the area closed down. Soon unemployment rates rose by 10 per cent in Ohio's Mahoning Valley. Property valuations dropped by 27 per cent, tax collections by 40 per cent, and sales by some $15 million (2). The combined cost of welfare, food stamps, and lost tax revenues attributable to the plant closing soon totalled over $70 million (33, 53).

The personal impact of unemployment partly depends on whether it is a shared experience, as in mass layoffs, or a solitary experience. But studies show that whatever the circumstances, we have been so socialized that when we lose jobs, we almost always blame ourselves and suffer severe loss in self-esteem. Harry Maurer, after interviewing hundreds of unemployed workers across the nation, wrote:

> Even when workers were axed by a willful employer or when hundreds were laid off at a time, the ache of personal failure is felt. Having absorbed a value system that glorifies professional success, unemployed Americans cannot help but thinking they fall short as human beings. And the more thoroughly they accept American mythology regarding beneficent competition, equal opportunity, and the entrepreneurial spirit, the deeper their shame. (50)

Dr. Harvey Brenner (11) and other researchers have shown that as unemployment rises, so do first admissions to psychiatric hospitals, suicide and homicide rates, alcohol consumption, deaths from cirrhosis of the liver, heart and vascular diseases, and infant and maternal mortality. Applying his findings to the period from 1970 to 1975, it was estimated that the U.S. economy lost some $21 million in income, deaths, and institutionalization for all types of unemployment-related illnesses. But no measure can possibly reflect the human cost in broken marriages, lost dreams, and discouragement.

Mental health centers, crisis "hot lines," and a host of other community services have corroborated Brenner's work in their reports of the impact of unemployment in recent years. As jobs declined, community services were flooded with requests for help. Family friction, sexual dysfunction, family violence, desertion, and divorce all increased. So did child abuse. After an extensive review of the literature, Dumont (27) concluded that "unemployment is a health crisis of tragic proportions. For people in this society, the loss of work represents not only financial insecurity, but a biopsychological assault of such magnitude that it must be counted as one of the great public health menaces of our time. . . . "

Other research, reviewed in more detail in Chapter 8, shows that although divorce and separation rates are about twice as high for blacks as whites, if their unemployment experience is held constant, the difference virtually disappears. These facts strongly suggest that it is not the matriarchal family system that primarily threatens the stability of black families, but the simple unadulterated fact of frequent joblessness.

Neither counseling services within the social welfare complex nor corporations have given the attention to this problem that it deserves (29). For many years social agencies were more likely to deal with intrafamily tensions than with work-related difficulties, and few communities yet have services designed explicitly to help jobless men and women deal with the involved psychological, physiological, vocational, retraining, and relocation problems they so often encounter. Considering that over 7 million workers are now jobless and seeking work and far more during an entire year, this group may well be the most severely underserviced in the population. Certainly, providing unemployment insurance — to just about half of the group — is only the first step.

As most Americans today have reason to know, some nations take preventive steps to reduce the risk of unemployment. In Japan workers have lifetime employment in many industries, and wages are so arranged as to create incentives for higher productivity and excellence. All over Europe, government and business have collaborated for years to stabilize employment and make permanent jobs for the "hard-to-employ." Fortunately, American businessmen are beginning to show more interest in the social inventiveness of their foreign colleagues, but so far neither their more democratic style nor the concept of "permanent" employment has gained much foothold in the U.S.

The Fiscal Crisis of Government

We have seen how large corporations contribute to the fiscal crisis of government in many ways. They reduce tax revenues by failing to provide enough jobs in the U.S., by demanding and receiving a long list of expensive subsidies, bailouts, and supportive services, by spending their profits acquiring new properties rather than creating new jobs and improving productivity. They add to the cost of government by failing to protect product quality or the safety and health of workers, thereby pushing government into expensive, abrasive regulatory activities.

But whenever the fiscal crisis of government is at the top of the agenda, social welfare is typically cast in the role of both villain and victim. All through the 1970s, services languished as one community and state after another either rejected necessary tax increases or enacted sharp tax reductions. Then, to protect the supply of jobs, cities almost gave away their birthright to attract industry — which as often as not demanded more and better services. Soon a predictable pattern of tax abatements for industry, tax increases for citizens was set in motion. The harm done to the social fabric was incalculable, as citizens, cities, and states were pitted against each other. Households without children soon decided that schools cost too much. People with steady, secure jobs were sure that the unemployed could find work if they really tried. The young came to resent paying for social security. Having never known life without it, they were sure that saving for their old age was a simple matter if only they could retain more of their present earnings. Able-bodied people, being unable to imagine that they would ever become disabled, faulted those who had this misfortune for relying on cash transfers or for demanding expensive adaptations in public transportation so that they, too, could work and participate in community life. Cities blamed states, and both faulted the federal government. In the maelstrom, national leadership first blamed citizens for losing confidence in America and then short-circuited the democratic process by rushing legislation through Congress in 1981 that mandated social welfare cuts in the first year alone of some $36 billion, with much more to come. If anyone doubted the power of big business to dominate government policy before this chain of events, it is difficult to see how the doubt could survive the happenings in Washington these years.

Perhaps never since the Civil War have democratic consensus-building efforts and citizen participation been more important to the national welfare.

References ————————————————————————————

1. AFL–CIO. *Memo From Cope* (January 2, 1978), p. 2.
2. Alperovitz, Gar and Jeff Faux. *Rebuilding America.* New York: Pantheon Books, 1984, pp. 147–148.
3. Associated Press News Release: Melville, N.Y. "Henry's Brother Speaks Out

Against Company Takeovers: Kissinger vs. Conglomerates." Cleveland *Plain Dealer,* June 9, 1978.

4. Barnet, Richard. "A Reporter at Large: the Search for National Security." *The New Yorker,* **57** (April 27, 1981), pp. 50–140.

5. ———. *The Lean Years: Politics in the Age of Scarcity.* New York: Simon and Schuster, Inc., 1980, pp. 139–141, 239, 249–251, 287, 290.

6. ——— and Ronald E. Müller. *Global Reach: The Power of the Multinational Corporation.* New York: Simon and Schuster, Inc., 1974, pp. 15, 182–183.

7. Berg, Alan. *The Nutrition Factor: Its Role in National Development.* Washington, D.C.: Brookings Institution, 1973.

8. Bluestone, Barry and Bennett Harrison. *The Deindustrialization of America.* New York: Basic Books, Inc., Publishers, 1982, pp. 42, 47, 145–146.

9. Booth, Heather and Steve Max. "Citizen vs. Corporation." *Social Policy,* **11** (May/June 1980), pp. 26–28.

10. Braithwaite, John. "Crime and the Abuse of Power in International Perspective." In *Report of the Interregional Meeting of Experts on Crime and the Abuse of Power: Offenses and Offenders Beyond the Reach of the Law.* New York: United Nations, July 9–13, 1979, pp. 22–23.

11. Brenner, M. Harvey, *Mental Illness and the Economy.* Cambridge: Harvard University Press, 1973.

12. Brody, Michael. "Can GM Manage it All?" *Fortune,* **112** (July 8, 1985), p. 25.

13. Burck, Arthur. "A Difference of Opinion: A Merger Specialist Who Hates Mergers." *Fortune,* **108** (October 19, 1981), pp. 221–228.

14. Carnoy, Martin and Derek Shearer. *Economic Democracy: The Challenge of the 1980s.* White Plains, N.Y.: M. E. Sharpe, Inc., 1980, pp. 87, 132–143.

15. Carter, Craig. "Uncuffing AT&T." *Fortune,* **112** (July 8, 1985), p. 127.

16. Clinard, Marshall B. and Peter C. Yeager. *Corporate Crime.* New York: The Free Press, 1980, pp. 38, 41–42, 253.

17. Cochran, Bert. *Welfare Capitalism — and After.* New York: Schocken Books, 1984, pp. 90–92, 99.

18. Commoner, Barry. *The Poverty of Power: Energy and the Economic Crisis.* New York: Bantam Books, Inc., 1976.

19. "The Cost of Auto Quotas." Editorial, *Washington Post,* February 21, 1985.

20. Dahl, Robert A. *Who Governs?* New Haven: Yale University Press, 1961.

21. ———. *Modern Political Analysis,* 3rd ed. Englewood Cliffs, N.J.: Prentice-Hall, Inc., 1976.

22. Dennis, Darienne L. and Royce D. Wolfe. "The International 500." *Fortune,* **111** (August 20, 1984), p. 201.

23. Domhoff, G. William. *The Powers That Be.* Englewood Cliffs, N.J.: Prentice-Hall, Inc., 1978.

24. ———. *Who Rules America?* Englewood Cliffs, N.J.: Prentice-Hall, Inc., 1967.

25. Drew, Elizabeth, "A Reporter at Large: Charlie." *The New Yorker,* **53** (January 8, 1978), pp. 32–64, 40.

26. ———. *Politics and Money: The New Road to Corruption.* New York: Macmillan Publishing Co., 1983, pp. 12–27, 156.

27. Dumont, Matthew P. "Is Mental Health Possible Under Our Economic System? No!" *Psychiatric Opinion,* **14** (May/June 1977), pp. 9–11, 32–33, 44–45.

28. Edsall, Thomas Byrne. *The New Politics of Inequality.* New York: W. W. Norton & Co., 1984, pp. 76–77, 130–136.
29. Figueira-McDonough, Josephine. "Mental Health Among Unemployed Detroiters." *Social Service Review,* **52** (September 1978), pp. 383–399.
30. Galbraith, John Kenneth. *Economics and the Public Purpose.* Boston: Houghton-Mifflin Co., 1973, pp. 43, 151–159, 218–222.
31. George, Susan. *How the Other Half Dies: The Real Reasons for World Hunger.* Montclair, N.J.: Allanheld, Osmun & Co., Publishers, 1977.
32. Gilder, George. *Wealth and Poverty.* New York: Basic Books, Inc., Publishers, 1981, p. 76.
33. Ginsburg, Helen. *Full Employment and Public Policy: United States and Sweden.* Lexington, Mass.: D.C. Heath & Co., 1983, pp. 85–103.
34. Grubb, W. Norton and Marvin Lazerson. *Broken Promises: How Americans Fail Their Children.* New York: Basic Books, Inc., Publishers, 1982, pp. 282–284.
35. Henderson, Hazel. *Creating Alternative Futures: The End of Economics.* New York: Berkley Publishing Corp., 1978, pp. 83–92.
36. Heslop, Allen. Ed. *Business–Government Relations.* New York: New York University Press, 1976, p. 12.
37. Huntington, Samuel P. *American Politics: The Promise of Disharmony.* Cambridge: The Belknap Press of Harvard University Press, 1981, pp. 7–8.
38. Infant Formula Action Coalition. "Infant Formula Fact Sheet." Circular to contributors. Minneapolis: INFACT, February 1984.
39. Knight, Robin. "Why U.S. Firms Say 'No' to Overseas Investing." *U.S. News & World Report,* **98** (December 3, 1984), pp. 58–59.
40. Kramer, Mark. "The Ruination of the Tomato." *The Atlantic,* **245** (January 1980), p. 75.
41. Lawrence, Steve. "Bar Wars: Hershey Bites Mars." *Fortune,* **112** (July 8, 1985), p. 53.
42. League of Women Voters. "Facts on Pacs." *The National Voter,* **34** (Fall 1984), pp. 1–8.
43. Lekachman, Robert. "A Cure for Corporate Neurosis." *Saturday Review,* **5** (January 21, 1978), pp. 30, 31.
44. ———. *Economists at Bay: Why The Experts Will Never Solve Your Problems.* New York: McGraw-Hill, Inc., 1976, pp. 160–185.
45. Lindblom, Charles. *Politics and Markets.* New York: Basic Books, Inc., Publishers, 1977, p. 356.
46. Loos, Barbara G. and Dennis J. Moulton. "The World's Largest Industrial Corporations." *Fortune,* **112** (August 19, 1985), p. 179.
47. Louis, J. C. and Harvey Yazigian. *The Cola Wars.* New York: Everest House, 1980, p. 176.
48. Magnet, Myron. "The Fortune 500: The Dollar Dampens the Profit Party." *Fortune,* **111** (April 29, 1985), pp. 252–316.
49. ———. "The Service 500: It's Shape Up or Shake Out in a Shook-Up World." *Fortune,* **111** (June 10, 1985), p. 170.
50. Maurer, Harry. *Not Working.* New York: Holt, Rinehart & Winston, 1979, pp. 4–5.

51. McWilliams, Wilson Carey. *The Idea of Fraternity in America.* Berkeley: University of California Press, 1973, pp. 558–569.
52. Mills, C. Wright. *The Power Elite.* New York: Oxford University Press, 1956, pp. 3–4.
53. Moberg, David. "Shuttered Factories — Shattered Communities." *In These Times,* **27** (June 1979), p. 11.
54. Müller, Ronald E. *Revitalizing America: Politics for Prosperity.* New York: Simon and Schuster, Inc., 1980, pp. 63–64.
55. Patton, Arch. "Why Corporations Overpay Their Underachieving Bosses." *Washington Post,* March 3, 1985.
56. Pauly, David, et al. "Antitrust, Reagan Style." *Newsweek,* **98** (July 6, 1981), p. 59.
57. Pechman, Joseph A. "Introduction." In Joseph A. Pechman., Ed., *Options for Tax Reform.* Washington, D.C.: Brookings Institution, 1984, p. 1.
58. Piore, Michael J. and Charles F. Sabel. *The Second Industrial Divide: Possibilities for Prosperity.* New York: Basic Books, Inc., Publishers, 1984, pp. 286–295.
59. Reich, Robert R. *The Next American Frontier.* New York: Times Books, 1983, pp. 140–175.
60. Reilly, Ann. "Reagan Turns a Cold Eye on Antitrust." *Fortune,* **112** (October 14, 1985), p. 31.
61. Robertson, James Oliver. *American Myth, American Reality.* New York: Hill and Wang, Inc., 1980, pp. 187–188.
62. Roeder, Edward. "Campaign Financing: The 'Good News' Is All Wrong." *Washington Monthly,* **17** (July/August 1985), pp. 47–48.
63. Sale, Kirkpatrick. *Human Scale.* New York: Coward, McCann & Geoghegan, Inc., 1980, pp. 303, 311–314.
64. Samuelson, Paul. *Economics,* 11th ed., rev. New York: McGraw-Hill Book Co., 1980, p. 104.
65. Seamonds, Jack A. "When States Go All Out to Lure Industry." *U.S. News & World Report,* **98** (May 20, 1985), p. 92.
66. Seidenberg, Robert. *Corporate Wives – Corporate Casualties?* New York: Anchor Books, 1975.
67. Serrin, William. "Let Them Eat Junk." *Saturday Review,* **7** (February 2, 1980), p. 19.
68. Servan-Schreiber, Jean-Jacques. *The American Challenge.* Trans. by Ronald Steel. London: Hamilton, 1968.
69. Silk, Leonard and David Vogel. *Ethics and Profits: The Crisis of Confidence in American Business.* New York: Simon and Schuster, Inc., 1976, p. 105.
70. Simon, William E. *A Time for Truth.* New York: Berkley Publishing Corp., 1978, pp. 245–246.
71. Struck, Myron. "U.S. Considers Changing Rule Aimed at Aiding Small Business." *Washington Post,* January 4, 1985.
72. Thurow, Lester C. *The Zero-Sum Society: Distribution and the Possibilities of Economic Change.* New York: Basic Books, Inc., Publishers, 1980, pp. 150, 194–211.
73. Tiedman, Klaus. "Combating Economic Crime in West Germany, with Special Regard to Organized Forms of Economic Criminality." In *Report of the Inter-*

regional Meeting of Experts on Crime and the Abuse of Power: Offenses and Offenders Beyond the Reach of the Law. New York: United Nations, July 9–13, 1979.

74. Truman, David B. *The Governmental Process,* 2d ed. New York: Alfred A. Knopf, Inc., 1971, Ch. 2.

75. Turner, Jonathan H. and Charles E. Starnes. *Inequality: Privilege and Poverty in America.* Santa Monica: Goodyear Publishing Co., Inc., 1976, pp. 89–119.

76. U.S. Bureau of the Census. *Statistical Abstract of the United States, 1979.* Washington, D.C.: U.S. Government Printing Office, 1979, p. 272.

77. Uttal, Bro. "Now, the Japanese Challenge in Microprocessors." *Fortune,* **112** (July 8, 1985), p. 110.

78. Vatter, Harold G. "The Position of Small Business in the Structure of American Manufacturing, 1870–1970." In Stuart W. Bruchey, Ed., *Small Business in American Life.* New York: Columbia University Press, 1980, pp. 142–168.

79. Ward, Barbara. *Progress for a Small Planet.* New York: W. W. Norton & Co., Inc., 1979, pp. 246–247, 261.

80. Williams, Monci Jo. "McDonald's Refuses to Plateau." *Fortune,* **110** (November 12, 1984), p. 34.

81. Worthy, Ford S. "The 500: The Fortune Directory of the Largest U.S. Industrial Corporations." *Fortune,* **107** (May 4, 1981), p. 322.

82. Wright, J. Patrick. *On a Clear Day You Can See General Motors: John Z. DeLorean's Look Inside the Automotive Giant.* Grosse Pointe, Mich.: Wright Enterprises, 1979, pp. 229–243.

CHAPTER 6

Poverty in America: Statistical Artifact or Reality?

As recently as the early 1960s, very little was known about poverty in the U.S. There were no lengthy census reports on the poor, nor any systematic yardstick for separating the poor from the nonpoor. But after Michael Harrington's (13) eloquent book, *The Other America,* appeared, everything changed as presidents, governors, and America's elite were shocked into awareness that the richest nation on earth had millions of impoverished citizens who lived in grossly inadequate housing, often went to bed hungry, and for want of money to buy shoes and warm clothes, had to keep their children out of school. Decisions about what should be done to solve the problem have run the gamut in the past several decades.

First there was the short-lived War on Poverty, which in combination with high employment, a zestful economy, and a host of other social welfare initiatives, caused the poverty count to fall by a third in five years, ending at 24.1 million. Except for 1973 and 1974, it has never been lower. Then the Nixon Administration proposed a negative income tax to set an income floor under families with children. When it failed to win support, the food stamp program was expanded to offset rising urban food costs. The next change occurred when the Carter Administration decided national defense urgently needed updating and the time had come to check the growth of social welfare. This was the beginning of restrictions in the food stamp program and social security disability benefits; social security taxes rose sharply; and stagflation seemed uncontrollable; all of which pushed the poverty roster up to 29.3 million by 1980. The Reagan Administration continued many Carter policies, but unlike the pragmatism of their predecessors, Reagan and his colleagues arrived in the White House with an ideology that was soon reflected in a spectacular arms buildup, sharp budget cuts and elimination of programs for the poor, tax increases for the poor and tax decreases for the rich, a devolution of authority and responsibility to the states, deregulation of industry, and a stream of decisions and proposals to sell national resources and to contract with the private market for many traditional government services. Combined with a long recession, poverty rates rose to heights not seen since the mid-1960s when the War on Poverty was just getting underway. Of all age groups, children under six years were the most likely to be poor.

In the following pages the controversy over how to define poverty, and how many people are poor will be reviewed. Then we discuss who the poor are, how poor they are, and the relative risks of being poor.

How Poverty is Defined and Measured _____

Development of Poverty Thresholds. Poverty has been defined in many ways. Lack of power, shortage of money, and self-defeating attitudes and styles of life are among the most common. But when the goal is to count the poor, a materialistic society with a penchant for "hard facts" rather naturally opts for an economic definition. From a range of alternatives, one such definition was chosen that fit already available census data: poverty would be measured in terms of pretax money income as defined by the Bureau of the Census.

In the early 1960s Mollie Orshansky of the Social Security Administration was already at work trying to develop a poverty index (23). She started with the "economy food budget," the cheapest of three budgets previously developed by the U.S. Department of Agriculture. Knowing that studies in the 1950s showed that American families spent about one third of their disposable (after-tax) income for food, she multiplied economy food budgets for different types of households by three to produce a series of poverty thresholds. No adjustment was made to reflect the difference between pretax and posttax income. Nor was it often emphasized that out of their small incomes, the poor, like everyone else, still had to pay taxes.

Orshansky's first poverty count appeared in 1963 (19), about a year before the War on Poverty got underway. By early 1965 her second report was published (20). Finally in 1969 her thresholds, with minor modifications, became the official series used by the Bureau of the Census in making yearly reports on the poverty population.*

In order to separate the poor from the nonpoor, the Bureau of the Census uses a set of income cutoffs that vary slightly depending on size of household, presence and number of children or other family members, and age of householders or family heads. It should be emphasized that only income, not financial need, is taken into account in applying poverty thresholds. This is one reason why some people believe poverty may be undercounted, not overcounted.

Absolute or Relative Poverty. Orshansky defined poverty in absolute terms as a subsistence level of living. Economy food budgets were not

_____
*All poverty data cited in this chapter are from these yearly publications unless otherwise noted. At this writing, the most recent full report is for 1984 income (39).

intended to provide sufficient nourishment for long periods of time. They were purely for temporary use, as in the event of an unexpected layoff of a few weeks. Experts at the U.S. Department of Agriculture estimated back in the 1970s, when food stamp standards were relatively higher than they now are, that only about one quarter of the families living on an economy food budget received adequate nourishment (17), and then probably only when mothers were superior planners, shoppers, and cooks. National studies of nutritional intake among infants have also shown that 13 per cent under one year of age were deficient in calcium, 28 per cent in vitamin A, and the vast majority in iron (8). It was malnourishment of this and even worse levels that kept pediatricians and nutritionists laboring so hard and devotedly to promote the food stamp and various child nutrition programs (15).

Each year thresholds are updated to keep pace with the cost of living, but no adjustment has ever been made to take improved standards of living into account And even cost-of-living adjustments leave a good bit to be desired. For example, since 1969 the consumer price index for what are essentially middle-income families has been used to update thresholds. But poor households have different consumption patterns than others. They must spend almost every cent on necessities, some of which have been among the most rapidly rising items in the consumer price index. We can see the result of this shortfall by comparing the poverty threshold for four person families in Table 6–1 with the median income of all four person families in 1959 and 1984. In the earlier year, the threshold represented about 48 per cent of median income; by 1984 the threshold had fallen to 34 per cent of the median. In other words, even though the cutoff point was raised each year to reflect price changes, average family income

TABLE 6–1. Poverty Thresholds in 1984

Size of Family Unit	Threshold
1 person (unrelated individual)	$ 5,278
Under 65 years	5,400
65 years and over	4,979
2 persons	6,762
Householder under 65 years	6,983
Householder 65 years and over	6,282
3 persons	8,277
4 persons	10,609
5 persons	12,566
6 persons	14,207
7 persons	16,096
8 persons	17,961
9 persons or more	21,247

Source: U.S. Bureau of the Census. *Current Population Reports, Consumer Income 1984,* Series P–60, no. 152, p. 122.

rose even more. So as the years passed, those families officially classified as poor fell progressively behind other families, incomewise. Or to shift our perspective slightly, part of the decline in poverty rates since 1959 was due to the erosion of the measure or definition of poverty. It is as though a yardstick that was once thirty-six inches long was cut back to twenty-five inches but was still called a yardstick.

This raises the question of whether poverty should be defined in absolute or relative terms. While Orshansky's absolute cash cutoffs may have been politic at the time, as has been argued, many people agree that how the poor fare is not simply a matter of whether they have enough to survive. When average family income is substantially above the poverty level and rises more rapidly, pressure on prices not only forces the poor to pay more, too, but pushes some right out of the market. This is one reason why public housing subsidies, food stamps, infant and maternal nutrition programs, school lunches and breakfasts, and Medicaid became necessary. Also, as expectations rise, concepts of need change across the income scale. This fact is often overlooked by critics who insist that poverty no longer exists in the U.S. "If you want to see real poverty," they often claim, "look at children in the streets of Calcutta." Naturally the poor in the U.S. have more food and more money than families in developing nations. But is India, Bangladesh, or Ethiopia a rational frame of reference for one of the most highly developed nations in the world? Is it even safe to condone such extremes of wealth as this criticism suggests? In very pragmatic terms, if "felt deprivation" rises dangerously, so will feelings of alienation, despair, discontent, and consequent civic disorders. Fortunately most people are uneasy and concerned when they learn that over one fifth of our children live in homes where parents earn too little to afford decent shelter, health care, or other necessities of life (30).

This line of reasoning leads to a relative definition of poverty. Victor Fuchs (10), Oscar Ornati (18), Lee Rainwater (24), and scholars at the University of Wisconsin's Institute for Research on Poverty (16) have proposed indexes representing some fixed share of a moving average, e.g. 40 or 50 per cent of median income or median disposable income. Since average incomes tend to reflect wage trends, which in turn influence prices, this type of index automatically corrects for rising costs and standards of living. To illustrate how much depends on the type of definition used, Plotnick and Skidmore (22) measured progress against poverty between 1964 and 1974, relying on an index representing 44 per cent of median income. In 1972 they counted 32.3 million poor people as compared with the official census count of 24.5 million. If a relative index set at 48 per cent of median income had been chosen initially, by 1983 the poverty threshold for four person households would have been about $12,100 instead of $10,178, and the poverty count would be about 48 million, not 35.3 million. A relative index would also serve as a better warning about the impact of programs and policies on the poor, and alert citizens to the fact that a booming economy and a war on poverty in the 1960s had been more than offset by recessions, inflation, prolonged high unemployment, and cut-backs in public benefits for the poor during the 1970s and 1980s.

The Significance of Income Concepts in Counting the Poor. The same controversy discussed in Chapter 4 as to what should be counted as income and at what stage income should be measured arises when the subject of poverty is broached. Efforts have been made to adjust census data to cover all types of money income, in-kind benefits, and taxes in order to secure a more realistic picture of poverty. In 1982, for example, using pretax income, the Bureau of the Census found 15 per cent of the population was poor (37). Adjusting for underreporting of income and noncash benefits priced at market value, the rate fell to 8.8 per cent (11). When a somewhat lower and probably more realistic value to recipients was substituted for market value, the poverty rate fell to only 12.7 per cent (26, 41). Which if any of these measures gives the "true" count is not yet clear.

In addition to the technical problems, some troublesome policy issues have yet to be resolved. Does it really make sense to add a value for all or most in-kind benefits to family income when the goal is to measure family poverty? The reason for skepticism on this score is perhaps best illustrated with health care. For many poor families public benefits do not conserve family income. They simply give access to care families otherwise would go without. Assume a tiny low birth weight baby is born into an impoverished family. With the remarkable technologies now available, the doctors and hospital save her life — at a cost of $40,000. As is done in all efforts to arrive at a "true" poverty count, that $40,000 is added to the parents' income, pushing the family into the upper-income group. But Medicaid money for the infant's care went to the hospital, doctors, nurses, medical supply and equipment firms, not to the infant's family. Furthermore since low birth weight babies are often left mentally retarded or otherwise disabled, the family may have unusual medical needs for the balance of her life. So, we have the anomaly of a statistically "well-off" but actually very poor family. This might not matter if poverty data were not used to frame poverty policy. That everyone close to the scene expects it to be was well illustrated by the outcry when it was announced in April 1984 that consultants would meet at the Bureau of the Census the following month to "perform a technical review of the procedures used to value noncash benefits." The list included conservative economists whose research in this area had been thoroughly discredited. Almost overnight, objections poured into Washington, primarily reflecting the fear that the Administration was intent on redefining poverty in ways that would arbitrarily lower the poverty count. The heat was so fierce that the meeting was cancelled (21).

Many experts in this field treat education in the same way. Does this economic logic fit our values? It seems to assume that education is an optional private consumption item that benefits only the individual, and that when the state provides or subsidizes schools, the cost — in excess of household taxes for this purpose, tuition, and whatever books and supplies families pay for — represents a gift to citizens. But state laws require youngsters to go to school because the nation needs and wants them to be educated. If they were not, our highly technological, industrialized economy would collapse, and the loss in human potentials would be incalculable. In other words, part of the cost should be attributed to "the public good." On balance it seems that economists have forgotten the purpose of their exercise. It is one thing to study how the public investment in education is allocated over income classes in order to identify and correct inequities. Similarly, measuring per capita educational costs over time can provide useful clues to changing standards of living. But what sense does it make to regard the public share of educational costs as personal income for the purpose of measuring the extent or depth of family poverty? Or to use the results to justify killing programs because "poverty no longer exists," thereby eliminating this "income increment" and as a consequence causing the poverty count to skyrocket again? The point is that unless econometric models reflect widely held values, they can be dangerously misleading. This is not a case of economists cautiously opting for value-free models. Their current ones are loaded with values, primarily reflecting an individualistic, free enterprise, private sector bias.

These unresolved issues help to explain why the Bureau of the Census publishes yearly reports on households receiving or covered by noncash benefits, but stops short of adding any value for them to family income. Since the Bureau collects little relevant data from families, instead relying on econometric models based on program reports regarding eligibility, cost, and actual coverage, the final product is of limited use. What is needed are reports showing the actual distribution by income class of all publicly supported or subsidized benefits and services, whether financed from direct expenditures or tax savings. Only then can we decide if the poor are getting too much, which seems to be the major worry.

How Poor are the Poor?

Median Income and Economic Mobility. For the poor, poverty thresholds are income ceilings. They tell nothing about the actual income of poor households. As a matter of fact, most have incomes well below the thresholds. In 1984 the median income of poor families was $5,455, about 21 per cent of the median income of all families, $26,433. And poor households were slightly larger. For unrelated individuals, many of whom are elderly women living alone, median income was only $3,453 among the poverty group.

Each year census reports publish income deficits — the difference between family income and poverty thresholds. Since 1968 median family deficits have ranged (in current dollars) from $993 to $3,696, reaching their lowest point in 1968 and their highest in 1984. On average, median income of poor families is about 50 per cent of the official thresholds. There is another way of looking at the situation. Between 1972 and 1984, the consumer price index rose by 146 per cent, median income of all families by 138 per cent, and median income *deficits* of poor families by 207 per cent.

The society of the poor is more egalitarian than the "other America." Racial and ethnic differences tend to disappear. In 1983 average income per family member varied by only $86 among poor black, white, and Hispanic families. Blacks and whites were within $14 of each other. Because of social security and SSI, poor families with elderly heads fared somewhat better. Their average per capita income of $1,752 gave them a $300 lead over their poor neighbors.

There is surprising mobility up and down the income ladder. Changes in economic status have been followed since 1968 when the Survey Research Center of the University of Michigan began collecting data through repeated annual interviews with a single, continuing sample of over 5,000 families. One analysis made of the longitudinal survey data shows that while 11.1 per cent of families in the bottom income quintile in 1971 were also there in 1978, and another 4.4 per cent had moved up only to the next quintile, slightly more, 4.5 per cent, were in the upper three quintiles. At the other end of the income scale, only 9.7 per cent of the families were in the highest quintile in both 1971 and 1978. While 5.9 per cent had only fallen one quintile, 4.4 per cent were scattered among the lowest three quintiles. In all, almost one quarter of the families moved at least two quintiles in either direction, which suggests that how the poor are treated should be of considerable concern to a great many people (6).

The panel study permits another measure of "persistent" poverty, which is much talked about today. Between 1969 and 1978, only 0.7 per cent of families were poor all ten years, while 2.6 per cent were poor for eight years. But almost a quarter of all families were counted among the poor for one or more years during this period (7). Not surprisingly, female-headed households, especially those headed by black women and Southerners — obviously overlapping groups — were most likely to be among the persistently poor. Disabled and rural residents were also among the more than usually vulnerable groups (7).

While changes in family composition often plunge people into poverty, whether or not they remain poor frequently depends on whether they find and are able to hold on to full-time jobs paying decent wages. With their heavy home responsibilities, this is more difficult for mothers with young children; nonetheless, the commitment among the poor to work is impressive. In 1983, when over 10 million men and women were jobless in almost every month, 60 per cent of all poor families had at least one wage earner. About a third had two or more employed members. Of poor married couples, 71 per cent of the "householders"* worked during the year as compared with just under half of all female family heads. Of those who worked, about half worked year-round, most of them full time. So why were so many poor? The Administration's failure to raise the minimum wage was part of the problem. Since many poor adults are relatively poorly educated and work in low-paid occupations, where the minimum wage is set can be more important than work effort in determining family income.

Food and Housing Supplements. It is often assumed that poor people routinely receive food stamps and housing subsidies. Unfortunately, being poor in the U.S. today too often means that families are homeless, go to bed hungry, and children die prematurely.

During 1983 only two fifths of poor households received food stamps. About four out of every five AFDC families were among the recipients, but over two fifths of all poor families with young children were not. Less than half of the 13.3 million poor youngsters received free or low-cost school lunches or breakfasts. The WIC program, which provides high nutrition supplements for pregnant and lactating women and their infants and young children, has waiting lists all over the nation. The only federal food program that Congress categorically refused to cut, it is nonetheless funded at levels that cover only one third of eligible families (38, 43).

All other food programs that helped so much to reduce hunger and malnutrition during the 1970s have been cut back in one way or another (4). Between 1982 and 1985 federal funds declined by $12.2 billion — despite the prolonged recession and rise of five million in the poverty population. The number of children receiving school lunches declined by 2.5 million after 1981, and 2,700 schools closed down both the lunch and breakfast programs because too few children any longer qualified under the new restrictions to make the program affordable. The majority of the "savings" in the food stamp program in recent years was due to the unprecedented decision to set benefit levels below the cost of the nutritionally deficient Department of Agriculture "thrifty food budget," the frame of reference for food stamp standards.† Few of us will forget the Administra-

---

*In recent years either the wife or husband could claim to be the "householder." Typically, the term refers to the husband.

† The Food Research and Action Council in Washington, D.C. recently checked food costs in eight major cities in order to learn what the "thrifty food budget" for a family of four, qualifying for $268 monthly in food stamps, would cost. The price ranged from $377.20 to $412.88, for an average of $384.48.

tion guidelines defining pickles and catsup as satisfying the vegetable requirement in school lunches.

Despite the ground swell of hunger centers and soup kitchens across the nation (43), in 1985 the prestigious Physician's Task Force on Hunger in America reported that hunger was epidemic in the U.S., afflicting at least 20 million people for at least part of every month. Clinics in poverty areas were finding cases of kwashiorkor and marasmus, two "Third World diseases" of advanced malnutrition, as well as gross vitamin deficiencies, "stunting," "wasting," and other health problems traceable to inadequate food. Second Harvest, an organization of food banks supplying soup kitchens and food pantries, reported a 700 per cent increase in the amount of food distributed since 1980 (43). The Children's Defense Fund, summarizing reports received from doctors all over the nation, found that thousands of youngsters were showing disturbing signs of stunted growth, dehydration, and diarrhea, and were abnormally underweight. Between 1981 and 1983 the children admitted to six hospitals in Cook County, Illinois, for conditions related to malnutrition rose by 26 per cent. After declining for three decades, infant mortality rates began levelling off, and for blacks actually rose. Now, as back in the 1950s, the rate for blacks is twice as high as for whites. Poverty, malnutrition, and the absence of early prenatal care have been identified repeatedly as the key causal factors (4).

These facts shed light on why pediatricians and nutritionists are pleading with federal officials, as they did in the 1960s, to increase appropriations for all food programs. In the process, they are reminding Congress that for every one dollar cut from food programs, experience confirms three dollars will be necessary to correct subsequent problems of malnutrition (14).

What about housing supplements for the poor? In 1983 just one seventh of poor households lived in public housing or subsidized rental housing (38). Their shelter cost (including utilities) was subsidized if it exceeded 30 per cent of net income — raised from 25 per cent in 1981. For at least the last fifteen years rising housing costs have had catastrophic effects on the budgets of the poor. By 1976 two fifths of low-income central city dwellers paid more than half of their income for housing (2). By 1985, as much as 70 per cent was sometimes necessary. To put this in perspective, in 1981 a financial planning firm serving relatively well-to-do families, reported their clients averaged a mere 10.8 per cent for shelter costs (9).

A long-standing but increasingly critical shortage of low-income housing has now collided with a rise in poverty, prolonged joblessness, and the failure of housing allowances in welfare grants to keep pace with inflation. The result has been described as an epidemic of homelessness. Federal cutbacks and threatened withdrawal from housing programs for the poor precipitated the crisis and continue to exaccerbate it. Despite the economic upturn, homelessness continued to rise during 1985.

Since the National Housing Act was passed in 1949, federal housing programs for the poor have never met their goals. During the 1970s Nixon, and then Ford, concluded that instead of constructing more public housing, the federal government should shift to rent subsidies. To this end new laws authorized the government to write fifteen-year contracts with landlords to build or otherwise provide rental units for eligible families.* By 1981, 1.7 million households were being helped by the program. Since then rents have been raised and the number of units has steadily declined. One section of the law targets the aged and handicapped. In 1979 it funded 20,444 units; by 1985 the number had dropped to 12,000. In New York City, 170,000 families declared eligible for public housing can expect to wait fifteen to eighteen years for units to become available. People now applying for public housing in Washington, D.C. can expect to wait ten years (4). Nonetheless, in 1986 the Administration asked for a two-year moratorium on new construction, expressed preference for a voucher program, which would "free" the poor to find their own "assisted" housing in the private market, and announced its wish to sell the profitable Federal Housing Administration, which provided the low-cost loans that turned the U.S. into a nation of homeowners.

Every recent year some 2.5 million people have been involuntarily displaced from their homes. Homeless people are very difficult to count. Estimates of the children alone range up to 660,000. A New York state task force reported that on a typical night in 1983, the state had from 40,000 to 50,000 homeless people, 85 per cent in New York City. About half slept in emergency accommodations provided by the state and local governments, churches, and synagogues; the balance slept in the streets, under bridges, in bus terminals, on park benches. During the cold winter some froze to death, including one in Washington, D.C. near the White House.

While deinstitutionalization of the mentally ill and mentally retarded, combined with widespread community refusal to have them lodged in group homes, has added to the number of homeless people, the most credible studies agree that poverty is the number one cause of homelessness. The typical homeless family is a mother with several young children (4). But joblessness, mortgage foreclosures, and evictions added a surprising number of two parent families to the group. The young and old, most people agree, have been the chief victims.

For fiscal 1986, the Administration proposed a moratorium on all new commitments for federally "assisted" housing, including the highly successful, Republican-initiated rent subsidy program.

Sources of Income. The poor are wonderfully ingenious in putting

---

*Unless Congress takes the necessary action, the first fifteen-year contracts will expire in 1991, losing 200,000 units. By 2001, 1.2 million units could be lost — more than one quarter of all government subsidized housing units.

TABLE 6–2.   Sources of Income for Poor Families

Earnings, earned benefits, private investments, and intrafamilial transfers	73.3%
AFDC, SSI, and general assistance	26.7%

Source: U.S. Bureau of the Census. *Current Population Reports, Consumer Income 1983,* Series P–60, no. 147, p. 142.

together viable "income packages" (25). They work when they can find jobs and can be spared from home. Some fatherless families get child support, though not nearly enough. Many households receive several cash transfers. Dividends, interest, and rentals help a few. More have small pensions or annuities, and a few even get alimony.

What share of their income is derived from each source? In 1983, of every $100 of income, $46.60 was earned, $23.20 came from AFDC or general assistance, $13.60 from social security, $6.20 from unemployment insurance, workers' compensation, or veterans' benefits, $5.20 from pensions and intrafamilial transfers, like child support, $3.50 from SSI, and $1.70 from dividends, interest or rentals. This helps to clarify a very important point. As Table 6–2 shows, *their own earnings, earned benefits, private investments, and help from relatives account for almost three quarters of their income.* Welfare payments account for just over one quarter.

The pattern is very similar for poor blacks and whites. What differences exist reflect the greater difficulty blacks have in finding work and their lesser likelihood of owning income-producing property. Age predictably makes for greater differences. While young people (with heads under twenty-five years of age) derive over half of their income from earnings, almost two fifths come from AFDC, SSI, or general assistance. Families with aged heads, on the other hand, receive almost three quarters of their income from social security.

The Taxes the Poor Pay.   For the last several years, the Bureau of the Census has turned its attention to the effect of taxes on income distribution. Using simulated models for allocating federal and state income taxes, property taxes, and social security taxes, it was estimated that in 1983 just under two thirds of poor households paid one or more of these taxes.

- 44 per cent paid social security taxes
- 33 per cent paid property taxes
- 13 per cent paid state income taxes
- 8 per cent paid federal income taxes (34)

Altogether, taxes represented 7 per cent of the gross income of the poor, reducing their average income from $4,480 to $4,250. For the two thirds actually paying taxes, the loss was greater, of course. When marginal tax rates were reduced for the next three years in 1981, a windfall that was to be very profitable for the rich, the Administration and Congress refused to index standard deductions, personal exemptions, or the earned income tax credit. The result by 1984 was a fivefold increase in the share of income paid in taxes by the poor. The Children's Defense Fund illustrated the contrasting impacts of 1981 tax decisions on corporations and the poor.

> Today, a family of four (two parents, two children) with earned income at the 1984 poverty line, $10,613, pays $1,076 in federal taxes: 10 per cent of its income. Five years ago, this same family with earnings at the 1979 poverty level paid less than 2 per cent of its income in federal taxes. . . . A single working mother with three children and a below-poverty income of $10,500 paid a higher federal income and social security tax (21 per cent) on a salary increase in 1984 than the wealthiest taxpayer paid on profits from the sale of stocks, bonds, or real estate (20 per cent). Indeed, on her $10,500 income, she paid $1,186 in taxes, more than Boeing, General Electric, Dupont, Texaco, Mobil, and AT&T altogether paid in 1983, although these corporations earned $13.7 billion in profits. (4)

In addition, of course, the poor, like everyone else, paid sales and excise taxes, which together are a fairly lucrative source of revenue for the states. Not until the 1985 tax year were some adjustments made to relieve low-income families, and then by indexing only personal exemptions and standard deductions to inflation. By 1986 public pressures for a fair tax system mounted to the point that it seemed likely that households below the poverty threshold would soon be free of all federal income tax liability.

Given their paltry incomes, how do the poor manage? One explanation is the sharing pattern often observed in the social networks of poor neighborhoods. Stack (29) studied the phenomenon in detail. When cash "windfalls" arrived — paychecks, small inheritances, welfare checks, occasional lottery payoffs — suddenly throughout the network utility bills, grocery bills, clothing bills, and rent were paid. This pattern meant that few incomes rose above the poverty level, but most people survived. Withdrawing from such networks is difficult for people who care. They not only risk isolation as "nonmembers," but have to cope with their own guilt about leaving kinfolk and friends behind.

The Risk of Being Poor

From March 1980 to March 1984, the poverty population grew by 6.8 million people to reach a total of 36.1 million, the highest since the early 1960s. But the highest poverty rate since 1965, 15.2 per cent, was in 1983, when over 11 million workers were jobless. Higher poverty rates tend to democratize incidence. Nonetheless, certain groups were still far more likely to be poor than others. Structural problems in our society, including deeply held biases and the willingness to condone extraordinarily high unemployment rates, make it simpler than it should be to predict which groups will suffer the highest risk of poverty. The poor population is a distillate of our failure to respect and plan for all people alike. Racism, sexism, unemployment, family breakdown, large families are all associated year after year with the highest poverty rates. When these factors interact, families are placed in multiple jeopardy, and poverty rates skyrocket accordingly.

Children are far more likely these days to be poor than any other age group. This was once the fate of the aged, but social security, especially its cost-of-living adjustments since the early 1970s, helped to reduce poverty rates for the aged from 35.2 per cent in 1959 to 14.1 per cent 1983. Children's poverty rates began at a lower level, 26.9 in 1959, declined to 13.8 by 1969, and rose fairly steadily to 21.7 by 1983. Almost half of all black children are poor, as are over a third of Hispanic children. But despite their lower rate, 16.9 in 1983, the 8.5 million poor white children dominate the group. Poor youngsters are disproportionately from female-headed families, which are four times more likely to be poor than two parent families. Even in good times, when all poverty rates decline, this general relationship is fairly constant. Because of the lifelong consequences of being raised in poverty, and the fact that almost three tenths live in families with incomes that are below 125 per cent of the poverty threshold, finding solutions to childhood poverty constitutes one of the most important challenges today. The cost of children as measured by the rise in poverty rates is dramatically illustrated with female-headed families. For black women the risk of being poor doubles with the first child. For white women, it goes up threefold. If mothers are also young (under twenty-five years of age), most are poor. The basic challenge is to find ways to stabilize the family; until that goal is achieved, better solutions are needed for the problems women experience raising children alone.

Blacks, native Americans, and families of Hispanic origin are America's poorest families. Published census reports rarely isolate native Americans, but rather lump them with Aleuts and Eskimos. Together these groups numbered about 1.4 million in 1983, with native Americans constituting three quarters of the total. While they are scattered over the nation, most live in western states, frequently residing in cities rather than on reservations. Historically, native Americans have suffered severe deficiencies in health, housing, education, and income (1, 12, 42). In the spring of 1980 their unemployment rate was double the national average, and over half of the adults twenty-five years or older had not graduated from high school. All three minority groups have a disproportionate share of families headed by women — 23 per cent for native Americans and Hispanics, and 43 per cent for blacks (40).

The U.S. population includes about 14.9 million persons of Hispanic

TABLE 6–3. Comparative Poverty Rates, 1983

	Families with			
	White Male Heads	Black Male Heads	White Female Heads	Black Female Heads
All families	7.0	16.2	28.3	53.8
Age of Head				
Under 25 years	14.7	29.9	62.5	84.0
25–34	8.4	14.7	45.3	61.1
35–44	6.7	14.5	26.6	51.1
45–54	5.2	13.4	18.4	43.3
55–59	5.5	20.1	17.4	32.1
60–64	6.6	11.4	13.3	47.7
65 and over	16.1	21.7	11.5	37.9
Family Size				
Two	5.6	14.0	21.4	44.4
Three	5.2	12.5	29.5	48.6
Four	6.8	13.9	43.8	63.8
Five	11.2	16.9	47.9	65.6
Six	15.8	21.4	51.2	73.8
Seven or more	23.7	46.9	48.0	76.7
Number of Children				
None	4.7	12.3	9.7	28.6
One	6.3	14.5	29.4	46.7
Two	8.2	16.1	42.7	57.9
Three	14.7	20.7	65.1	80.9

Four	21.6	23.3	67.4	79.2
Five or more	34.9	66.7	74.3	90.8
Education of Head				
None	33.3	44.4	—	—
Under 8 years	20.2	29.6	41.2	54.2
8 years	10.2	29.4	34.6	58.5
High School				
1–3 years	10.7	20.0	42.2	67.1
4 years	6.1	12.4	21.7	48.9
College, 1 or more years	3.0	5.0	14.2	27.9
Work Experience				
Worked during year	5.6	10.2	18.1	33.5
50–52 weeks	3.5	5.9	7.3	16.1
Full-time	3.3	5.2	4.6	11.1
Did not work	13.1	35.3	46.0	77.6
Number of Workers				
None	14.6	44.9	63.7	89.8
One	10.5	24.3	25.3	41.0
Two	4.2	7.2	7.6	25.2
Three or more	2.9	6.2	5.6	16.7

Source: U.S. Bureau of the Census. *Current Population Reports, Consumer Income 1983,* Series P–60, no. 147, Tables 11, 17, 18, 26.

origin, with Mexicans dominating the group. The poorest are the Puerto Ricans, most of whom live in large eastern cities, especially New York, where the cultural shock of racism, which is rare in Puerto Rico, the scarcity of suitable jobs, and their educational and language handicaps have contributed to profound family disorganization (32). Cordasco and Bucchioni (5), Rogler (27), Sexton (28), and Thomas (31) have all written vivid accounts of the hardships many suffer here as well as in Puerto Rico.

The future of native Americans may be brighter than for other minority groups. Their legal success in pressing land claims and fishing and timber rights has resulted in sizeable awards, which in turn stimulated remarkable economic and community development — and a new sense of pride (3). The accomplishments of the Passamaquoddy and the Penobscot in Maine have been particularly noteworthy. In addition to their own job-creating projects, they have become a major financial resource for state development.

Table 6–3 shows the risk of being poor for blacks and whites with a range of ages, education, and levels of employment. Primarily organized around family heads, this exercise focuses on relative risk, in the process highlighting groups in multiple jeopardy. A glance at the top line of figures shows that as compared with white males, families headed by black men are twice as likely to be poor. But families headed by white women run four times the risk of those headed by white men, and for those headed by black women the risk is almost eight times higher. These facts strongly suggest that sex now outweighs race as a poverty predictor.

What were the factors that pushed rates up between 1980 and 1983 even for the favored group of white two parent families? If the father had little or no education or the family was unusually large, the risk of poverty rose sharply. Even joblessness, youth, and old age took second place to these two handicaps. How did black men lower their risk of poverty over the years? By getting a college education, maintaining a stable marriage, working steadily year-round in full-time jobs, and having two or more paid workers in the family. It also helped to have no more than two children.

How blacks do in comparison with whites depends so significantly on the interaction of employment patterns and family structure that the progress of steadily employed intact families is obscured when median incomes of the two races are compared. For many reasons the rate of family formation is lower and the rate of family disruption is higher among blacks than whites. The disproportionate share of black families headed by women in recent years has had a very depressing effect on the median income of black families. By way of illustration, back in 1964 black median income was 54 per cent of white. But it reached parity for a group of young black and white families with employed husbands under thirty-five years of age who had working wives (33). In 1975, in the North Central region, when all white and black married couples with both spouses working were compared, blacks inched beyond whites (35). Black family median income represented 101.3 per cent of the white family median. Black and white families in this group had yearly incomes of $18,264 and $18,028, respectively. White wives contributed less to family income than black wives, and blacks may have surpassed whites in work effort. In any event, this is refreshing evidence that, given equal opportunity to work steadily at decent wages, black and white families turn out to be equivalent in earning capacity. Even the long recession in the early 1980s, with its depressing effect on wages, did not mar this record. In 1983, black median family income was 96 per cent of the white median for married couples consisting of a husband between thirty-five and forty-four years of age, who worked full time, year-round, and an employed wife (36).

Obviously having two able-bodied working adults in the home makes for a vast difference, not only in income but in feelings of mutuality and security as well as the hope that their work effort will result in a better future. The tragedy for many minority group families is the inordinately high rates of unemployment that persist from one year to the next — usually more than double, sometimes treble, the rates for whites. When jobs disappear in a sluggish economy, minority group workers are far more vulnerable than whites even when fair employment laws are rigorously enforced. Economic booms and busts, and racial biases of fellow workers, employers, and neighbors cannot help but place special strains on personal health and family structure. The effect of these interactions on black families is so significant that it will be examined in detail in the next chapter.

References

1. American Indian Policy Review Commission. *Final Report*, Vol. 1. Washington, D.C.: U.S. Government Printing Office, 1977, pp. 83–95.
2. Boynton, Robert Paul. *Occasional Papers in Housing and Community Affairs*, Vol. 4. Washington, D.C.: U.S. Department of Housing and Urban Development, July 1979.
3. Brobeur, Paul. "Annals of Law (Indian Land Claims)." *New Yorker*, **58** (October 11, 1982), pp. 76–155.
4. Children's Defense Fund. *A Children's Defense Budget: The Analysis of the President's FY 1986 Budget and Children*. Washington, D.C.: Children's Defense Fund, 1985, pp. 8–9, 83–98, 129–140.
5. Cordasco, Francesco and Eugene Bucchioni. Eds. *The Puerto Rican Experience*. Totowa, N.J.: Littlefield, Adams & Co., 1973.
6. Duncan, Greg J. and James N. Morgan. "An Overview of Family Economic Mobility." In Greg J. Duncan, Ed., *Years of Plenty, Years of Poverty*. Ann Arbor, Mich.: University of Michigan, Institute for Social Research, 1984, p. 13.

7. Duncan, Greg J., Richard D. Coe, and Martha S. Hill. "The Dynamics of Poverty." In Greg J. Duncan (6), pp. 41, 49.
8. Edelman, Marian Wright. *Portrait of Inequality: Black and White Children in America.* Washington, D.C.: Children's Defense Fund, 1980, p. 97.
9. Freund, William O. H. "Planning Perspectives: Figuring Your Personal Budget." *Investor News,* 3 (January 1981), p. 2.
10. Fuchs, Victor. "Redefining Poverty." *Public Interest,* 8 (Summer 1967), pp. 88–95.
11. Gottschalk, Peter and Sheldon Danziger. "Macroeconomic Conditions, Income Transfers, and the Trend in Poverty." Mimeographed. Madison: University of Wisconsin, Institute for Research on Poverty, September 1983, p. 13.
12. Hagan, William T. *American Indians,* rev. ed. Chicago: University of Chicago Press, 1979.
13. Harrington, Michael. *The Other America: Poverty in the United States.* New York: Macmillan Publishing Co., Inc., 1963.
14. King, Seth S. "Doctors Say Federal Food Plans Have Slashed Gross Mulnutrition." *New York Times,* May 1, 1979.
15. Kotz, Nick. *Let Them Eat Promises: The Politics of Hunger in America.* Garden City: Doubleday & Co., Inc., 1971, pp. 7–8.
16. Lampman, Robert J. *Ends and Means of Reducing Income Poverty.* New York: Academic Press, Inc., 1971, pp. 51–57.
17. Marmor, Theodore R. Ed. *Poverty Policy.* New York: Aldine Atherton, Inc., 1971, p. 6.
18. Ornati, Oscar. *Poverty Amid Affluence.* New York: Twentieth Century Fund, 1966, pp. 3–26.
19. Orshansky, Mollie. "Children of the Poor." *Social Security Bulletin,* 26 (July 1963), pp. 3–13.
20. ―――. "Counting the Poor: Another Look at the Poverty Profile." *Social Security Bulletin,* 28 (January 1965), pp. 3–29.
21. Pear, Robert. "U.S. Weighing Change in Poverty Program." *New York Times,* November 23, 1984.
22. Plotnick, Robert D. and Felicity Skidmore. *Progress Against Poverty: A Review of the 1964–1974 Decade.* New York: Academic Press, Inc., 1975, pp. 82, 85.
23. Poverty Studies Task Force. *The Measure of Poverty.* A Report to Congress as Mandated by the Education Amendments of 1974. Washington, D.C.: U.S. Department of Health, Education, and Welfare, 1976, pp. 5–11.
24. Rainwater, Lee. *What Money Buys: Inequality and the Social Meaning of Money.* New York: Basic Books, Inc., Publishers, 1974, pp. 147–158.
25. Rein, Martin and Lee Rainwater. "Patterns of Welfare Use." *Social Service Review,* 52 (December 1978), pp. 511–534.
26. Rivlin, Alice M. Ed. *Economic Choices 1984.* Washington, D.C.: Brookings Institution, 1984, pp. 160–161.
27. Rogler, Lloyd H. *Migrant in the City.* New York: Basic Books, Inc., Publishers, 1972.
28. Sexton, Patricia Cayo. *Spanish Harlem: Anatomy of Poverty.* New York: Harper & Row, Publishers, 1965.
29. Stack, Carol B. *All Our Kin: Strategies for Survival in a Black Community.* New York: Harper & Row, Publishers, 1974, pp. 32–45.

30. Sundquist, James L. "Has America Lost Its Social Conscience — and How Will It Get It Back?" Paper delivered at the Conference on the National Social Conscience, Florence Heller School, Brandeis University, November 21, 1985.
31. Thomas, Piri. *Down These Mean Streets.* New York: Alfred A. Knopf, Inc., 1967.
32. U.S. Bureau of the Census. *Current Population Reports, Population Characteristics 1979,* Series P–20, no. 354, p. 12.
33. ————. Current Population Reports, *Special Studies 1790–1978,* Series P–23, no. 80, pp. 27, 43.
34. ————. Current Population Reports, *Special Studies 1983,* Series P–23, no. 143, pp. 2–4.
35. ————. Current Population Reports, *Consumer Income 1975,* Series P–60, no. 111, Table 2A.
36. ————. Current Population Reports, *Consumer Income 1983,* Series P–60, no. 146, Table 23.
37. ————. Current Population Reports, *Consumer Income 1983,* Series P–60, no. 147.
38. ————. Current Population Reports, *Consumer Income 1983,* Series P–60, no. 148, pp. 20, 30, 33.
39. ————. Current Population Reports, *Consumer Income 1984,* Series P–60, no. 152, pp. 5, 105, 111.
40. ————. *Statistical Abstract of the United States 1985.* Washington, D.C.: U.S. Government Printing Office, December 1984, pp. 33–34.
41. ————. "Estimates of Poverty Including the Value of Noncash Benefits: 1979 to 1982." *Technical Paper 51.* Washington, D.C.: U.S. Government Printing Office, 1984, p. 3.
42. Urban Associates, Inc. *A Study of Selected Socio-Economic Characteristics of Ethnic Minorities Based on the 1970 Census,* Vol. 3: American Indians. Washington, D.C.: U.S. Department of Health, Education, and Welfare, 1974.
43. Woodside, William S. "Hunger in America is Real." *Fortune,* **111** (June 24, 1985), pp. 127–128.

CHAPTER 7

Women and Children Last: Racism and Sexism

Introduction

In 1984, over half of the children growing up in fatherless families were poor, as contrasted with one seventh of those in two parent families. Children of black and Hispanic origin without fathers at home had the worst odds — over two thirds were poor. These findings heralded nothing new. Long before the first poverty count provided systematic evidence, it was clear that the fortunes of children largely depended on their race, ethnic origin, and whether they lived with both parents or only their mother.

Since 1970 the number of fatherless families more than doubled, whereas two parent households with children decreased by 2 per cent. Simultaneously, the number of children living in homes without fathers pushed up from 9 to over 12 million, while those in two parent homes declined by more than 12 million. The convergence of these trends with stubbornly high poverty rates for female-headed families has stimulated shelves of research but no consensus about solutions. One reason for the stalemate is that every question runs headlong into value issues that Americans differ about passionately. The question of whether the future will bring more or fewer one parent families leads into conflicts regarding the role of racism, sexism, immorality, parental irresponsibility, and even government policies in stimulating their growth. Questions about why so many are poor raise issues around work, welfare, and child support. Questions about why potentially helpful community services are in such short supply lead to disagreements about whether one parent families are a normal structure, simply seriously underserviced, or are instead a pathological reflection of social disorganization.

While political debates wax and wane, social scientists persist in efforts to sort fact from fiction. In this chapter we review their conclusions about why households headed by women have increased, why so many are poor, what their problems reflect about American values and institutional lag, and major suggestions about how destructive trends might be reversed.

116

Why Have Households Headed by Women Increased?

In 1940 women headed one in every seven American households. By 1981 they were responsible for more than one in every four. Many factors shaped this trend. Among the most important were the "splitting-off" phenomenon, postponement of marriage, increased marital disruption, the rising number of illegitimate births among teenagers, and interacting with all of these forces, the persistently high unemployment rates among young people, especially blacks.

The "Splitting-Off" Phenomenon

In large part the trends reflect the rising pattern of living alone or with friends rather than relatives (4). Beginning in the 1940s, widows and widowers of all ages began breaking with the doubling-up pattern of the depressed 1930s. Instead of joining relatives when spouses died, they opted for privacy and independence.* This does not mean that all such decisions were voluntary. There was often a push out of relatives' homes as well as a pull toward independence. But at least social security, private pensions, life insurance, and eventually SSI, as well as better health and special housing for the aged, made separate living arrangements feasible for many. Because they live longer, more women than men were caught up in this trend.

The process of splitting off, and thereby dividing rather than pooling resources, also increased the number of poor people. What was often sufficient for a collective household provided a bare minimum once members went their separate ways. By the end of the 1970s, about three out of every ten persons of sixty years and older lived alone or with nonrelatives. About three quarters of the group were women, and almost three out of every ten were poor.

After World War II, young singles began moving out of parental homes earlier, as their European peers had done in such droves between the two world wars. They migrated from farms and small towns to large cities and made their own design for living. For many the lure of better jobs was of less moment than the wish to be free of parental controls. The drive was toward personal autonomy and independence, and in due course peer relationships often replaced family ties (59).†

---

*Haraven (31) reports that back in the nineteenth century widows often took in roomers and boarders rather than doubling up with relatives. The pattern apparently tends to be cyclical, coinciding closely with economic conditions.

†In 1972 for daughters and 1974 for sons, this trend began to reverse. By 1984 over half of the sons between twenty and twenty-four years of age lived with their parents, as did just over two fifths of the daughters in this age group. The Bureau of the Census ascribes this change to the postponement of marriage and the increase in children returning home after divorce or marital separation (69). It seems likely that the severe recessions in the 1970s and early 1980s should also be included.

This splitting-off phenomenon also played a role in the growth of households of women and children. Both blacks and whites helped to shape the trend, but for many reasons black children are more likely than white to grow up without fathers at home. As the 1980s began, of families with minor children, about half of the black families and only one seventh of the white families were headed by women. Some people blame AFDC, not necessarily because it helps mothers and children, but because it excludes most intact families, thereby discouraging family formation and encouraging family breakdown (3). While logic and a good bit of evidence support these charges, it is difficult to know what share of responsibility for the rise in female-headed households can be laid at AFDC's door, for the fact is that many social forces operating today have exactly the same effect on the family system of the poor.

The Postponement of Marriage

Since the procreation of children operates independently of marriage, the number of female-headed families with children depends to some extent on when women marry. A society that blazons sex from TV screens, billboards, and magazine racks asks for trouble if marriage is unduly delayed. In 1960 three out of every ten women between the ages of twenty and twenty-four were single; by 1984, the proportion had doubled. Since 1970 the median age at the time of their first marriage rose for men from 23.2 years to 25.5 and for women from 20.8 years to 23.3. By the end of this period, too, around 2 million unmarried couples lived together, almost four times more than in 1970. As a group, they tend to be younger than married couples, and three out of every ten had children in the home.

Whether young people have rejected or simply postponed marriage is not clear, but one relationship is confirmed. At every educational and age level, the likelihood that men have ever married is directly related to their income (63). Since the late 1960s the job market has been particularly rough on young people. With an economy incapable of generating enough jobs for unskilled, inexperienced people in good times, even before the baby boom came of age, the flood of youth into the labor market during years of recession compounded an already difficult problem. Even when the economy rallied and jobs opened up, unemployment rates for youth, especially if they were black, remained high. In such situations most people are sensible—they postpone taking on long-term commitments. Because blacks are more likely to be poor, this means that at every age level a larger share of black than of white men has avoided marriage.

Another development occurred during the past fifteen years that reduced the likelihood of early marriage. Increasingly, high school graduates went on to college. The unanswered question is whether most will marry shortly after leaving college or continue to pursue their independent ways.

Skewed sex ratios also played a role in the postponement of marriage. In a monogamous society, for marriage to be a realistic option for everyone who wishes to marry, a fairly good numerical fit is necessary between the sexes. Glick (65) explains that because of the post–World War II baby boom, which lasted from 1945 to 1961, peaking in 1957, women were about 5 to 10 per cent more numerous than men at those ages when most first marriages occur.* So more young women than usual remained single. By now the gap is narrowing, and this reason for delaying marriage should begin to fade.

But sex ratios are skewed for other reasons that warrant less optimism. From conception, male mortality rates are significantly higher than female rates, and only very recently has the gap begun to narrow. Back in 1940 the difference between the sexes in life expectancy at birth was only 4.3 years. In 1978 it was 7.7 years; by 1983 it had declined slightly to 7.1 years. In these forty-three years, heightened ability to control infection significantly reduced maternal mortality, and more women as a consequence lived out a "normal" life span. But our highly competitive, urban, industrialized life continues to take its toll of men, and at all ages the gap in life expectancy between the sexes is greater for blacks than whites.

In his study of national mortality patterns, Preston (54) concluded that the gap between the sexes affects " . . . the chances of marriage, the expected length of widowhood, and a host of other social and demographic variables." Of all causes of death, he found that eliminating violent deaths would have the greatest impact on sex ratios. In 1977 suicide, homicide, and accidents — mainly involving motor vehicles — accounted for two thirds of the 93,000 deaths between the ages of fifteen and thirty-five. By 1982, after several years of experience with a national 55 miles per hour speed limit, motor vehicle accidents were a less prominent cause of death. But still many young — often drunken — drivers and their friends were involved in such accidents. Men are about three times more likely than women to commit suicide or to die in accidents, and almost four times more often are victims of homicide. And while suicide rates for young white men surpass those of their black counterparts, the latter are rising rapidly.

In the process many widows are left behind. In a national survey of marital patterns made in 1975, about one third of the 7 million women whose first marriages ended with their husbands' deaths were found to be under forty years of age at the time (64). Four fifths were left with children under eighteen years of age. The threat of widowhood was particularly grave for black women. Between ages thirty-five and fifty-four, they were almost three times more likely to be widowed than white women. Other studies show that more time elapses before black widows and divorcees

---

*If marriages and remarriages are both taken into account, men tend to marry women about four years younger.

remarry, and fewer ever do so (8, 60). For some this is a matter of choice, but there is little doubt that it also reflects the shortage of eligible men who can afford to marry women with children.

Marital Disruption

While three out of every four adults queried yearly since 1973 claim that they enjoy a "very great deal" or a "great deal" of satisfaction with family life (66), the U.S. has the highest divorce rate among industrialized nations. Currently, for every two marriages each year, one couple is divorced.* The number of children involved rose from 463,000 in 1960 to over 1 million by the early 1970s and has stayed at or above that level ever since. In recent years it has been estimated that by their sixteenth birthday, one half of all children will have spent part of their childhood in a single parent home. By 1984, just over one fifth of them — 14.0 million — lived with only one parent. One study shows that most have little or no contact with the separated parent, even when he or she lives nearby (24). With divorce and separation rates so much higher for blacks than for whites, it should come as no surprise that far more black than white children are growing up in one parent homes — 53 per cent as compared with 17 per cent.

The easing of divorce laws explains part of the sharp upturn. Beginning with California's adoption of no-fault divorce in 1970, 49 states enacted somewhat similar laws. Designed to reduce bitterness and strain, the new statutes make it unnecessary for marital partners to sue each other. Instead, in effect, they sue the marriage for having failed them (58, 74). California now expedites the process by granting divorces to several hundred couples simultaneously. One such scene shown on television rather resembled a picnic moved indoors because of rain — except for occasional bewildered, forlorn faces in an otherwise lighthearted throng. By the mid-1980s serious questions were being raised about the support arrangements in no-fault divorces. As Lenore Weitzman (73), who was recently honored by the Congressional Caucus on Women's Issues in Washington, D.C. for her remarkable ten-year study of the consequences of the California law, commented, "I think if more people knew about the current results of the system of divorce, they would invest more in their marriages" (25).

A few years back the great worry was how long divorce rates would continue to rise. Rheinstein (55) expected them to level off soon. He

---

*This does not mean that the traditional family system is disappearing. The preponderance of couples are still in their first marriage (64). But children are particularly vulnerable for several reasons. Divorced people tend to be younger and are more likely than couples in their first marriage to have children in the home. Also, the number of children rises with the number of remarriages, and in turn remarriages are now more prone to divorce than first marriages.

pointed out that for many years separation was the poor man's divorce. Then free or low-cost divorce became available to the poor, and couples queued up to have their long-fractured unions dissolved.* Once the courts disposed of the backlog, he predicted, divorce rates would decline. Goode (29) also called attention to the positive relationship between easing the sanctions against divorce and rising divorce rates. This relationship, too, could easily be stronger during the first years of no-fault divorce laws. Whether due to these or other factors, between 1980 and 1984, the divorce rate dropped 8 per cent below the record high in 1979. Only time will tell if this is a temporary lull or the beginning of a long-term reversal.

The Interaction of Unemployment, Racism, and Marital Instability. Until black unemployment rates decline significantly, divorce and separation rates among black families may well continue to rise. Social science research leaves little doubt of the adverse effects of joblessness on family life. By 1981, after two years of deepening recession, for blacks the divorce ratio† — the number of divorced persons for every 1,000 husbands and wives in intact marriages — had soared to 233 as compared with 100 for whites. If divorced and separated persons are added together, the black ratio jumped to almost four times the white ratio. What accounts for the marked difference? Several years back Ross and Sawhill (56) made an exhaustive search for the answer. Of all variables studied, the unemployment experience of husbands turned out to be the best predictor of marital disruption. When unemployment history was held constant, the difference between black and white divorce and separation rates almost disappeared.

While national efforts to check inflation by inducing recessions hurt everyone thrown out of work, blacks consistently have more frequent and longer bouts of joblessness than whites and more likelihood of being poor. Since 1954 unemployment has increasingly plagued black teenagers and now follows them into early adulthood. This is not simply a prolonged effect of recession, but part of a long-term deterioration that continued even during periods of economic upturn. In fact, for young whites, unemployment rates were fairly stable during the 1970s, whereas they rose considerably for young blacks. With worsening conditions in the 1980s, by July 1982, 49.7 per cent of black teenagers in the labor force looked for work in vain.

---

*In some negative income tax experiments during the 1970s, many couples soon filed for divorce. The conclusion was reached that national income guarantees would have an adverse effect on the family system. While divorce rates might well rise if payments were high enough to give marital partners a real option between staying in a bad, even dangerous, marriage or living independently, it should also be kept in mind that experience has repeatedly confirmed that whenever new, greatly needed services are offered, they are inundated for a spell, and then applications gradually level off.

† Unlike the divorce rate, the divorce ratio is affected by the incidence of first marriage and remarriage of previously divorced persons, as well as by the incidence of divorce. The two indexes are currently moving in opposite directions.

Then there is the interaction between school dropout rates and unemployment to consider. Half of all students between ages sixteen and twenty-four are in the labor force. For some, staying in school depends on whether they find jobs. But in the fall of 1979, 49 per cent of black elementary and high school students were unemployed as compared with only 14 per cent of their white counterparts. Among high school graduates under twenty-four years of age, 8 per cent of whites were jobless as compared with 23 per cent of blacks. Despite discouragement with the job market that had led to lower labor force participation among black than white college students, the former were still more likely to be unemployed. In commenting on this situation, Young (76) refers to " . . . the limited employment opportunities in the inner city where blacks are concentrated, and the isolation of many colleges in rural areas where the chances of employment are slim." Inevitably, too, she adds, " . . . high unemployment rates among black students . . . eventually discourage job seeking."

The story is the same for many blacks all through their working lives. Typically, their unemployment rate is double the white rate. Are these different patterns due to race discrimination? Many attempts have been made to place the blame elsewhere. Bowers (6) looked particularly at the gap between black and white youth rates. In the process, he examined the effect of an overcrowded "baby boom" labor market, the "pricing out" of youth by rising minimum wages, swelling school attendance, and the influx of women into the labor market. But none of these explained more than a small fraction of the gap. Doeringer and Piore (16) have advanced a "dual labor market" theory to explain the employment gap at all ages. They believe that instead of a single line of job seekers at employment offices, in effect there are two lines, one consisting of experienced white males, the other made up of blacks, youths, and women. Only after the first line is exhausted do people in the second have a serious chance of being hired, they suggest. Thurow (61) speculates that the unwillingness of some whites to work alongside, let alone under, blacks may be as important a deterrent as employer bias.

Bouts of unemployment wreak all kinds of havoc in marriage, a fact now richly documented in the literature (26). Demographers point out that as family income rises toward the median for all families, marital stability also rises. But so many blacks earn so little or work so irregularly that their family median is less than 60 per cent of the white median. Noting the relationship between unemployment, school dropouts, and marital instability, Glick (27) points out that if married couples are both either high school or college graduates, the odds of divorce are relatively low. But for school dropouts at either level, the risk of marital disruption jumps drastically. The psychological damage of joblessness may well be even more undermining than physical deprivation. Despite handicaps in the labor market, the ability of black men to provide regular family support is judged by standards and expectations prevailing in the dominant white culture. Far more often than is true for blacks, white husbands and fathers can count on steady, decent incomes that rise fairly predictably each year, a fact that contributes significantly to marital stability (10). Hannerz refers to the problems this contrast creates for black men in the ghetto.

> The ghetto dwellers know mainstream culture but have little chance of living in line with it. . . . A man in the ghetto knows, for instance, that according to mainstream culture a man should be his family's breadwinner, he should provide it with a satisfactory status in the society's system of social ranking, and he should be a knowledgeable advisor to all its members. But as much as he thinks that all this sounds good, he cannot play the part very well when he is poorly paid or even unemployed, when his job is generally held in low esteem, and when he has little education. (30)

As Liebow (44) so sensitively illuminated in *Tally's Corner,* the harm done to self-esteem by prolonged and often unsuccessful efforts to find a permanent and pleasing niche in the labor market in a society where most white men succeed greatly reduces the odds that black men and women will enjoy enduring unions.

Illegitimacy and Teenage Pregnancy

In 1984, of every 100 fatherless families,* sixty-five mothers were divorced or separated, twenty-eight were unmarried, and seven were widows. Since 1970 the number of unmarried mothers with young children has grown eightfold. White women contributed disporportionately to this increase.

Illegitimate births rose from 399,000 to 737,893 between 1970 and 1983, when just over half were born to white women. Black illegitimacy rates, which have been falling for years, were still four times higher than the rising white rates. Recently, such births have increased for all age groups from fifteen to forty years, but by far the most worrisome group is the teenagers. Whether married or single, the adverse social and economic consequences of early parenthood in these days when the social maturation process extends for many young people through their early twenties are so grave and for many women so intractable that special attention is being focused on them from many directions.

Every recent year, over a million teenagers have become pregnant. Three out of four pregnancies are unplanned, unintended, or unwanted. Almost seven out of ten first babies are conceived out of wedlock. In all,

---

*This count refers to "family groups," an all-inclusive classification available in recent census reports to embrace female-headed *families, related subfamilies,* and *unrelated subfamilies,* in this instance, all with children under eighteen years of age at home.

about 500,000 babies are born, about half to unwed mothers. The balance of pregnancies are terminated by spontaneous or, far more often, induced abortions. Mothers fifteen years or younger have about 34,000 babies yearly.

The U.S. has the highest teenage pregnancy rates among developed nations. In this regard, we more nearly resemble developing nations. Our rates are twice as high as those in Canada, England, and France, almost three times higher than in Sweden, and seven times higher than in the Netherlands. Yet careful investigators confirm that teenagers in Europe are about as likely as ours to be sexually active (38). As a matter of fact, our teenage *abortion* rate is higher than teenage *pregnancy* rates in some European countries.

Considerable effort has been made to bring the problem to public attention, but until the sharp philosophical controversies over causes and solutions are resolved, no consistent, effective national policy is likely to emerge.

In the meantime a great deal has been learned about the magnitude of the problem, preventive measures used by teenagers, and the consequences of early childbearing. Considered an epidemic by some and the nation's primary population problem by others, it is the major cause of school dropouts, a significant factor in child abuse, and a key obstacle to reducing infant and maternal mortality (9, 22, 51). Whether or not teenagers marry, having a child at this early age typically results in prolonged poverty, high divorce rates, and a greater risk of poor health, given the depressed living standards of most teenage households (14, 15, 21, 50).

Family planning specialists estimate that half of all teenagers are sexually active, with a somewhat higher proportion of boys than girls. The rise in premarital sex after World War II is held by historian Edward Shorter (59) to be nothing short of a premarital sexual revolution. It was worldwide and remained essentially uncurbed until the birth control pill came on the market during the 1960s; then in some countries the phenomenon became less apparent. In 1982, over 90 per cent of sexually active married women with a risk of unwanted pregnancy used some type of contraceptive. But among sexually active teenage girls, only seven out of every ten used any preventive method, and about two fifths of the group who did use one of the less effective methods (1). Zelnik and Kantner (62) concluded after their 1979 survey that facts such as these reflected widespread misinformation about sex, mistrust of the pill, and lack of access to medically prescribed contraceptives.

In stressing the need for more and better sex education, the late Frederick Jaffe (35) recalled Gallup polls showing that over three quarters of Americans favored sex education in the schools, but due to objections of a small minority, 16 per cent, "current sex education," he concluded, "ranges from none to inadequate." By now there are some shining exceptions. In an increasing number of communities, comprehensive health services, including family planning services, are offered in clinics located in or nearby public high schools and junior high schools. The first such program, the St. Paul Maternal and Infant Health Care Project, was organized more than a decade ago. Now located in schools around the city, clinics offer prenatal and postpartum care, a full range of reproductive health services, sex education and counseling, and a wide variety of general health services — to reduce the likelihood of clinics or users being stigmatized. These clinics are now used by most of the student body. They have achieved remarkably high contraceptive continuation rates, and between 1976 and 1984, birthrates dropped from 59 to 26 per 1,000 female students in the participating schools. The program has become a model for others organized around the country; altogether they are regarded as one of the most promising breakthroughs in recent years (18).

Once pregnant, what do teenagers do about it? The answer depends in part on what they can afford and where they live. Relevant services are not evenly distributed, nor are all doctors willing to perform abortions. Now that federal funds cannot be used for this purpose, there are far fewer free or low-cost services available. Between 1977 and 1981, federal restrictions caused the number of abortions (for all age groups) funded by the federal government, to fall from 300,000 to 17,983. Some states promptly compensated by appropriating their own funds, with the result that 210,000 abortions were publicly financed in 1982, with state money paying 90 per cent of the cost (28). But in most states, family income either determined which women had to bear unwanted babies or caused medically undesirable delays in performing abortions, as poor women struggled to raise the necessary funds (34). As usual, the poorest among them — blacks — were the primary victims.

Still other problems arose when conservative congressmen undertook to decide the precise moment when life begins, in order to draft a constitutional amendment outlawing any interference with pregnancy from that moment. After divisive public hearings on the subject, both its potential for splitting the Republican Party and the difficulty in phrasing an amendment that would survive court challenge resulted in shifting the focus back to teenagers. In February 1982, the U.S. Department of Health and Human Services proposed a regulation requiring family planning clinics funded under Title X of the Public Health Act to notify parents before prescribing contraceptives for teenagers. Soon dubbed the "squeal rule" by the media and teenagers, it stimulated some 65,000 letters to Washington, one of the most voluminous public responses to a proposed rule ever recorded (41). Letters ran about four to one against the regulation, and although it was not yet in effect, teenage attendance at clinics fell off sharply. In the ensuing debate it emerged that many family planning clinics routinely tried to persuade teenagers to confide in their parents, that many did so voluntarily, and that clinics commonly scheduled activities for parents (23). The girls who wanted their privacy protected, however, insisted that unless visits were confidential, they would "go it alone," which to family planning specialists foreboded more illegitimate pregnancies. The controversy continues. Family planning funds through Title X of the Public Health Act are under siege year after year, federal funds have been denied to international voluntary agencies that use any of their own funds for abortions, and in 1984 alone at least 161 acts of violence were committed against abortion clinics, women trying to use them, and doctors working for them. The crimes range from physical damage and harassment to arson, kidnapping, and alleged murder.

In the meantime, teen abortion rates rise while those in European countries remain constant or fall. What are they doing differently? First, they confront the fact of teenage sexuality openly and dispassionately in public forums, the media, and policy-making bodies. Second, they have agreed to provide a full range of educational, counseling, and reproductive health care services, including abortion, to all ages including teenagers. Third, they make contraceptives easily accessible at low cost through their national health services, and sometimes in the schools, supermarkets, and vending machines. The most comprehensive program was initiated in Sweden in 1975 when a law making abortions freely available to women of all ages became effective. Feeling that an abortion was a most unfortunate introduction to sexuality for adolescents, the Swedes promptly embarked on a program that simultaneously linked improved education about sexuality and its place in human relationships with contraceptive services for teenagers through the schools and the health care system. The strategy succeeded remarkably. As of 1974, the U.S. and Sweden had virtually identical adolescent abortion rates; but by 1981, the Swedish rate had declined by 27 per cent while the U.S. rate had grown by 59 per cent (17, 38).

What other options do mothers have? Marriage between conception and birth has always been a favored solution for illegitimate pregnancy. But after the early 1960s, when over half of the women who conceived out of wedlock married before their babies were born, this solution steadily declined in popularity until by 1980, less than two fifths elected it — about half of the white women and less than one tenth of black women. Both the likelihood of marrying before the birth and the rapidity with which women marry after childbirth vary with age and race. About 18 per cent of the mothers under eighteen years of age marry within a year, and almost 40 per cent marry within three years. At all ages, the rate for white women is about double the rate for black women (53).

For some women, surrendering the baby for adoption is the answer. Traditionally white illegitimate babies were the major source of supply for the adoption market. Black mothers rarely had this option, since adoption agencies were dominated by whites who assumed that black babies were essentially unadoptable and that black families were strongly opposed to this solution. They were proved wrong on both counts when blacks began organizing their own services, but by then the accumulation of unwanted black babies far surpassed the limited resources (5). The National Urban League still hopes to change this situation, but sad and forlorn black youngsters continue to pile up in the nation's dismal child care institutions.

In the meantime, during the 1960s, to the consternation of hopeful adoptive parents, white women began refusing to relinquish their infants. In 1976 Jenkins (36) estimated that this was true for as many as 85 per cent. By 1978, 93 per cent of teenagers kept their infants. The result is a thriving new industry blazoned by such headlines as "Babies for Sale" (47). Rewards of $10,000 or higher have been reported for carrying babies to term and releasing them for adoption, but so far motherly instincts seem to be prevailing.

Many people persist in holding the mere existence of AFDC and/or "rising benefits during the 1970s" responsible for stimulating illegitimacy. But it so happens that caseload growth levelled off during the decade and benefits fell by a third in real value. Also, careful research has shown that states with higher benefits tend to have lower illegitimacy rates than states with lower benefits (19). On the other hand, it is true that AFDC does provide an option to women so that fewer are forced into marriage and more can leave abusive, indifferent, irresponsible husbands. But there is no evidence that this option encourages repeated illegitimacies — 86 per cent of unmarried mothers on AFDC in the late 1970s had only one child (49).

Charles Murray's widely read book, *Losing Ground* (52), raises a somewhat different issue. He claims that the U.S. Supreme Court decision in *King* v. *Smith* in 1968, by opening the doors in unprecedented fashion to unmarried mothers and their children, sent a new message to the poor to the effect that immorality and irresponsibility would be rewarded with AFDC eligibility, while equally poor families with stable marital unions would continue to be ineligible. In Murray's view, this decision immediately turned a "popular" program into a pariah, caused the AFDC caseload to skyrocket, and undermined the morals, ambition, and responsibility of the poor, doing them untold damage. AFDC, he writes, was intended for widowed families, but in effect they were now shoved aside by the burgeoning group of unmarried women with children. The best solution would be to repeal the program, in his view. It is unfortunate that Murray clouds an important issue with so many historical errors. From the beginning AFDC was designed for children who were needy because of the death, continued absence, or mental or physical incapacity of a parent. By 1939 every state with an AFDC program helped some illegitimate children (2). Furthermore, if Murray had any evidence of the "popularity" of AFDC — at any time — many historians would welcome it. The program has survived in an atmosphere of hostility, indifference, and despair only because no one could sell policy makers or the public on a better alternative. The point that Murray might better have made is that it was unfortunate that after *King* v. *Smith,* Congress did not immediately *require* all states to extend eligibility to needy intact families with an unemployed parent. The fact that about half of the states (those with higher than average illegitimacy rates on the whole) failed to pick up this option when it became available in 1961 is the reason for the contrary messages to the poor that Murray complains about. But he is strangely silent on the effects of unemployment on programs for the poor or on their family structure. Nor does anything in his book explain why the far more generous welfare states in Europe have lower teenage pregnancy and abortion rates than the U.S., or how our economy with over 8 million unemployed workers could absorb some 3.2 million more poorly educated, unskilled AFDC mothers. Whether the goal is to reduce illegitimacy or to reform or repeal welfare programs, these issues have to be addressed seriously and with reliable evidence.

So far as illegitimacy is concerned, probably Shirley Hartley (32), in her well reasoned, impressively documented study, sheds the most light on this problem in the U.S. She points out that — in a sexist culture where adolescents are little planned for or supervised, have an ill-defined role (unless they are students) and too few jobs, and receive little adequate sex education, only sporadic fertility control services, and insufficient information about feasible alternatives — high teenage illegitimacy rates are predictable. The scientists who studied European programs for teenagers essentially concur. They were perplexed when they tried to apply their findings to the U.S. Despite our claims to the contrary, everything pointed, they found, to a nation with a pronatalist policy — the very unequal distribution of income, a depth of poverty unknown in Europe, an inconsistent, gap-ridden service structure, and a strong tendency to exhort and moralize rather than to confront the problem openly and objectively in order to settle on effective solutions.

Why are Fatherless Families so Poor? _____

Mothers with young children but no husbands at home rely chiefly on three sources of income — earnings, public cash transfers, and intrafamilial transfers like child support payments, alimony, and contributions from various relatives. All three support systems are permeated with anachronistic, sexist attitudes that leave women and children with the short end of the stick.

The World of Work

As compared with two parent families, those headed by women have fewer wage earners, lower wages, and higher rates of unemployment (42). Lone mothers are less often free to work full time, but many who would like to do so can only find part-time jobs.

In the spring of 1984, 67 per cent of all women who headed families with children under eighteen years of age were in the labor force (33). The proportion varied somewhat with the marital status of mothers and the number and age of the children. Just under four fifths of divorced mothers, around three fifths of separated and widowed mothers, and slightly less than half of unmarried mothers (who were more likely to have preschool children) had jobs or were seeking them. For all groups, the rates rose, often substantially, if the children were all six years or older or if there was only one child. There is nothing remarkable in the fact that mothers left with children to care for find paid work when possible. What is different today from twenty years ago is the high labor force participation of mothers with very young children, under three years of age. The rates range from 40.1 per cent for unmarried mothers to 55.5 per cent for divorcees, who tend to be older, better educated, to have better-paying jobs, and can probably afford more reliable child day care than other mothers in this group (37).

Their impressive commitment to work is further reflected in the fact that the preponderance of these mothers — from 67 per cent of the widows to 88 per cent of the divorcees — work in full-time jobs, and even the few who work part-time, tend to do so year-round.

But they also have unusually high unemployment rates. While under 7 per cent of the mothers in intact marriages were jobless in early 1984, 10 per cent of widowed and divorced mothers, 18 per cent of separated mothers, and 29 per cent of unmarried mothers were searching in vain for jobs. The job market was particularly unwelcoming to young unmarried mothers with preschool children. One third were unemployed. To make matters worse, far fewer families headed by women, as compared with two parent families, have multiple wage earners — 22 per cent and 67 per cent respectively. This means that when mothers lose their jobs, there is far less likelihood of other wages coming into fatherless homes to cushion the blow. Combined with welfare cuts, these facts help to explain why the typical homeless family in recent years was a mother with several young children and why the poverty rates for fatherless families either remain stubbornly high or rise (12).

In 1981, full-time women workers earned only 65 per cent of what men earned (57). By 1983, median earnings for mothers maintaining households with children averaged $256 weekly as compared with $400 for male householders with children — 64 per cent. A survey of all full-time workers in 200 occupations in 1983 tells much the same story (48). One of the chief problems is the sexist clustering in the labor market. While affirmative action programs during the 1970s were effective in increasing the number of women in predominantly male professions, about half of all men and women still work in jobs that are dominated by one sex, and many of the twenty occupations that are expected to grow the most by 1990 are those that traditionally employ eight or nine women to every man. Even when women work in male-dominated settings, they are clustered in the lowest-paid jobs (75). While part of the wage gap is due to differences in education, experience, and length of time in the labor market, sex segregation is blamed for about 30 to 40 per cent of the gap. Evidence confirms, for instance, that where women work is not simply the outcome of free choice in an open market. Instead what most women encounter are constraints in premarket education and training that narrow their choice to a few alternatives, and in the job market they are effectively segregated into lower-paid work. Aggressive affirmative action policies in the 1970s, strongly supported by distinguished public leadership, helped to open many doors to women in such male-dominated occupations as banking, computer programming, law, bus driving, mining, and bartending. But the recent policy reversals, the withdrawal of federal leadership, and the decision of the Employment Opportunity Commission to pursue individual rather than class action suits have already had a negative impact on women's job opportunities. Fewer educational loans and scholarships, social stereotyping, veterans' preference, departmental rather than plantwide seniority rules, and the practice of paying men more than women for jobs requiring essentially equivalent education, training, skill, and experience are among the chief obstacles that are likely to remain in place while the current civil rights climate prevails.

But mothers will continue to be handicapped in the labor market until more child care and preschool services are provided, more flexible and realistic arrangements are made for mothers to stay home around childbirth or when children are sick, and hours of work are better adapted to family needs. Alternatives available in other industrialized nations deserve more attention in the U.S. In 1980 Kamerman (39) reported on services for working mothers in five European nations — France, East Germany, West Germany, Hungary, and Sweden. In all except West Germany, a higher proportion of mothers were employed than in the U.S.; the share rose to over four fifths. All five nations provide tax-free family allowances, ranging from $300 to $600 yearly per child. Most European nations also define childbirth and illness of children as social risks causing temporary unemployment, thereby qualifying mothers for wage replacement benefits and full protection of jobs, seniority, and pension entitlement. Paid maternity leaves range from three months in Denmark to nine months in Sweden and three years in Hungary. In Sweden both fathers and mothers are eligible, and benefits can be prorated to cover full- or part-time leaves. Typically, mothers remain out of work for about six months, beginning several weeks before the baby is expected. Cash benefits usually equal most or all of "covered" wages, the share of wages subject to social security taxes.

As for substitute child care services, in Europe most children between three and six years of age attend all day preschool programs associated with the educational system. This is true whether mothers work or not, since the experience is widely regarded as beneficial for children. For most families with working mothers, child care is available during normal work hours for children from two-and-a-half or three years of age, although fairly extensive programs also serve toddlers.

Conversely, in the U.S. only about half of the three- and four-year-olds in middle- and upper-income families, and three tenths of those in low-income families are currently in some type of day care. (The mothers of about half of the children in better-off families are not employed.) Just over a third of the children under three years of age with working mothers were in family day care or day-care centers in the late 1970s. While more recent information is spotty, from all directions evidence pours in regarding the "millions" of mothers who would work if only they could find affordable, reliable care for their children (12). Federal funds for this purpose were cut substantially in the early 1980s, with reductions in Title 20 of the Social Security Act, the Child Care Food Program, and the elimination of CETA, which funded wages of many day-care workers. These reductions were followed by budget cuts in thirty-two states and the lowering of standards in twenty-five. Only when anxiety mounted over reports of child abuse in day-care centers and investigations exposed the very low wages paid child care workers (87 per cent receive less than the minimum wage), was there sufficient concern to cause Congress to restore some funds. But apparently some half million children under six years of age and another 5 million school children under ten years are in need of full-time or after-school day care (11, 40, 72).

The average yearly cost of full-time care in day-care centers is now $3,000. The price mounts steeply in private, for-profit centers, which provide most of the care for preschoolers. The largest, KinderCare, charged $5,000 per child in 1984 (45). Considering the low wages of many women, unless this service is subsidized, paid work is often not a viable option. Nor has the child care tax credit helped many low-paid mothers since most earn too little to use it. Only if it is turned into a refundable credit will it help the families who need it most. To add to the problem, AFDC since 1981 has only permitted $160 monthly in child care expenses to be taken into consideration in determining eligibility. If they have to make private arrangements, this ceiling would not cover the cost of even one child for a full month. Child care experts believe the cutback in public subsidies has resulted in considerable "underground" child care, which means lost tax revenues and unlicensed, unregulated arrangements for children.

Public Cash Transfers

Public cash transfers are far more important to women than to men. About eight out of every ten female-headed families receive some type of transfer, as compared with only four out of every ten of their male counterparts. While the transfers women receive are lower on the average, they constitute a higher share of income, about one third as compared with one tenth for male-headed families.

One reason that two parent families receive higher benefits is that over 95 per cent of their transfer income is derived from universal programs paying wage-related benefits. This is true for only 70 per cent of women, and with lower wages, whether benefits are universal or selective makes less difference for women so far as relative amounts are concerned. In other words, the disadvantages experienced by women in the labor market follow them through life. But the social insurances present other problems for women. Women are less likely to qualify for unemployment benefits since they have shorter work histories and more part-time and irregular work. Domestic work was not covered in most states until Congress amended the Unemployment Insurance Act in 1977. Even now only 15 per cent of service workers are covered. In many states women have been disqualified for leaving work without "good cause" when they moved with their husbands, who were transferred or found better jobs elsewhere, or when their children had prolonged illnesses. In recent years the sex gap in the share of unemployed workers who qualify for benefits has widened (20).

The social security system is also riddled with pitfalls for women who head households. The problems have less to do with sex perhaps than with the quaint assumptions built into the program: that (a) all families have two parents, one a homebound mother and the other a steadily employed father (70); and that (b) families with young children need less per capita to live on than aged couples. Family benefit ceilings are one culprit. As of 1980 no family could receive more than 150 to 188 per cent of the former worker's benefit, known in social security jargon as the primary insurance amount (PIA). The formula for calculating family benefits provides least help to large families and those with low-wage earning fathers. A 1971 study, the most recent available, showed the outcome of this formula for beneficiary families of different sizes (2). Only 32 per cent of widows with one or two children were poor, as compared with 49 per cent with three children and 70 per cent with four or more. In 1982, widows with two children received benefits averaging $885.50 monthly, but for those with three or more children, benefits dropped on the average to $867.90. At the same time, aged *couples* averaged $702.50. According to social security logic, this makes sense but it scarcely adds up to a promising anti-poverty policy for children. To make matters more difficult for mothers with children between eighteen and twenty-two years of age, in 1981 the Administration convinced Congress to phase out benefits for students in this age group. Between the end of 1980 and September 1985, eighteen- to twenty-two-year-olds receiving social security benefits dropped from 733,758 to 67,000, for a loss monthly of about $127 million, and soon the small remnant will be phased out, too.

Another of many inequities in the system arises in connection with the duration of marriage. Divorced mothers must have been married to the wage earner for ten years in order to qualify for benefits on his earnings record. But widowed mothers qualify after nine months of marriage. Today, of course, divorcees not only greatly outnumber widows among relatively young women, but since close to two thirds of all women whose marriages end in divorce are under thirty years of age at the time, their chances of having been married for ten years are slim. Until the last few years, a twenty-year marriage was required. As for unmarried mothers, under no circumstances can they receive benefits on the earnings record of the child's father. Whether the child qualifies depends on whether the insured father acknowledged paternity, provided support, or was ordered by the court to do so.

Quite naturally, too, women are far less apt than men to qualify for veterans' benefits, and they often lose out in efforts to secure public employment because of veterans' preference laws. They may rank first so far as merit, education, and experience are concerned but be shunted aside by veterans at the bottom of civil service lists. This is one reason why women's organizations were disappointed with the decision of Congress, upheld by the Supreme Court, to exclude women from the draft.

So, what are fatherless families left with? AFDC — the least popular, least predictable, and least generous of cash transfers available everywhere in the nation, and the program most permeated with offensive social controls. Since states set standards of assistance, they vary widely, often bearing little relationship to family needs or the states' fiscal capacity. In October 1984, when monthly social security checks for widows with two young children averaged about $944, the monthly maximum AFDC payment for a family of three persons with no other income was $96 in Mississippi, $167 in wealthy Texas, $276 in Ohio, $417 in neighboring Michigan, and $555 in sunny California, the only state that requires periodic cost-of-living adjustments in AFDC.

Back in 1973, there were 84 AFDC children for every 100 poor children. Today the ratio has dropped to 53 per 100. The policy changes that brought about this decline in coverage in the main restored limitations that had been removed during the 1960s in order to make the program more realistic, supportive, adaptive, and stabilizing for families and communities.

Anyone familiar with public aid and poor families could predict that the policy reversals had a high probability of raising school dropout rates for AFDC children, making marriage to their mothers more hazardous, financially, for men,* significantly reducing cash benefits and services to poor fatherless families, and making many working poor families ineligible for AFDC. The redirection of policy in 1981 also meant that in the prolonged recession that quickly followed, AFDC was inevitably less useful to communities, as well as families. Where the caseload had once grown during recessions, thereby helping to maintain community purchasing power, it no longer had this adaptive potential.

One of the great tragedies in AFDC is its failure to encourage, let alone require, mothers to finish their education in order to qualify for decent and desirable jobs as their children grow older. Instead, most mothers have been required for some years to work or enroll in work training programs, which rarely lasted long enough to overcome serious educational and skill deficiencies. But some states or localities always made it possible for mothers to complete their formal education, including college if they won scholarships and maintained good grades. At Cleveland State University, for example, AFDC mothers were preparing to be social workers, health technicians, lawyers, and teachers, to list only a few of their career goals. Every year some graduated and found steady jobs, happily bidding goodbye to a life of dependency. But since 1981, with strong federal encouragement, numerous states have established programs requiring all but mothers with very young children to "work off" their welfare checks. For mothers in school, this promises to be a disaster. Raising children alone leaves barely enough time to study, without also having to "work off" welfare checks at subminimum wage rates.

Intrafamilial Transfers

On August 16, 1984, President Reagan signed P.L. 98–378, the Child Support Enforcement Amendment, denouncing as he did so the "devil-may-care" attitude of too many "parents." For scores of women the occasion marked a rare victory in the long struggle to enlist the power and prestige of the federal government in efforts to require the states to enforce their parental liability laws. For days after the event, newspapers reported that only a third of mothers with young children received child support and just two thirds of this group received the full amount due. This helped to explain the disproportionate poverty of fatherless families and why so many had to turn to welfare for help. The new law if enforced properly, it was explained, could accomplish a great deal for women. That it was passed

---

*Marriage is by far the most likely way for women to improve their income status. Details of these policy shifts are discussed in Chapter 9.

unanimously in both houses of Congress—during an election year—confirmed the importance of the women's vote to both Democrats and Republicans.

Why have so few fathers supported their children after leaving home? The principle of parental liability for child support has long been a fixture in the statutes of every state in the nation. Courts can determine how much fathers should pay and issue orders to that effect, or parents can negotiate voluntary written agreements. The obligation to pay is enforced for the most part through criminal provisions that make default a misdemeanor, or through the contempt power of the court. The penalty for nonpayment may be a fine, imprisonment, or both. Laws requiring bonds to be posted and permitting liens against property if fathers default or seem likely to do so are not uncommon (13). Also, for many years interstate compacts have been in place that permit courts to settle support problems when fathers move across state lines.

This suggests a fairly airtight system that guarantees continuing support to most children of divorced, separated, and unmarried fathers. But the evidence suggests otherwise. While some fathers conscientiously support their children after families break up, and a few do so very generously, the child support system has never coped well with the men who do not. Women have long complained that once fathers leave the home, they pay too little and very unpredictable child support, and that courts show little interest in the matter. These are some of the reasons why women often decide, if it is at all feasible, to manage alone (46). But why should it be necessary? Why are so many men permitted to evade this legal and moral responsibility? The first loophole is that in about two fifths of the cases, courts refuse to issue support orders. In recent surveys by the Bureau of the Census (67, 68), it was found that the share rose to three fifths for poor families. While no questions directly probed for the reasons, authors of the second report listed some that came to mind. Judges may see no point in issuing support orders if fathers are too poor to comply, which is clearly true for a sizeable group in these years of high unemployment. Mothers may have waived support in lieu of property settlements. Unmarried mothers may have failed to establish paternity before the relatively short statutes of limitation in this area took effect. The whereabouts of fathers may not have been known. Mothers, anticipating how uncooperative and angry fathers would be if support issues were raised, may have preferred to postpone confronting the problem. While all of these points have merit, many women would also fault the courts. Why, many have asked, when they return to court to petition judges to issue support orders, are they so often brushed aside? When former husbands remarry and father more children, why are second families almost always favored over first families? And why are women so often treated by court personnel as nagging, unreasonable harridans when they press for support?

One interesting fact, confirmed repeatedly over the years, is that fathers are far more likely to comply with voluntary support arrangements than with court orders. The findings of the 1981 survey are a case in point. While only one third of the women with court orders in effect received the full amount due and another third received nothing at all, two thirds of those with written voluntary agreements were paid in full and only one eighth received nothing. Furthermore, at all income levels voluntary agreements are associated with higher support payments. Nonetheless, most couples rely on courts to set payment levels and issue orders, and public welfare agencies have always favored this approach. It seems possible that if more marriage counseling were available at the right time, more couples might succeed in arriving at mutually acceptable arrangements without resorting to the courts.

The second loophole is that when men fail to pay or pay less than ordered, many courts simply fail to follow up on the matter. And, of course, fathers know this. In some jurisdictions, occasional roundups are staged, which result in a few men going to jail. But as some women have pointed out, even a few days in jail may cause jobs to be lost, thereby making a long-term solution even more remote. The proportion of defaulting fathers against whom legal action of any type is taken has varied widely among jurisdictions. Courts were believed over the years to be more zealous in the years immediately following a divorce when as "many" as 15 or 20 per cent of delinquent fathers might be "pursued," but even to secure this limited help women had to take the initiative. Until the recent surveys, people close to the scene conjectured that, once support was ordered or agreed upon, compliance rates were very low. But recent surveys suggest a better record than expected. About seven out of every ten men scheduled to pay child support in the survey years did so, and about half of the group paid in full. The surveys also suggest that the long-noted decline in support payments as the years pass following a divorce may reflect a decline in support orders, not a decline in paternal concern or compliance.

Both problems, the shortfall in support orders and the failure to follow up on defaulting fathers, have more serious consequences for black than white families. In 1981 support orders were awarded to only a third of black families in contrast to seven tenths of whites, and fewer than a quarter of black mothers received payments as compared with almost three fifths of the white mothers (68). But earlier research has shown that when income is held constant, black fathers turn out to be as conscientious as white fathers or more so, and poor men at least as conscientious as better-off ones (43). Unfortunately, in the real world income is not held constant; nor are marital disruption rates.

The level of support payments has been shockingly low for most families following divorce or separation, especially when courts set the amount. A ten-year study of the impact of California's no-fault divorce law by Lenore

Weitzman (73) found that divorced women and their children experienced a 73 per cent drop in their standard of living during the first year following the divorce, while their husbands enjoyed a 42 per cent rise in theirs. In an interview with Marilyn Gardner (25) of the *Christian Science Monitor,* Weitzman commented

> When I first found cases of middle-class women who had been cut off with no support or minimal support and were told to go out and get jobs after being homemakers and mothers for 25 years — and who lost their homes so the house could be sold (to divide the proceeds in half) — I thought they were exceptions. And when I saw the low child-support awards and the women who couldn't collect, I thought "Oh, they probably had a bad attorney or got the wrong judge." I had a hard time realizing how normal it was for women to be suffering, really suffering as the result of divorce. . . . The evidence is just inescapable that some lawyers and judges are saying "Well, if women want equality, we'll give them equality."

She recommends a redefinition of marital property to include not only tangible assets but career assets such as pensions, health insurance, education, and professional licenses. "Marriage is a partnership," she points out. "If two people really believe in the partnership, everything they acquire during the marital partnership should be joint property and should be equally divided."

The 1981 survey found that support payments averaged only $2,106 for the year. There is a rough relationship between the amount paid and family size, varying from $1,373 for one child to $2,455 for four or more children. In the few years elapsing since the first survey of this type in 1978, support payments declined in real value by 16 per cent.

Virtually all efforts to improve the situation were stimulated by the desire to conserve public funds by forcing more absent fathers of AFDC families to take over their support. After milder steps proved ineffective, Congress decided in the mid-1970s to require states to establish agencies to enforce support obligations in behalf of welfare families. Simultaneously, the states were given financial incentives (at the expense of families) to do so. The law also opened social security and income tax records to help the new Offices of Child Support, to be organized across the nation, in locating absent fathers, and permitted garnishment of federal wages and stipends to pay delinquent support orders. The most important departure from the past was that for a small fee non-AFDC mothers could also use the service. The mothers above the poverty line whose support payments are in arrears or never arrive are five times more numerous than those below the poverty line. As a result of this new initiative, $1.3 billion was collected in 1979 alone from delinquent fathers — 55 per cent in behalf of 500,000 nonwelfare mothers who sought help, and 45 per cent from the absent fathers of 750,000 AFDC families. By 1984, $214 billion had been collected, and about 185,000 families had been able to leave the welfare rolls (71).

During its first year in office, the Reagan Administration convinced Congress to strengthen collection procedures in regard to AFDC absent parents. The new law gave the IRS authority to intercept income tax refunds due parents who were over $150 and three months in arrears, and permitted states to deduct child support owed to AFDC families from unemployment insurance payments. Also, by requiring that the income of all step-parents be taken into account in determining eligibility for AFDC, rather than the income of only those liable by state law, the number of adults who could be charged with nonsupport was significantly increased. But the new law was of less help to nonwelfare families, since it required that they pay the full cost of collection, not simply a nominal fee as they had in the past. For some low-income mothers, this could be a great hardship.

States soon began strengthening their laws by such measures as directing the courts to issue support orders with automatic withholding provisions or by reinstituting the authority to take liens on the homes of absent parents of AFDC children, a common approach some years ago. Some also withheld state income tax refunds.

But the impact of stronger laws was considerably muted by the deep and prolonged recession and the cut in federal funds for social welfare. Keeping up with support payments was impossible for thousands of fathers who were out of work, and enforcement staffs were cut at both the federal and state levels. During 1981, when six million parents requested the new child support agencies to enforce delinquent support orders, their ability to do so was sharply curtailed, and, even so, the courts were overwhelmed by the deluge. In tiny Connecticut alone, nonsupport cases were pouring in at the rate of 1,100 monthly. A New Jersey official reviewed his records and concluded that "A divorced woman today has only a 10 per cent chance of being paid on time and in full." (7) The situation was so critical by the late summer of 1982 that hundreds of women over the nation were organizing protest groups.

The new law signed by the President in August 1984, and effective on October 1, 1985, was largely the result of the efforts of thousands of women to bring their plight to public attention. Census reports on the poverty population and the scope of nonsupport deserve a hefty share of credit, too.

The new law requires that

- States must notify employers that if parents are up to one month in arrears in court-ordered child support payments, arrangements must be made to withhold support payments from wages, and the sums collected must be forwarded to the appropriate state agency.
- All child support orders issued or modified after October 1, 1985 must permit withholding of wages whenever parents become delinquent.
- If employers or states fail to comply, they will be held responsible for the sums involved.

- States must change their laws, if necessary, to extend the statute of limitations for establishing paternity and for suing unmarried parents for support to eighteen years.
- States may require absent fathers to give security, post bond, or give some other guarantee to insure prompt payment of overdue child support where there has been a pattern of delinquency.
- Henceforth, child support obligations are to take priority over commercial debts and other legal claims pending against an employee's wages.
- The same location and collection services must be guaranteed to non-welfare and welfare families. If the former are not already registered with the local child support enforcement agency, they may do so by telephone. If they prefer they may pursue a private legal action to collect support.
- If families lose eligibility for AFDC because of an increase in child support, they must be continued on Medicaid for at least four months; the fifty dollars child support disregard available since 1984 is to be continued in determining eligibility and setting grant levels.

The effective date of the law was set for October 1, 1985, but loopholes could delay implementation for at least one year, and considering the resistance this law will generate, even further delays can be anticipated. Also, ample experience confirms that even laws with "teeth" in them may sound far more forceful on paper than they turn out to be in fact, and unless procedures are cautiously shaped to protect due process, untold numbers of court challenges are predictable. Nonetheless, the new law is one large step toward achieving equity between men and women.

References

1. Bachrach, Christine A. "Contraceptive Practice Among American Women." *Family Planning Perspectives,* **16** (November/December 1984), pp. 253–259.
2. Ball, Robert. *Social Security: Today and Tomorrow.* New York: Columbia University Press, 1978, p. 140.
3. Bell, Winifred. *Aid to Dependent Children.* New York: Columbia University Press, 1965, pp. 174–198.
4. Beresford, John C. and Alice M. Rivlin. "Privacy, Poverty, and Old Age." *Demography,* **3** (May 1966), pp. 247–258.
5. Billingsley, Andrew and Jeanne M. Giovannoni. *Children of the Storm: Black Children and American Child Welfare.* New York: Harcourt Brace Jovanovich, Inc., 1972, pp. 129–209.
6. Bowers, Norman. "Young and Marginal: An Overview of Youth Unemployment." *Monthly Labor Review,* **102** (October 1979), pp. 4–16.
7. Brooks, Andrée. "Child Support: A Growing Problem of Nonpayment." *New York Times,* June 14, 1982.
8. Bumpass, Larry and Ronald Rindfuss. "Children's Experience of Marital

Disruption." Discussion Paper #512–78. Mimeographed. Madison: University of Wisconsin, Institute for Research on Poverty, 1978.

9. Card, J. J. and L. L. Wise. "Teenage Mothers and Teenage Fathers: The Impact of Early Childbearing on the Parents' Personal and Professional Lives." *Family Planning Perspectives,* **10** (July/August 1978), p. 199.

10. Cherlin, Andrew. "Work Life and Marital Dissolution." In George Levinger and Oliver C. Moles, Eds., *Divorce and Separation: Context, Causes, and Consequences.* New York: Basic Books, Inc., Publishers, 1979, p. 194.

11. Children's Defense Fund. *Black and White Children in America.* Washington, D.C.: Children's Defense Fund, 1985, p. 54.

12. ———. *A Children's Defense Budget: The Analysis of the President's FY 1986 Budget and Children.* Washington, D.C.: Children's Defense Fund, 1985.

13. Clark, Homer H., Jr. *Domestic Relations: Cases and Problems.* St. Paul, Minn.: West Publishing Co., 1974, pp. 369–394.

14. Coombs, L. D. and R. Freedman. "Premarital Pregnancy, Childspacing and Later Economic Achievement." *Population Studies,* **24** (November 1970), p. 389.

15. Cutright, Phillips. "Timing of the First Baby: Does It Matter?" *Journal of Marriage and the Family,* **35** (November 1973), pp. 585–597.

16. Doeringer, Peter B. and Michael J. Piore. *Internal Labor Markets and Manpower Analysis.* Lexington, Mass.: D. C. Heath Co., 1971.

17. "Doing Something About Teenage Pregnancy." Editorial. *Family Planning Perspectives,* **17** (March/April 1985), pp. 52–53.

18. Dryfoos, Joy G. "School-Based Health Clinics: A New Approach to Preventing Adolescent Pregnancy." *Family Planning Perspectives,* **17** (March/April 1985), pp. 70–82.

19. Ellwood, David T. and Mary Jo Bane. "The Impact of AFDC on Family Structure and Living Arrangements." Report to the Department of Health and Human Services. Mimeographed, 1985.

20. Fineshriber, Phyllis H. "Unemployment Insurance Inequities Among Women Deepen." *Monthly Labor Review,* **102** (April 1979), p. 44.

21. Freedman, Deborah S. and Arland Thornton. "The Long-Term Impact of Pregnancy at Marriage on the Family's Economic Circumstances." *Family Planning Perspectives,* **11** (January/February 1979), pp. 6–21.

22. Furstenberg, Frank F., Jr. "The Social Consequences of Teenage Pregnancy." *Family Planning Perspectives,* **8** (July/August 1976), p. 148.

23. ———, Roberta Herceg-Baron, Dorothy Mann, and Judy Shea. "Parental Involvement: Selling Family Planning Clinics Short." *Family Planning Perspectives,* **14** (May/June 1982), pp. 140–144.

24. ——— and C. W. Nord. "The Life Course of Children of Divorce: Marital Disruption and Parental Contact." Paper presented at the annual meeting of the Population Association of America, San Diego, April 29–May 1, 1982.

25. Gardner, Marilyn. "Sociologist Says No-Fault Divorce Burdens Women." *Christian Science Monitor,* October 21, 1985.

26. Glick, Paul C. and Karen Mills. "Black Families: Marriage Patterns and Living Arrangements." Paper presented at the W. E. B. DuBois Conference on American Blacks, Atlanta, October 3–5, 1974.

27. ——— and Arthur J. Norton. "Marrying, Divorcing, and Living Together in the U.S. Today." *Population Bulletin,* **32** (October 1977), pp. 9–11.

28. Gold, Rachel Benson. "Publicly Funded Abortions in FY 1980 and FY 1981." *Family Planning Perspectives,* **14** (July/August 1982), pp. 204–207.
29. Goode, William J. *World Revolution and Family Patterns.* New York: The Free Press, 1963, pp. 81–86.
30. Hannerz, Ulf. "The Notion of Ghetto Culture." In John F. Szwed, Ed., *Black America.* New York: Basic Books, Inc., Publishers, 1970, p. 102.
31. Haraven, Tamara K. "Family Time and Historical Time." *Daedalus,* **106** (Spring 1977), p. 65.
32. Hartley, Shirley Foster. *Illegitimacy.* Berkeley: University of California Press, 1975, pp. 251–258.
33. Hayghe, Howard. "Working Mothers Reach Record Number in 1984." *Monthly Labor Review,* **107** (December 1984), pp. 31–33.
34. Henshaw, Stanley K. and Lynn S. Wallisch. "The Medicaid Cutoff and Abortion Services for the Poor." *Family Planning Perspectives,* **16** (July/August 1984), pp. 170–180.
35. Jaffe, Frederick S. "Teenage Pregnancy: A Need for Education." In *Today's Girls: Tomorrow's Women.* A National Seminar. New York: Girls Clubs of America, 1979, pp. 24–25.
36. Jenkins, Gladys. "The Single Parent Family: An Overview." In *Proceedings of the Changing Family Conference.* Ames, Iowa: Iowa State University, Division of Continuing Education, 1976.
37. Johnson, Beverly L. and Elizabeth Waldman. "Most Women Who Maintain Families Receive Poor Labor Market Returns." *Monthly Labor Review,* **106** (December 1983), pp. 30–34.
38. Jones, Elise F. et al. "Teenage Pregnancy in Developed Countries: Determinants and Policy Implications." *Family Planning Perspectives,* **17** (March/April 1985), pp. 53–62.
39. Kamerman, Sheila B. "Child Care and Family Benefits: Policies of Six Industrialized Countries." *Monthly Labor Review,* **103** (November 1980), pp. 23–28.
40. ————. "Child Care Services: A National Picture." *Monthly Labor Review,* **106** (December 1983), pp. 35–39.
41. Kenney, Asta M., Jacqueline D. Forrest, and Aida Torres. "Storm Over Washington: The Parental Notification Proposal." *Family Planning Perspectives,* **14** (July/August 1982), pp. 185–197.
42. Klein, Deborah Pisetzner. "Trends in Employment and Unemployment in Families." *Monthly Labor Review,* **106** (December 1983), pp. 21–25.
43. Krause, Harry D. *Child Support in America: The Legal Perspective.* Charlottesville, Va.: The Michie Co., 1981, pp. 281–298.
44. Liebow, Elliot. *Tally's Corner: A Study of Negro Streetcorner Men.* Boston: Little, Brown & Co., 1966.
45. Magnet, Myron. "What Mass-Produced Child Care is Producing." *Fortune,* **110** (November 28, 1983), pp. 157–174.
46. Mayleas, Davidyne. *Rewedded Bliss: Love, Alimony, Ex-Spouses, and Other Domestic Blessings.* New York: Basic Books, Inc., Publishers, 1977.
47. McTaggart, Lynn. *The Baby Brokers: The Marketing of White Babies in America.* New York: The Dial Press, 1980.
48. Mellor, Earl F. "Weekly Earnings in 1983: A Look At More than 200 Occupations." *Monthly Labor Review,* **108** (January 1985), pp. 54–59.
49. Millman, Sara and William D. Mosher. "Selected Demographic Characteris-

tics of Teenage Wives and Mothers." *Advanced Data from Vital & Health Statistics of the National Center for Health Statistics,* **61** (September 26, 1980), pp. 1–11.

50. Moore, Kristin A. and Richard F. Wertheimer. "Teenage Childbearing and Welfare: Preventive and Ameliorative Strategies." *Family Planning Perspectives,* **16** (November/December 1984), pp. 285–289.

51. Mott, Frank L. and William Marsiglio. "Early Childbearing and Completion of High School." *Family Planning Perspectives,* **17** (September/October 1985), pp. 234–237.

52. Murray, Charles. *Losing Ground: American Social Policy, 1950–1980.* New York: Basic Books, Inc., Publishers, 1984.

53. O'Connell, Martin and Carolyn C. Rogers. "Out-of-Wedlock Births, Premarital Pregnancies and Their Effect on Family Formation and Dissolution." *Family Planning Perspectives,* **16** (July/August 1984), pp. 157–162.

54. Preston, Samuel H. *Mortality Patterns in National Populations.* New York: Academic Press, 1976, pp. 172–178.

55. Rheinstein, Max. *Marriage Stability, Divorce, and the Law.* Chicago: University of Chicago Press, 1972, pp. 261–276.

56. Ross, Heather L. and Isabel V. Sawhill. *Time of Transition: The Growth of Families Headed by Women.* Washington, D.C.: The Urban Institute, 1975, pp. 39–60.

57. Rytina, Nancy F. "Earnings of Men and Women: A Look at Specific Occupations." *Monthly Labor Review,* **105** (April 1982), pp. 25–31.

58. Sell, Kenneth D. "The Divorce Law, Reform and Increasing Divorce Rates." In J. Gipson Wells, Ed., *Current Issues in Marriage and the Family,* 2d ed. New York: Macmillan Publishing Co., Inc., 1979, pp. 290–308.

59. Shorter, Edward. *The Making of the Modern Family.* New York: Basic Books, Inc., Publishers, 1977, pp. 108–120, 269–282.

60. Sutton, Gordon F. "Measuring the Effects of Race Differentials in Mortality Upon Surviving Family Members." Madison: University of Wisconsin, Institute for Research on Poverty, Reprint 268, 1977.

61. Thurow, Lester C. *Generating Inequality: Mechanisms of Distribution in the U.S. Economy.* New York: Basic Books, Inc., Publishers, 1975.

62. United Press International Release: Baltimore. "Half of Teen Girls Have Sex, Says Study." *Cleveland Press,* October 17, 1980.

63. U.S. Bureau of the Census. *Current Population Reports, Population Characteristics 1975,* Series P–20, no. 287, Table 9.

64. ———. *Current Population Reports, Population Characteristics 1975,* Series P–20, no. 312, Tables A and O.

65. ———. *Current Population Reports, Special Studies,* Series P–23, no. 78, 1979, pp. 1–6.

66. ———. *Current Population Reports, Special Studies,* Series P–23, no. 104, 1980, p. 1.

67. ———. *Current Population Reports, Special Studies 1978,* Series P–23, no. 112, Table A.

68. ———. *Current Population Reports, Special Studies 1981,* Series P–23, no. 140, p. 2.

69. ———. *Current Population Reports, Special Studies 1983/1984,* Series P–23, no. 145, p. 18.

70. U.S. Department of Health, Education, and Welfare. *Social Security and the Changing Roles of Men and Women.* Washington, D.C.: U.S. Government Printing Office, 1979.

71. U.S. Department of Health and Human Services. *Child Support Enforcement.* 9th Annual Report to Congress for the Period Ending September 30, 1984. Washington, D.C.: Office of Child Support Enforcement, December 1984.

72. Watson, Russell et al. "What Price Day Care?" *Newsweek,* **104** (September 10, 1984), pp. 14–22.

73. Weitzman, Lenore. *The Divorce Revolution — The Unexpected Social and Economic Consequences for Women and Children.* New York: Macmillan Publishing Co., Inc., 1985.

74. Wheeler, Michael. *No-Fault Divorce.* Boston: Beacon Press, 1974.

75. Young, Anne McDougall. "Median Earnings in 1977 Reported for Year-Round, Full-Time Workers." *Monthly Labor Review,* **102** (June 1979), pp. 35–40.

76. ————. "School and Work Among Youth During the 1970s." *Monthly Labor Review,* **103** (September 1980), pp. 44–47.

CHAPTER **8**

Ideologies of Poverty and Inequality

Why is it that so many Americans not only easily accept poverty amidst plenty but regard extremes of wealth as normal and inevitable? And why do other Americans flatly disagree on both counts? Where and when did such attitudes and beliefs originate? Are they modern inventions or do they have an intellectual history?

By and large our attitudes about poverty have been in the public domain ever since theories were developed to rationalize extremes of power and privilege at the beginning of the Industrial Revolution. Toward the end of the eighteenth century questions about poverty became a major preoccupation. Was it inevitable? What caused it? What, if anything, should the state do to relieve the misery of the poor? Efforts to answer such questions generated many theories, some of which profoundly influenced government policy on both sides of the Atlantic. A few still survive as the core of conflicting belief systems today. In this chapter several theories that had an enduring effect on our attitudes toward poverty and the poor are examined: Malthusian population theory, Owenism, Social Darwinism and its twentieth-century progeny, the eugenics movement and its recent genetics counterpart.

Malthusian Population Theory

After Thomas Robert Malthus (1766–1834) advanced his theory of population, economics soon became known as the dismal science. Malthus was the son of a comfortably situated liberal English landowner, a friend of egalitarian philosophers like Rousseau, Condorcet, and William Godwin. After attending Cambridge, where he earned a divinity degree and the M.A., young Malthus settled in a parish near his father's home, and became known as a kindly, sincere Christian minister. But his views of the poor were harsh and unyielding and gave rise to a grim and dour population theory that boded no good for the poor (43).

Like other well-educated men of his time, he was keenly aware of the social upheaval brought about by the French Revolution, the deepening disorders in England at the onset of the Industrial Revolution, and the sudden increase in population and poverty during the last quarter of the eighteenth century. After years of crop failures, famine was widespread. The liberal reform proposal, championed by his father and Prime Minister Pitt, would extend to the entire nation what became known as the Speenhamland plan. This was a system of wage subsidies designed to bring the income of agricultural workers up to a survival minimum (35). Young Malthus passionately opposed the idea. He was sure it would depress wages further, stimulate population growth, and bankrupt the nation. With his broadminded father's encouragement, he wrote and published his first *Essay on Population* in 1798. Eventually it was revised five times, but his core theory remained unaltered (13).

Malthus held that population increases geometrically while food supply increases only arithmetically. Therefore, population growth always outstrips food supply, and the masses are doomed to exist at the edge of starvation. Only two events could change the outcome: a decline in fertility or a rise in mortality. He did not expect the former — "toward the extinction of passion between the sexes, no progress whatever has hitherto been made." (34) Nonetheless, in Christian charity, the poor should be exhorted to practice moral restraint — which translated into continence and postponement of marriage and childbirth. Otherwise, "positive" checks — famine, war, pestilence, vice — would determine the outcome. Later he added emigration to the list. To make his message even more dismal, Malthus insisted that if technical breakthroughs increased the food supply, procreation would rise and temporary gains would soon be lost. In other words, the terrible misery of the poor was not the result of unjust social or economic institutions, as egalitarian philosophers and his father contended, but was the inevitable consequence of a natural law which makes food necessary to sustain life, and the power of the population to increase substantially greater than the power of the earth to provide subsistence (7, 37).

Malthus favored repealing the Poor Laws. Any child born one year thereafter, he suggested, should forever be disqualified from public aid, although a two-year grace period might be permitted illegitimate children. During his early years he also opposed wage increases, but later came to believe they might encourage "prudence," especially if workers were better educated (14). But his opposition to the Poor Laws was unchanging. It was true, he agreed, that if all relief were withheld, "nature" would take its course, and mass death would result. But survivors would have learned the virtues of moral restraint and self-reliance (35).

Malthus's essays attracted storms of criticism and extravagant praise. How could a religious man be so hard on the poor, some people queried? He responded that a beneficent Creator rewards with happiness in this life as well as the next those who resist temptation and overcome difficulties.

Where was proof for his theory, others asked? Malthus set off for Europe to gather such data as might be available. He never succeeded in proving the arithmetic – geometric progression, but he remained adamant that population must eventually outstrip food supply, and he continued working for the repeal of the Poor Laws. He triumphed in 1834, the year of his death, when the harshest Poor Law in England's history was enacted. Henceforth, no outdoor relief (aid to families in their own homes) was to be provided. Instead dependents, or paupers as they were then called, were to be sent to the poorhouse. There, sexes were to be segregated, everyone was to work, and living conditions were to be made as grim and harsh as possible in order to deter others from applying. This "reform" quickly crossed the Atlantic and remained the major American public anti-poverty policy until the Depression of the 1930s.*

Evidence For and Against Malthusian Theory.   No one quarrels with Malthus about the fact that in a finite space nothing, including man, can increase indefinitely, and many agree that there is cause for alarm about population trends. Even the current decline in fertility may have come too late to ease pressures on the food supply. One reason is that population has not merely grown exponentially, as Malthus predicted; it has exploded (29). During human history, the rate of growth increased from 2 per cent per millennium to 2 per cent per year (21). From the beginning of human society to 1825, population grew to 1 billion. By 1930 it numbered 2 billion. Thirty years later, in 1960, there were 3 billion people in the world. Fifteen years later, in 1975, the 4 billion mark was passed. Current estimates suggest a population of 5.8 billion by 2000, with about four fifths in developing nations and one fifth in developed nations.

But is the shortfall in food production a major problem, and is overpopulation by the poor the cause of whatever scarcity exists?

1. The Irish Potato Famine.   Perhaps the Irish potato famine gave the greatest credibility to Malthusian theory. At the beginning of the eighteenth century, 2 million people lived miserably on small grains in Ireland. A few years later the potato was introduced. At first people were better fed, but then the age of marriage dropped drastically, babies proliferated, and by thirty most women were grandmothers. By 1841 the Irish numbered 8 million, and people were no better nourished than before the potato arrived. Then disaster struck. In 1845 and the next four years, the potato crop failed. In those years, 2 million people starved to death. Another 2 million emigrated to slums in England and the U.S. (34), with about 200,000 dying of starvation or cholera at ports of embarkation or in transit

---

*"Outdoor" relief did not entirely disappear either in England or the U.S., probably because politicians could not survive nor well-off families sleep comfortably with such harsh public policies. Also, it has always been more expensive to maintain people in institutions than in their own dwellings.

on what became known as "coffin" or "fever" ships (7). Soon Ireland's population was halved, and has remained at or below that level down to the present.

2. Food Supply Trends. Malthus was so preoccupied with the fecundity of the poor that he overlooked the potential fecundity of science. Since his death, food production has well outstripped population growth. The transformation was brought about by two resources — mechanical energy from fossil fuels and scientific and technical knowledge. While easing pressures on the food supply, they have also broadened the list of resource systems that must be taken into account in any plausible theory. No longer are we solely concerned with the natural capacity of the earth to produce food. For instance, in 1974 Revelle (47) estimated that if all arable land were cultivated at maximum efficiency, the earth and technology could probably feed 40 to 50 billion people. But long before that number is reached, population density and pollution would create intolerable stress, and vital, nonrenewable resources used in our high technologies might well be exhausted. This is one reason why China's largely organic, muscle-powered agriculture is of such interest (10).

3. "Misery" as a Population Check. Malthus was wrong on another score. Except in the short run, "misery" is not the most powerful inhibitor of population. When high infant mortality rates prevail, couples have more, not fewer, children. Fertility rates decline as per capita income rises, leading to better education, housing, health care, and rising expectations. These findings have led to a theory of *demographic transition,* which is the strongest competitor with Malthusian theory today. It holds that changing patterns of social behavior act to limit population before it is rudely cut back by famine or disease. The theory posits a three-stage demographic evolution. First, in undeveloped societies, population is stabilized by high birth and death rates. Then, as nations develop, modern sanitation and disease prevention swell the population. But as the middle class grows, people experiment with family limitation to improve their income status. Soon they become models for others, and birth rates decline. This leads to the third stage. Through social planning, birth and death rates approximate consciously selected levels reflecting popular preferences regarding family size. Once again, the theory holds, population growth achieves a degree of stability (7).

4. Is Consumption by the Poor the Problem? Malthus entirely overlooked an issue that troubles population specialists today — the strong, direct relationship between consumption and income. It is not poor but rich families, and not poor but rich nations that make the greatest per capita claim on resources. It is also the rich whose consumption and production patterns reflect the greatest waste (36). Hundreds of examples come to mind. People over the poverty line have five times more impact on resources than those below. "At the cutting edge," Keyfitz (29) writes, "the increase in affluence has much more effect than the increase in population." Each year, Lekachman (30) reports, "Americans use up 40 per cent of the world's output of raw materials, an appalling testimonial to the cult of the car and the national appetite for packaged merchandise." In 1975 the energy consumed per capita in the U.S. was almost six times the world average and double the consumption rates in France, West Germany, Denmark, Norway, or the United Kingdom (61). With 5.3 per cent of the world's population, in 1976 we consumed 30 per cent of the energy, 20 per cent of the steel, 21 per cent of nitrogenous fertilizers, 39 per cent of the newsprint, and 16 per cent of the sugar (64). The average American consumed 314 eggs per year, as compared with eight for the average person in India (2).

Agricultural researchers despair over the inefficiency of our highly mechanized fossil-fuel farming (22). While China's entire grain harvest goes to feed her 800 million people, more than half of ours is fed to cattle, hogs, chicken, sheep, and other livestock. Except for hogs, all could prosper on food unfit for human consumption and on land unfit for human crops. They yield only about one unit of food energy for humans for every four to seven units of caloric intake. But the meat, poultry, and dairy industries were developed to maximize profits, not to maximize the efficient use of valuable resources (12).*

In international forums called to discuss population, food, and energy problems during the 1970s, the U.S. was charged repeatedly with profligate waste and overuse of the world's precious resources. The fear among "world watchers" is not only that some resources will become exhausted but that as they dwindle and costs rise, international tensions and inequality can only increase.

The Impact of Malthusian Ideology on Social Welfare. Old ideas, however unfounded, die hard. Not only did Malthus influence public welfare for 100 years, but remnants of his biases about the poor are still found in the public psyche and public policy. Two myths have particularly strong staying power.

1. Myth: The Poor Beget Children to Secure Public Welfare. This myth starts with an assumption that poor women have many more children than better-off, more responsible ones. But in 1981, the difference amounted to only half a child. The average number of children in American families with children was 1.9 as compared with 2.4 for all poor families (60). AFDC

---

*Barry Commoner (9), writing about the effect of affluence and population growth on environmental pollution, claims that together they account for only one quarter of the increase in pollution since World War II. By far the more important cause comes from technological changes in industry — the heavy dependence on nitrogen fertilizers and pesticides in agriculture, the use of phosphates in laundry, great quantities of lead and nitrogen oxide from automobiles, and the proliferation of containers, from aerosol cans and beer bottles to nondegradable plastics.

families now average about 2.1 children (11). It is true that families with large numbers of children are somewhat more apt to be poor than others, but the recent trend toward smaller families cuts across income lines. So does the presence of large numbers of children. In 1979, for example, among families with five or more children, 10 per cent had incomes under $5,000 and 30 per cent had $25,000 or more (59).

Do poor women have more children in order to raise their welfare grants? No one has offered a scintilla of proof that poor women have welfare in mind as they conceive children. At best, it is assumed that programs like AFDC and social security reduce the need for cautious family planning. In point of fact, where a full range of family planning services was provided to AFDC mothers in the late 1960s, few had additional children while receiving public aid. This was a vivid change that showed up when reading AFDC records over a span of ten or fifteen years. The subsequent rise in illegitimate births among teenagers has somewhat changed the picture, although there is still no evidence that the availability of AFDC has brought about the increase. Changed social mores coupled with scarce or ineffective preventive services are more likely responsible.

Perhaps the best evidence comes from other industrialized nations with family allowances. Whenever they are proposed for the U.S., fears over their presumed pronatalist impact are resurrected. But what bothers Europeans most is the continued decline in birthrates. France, with the most generous family allowances and a variety of reinforcing family benefits, hoped to stimulate birthrates after World War II. Initially she experienced about the same increase as the U.S. (51). But by mid-1978, the "peril of the declining birthrate" so obsessed some French leaders that a bill was introduced to give extra votes to citizens with large families (28, 54). All over Europe the trend is the same (61). Zero population growth will occur there well ahead of the U.S., experts predict. Canada has provided both children's and youth allowances, but her rates are strikingly similar to ours.

Nonetheless, the fear that the poor exploit public benefits by having more children lingers. About half of the state AFDC programs set family ceilings, as does social security. They help families of any size, but beyond the family ceiling no upward adjustment is made for additional children. In the mid-1970s members of the House Ways and Means Committee proposed amending AFDC law to prohibit any adjustment for family size. Some states have argued for Draconian measures to limit childbearing among poor families (3, 62). Often they are described as "options." For example, women who apply for AFDC may "choose" to practice birth control or lose custody of their children. Or they may "choose" between sterilization or going to jail. At one time Connecticut considered paying a bonus of $300 to welfare mothers who consented to sterilization.

2. *Myth: Americans Give Too Generously to Developing Nations.* Many Americans believe that we show reckless generosity in providing food to

poor nations. At least in part their objections reflect the Malthusian view that such help is futile and self-defeating. The hitch is that the basic premise is wrong. Americans are less generous than some other nations in this regard. For years it has been proposed that rich nations should strive toward a target transfer of 0.7 per cent of GNP to poor nations to help in technical development, with 84 per cent going in the form of grants or low interest loans with long repayment terms. Norway, Sweden, and the Netherlands exceeded this target by 1976 and proposed reaching 1 per cent by 1980. The U.S. is well behind. "It is ironic," Barbara Ward writes,

> that in 1976 the three strongest western economies — West Germany, with aid at 0.31 per cent of GNP, the U.S. with aid at 0.25 per cent, and Japan with aid at 0.20 per cent were proportionately among the smallest givers. On an even more niggardly scale, the centrally planned economies gave less than 0.1 per cent. At the other extreme, Kuwait's percentage was 3.23, that of Saudi Arabia 5.77, and OPEC donors as a group 2.14. (63)

While the U.S. is the largest exporter of food, the vast majority of our exports are sold, not given away. And sold at prices developing nations cannot afford (12). In 1976, we exported agricultural products valued at $23 billion, $1 billion of which was distributed through the Food for Peace program. Only $265 million was donated outright. More recently we agreed to double our food aid commitment to developing nations under one program, the Food Aid Convention, but this still involves only a very minor share of total agricultural exports. In reporting this increase, Tweeten wrote that millions of people in developed and developing nations

> . . . will die prematurely in the next decade from diseases associated with malnutrition. In developed countries the principal problem will continue to be overeating — a factor in cardiovascular and other diet-related diseases that account for over half of the deaths in the U.S. In developing countries the principal malnutrition problem will continue to be inadequate calorie and protein consumption — a factor in premature death from . . . diseases that ordinarily do not kill. . . . The fact that few people die of outright starvation does not diminish frustration over a world stubbornly separated into camps of overnutrition and undernutrition. Both "camps" could gain by sharing. (58)

The problem, in other words, is not so much scarcity of food as its maldistribution. By 1980 the United Nations World Food Council announced that twenty nations around the world were threatened with famine. Seventeen were African countries where 1 million were expected to die by the end of the year from starvation and many more millions to develop acute malnutrition with lifelong effects (46). By 1986 widespread famine had resulted in worldwide voluntary fund-raising drives to provide food for millions of starving and often homeless people.

Owenism: Change the Environment and Change the Man _____

Robert Owen (1771–1858), cotton spinner, businessman, socialist re-former, community builder, and trade unionist, was born in Newton on the banks of the Severn in Wales. He had to leave school at nine years of age to work as a draper's assistant. By nineteen he was managing a cotton mill, which became known for its superior fabric and excellent management.

New Lanark: Testing Ground for a Theory. When Owen was twenty-nine, he and several partners bought the New Lanark mills in Scotland, where 2,000 workers were employed. They included 500 children who had been brought at five or six years of age from poorhouses in Glasgow and Edinburgh. The former proprietor, whose daughter Owen soon married, had treated the youngsters well, but conditions in the mill town were deplorable. Housing was decrepit, education and sanitation were virtually unknown, and crime and vice abounded.

From an early age Owen believed that human beings were primarily shaped by their environment. If children were reared in healthful, whole-some conditions, he expected they would become exemplary, happy, and fulfilled citizens. It was poverty, neglect, exploitation, and disrespect that dehumanized people (44). New Lanark was to become the testing ground for this theory. Greeted at first with suspicion, Owen gradually won the workers' confidence, especially after he kept everyone on at full pay during a widespread economic crisis. Until business conditions improved, workers cleaned and repaired machinery and bettered conditions around the mills (41).

Owen opposed paid work for children under ten years of age and refused to accept more pauper children. He established nurseries, provided free elementary education for youngsters between five and ten years, and low-ered working hours for youth under eighteen. He prohibited the cruel punishments commonly meted out in factories at the time. He set up sickness and retirement funds, supported by regular contributions from owners and workers. Housing was greatly improved, with separate living quarters for each family, and communal kitchens and dining areas. Trou-bled by drunkenness and high prices for shoddy goods, Owen set up stores where goods were sold just above cost and liquor sales were supervised (19).

New Lanark became a Mecca for visitors from around the world and was written about with glowing praise (45). The schools were admired for the freedom permitted children in a curriculum interspersed with nature walks, singing, and dancing, unheard-of frivolities at the time, and also because punishment and denigration were outlawed in favor of encourage-ment and daily evaluation (20). While Owen was undoubtedly paternalis-tic, the new self-respect and amiability of both children and adults impressed even the skeptics (41). New Lanark also thrived as a business venture. Even though he and his partners, Jeremy Bentham and Quaker William Allen, took only 5 per cent in profits rather than the customary 20 per cent, Owen became a rich man (48).

Efforts at Social Reform. In 1813 Owen published *A New View of Society,* spelling out his beliefs about the malleability of man and his ideas about social reform. To reduce involuntary unemployment and improve the quality of life, he proposed decentralizing production in small cooperative communities with from 1,200 to 2,000 members. By locating factories in rural areas, agriculture and manufacturing could be coordinated on a human scale and provide year-round employment. Since only producers would share in the rewards, everyone would be inspired to produce (14, 44). Using his New Lanark experiment as a guide, he recommended that men be chiefly responsible for factory work while women performed domestic work, including meal preparation in communal kitchens. All youth and adults were to do agricultural work in order to feed and clothe the community. Children were to live in dormitories after their second year, where they would be closely supervised by carefully selected women. While youngsters were free to visit their parents, Owen was convinced that family control over children should give way to a larger community control. He favored stiff fines for drunkenness and suggested that illegitimacy should be handled by imposing fines on both parents, which would be deducted from their weekly pay and transferred to a poor fund (19).

Owen was naturally at loggerheads with Malthus, although he agreed that the "dole" destroyed men's spirit and will.* As an immediate step, Owen favored public works programs to employ able-bodied men on road and canal improvements. From 1813 to 1824 he tried to convince fellow industrialists and Parliament to adopt his reforms. His educational ideas seemed likely to prevail until opponents inquired into his nonconformist views on family and religion. When it became known that he favored community control of children from an early age and rejected the established church, Owen saw his supporters melt away like snow on a warm spring day. Later Marx was to dub Owenism "utopian socialism" because of Owen's naive assumption that industrialists and other wealthy people would ever voluntarily share with the masses.

*In taking exception to Malthus, Owen pointed out that "the population of the world is ever adapting itself to the quantity of food raised for its support; but [Malthus] has not told us how much more food an intelligent and industrious people will create from the same soil, than will be produced by one ignorant and ill-governed. It is, however, as one to infinity. . . . Food for Man may also be considered as a compound of the original elements, of the qualities, combination, and control of which, chemistry is daily adding to our knowledge; nor is it yet for man to say to what this knowledge may lead or where it may end." (44) Later, in 1817, he carried the argument further. "There can be no doubt that it is the artificial law of supply and demand arising from the principles of individual gain in opposition to the general well-being of society, which has hitherto compelled the population to press upon subsistence." (44)

Socialist Communities in America.   In 1824 Owen decided to go to the U.S. where he expected a warmer welcome for his model communities and other reforms. He was enthusiastically invited to address Congress* and soon purchased the town that he renamed New Harmony in Indiana from the Rappites. In time other Owenite communities were organized. None actually conformed to Owen's prescriptions about size, range of occupations, funding, communal facilities, or housing arrangements. Only their schools were modeled closely after New Lanark's. In the eagerness to get underway, for example, instead of waiting until 1,000 to 2,000 members materialized, communities sprang up with as few as twelve or twenty members. And while they were planned chiefly as agricultural towns, often members had no experience in farming or animal husbandry. Nor did they always market produce to earn money for other necessities.

Few Owenite communities lasted for long. Schisms developed over details of communal living, handling of property and capital, democratic control, and philosophic and moral issues. When this happened, groups often broke off and set up new communities. In the process, few failed in the sense of going bankrupt or losing their initial investment, although Owen lost a fortune at New Harmony, which he purchased outright and either sold or leased to members. When the community dissolved he was left with a great deal of land and no current buyers.

Owenite communities were part of a fairly widespread "communitarian" movement that proved to be an enormous boon to pioneers. These socialist experiments served a valuable transition role for families who lacked capital and equipment and yearned for companionship and the security of numbers on dangerous frontiers (19). Also, many provided a remarkable experience in direct democracy. Members often debated endlessly because they were deeply involved in the fate and quality of their community. Observers were impressed with the forthright quality of discussion and its amiability, both at such odds with widespread frontier violence.†

Owen returned to England in 1829** and turned his energies to orga-

---

*His two addresses on February 25 and March 7, 1825, are published in a collection assembled by Oakley C. Johnson (27).

†Some nineteenth-century "communes" lasted longer and made considerable money. Bethel in Missouri began in 1844 with $30,000 in assets and dissolved thirty-six years later with $3 million. Hopedale in Massachusetts began with less than $5,000 in 1841 and disbanded in 1856 with a quarter of a million in assets. The Wisconsin Phalanx increased its assets from a bare $1,000 to $33,000 between 1844 and 1850. When the Amana communities in Iowa dissolved after ninety years, they had more than $2 million to share among members (50). Altogether scholars have identified about 130 communities of this type in the U.S. before the Civil War and many others in Ireland, Wales, and England (4).

**His four sons chose to remain in New Harmony and become American citizens. One, Robert Dale Owen, while a member of the Indiana legislature, succeeded in getting passed a married woman's property act and laws authorizing the public school system and allowing more freedom to divorce. As a member of Congress, he drafted the bill founding the Smithsonian Institution. He was also a prominent Abolitionist and was credited with influencing President Lincoln to issue the Emancipation Proclamation (27). A second son, David Dale Owen, was the first U.S. Geologist and in that capacity organized the U.S. Geological Survey.

nizing workers' cooperatives and trade unions. By then he was convinced that until labor gained in strength, no improvement in working conditions could be expected. Despite his strong convictions and tireless work, by that time he was probably too much a pacifist and patriarch to inspire or lead a vigorous workingmen's movement (56). With the passage of the repressive 1834 Poor Law, which caused citizens to erupt in outrage and set the stage for class struggle, he returned to his lifelong interest in cooperatives and a benign classless society. The day for men like Marx and Engles had arrived in England.

The Impact of Owenism. In our time, many of Owen's reform proposals have become commonplace: better wages, improved working conditions, prohibitions on child labor, shorter working hours, trade unions, public works programs, nursery schools and day care (still too limited for Owen's taste), public education, retirement pensions, sick pay, better housing, more rights for women and children, more equal sharing between the sexes, a more secular society, a looser family structure, easier divorce, and innovative alternative styles of living.

His community experiments have served as valuable lessons for organizers of New Towns and communes. He has been resurrected as a latter-day hero in developing nations, in part because he was firmly convinced that people should have the same rights and be treated similarly without respect to race or ethnic origin. But his great vision, a classless society without poverty, ran headlong into the competing ideologies of capitalism, individualism, Malthusianism, and social Darwinism, which was soon to burst on the horizon.

Social Darwinism

Herbert Spencer (1820–1903), father of social Darwinism and favorite philosopher of America's Gilded Age, was born in England of a lower-middle-class Nonconformist family. Having rejected an opportunity for a university education, he began working at the age of seventeen as a railroad engineer. At twenty-six he joined the editorial staff of the *Economist,* an English weekly, and began a long writing career during which he produced many turgid volumes of social philosophy.

Survival of the Fittest and Laissez-faire Capitalism. Spencer was a lifelong, implacable foe of the state and a fanatical protector of individualism. Drawing upon Malthusian theory, he became preoccupied with the idea of evolution and progress. He reasoned that with constant competition for insufficient sustenance, the most favored variations in the species would inevitably survive while the least favored would be destroyed. From this notion he soon conceptualized society as an organism that constantly evolves toward perfection by "excreting its unhealthy, imbecile, slow, vacillating, faithless members to leave room for the deserving." (31) He thereby gave natural selection through competition the status of natural law. The weak lose the struggle and die out; and it is best that they should. "Survival of the fittest" became the watchword for individuals and social institutions that wished to strive toward perfection. By definition, the wealthiest and most powerful were the "fittest." (24)

Spencer's first book, *Social Statics,* published in 1852, six years before Darwin's *Origin of Species* appeared, was a vigorous attack on state involvement in social reform. State intervention was not merely futile since men could not expect to reverse a natural law; it was also harmful to the well-being and progress of society. Spencer viewed laissez-faire capitalism as nature's way of improving the race. Businessmen who bested their competitors by fair means or foul thereby proved themselves to be the fittest to enjoy power and wealth. The sole functions of the state should be to protect citizens from assault and to protect their right to enjoy the fruits of their success. Other forms of state intervention, he insisted, dangerously interfered with the working out of evolutionary laws and would disastrously weaken the species (5).

Spencer opposed public education, public housing, public health and sanitation, public aid, and even a public mail system. Initially, he repudiated the idea of private charity. But when even enthusiastic supporters accused him of being hard-hearted, he relented and agreed that voluntary charity could be condoned since it encouraged the Christian virtue of altruism and afforded the wealthy an opportunity to gain in grace (57).

Spencer's Capture of America.   From 1870 to approximately 1890, social Darwinism, as Spencerian pseudophilosophy was dubbed, was read and talked about "by the whole intelligent world." Spencer's books were translated into countless languages including Sanskrit and Mohawk (42). His beliefs fell on the most fertile soil in the U.S. They literally swept the nation. When he resigned as a professional journalist to devote the rest of his life to philosophy, his American admirers sent $7,000 and a gold watch as an expression of gratitude. Visiting the U.S. in 1882, he was lionized by the wealthy and powerful and hailed as a prophet. For a generation, social Darwinism was the orthodox doctrine in the social sciences. Preached from thousands of pulpits, taught in university classrooms, it was accepted as standard doctrine in newspaper offices (15).

In the post-Civil war years, when vast fortunes were accumulating and the conspicuous consumption of wealthy tycoons contrasted so shockingly with the squalor and misery in the slums, Spencerian theory provided the perfect justification for unbridled competition and selfishness. The "jungle character of the economic struggle was frankly admitted," Lerner (32) reports, "but it was justified on the ground that Nature decreed it."* Spencer's disciples were assured a future of unlimited progress and universal happiness, so long as they did nothing to interfere with natural law.

American Social Darwinists. An English detractor once commented about Spencer, "Happily for the majority of the world, his writing is unintelligible; otherwise his life would have been spent in doing harm." (42) Little did he realize what effective, enthusiastic interpreters Spencer would attract in the U.S. His views were popularized primarily by William Graham Sumner, Yale professor, Josephine Shaw Lowell, self-styled "scientific philanthropist," and Andrew Carnegie, self-made steel tycoon whose autobiographical and exhortative writings reached millions.

Sumner was profoundly pessimistic about the human condition. In his teaching and writing he brought together three great traditions of western capitalistic culture—the Protestant ethic, doctrines of classical economics, and Darwinian natural selection. To Sumner, "strong" and "weak" became synonymous with industry and indolence, frugality and extravagance, material success and pauperism. It all fit very neatly into his puritanical free-enterprise ideology. Both he and Lowell believed that the fate of the nation and the (white) race depended on following Spencerian prescriptions.

But during the last three decades of the nineteenth century, America was plagued with economic depressions, and the misery of the poor combined with the kindliness of many Americans precluded doing nothing in the face of such distress. Finally, in the 1880s, Lowell founded the Charity Organization Society (COS) to investigate poor families applying for help at various community organizations (1).† If applicants could pass rigorous tests devised to screen the "worthy" from the "unworthy," they were referred to cooperating agencies for direct assistance. Later the Society began giving direct relief with such stringent barriers, Bremner (5) reports, that if prospective contributors asked Lowell how much of their donation would go to the poor, she could answer proudly, "Not one cent."

Sumner and Lowell were especially alarmed for the middle class, which they perceived as a promising collection of initially poor, independent, proud citizens who had achieved modest amenities and security through

*People may well have been in great need of consolation since their fundamental beliefs about the nobility of man and his creation by God had been so thoroughly undermined by the theory of evolution. Muggeridge and Adams (42) speculate that Spencer had "hit upon a formula which made sense of everything" and furnished a "new scientific creed which . . . gratified a generation that was dumbfounded to find themselves no longer the children of God, but members of a brute creation."

†COSs eventually proliferated around the nation, and were the precursor of the Family Welfare Association of America and its many member agencies, which became the major site of voluntary social casework in the U.S.

diligent struggle. If public services were adopted, the "backbone" of America would have to cut back its hard-won gains to help bear the cost. Worse yet, the mere existence of public services might well sap the spirit of self-reliance (33). To exact this price to help people unfit for survival was absurd. In summarizing social Darwinism, Montagu (39) tersely noted that "human life was not only not sacred, it was perpetually on trial, and if found wanting, must perish."

As the infant reform movement that eventually led to the social security system got underway at the turn of the century, Spencer wrote one of his final maledictions.

> I have in so many places commented on the impolicy, and indeed the cruelty, of bequeathing to posterity an increasing population of criminals and incapables, that I need not here insist that the true beneficence will be so restrained as to avoid fostering the inferior at the expense of the superior. . . . Having, by unwise institutions, brought into existence large numbers who are unadapted to the requirements of social life, and are consequently sources of misery to themselves and others, we cannot repress and gradually diminish this body of relatively worthless people without inflicting much pain. Evil has been done and the penalty must be paid. Cure can only come through affliction. The artificial assuaging of distress . . . is a kind of social opium-eating. . . . The transition from State-beneficence to a healthy condition of self-help and private beneficence, must be like the transition from an opium-eating life to a normal life — painful but remedial. (53)

A year later, in 1905, when the U.S. Supreme Court in the case of *Lochner* v. *New York* struck down a law limiting work in bakeries to ten hours daily and sixty hours weekly, Justice Holmes (25) in a notable dissent wrote, "The Fourteenth Amendment does not enact Mr. Herbert Spencer's *Social Statics.*" By that time many intellectuals had repudiated social Darwinism, but in preceding decades lecture tours took the Spencerian gospel into towns and hamlets all over the nation. They attracted everyone within traveling distance and turned them into believers. When the doctrine was repudiated by scholars, word spread much more slowly, if at all.

Impact of Social Darwinism. Many people agree that social Darwinism is still very much alive in America. By the end of the nineteenth century, it had become the rationale for imperialistic policies against Spain. In Washington, D.C., Green (17) writes, it had become the excuse for racism. Under the influence of intellectuals, people came to believe that discrimination against blacks in public aid was essential to long-term progress and immediate community welfare. In the first decade of the century it generated the eugenics movement. William Ryan (49) sees remnants of it in the American tendency to "blame the victim." Still others see it currently reflected in the genetic theories of Jensen, Shockley, Herrn-stein, and their followers, as well as in the current Libertarian movement and Reaganomics.

The Eugenics Movement. Darwin's cousin, Francis Galton, laid the foundations of the eugenics movement with the publication in 1869 of *Hereditary Genius,* which soon caught the public fancy. It was followed in 1877 by *The Jukes,* written by American Richard Dugdale, who had served as visitor to New York's penal system. Having noticed that one family seemed to have contributed an undue number of members to the prison population, he traced it back for five generations. His findings convinced him that crime, pauperism, and disease were somehow transmitted from one generation to the next, and were closely associated with licentiousness, feeblemindedness, intemperance, and mental disorder. At the same time he took care to note that some members of the Jukes family who were removed to better environments turned out to be fine citizens (6). But the first message was the one that drew attention. In the following years, countless similar family studies were reported, each confirming that poverty and all of its correlates were inherited.* The result was social hysteria somewhat akin to the Salem witch trials two centuries earlier. The urgent need, professionals and laymen alike agreed, was to protect society from mental defectives, and the first place to screen them out was among immigrants. By 1912 the Eugenics Record Office, in conjunction with immigration and public health authorities, established an inspection station at Ellis Island, the usual port of entry.

Intelligence tests became routine. But it quickly became apparent to cautious observers that something was seriously amiss. About four fifths or more of incoming Jews, Hungarians, Italians, and Russians, and later half of the army recruits during World War I, were classified as feebleminded (38). Years before the problem was sorted out, though, virtually all poor, black citizens were similarly lumped among the mental defectives. The moment of glory for the eugenics movement came in 1924 with the passage of the Immigration Restriction Act, which set severe limitations on the admission of non-Europeans as well as southern and eastern Europeans. Not until it became painfully apparent how much the preoccupation with racial purity had contributed to the atrocities in Nazi Germany did the eugenics movement drop from sight.

---

*An equally famous book, *The Kallikak Family,* was written by Henry H. Goddard in 1912. He traced "good" and "bad" strains of this family back to a Revolutionary War soldier who had an affair with a feebleminded servant girl before his marriage to a young lady of impeccable Spencerian credentials. Goddard counted up for his astonished readers hundreds of worthless descendants of the servant girl and an equally impressive number of outstanding achievers among the wife's descendants. It was as much a morality lesson as an attempt at scientific investigation, but generations of college students were introduced to the study of heredity with accounts of the Jukes and the Kallikaks.

Current Genetic Theories of Black Inferiority. "The latest episode of this recurring drama," writes Stephen Jay Gould (16), began in 1969 when Arthur Jensen (26) published his article, "How Much Can We Boost IQ and Scholastic Achievement?" His first sentence announced, "Compensatory education has been tried, and it apparently has failed." Jensen, like many of his predecessors, based this conclusion on studies of identical twins, part of whom had been separated early in life and raised in different environments. He concluded that 80 per cent of intelligence, as measured by intelligence quotients (IQs), is inherited. On the average, IQs of blacks are fifteen points lower than whites'. So blacks are genetically inferior, and money spent on compensatory education is futile.

In 1974, like-minded William Shockley, Nobel laureate in physics who recently turned his attention to genetics, advocated hefty bonuses for eugenic sterilization. Worried about the proliferation of the "unfit poor," he proposed paying individuals so classified $1,000 for each point they fell below 100 IQ, if they agreed to be sterilized. People who paid income taxes would not qualify for the bonus, this being Shockley's formula for separating the poor from the nonpoor. The bonus would be placed in a trust fund which would dole out money to individuals over their lifespan. In promoting his idea, he claimed that "$30,000 put in a trust for a 70 IQ moron potentially capable of producing twenty children might return $250,000 to taxpayers in reduced costs of mental retardation care" (52). On the other side of the ledger, confident of the genetic superiority of Nobel laureates like himself, Shockley invited them to contribute to a sperm bank. The first baby resulting from this elite insemination program was born in April 1982. Shortly thereafter it was revealed that both the mother and her husband had served time in a federal prison for fraudulently securing loans and credit cards. They had also lost custody of the mother's children by a previous marriage following allegations of child abuse. Apparently confident that male genes would dominate and that the home environment was unimportant, the spokesman for the sperm bank conceded that the screening of mothers "was less than thorough," but he was not particularly troubled by the revelations (55).

In the meantime, Harvard psychologist Richard Herrnstein (23), a colleague of Jensen and Shockley, published his view of the relationship between IQs and meritocracy. He began with the premise that IQ tests measure intelligence, and that IQ is genetically determined. He then claimed that income and wealth are distributed among Americans in direct relationship to their IQs. Because of this, he maintains, America is fast becoming a "hereditary meritocracy" — a society stratified on the basis of inherited differences in IQ. The most capable, intelligent citizens, in his view, receive the greatest material rewards, as they should to maintain their incentives to take on the "burdensome task of leadership."

By now countless scientists have examined and refuted the work and logic of Jensen, Shockley, and Herrnstein. It is widely recognized that no one quite knows what the "intelligence" measured by intelligence tests is. But whatever it is, IQs are better correlated with success in school than with success in life. And the tests from which they are derived are consistently biased in favor of white middle-class children and adults. It is not hard to see why. Most tests of this sort were developed and standardized by using them with middle-class white children in northern school systems. Among other items, they include a great many that reflect information taught in those school and vocabulary typical of reasonably educated, white, middle-income families. If the tests tap innate abilities, no one knows exactly which ones, nor to what extent this might be true. Jensen's 80 per cent is considered wildly inflated. But even if IQs are inherited, this does not mean, as he seems to imply, that they are "fixed" or "immutable," beyond the reach of environmental modification. On the contrary, many inherited traits are regularly modified or neutralized, as with eyeglasses for poor sight or insulin for diabetes. In a collection of essays edited by Ashley Montagu (40), authors cite many studies showing that compensatory education and services have raised IQs significantly. For that matter physicians, too, have discovered treatments for mental-deficiency-related nutritional problems that restore people to normal functioning.

Noam Chomsky, noted linguist and philosopher, has challenged Herrnstein's claims that society must distribute the greatest rewards to the brightest people to assure their taking on "the burdensome task of leadership." This assumes that the satisfaction and respect enjoyed by people involved in interesting, socially useful, effective work have no intrinsic value. People work only for material gain in Herrnstein's world. If rewards are not high enough, bright people will opt to vegetate. Chomsky scoffs at this notion. "I doubt very much," he writes (8), "that Herrnstein would become a baker or lumberjack if he could earn more money that way." Thousands of college professors, writers, artists, and social workers undoubtedly agree — as they pay the plumber's bill.

Chomsky carries the argument further by challenging Herrnstein's notion that occupations are rewarded in direct relation to their value and benefit to society. Instead, he suggests, pay differentials reflect the relationship of workers to wealth and power. "Is it obvious," Chomsky asks, "that an accountant helping a corporation to cut its tax bill is doing work of greater social value than a musician, riveter, baker, truck driver, or lumberjack? Is a lawyer who earns a $100,000 fee to keep a dangerous drug on the market worth more than a farm worker or a nurse? Is a surgeon who performs operations for the rich doing work of greater social value than a practitioner in the slums who may work harder for much less extrinsic reward?" (8)

Chomsky concludes his criticisms of Herrnstein's logic by examining the alleged relationship between race and intelligence. Like many other scholars, he points out that except in a racist society, the mean IQ of individuals of any particular race has absolutely no significance. The differences within groups in the population are still far greater than the reported difference between black and white mean scores. Herrnstein's work, Chomsky concludes, appears to raise questions of great moment for our society only because it is useful to those who seek to justify the perpetuation of racial discrimination. He cites Marvin Harris's conclusion in *The Rise of Anthropological Theory* to put the whole subject in perspective:

> Racism also has its uses as justification for class and caste hierarchies; it was a splendid explanation of both national and class privilege. It helped to maintain slavery and serfdom; it smoothed the way for the rape of Africa and the slaughter of the American Indian; it steeled the nerves of the Manchester captains of industry as they lowered wages, lengthened the work day, and hired more women and children. (18)

References

1. Axinn, June and Herman Levin. *Social Welfare: A History of the American Response to Need.* New York: Harper & Row, Publishers, 1975, pp. 89–93.
2. Barnet, Richard J. and Ronald E. Müller. *Global Reach: The Power of Multinational Corporations.* New York: Simon and Schuster, Inc., 1974, p. 179.
3. Bell, Winifred. *Aid to Dependent Children.* New York: Columbia University Press, 1965, pp. 67–75.
4. Bestor, Arthur Eugene. *Backwoods Utopias.* Philadelphia: University of Pennsylvania Press, 1950.
5. Bremner, Robert H. *From the Depths: The Discovery of Poverty in the United States.* New York: New York University Press, 1956, pp. 19, 51–52.
6. Bruno, Frank J. *Trends in Social Work: 1874–1956.* New York: Columbia University Press, 1957, pp. 49–50.
7. Chamberlain, Neil W. *Beyond Malthus: Population and Power.* New York: Basic Books, Inc., Publishers, 1970, pp. 1–4, 5, 8–9.
8. Chomsky, Noam. "The Fallacy of Richard Herrnstein's IQ." *Social Policy,* **3** (May/June 1972), pp. 19–25.
9. Commoner, Barry. *The Closing Circle: Nature, Man, and Technology.* New York: Alfred A. Knopf, Inc., 1972.
10. Critchfield, Richard. "China: World's No. 1 Rice Producer is Fast Becoming World's No. 1 Grain Producer." *Christian Science Monitor,* September 16, 1980.
11. Duvall, Henrietta J., Karen W. Goudreau, and Robert E. Marsh. "Aid to Families with Dependent Children: Characteristics of Recipients in 1979." *Social Security Bulletin,* **45** (April 1982), pp. 3–9, 19.
12. Ehrlich, Paul R. and Anne H. Ehrlich. *The End of Affluence: A Blueprint for Your Future.* New York: Ballantine Books, Inc., 1974, pp. 187–193.

13. Flew, Anthony. Ed. *Malthus: An Essay on the Principle of Population.* Harmondsworth, Middlesex: Penguin Books Ltd., 1970, pp. 7–17.
14. Garraty, John A. *Unemployment in History: Economic Thought and Public Policy.* New York: Harper & Row, Publishers, 1978, pp. 68, 97.
15. Goldman, Eric F. *Rendezvous with Destiny.* New York: Random House, Inc., 1956, pp. 70–71.
16. Gould, Stephen Jay. "Racist Arguments and IQ." In Ashley Montagu, Ed., *Race & IQ.* New York: Oxford University Press, 1975, pp. 145–150.
17. Green, Constance McLaughlin. *Washington, Capital City: 1879–1950,* vol. 2. Princeton: Princeton University Press, 1963, pp. 69–70.
18. Harris, Marvin. *The Rise of Anthropological Theory.* New York: Thomas Y. Crowell Co., 1968, pp. 100–101.
19. Harrison, John F. C. *Quest for the New Moral World.* New York: Charles Scribner's Sons, 1969, pp. 151–157, 158, 176–177.
20. Harrison, John F. C. *Utopianism and Education: Robert Owen and the Owenites.* New York: Columbia University Teachers' College Press, 1969, Introduction.
21. Hauser, Philip M. "The Population of the World: Recent Trends and Prospects." In Ronald Freeman, Ed., *Population: The Vital Revolution.* Garden City: Doubleday & Co., Inc., 1964, pp. 15–29.
22. Henderson, Hazel. *Creating Alternative Futures: The End of Economics.* New York: Berkley Publishing Corp., 1978, pp. 83–105.
23. Herrnstein, R. J. *IQ and the Meritocracy.* Boston: Little, Brown & Co., 1973.
24. Hofstadter, Richard. *Social Darwinism in American Thought.* Boston: Beacon Press, 1955, pp. 31–50.
25. Holmes, Justice Oliver Wendell. *Lochner* v. *New York,* 198 U.S. 45.
26. Jensen, Arthur R. "How Much Can We Boost IQ and Scholastic Achievement?" *Harvard Educational Review,* **39** (Winter 1969), pp. 1–123.
27. Johnson, Oakley C. *Robert Owen in the United States.* New York: Humanities Press, 1970, pp. 1–4.
28. Kandell, Jonathan. "Former French Premier Seeks to Spur Lagging Birthrate." *New York Times,* June 6, 1978.
29. Keyfitz, Nathan. "World Resources and the World Middle Class." *Scientific American,* **235** (July 1976), pp. 28–35.
30. Lekachman, Robert. *Inflation: The Permanent Problem of Boom and Bust.* New York: Random House, Inc., 1973, p. 50.
31. Lens, Sidney. *Poverty: America's Enduring Paradox.* New York: Thomas Y. Crowell Co., 1969, p. 188.
32. Lerner, Max. *America as a Civilization,* vol. 2. New York: Simon & Schuster, Inc., 1957, p. 722.
33. Lubove, Roy. *The Struggle for Social Security.* Cambridge: Harvard University Press, 1968, pp. 116–117.
34. Malthus, Thomas Robert. *Population: The First Essay,* with a Foreward by Kenneth E. Boulding. Ann Arbor: University of Michigan Press, 1959, pp. 5, ix.
35. Marcus, Steven. "Their Brothers' Keepers: An Episode From English History." In Willard Gaylin, Ira Glasser, Steven Marcus, and David Rothman, *Doing Good: The Limits of Benevolence.* New York: Pantheon Books, Inc., 1978, pp. 46–49, 51.

36. Mayer, Jean. "Toward a Non-Malthusian Population Theory." *Columbia Forum,* **12** (Summer 1969), p. 5.

37. McCleary, G. F. *The Malthusian Population Theory.* London: Faber & Faber, Ltd., 1953, pp. 23–50.

38. Miringoff, Marque-Luisa. "The Impact of Population Policy Upon Social Welfare." *Social Service Review,* **54** (September 1980), p. 306.

39. Montagu, Ashley and Edward Darling. *The Prevalence of Nonsense.* New York: Harper & Row, Publishers, 1967, p. 8.

40. Montagu, Ashley. Ed. *Race & IQ.* New York: Oxford University Press, 1975.

41. Morton, A. L. *The Life and Ideas of Robert Owen.* New York: International Publishers, 1969, pp. 96, 102–103.

42. Muggeridge, Kitty and Ruth Adams. *Beatrice Webb: A Life, 1858–1943.* New York: Alfred A. Knopf, Inc., 1968, pp. 38, 39, 87.

43. Notestein, Frank W. "Introduction." In *Three Essays on Population: Thomas Malthus, Julian Huxley, and Frederick Osborn.* New York: New American Library of World Literature, A Mentor Book, 1960, pp. vii–x.

44. Owen, Robert. *A New View of Society and Other Writings.* Introduction by G. D. H. Cole. London: J. M. Dent & Sons, Ltd., 1963, pp. 22–38, 85, 175–180, 181.

45. Pollard, Sidney. "Introduction." In Sidney Pollard and John Salt, Eds., *Robert Owen: Prophet of the Poor.* Lewisburg: Bucknell University Press, 1971, pp. i–xi.

46. Profitt, Nicholas. "The Grim Famine of 1980." *Newsweek,* **96** (August 25, 1980), pp. 48–49.

47. Revelle, Roger. "Food and Population." In *The Human Population, A Scientific American Book.* San Francisco: W. H. Freeman and Co., Publishers, 1974, pp. 119–130.

48. Robertson, A. J. "Robert Owen, Cotton Spinner: New Lanark, 1800–1825." In Sidney Pollard and John Salt, Eds., (45), pp. 145–165.

49. Ryan, William. *Blaming the Victim,* rev. New York: Vintage Books, 1976.

50. Sale, Kirkpatrick. *Human Scale.* New York: Coward, McCann & Geoghegan, Inc., 1980, p. 401.

51. Schorr, Alvin L. "Income Maintenance and the Birth Rate." *Social Security Bulletin,* **28** (December 1965), pp. 22–30.

52. Shockley, William. "Sterilization: A Thinking Exercise." In Carl Jay Bajema, Ed., *Eugenics: Then and Now.* Stroudsburg, Pa.: Doidon, Hutchinson & Ross, 1976, p. 166.

53. Spencer, Herbert. *The Principles of Ethics,* vol. 1. New York: D. Appleton and Co., 1904.

54. Spengler, Joseph J. *France Faces Depopulation,* Postlude Edition. Durham: Duke University Press, 1978.

55. "The Sperm Bank Scandal." *Newsweek,* **100** (July 26, 1982), p. 24.

56. Tawney, R. H. *The Radical Tradition.* New York: Random House, Inc., 1964, pp. 38–39.

57. Trattner, Walter I. *From Poor Law to Welfare State: A History of Social Welfare in America,* 2d Ed., rev. New York: The Free Press, 1979, pp. 77–78.

58. Tweeten, Luther. "The Hard (and Sometimes Hopeful) Facts About This Hungry World." *Worldview,* **21** (December 1978), pp. 18–19.

59. U.S. Bureau of the Census. *Current Population Reports, Consumer Income 1979,* Series P-60, no. 129, Table 25.

60. ——— . ——— , *Consumer Income 1981* (Advance Report), Series P-60, no. 134, Table 18.

61. ——— . *Statistical Abstract of the United States 1979.* Washington, D.C.: U.S. Government Printing Office, 1979, pp. 884–889, 905.

62. U.S. Commission on Population and the American Future. *Population and the American Future.* New York: New American Library, 1972, pp. 159–160.

63. Ward, Barbara. *Progress for a Small Planet.* New York: W. W. Norton & Co., Inc., 1979, p. 250.

64. *World Statistics in Brief 1978.* New York: United Nations, 1978, pp. 214–217.

CHAPTER 9

Anti-poverty Strategies: Cash Transfers

Introduction

Proposals for reducing or ending poverty by funneling more money to the poor are not in short supply. During the 1960s when a government-guaranteed income floor under all households seemed within reach, the first question was whether to wipe the slate clean and create a monolithic income maintenance program or press for incremental improvements in the current pluralistic system. As the cost of the War in Vietnam mounted, the focus narrowed to families with young children, and debates shifted to the relative merits of family allowances and negative income taxes. The latter seemed likely to prevail when Nixon proposed his Family Assistance Program (FAP), a negative income tax with a built-in work incentive. But it failed to win either Congressional or popular support.

During the 1972 presidential campaign, Democratic candidate George McGovern flirted disastrously with a plan to distribute yearly subsidies of $1,000 to everyone, but after fellow Democrats challenged his cost estimates, the idea was tabled. When Jimmy Carter entered the scene, he submitted a more comprehensive, tidier version of Nixon's FAP, only to see it die with scarcely a nod from a disaffected Congress. That signaled the end of large-scale reform efforts in the 1970s.

In the meantime, Congress and the White House agreed to enlarge the food stamp program, created Supplemental Security Income (SSI) patterned after a negative income tax, sponsored impressive studies of anti-poverty programs and problems (56), made unemployment benefits taxable when adjusted gross income reached $20,000, and increased manpower and training efforts through the Comprehensive Training and Employment Act (CETA). More to lure low-income households to file tax returns and to offset rising social security taxes than to reduce poverty, a modest low-wage earner's refundable tax credit was added to the federal income tax.

The federal government also launched negative income tax experiments to test the impact of income guarantees on work effort. While the experiments often raised more questions than were answered, they provided little cause for alarm that a modest income floor would reduce the productivity of poor Americans significantly. But the interest in reform had largely evaporated by the time results were known (33, 35). Except for a few highly publicized reactions exaggerating negative findings and a spate of reports written for experts, the brief honeymoon with a negative income tax seemed to be over.

In the following pages a model for social policy analysis is first discussed and then relevant parts of it are used to analyze the strengths and weaknesses in our cash transfer system.

A Model for Social Policy Analysis _____

Systematic policy analysis requires a frame of reference, usually called a model or paradigm. If the goal is to evaluate a pluralistic cash transfer system as an anti-poverty strategy and to learn why it falls short of expectations, then the model should include both evaluative criteria for measuring performance and program characteristics most likely to influence performance.

Evaluative criteria inevitably reflect value judgments about the role of cash transfers in a wealthy, democratic society. In our view, they should reach all people in need and do so promptly, efficiently, and accurately. They should be fair and equitable. Benefits should be adequate, predictable, and adaptable, keeping pace with price or wage changes, so that people can plan realistically. Finally, cash transfers should be so designed as to encourage social cohesion among families and friends. Experience suggests that these standards are more apt to be achieved when citizens play an active role in policymaking and review.

Table 9–1 presents a model that takes these variables into consideration. Criteria for measuring performance appear in the left column. They include coverage of the population at risk, equity, adequacy, predictability, adaptability, social cohesion, efficiency, and accountability. Key program characteristics are listed in the right column. They include program auspices, administrative arrangements and degree of discretion, stated organizational goals, financing arrangements, benefit structures, eligibility rules, work incentives and disincentives, citizen participation, reporting, research, and feedback, planning mechanisms, and, finally, manifest and latent consequences. Not all criteria and program characteristics will be germane in every analysis, and others may be necessary in some. But these variables usually explain the variance in program outcomes.

The meaning or significance of several items may not be self-evident. "Stated organizational goals" is a case in point. It is listed to draw attention to the fact that the goals stated in public laws may be quite different

Table 9-1. Model for Program and Policy Analysis and Evaluation[a]

Criteria	Program Characteristics
Coverage of the population at risk	Auspices (public, private, voluntary nonprofit)
Equity	Administrative structure and discretion
Adequacy	Stated organizational goals
Predictability	Financing arrangements
Adaptability	Benefit structures
Encouragement of social cohesion	Eligibility rules and procedures
Efficiency: Accuracy	Work incentives and disincentives
Promptness	Arrangements for user/public participation
Simplicity	Reporting, research, and feedback
Accountability: Program	Planning mechanisms
Fiscal	Manifest and latent consequences

[a]Typically, this model would be used only after societal values, unique characteristics of the population, major historical influences, and attitudes toward government have been spelled out for given regions or nations. While the model is intended to be used to analyze cash transfers, with minor additions and modifications, it can be adapted to use in analyzing social services. For other models see Eveline M. Burns (7, 62), David Gil (16), and Robert Morris (29).

from those a given analyst has in mind, and it is well to be clear about this from the outset. AFDC is a good illustration. While commonly evaluated as an anti-poverty strategy, state programs are funded well below poverty levels and the parent legislation, Title IV of the Social Security Act, makes no reference to poverty-reduction goals. Instead it says, in effect, that the intent is to keep poor homes with children intact and to assure movement from welfare rolls to payrolls when this is possible without harming children. At best, ending poverty may be a by-product, but it is far from a consistent outcome. Many families are dropped from welfare without any material change in financial circumstances.

The item, "manifest and latent consequences," is derived from sociology and is best explained in Robert Merton's (28) seminal essay on the subject. A manifest consequence is a planned, openly acknowledged, anticipated consequence or outcome. In public cash transfers, manifest functions are spelled out in purpose clauses of public laws or other formal statements of legislative intent. Conversely, latent consequences are outcomes or impacts that were unplanned, unacknowledged, or unanticipated. Again using AFDC as an example, as was noted, one purpose of the program was to keep poor families together rather than forcing them to break up because of poverty. To the extent that programs serve this purpose, it would be a manifest consequence. But Bell's (3) study of AFDC eligibility rules showed that some were barely disguised devices for disproportionately rejecting black and illegitimate children. This was a latent consequence since nowhere in the parent legislation was there any mention of an intent to exclude needy children on moral or racial grounds. Identifying both types of consequences provides insights about why programs are shaped as they are. In the case of AFDC it became apparent that when the federal government entered the welfare scene in the 1930s, the law was meticulously negotiated to permit states maximum flexibility and discretion. They controlled financing levels, staffing patterns, administrative procedures, standards of need, appeals, and many eligibility rules. Quite naturally AFDC soon reflected state and local prejudices and wage structures. Not until the U.S. Supreme Court handed down a unanimous decision in *King* v. *Smith* (22) in 1968 was the rampant racism in AFDC effectively reduced. Within the next few years, as a direct result of the decision, between 500,000 and 1,000,000 children and parents, most of them black, became eligible for grants. But it was Merton's illuminating concepts and research paradigm that made the investigation leading to the court challenge so useful.

The Cash Transfer System

The cash transfer system is generally considered to include social security, unemployment insurance, workers' compensation, veterans' welfare, AFDC, SSI, state – local general assistance, and a group of nutrition programs, most notably food stamps, school lunches, and the Women, Infants, and Children Program (WIC).* But to secure a full grasp of publicly subsidized income protection schemes, the list should also include the job-related pensions and annuities that cover about half of the employed workers in the private sector and most government employees. Occasionally included, too, are several tax-deferred savings plans, like the Individual Retirement Accounts (IRAs) which became available fairly recently and are already being reconsidered by Congress.

Our cash transfer system has often been faulted for its incomplete coverage, unequal benefits to people in like economic circumstances, and for creating work disincentives. From the late 1970s to the early 1980s, the predictability of the largest program, social security, was called into question, but happily that issue is largely resolved. Far less attention is paid to the strengths and accomplishments of the system. Starting with this side of the ledger will serve to highlight why nations have come to rely on cash transfers so heavily.

Strengths and Accomplishments

The cash transfer system has helped U.S. capitalism through some very troubled times. Depending on one's perspective, this may or may not be a

---

*Medicare, Medicaid, public housing subsidies, and subsidized rental housing are sometimes included. They will be discussed in Chapter 10.

virtue, but in a conservative, business-oriented nation, it would be short-sighted to overlook it. Recurring recessions would have been far more disruptive for families, large and small business firms, and communities without the cushion of purchasing power provided by cash transfers. The recent recession, following so closely on sizeable cuts in most programs for the poor, provided a foretaste of what could happen in an industrialized nation without such programs. As it was, thousands of homeless families were wandering over the nation searching for jobs, child malnutrition rose alarmingly, the poverty count soared, and small business bankruptcies reached heights unknown since the 1930s.

Cash transfers are also stabilizing social forces. The fact that they provide financial assistance when earnings cease helps to keep families together and children in school. They help in maintaining law and order by muting urban and racial frustrations. When ghettos ignited in the 1960s, AFDC came to the rescue. The caseload tripled in that decade, only to level off after order was restored (36).

In addition to being a remarkably successful anti-poverty program for the aged, the social security system performs another societal function that is often overlooked. As the most popular program and the bedrock of our income strategy, it has become an instrument Congress can use to compensate for unresolved problems in the marketplace, for failures in economic policy, and for shortfalls in less popular cash transfers. One illustration is the decision made in 1956 for women, and 1961 for men, to permit retirement between the ages of sixty-two and sixty-five with actuarially reduced benefits. With continuing age discrimination in the job market, a serious shortage of jobs, no long-term unemployment insurance, and inadequate and incomplete health care coverage, offering the option of early retirement was a boon to the nation as well as to the individuals and families involved. By 1982, when nine out of ten newly retired beneficiaries opted for early retirement, just under half who retired at the earliest possible age listed poor health, compulsory retirement, loss of jobs, or bad business conditions as their reason (44).

From a family perspective, by 1983 over half of all families relied on cash transfers for part or all of their income (53), with social security, pensions, and annuities being by far the most important sources. About the same proportion of individuals living away from their families also depended to some extent on cash transfers. Whether young families today can appreciate what this means in terms of freeing the earnings of young and middle-aged couples for buying homes, paying for their children's education, enjoying pleasant holidays, purchasing clothes — rather than fully supporting their aged parents — is not at all certain, although all age groups seem grateful that the aged can more often today live active, independent lives which was rarely the case several generations ago. That social security and improved pensions and annuities have made these different living arrangements possible, and played a part in the improved health status of the aging, is seldom questioned; but for generations that have not experienced the very different circumstances that prevailed through most of the history of the human race, it is easy to object to the cost or assume that they will find the self-discipline and will earn sufficient to plan independently for their retirement. Socializing the basic cost does not obviate the need to save and plan; but by guaranteeing a basic floor of protection, it relieves a great deal of anxiety and contributes remarkably to a sense of community.

The much criticized means-tested programs also have beneficent consequences for all of us. Food stamps alone help some 18 million people and their communities cope with high unemployment and high food costs. With over a fifth of our children living below the poverty line, nutrition programs make the difference between strong and healthy bodies and minds or expensive, lifelong handicaps that result from malnutrition at the early developmental stages. In turn, AFDC has helped generations of poor children to go to school regularly — and its alumni include college presidents, lawyers, doctors, professors, social workers, and successful businessmen.

Before the Social Security Act and its welfare predecessors, few states showed any consistent regard for the income status of blacks or for any but some very cautiously selected fatherless families. By 1980 most blacks and many women had come to regard the federal government as a far better protector of equal rights and due process than state or local governments or private enterprise. It is too early to foretell what will happen to the bond between citizens and government if administrations in Washington persist in helping the rich at the expense of the poor, in undermining faith in the intentions of government by renewed efforts to discredit social welfare programs, or in trying to narrow the functions of the federal government to consist almost solely of national security. But however far they fall short of their ideal values in daily life, Americans have an enduring pride in their sense of fair play, the superiority of their form of government, and their compassion for the poor and vulnerable. It seems unlikely that these cornerstones in their cultural heritage can be uprooted within a few years.

Shortcomings of the Cash Transfer System

Gaps in Coverage. If the goal is to reduce or prevent poverty, a cash transfer system that grows haphazardly and for the most part distributes benefits only to certain categories of workers or households is bound to fall short of expectations.

1. Food Stamps — The Only Noncategorical Program. So long as they have cooking facilities or eat in approved congregate facilities, the only eligibility requirements for food stamps are that income must fall below defined levels and adult applicants must register for work except when they are over sixty years of age or responsible for a child under twelve years.* Given this broad coverage, and the fact that the market value of stamps received by each household rises inversely with income and directly with household size, the program has helped remarkably to equalize purchasing power between low-income male- and female-headed families, blacks and whites, and different regions of the country (27).

But it falls far short of covering all poor households. Initiated as a pilot project in the early sixties to help the very poor, by 1969 the program reached 2.9 million people. Then Nixon pressed for higher income standards as urban food costs rose, and by 1976 an average of 18.6 million participated each month. But many poor families did not. A major reason for the shortfall was that most people had to pay something for the stamps, and accumulating enough cash to do so proved impossible for many. The hostility experienced at grocery counters, the time lost in complying with certification requirements, and transportation problems also played a role. In 1977 the law was amended to permit the "bonus value," the difference between the face value of the stamps and their purchase price, to be distributed directly. Then income limits were cut back several times in the late 1970s in order to target the poor more effectively, with the result that food stamp users declined by 2.5 million by 1978. But worsening economic conditions soon pushed the caseload up to new heights.

Determined to constrain the growth of social welfare programs, the Reagan Administration reduced income limits, retained the 1974 assets ceiling, excluded strikers, increased reporting requirements, changed accounting procedures in ways that delayed certification for many families, and reduced food stamp benefits. By 1983 the food stamp beneficiary count was 1 million short of the 1981 level, when 2.5 million fewer workers were jobless. While the program in 1983 was somewhat better targeted toward the poor, because of the cutbacks the proportion of poor persons receiving food stamps was unchanged — 45.9 per cent in 1980 and 45.0 per cent in 1983. But in those few years, the proportion of the poor with children under six years of age who received food stamps declined, and it was this group that so worried pediatricians and parents.

2. Categorical Programs. All other cash transfers are categorical. In 1979 the Census Bureau examined the distribution of three major programs — social security, SSI, and public assistance.† While 29 per cent of families received one or more of these benefits in 1978, 40 per cent of those with incomes below the poverty threshold received none at all (52). The group included

---

*1980 amendments restricted the eligibility of students, and 1982 amendments excluded strikers and boarders.

†Public assistance includes AFDC, state–local general assistance, and emergency assistance.

- 46 per cent of poor white and 26 per cent of poor black families
- 54 per cent of poor male-headed and 26 per cent of poor female-headed families
- 41 per cent of poor families with children and 35 per cent of poor childless families
- 45 per cent of poor families with heads under sixty-five years of age as compared with 7 per cent of those with older heads

In addition, while almost half of *all* unrelated individuals received at least one of the three benefits, more than half of the *poor* members of this group received none at all. This was true for almost three out of every four under sixty-five years of age and only one in twenty of their older counterparts.

Unfortunately, comparable data are not available for more recent years, but what changes have occurred that would influence coverage of the population at risk have had a negative, not a positive, effect. In programs providing noncash benefits, whether means-tested or not, for example, coverage of the poor in 1983 was at about the 1980 level or had declined somewhat (52, 54).

Gaps in coverage primarily reflect the failure to provide programs for intact families with children and for singles and childless couples in their productive work years, some of whom may be unemployed or underemployed part or all of the year. They may not qualify for unemployment compensation because they work part-time or irregularly, only recently joined the labor force, have already exhausted unemployment benefits, or were disqualified for various reasons. Recent eligibility restrictions further limit the program's usefulness. In the fall of 1980, just over half of the unemployed received unemployment benefits. In the fall of 1985, only three tenths did so. This is a major blow to intact families. Even with such limited coverage, 8.9 million children were in households receiving unemployment benefits in the spring of 1984, which makes it the largest family income support program in the nation (54).

Similarly, despite proliferation of programs for sick, disabled, and handicapped persons, many still fall or are pushed through the cracks. Restrictive definitions of disability and long waiting periods — before applications can be filed and before benefits, if any, become available — cause a good bit of the problem. In workers' compensation, less than a quarter of income loss due to work-related illnesses and injuries is ever compensated, and from 40 to 50 per cent of the cash flow generated by premiums is absorbed by administrative expenses and insurance company profits (4). Often the sheer proliferation of programs creates problems since benefits received from one program may be offset — to the recipient's dismay — by those from another. Only a few states have temporary sickness and disability insurance for residents; otherwise, except for job-based sick leave provisions, which are far from universal, no cash benefits at all may be available to replace lost wages. Integrating all programs into social security and enacting a national health care program would bring some order to the system and give it far more credibility; but both the present political climate and the strong opposition to basic reform on the part of large employers and private insurance companies suggests that few improvements can be expected at all soon.

On balance, by far the most serious fault in the cash transfer system in the 1980s is the incomplete coverage of the population at risk of severe income loss or persistent poverty.

Inequitable and Inadequate Benefits. Benefits vary widely among programs, differ for people in like circumstances, and are often lowest for the poorest. In late 1985, a year spotted with state benefit increases, monthly AFDC grants for mothers with two young children and no other income ranged from $96 in Mississippi to $579 in New York (59) while social security benefits for a widow with two children averaged about $1,019 (21). Retired couples received social security checks averaging $776 (46), while a couple with no other income and maintaining their own household received $472 from SSI. In July 1985 unemployment benefits, including dependents' allowances in the few states that paid them, averaged about $541.42 monthly (49), while workers' compensation benefits for temporary total disability, by far the major type of award, ranged from $546 in Mississippi to $2,511 in Iowa (48).* Perversely, benefits tend to be considerably lower for far more serious permanent disabilities or the death of a worker (4).

As one possible test of adequacy, how do these benefits compare with the poverty threshold? In 1985, federal "poverty guidelines," which are used for administrative purposes pending updating of official thresholds, were $7,050 for couples, $8,850 for three person families, and $10,650 for four person households (11). If monthly payments from the various programs are annualized, only three turn out to be above the poverty threshold, the two social security payments and Iowa's benefit for temporary total disability, which would seldom if ever be given for a whole year.† At the bottom of the scale are the poor children in Mississippi who, with their mothers, receive only 13 per cent of the poverty threshold. One reason for the vast difference between family benefits in AFDC and social security is that federal law does not require cost-of-living adjustments in AFDC, nor does it have anything to do with setting standards initially. Between 1972

*The average 1983 social security benefit for widows with two children was adjusted for cost-of-living increases through 1985. Unemployment insurance and workers' compensation weekly benefits were multiplied by 4.33 to derive monthly benefits.

†Iowa's benefit is almost twice as large as average weekly earnings (1), which would impress most people as creating a work disincentive. The explanation for such generous benefits, according to Berman (4), is that employers often try to co-opt the largest group of beneficiaries in order to ward off pressures toward more expensive basic reforms.

and 1984, in real value AFDC payments fell 22 per cent behind the consumer price index, while social security beneficiaries received a relative windfall of upward adjustments.

Within the benefit structures of each program lie more variations on the theme. Both equity and adequacy are undone by family ceilings, ratable reductions,* waiting periods, the absence of national standards, status-sensitive benefit formulae,† the failure to pay dependents' allowances, various penny-pinching methods of calculating welfare grants, the failure to require cost-of-living adjustments in all programs, wage-related benefits, and the fear of work disincentives. The last two deserve more attention.

Wage-related Benefits. From an anti-poverty perspective, standardized, wage-related benefits in social security and unemployment insurance generate very perverse benefit structures. From the former worker's point of view, benefits paying reasonable wage replacement rates are logical and desirable. But in the process those who earn the highest wages receive the highest benefits, while the most poorly paid stay at the bottom of the scale. In other words, the benefit structure perpetuates traditional income disparities found in the wage structure and private insurance.

Regressive social security taxes add to the problem. In 1986 employees and employers each paid 7.15 per cent of the first $42,000 in earnings.** Both the tax rate and earnings base are scheduled to rise through the rest of the century, and obviously the higher the earnings base rises over average earnings, the less regressive the tax becomes. But it is still true that whether someone earned $42,000 or $1,000,000 in 1986, the same social security tax was due — $3,003, which makes the millionaire's effective tax rate 0.3 per cent as compared with 7.15 per cent for everyone earning $42,000 or less. Another feature adds to the regressivity. Employees pay income taxes on gross wages, including the share for social security taxes, but when employers pay corporation income taxes, social security benefits are first deducted as business expenses.

Wage-related benefits in conjunction with regressive taxes raise many

---

*In AFDC about half of the states pay only a percentage of their own standard.

†The reference is to such statuses as *divorced wife, widow, disabled widow, widow with children, essential person, disabled worker,* and the like. Each may receive somewhat different benefits.

**To keep these rates in perspective, in the Ohio State Teacher Retirement System, which is held in very high regard by pension specialists, in 1986 employees paid 8.75 per cent of their entire salary while employers paid 14.0 per cent of their payroll, for a combined "contribution rate" of 22.75 per cent, as compared with a combined social security tax rate in 1986 of 14.30 on earnings up to $42,000. Ohio public employees have never been covered by social security, but in addition to compulsory payments into the state retirement plan, some employees also contribute to TIAA–CREF or other annuities or savings plans.

issues. But it is important to keep in mind that social insurances were not designed to end mass poverty. Nor can any occupationally based benefit ever hope to do so especially in a country without a guaranteed right to work. Even in nations that strive seriously toward full employment, universal family allowances, national health care systems, and a panoply of community services available to everyone have been regarded as essential underpinnings to social insurance. So it is not wage-related benefits that are at fault, but rather the failure to take all major causes of poverty into account and to assure an income floor under all households.

Attempts are made to modify the direct relationship between wages and benefits in both social security and unemployment insurance. Until recently, the relatively low taxable earnings base made for a narrow range between minimum and maximum benefits. But this anti-poverty feature will gradually be lost in social security as the taxable earnings base shoots upward. The second modification comes from weighting benefits of low-wage earners so that they always receive the best return on their investment. Writing in 1984, Kuttner (24) claimed that a worker earning the minimum wage during his entire working years would receive benefits reflecting a 52 per cent return on his investment — as compared with a 31 per cent return for workers earning the equivalent of the taxable earnings base. Dependents' allowances also bring about some vertical and horizontal redistribution — from small to large families, which tend to be among the poorest.

To reconcile a decent income floor with realistic wage-related benefits, in the process reducing tax burdens on poor workers, some people favor shifting to a "double-decker" system (2). In one variant of this approach, the lower deck, consisting of a flat minimum payment for all workers, would be supported from general revenues generated by progressive income taxes while the upper deck, paying wage-related benefits, would be financed by employers and employees, as at present. This approach would have the advantage of permitting more nearly adequate minimum benefits and more realistic wage replacement for better-off workers. If such a reform were adopted, it would be logical to set minimum benefits no lower than poverty thresholds (58). To some extent, the present combination of social security and employer-provided pensions, enjoyed by millions of Americans, accomplishes the same goal, except that pensions are proving to be much more vulnerable than employees anticipated, as will be discussed later.

Work Incentives and Disincentives. The fear that cash transfers will create work disincentives results in untold efforts to keep a "reasonable" gap between benefits and potential earnings, and to make sure that if jobs are available, unemployed workers promptly accept them.

1. Unemployment Insurance and AFDC. Work disincentive effects have been studied exhaustively in unemployment insurance (18, 30), AFDC (9, 13, 20, 45), and various negative income tax experiments (33, 35). Garfinkel and Plotnick (15) estimate that unemployment benefits prolong periods of joblessness by only between 0.21 and 0.72 per cent of total hours worked, and that the loss in economic efficiency attributable to the program is less than one tenth of 1 per cent of total earnings. But skeptics abound, and a fair number are in Congress. In 1980, they eliminated benefits to workers who leave jobs "voluntarily," are fired for "misconduct," or are laid off from CETA jobs. States have long disqualified the first two groups for brief periods, but if after some time, people are still searching unsuccessfully for work, economic conditions were assumed to be at fault, and benefits were approved. Now states have no choice. Yet both "voluntary quits" and "misconduct" are subject to interpretation. Does a woman who suffers sexual harassment on the job and finally abandons hope of corrective action, leave "voluntarily?" Is this also the case with workers who leave to accompany spouses whose jobs were summarily transferred? And should an employer's allegation of "misconduct" always be accepted at face value? The AFL-CIO and many workers think not.

Repeated studies have shown little change in AFDC employment rates since cash work incentives and work and training requirements were introduced during the late 1960s (13, 14, 23). This is partly because poor education, few work skills, heavy home responsibilities, and scarce day-care services add up to only irregular work and low earnings for many AFDC mothers, and the help offered through work and training programs was usually too limited to make much difference (8, 19, 32, 43). But a small number of current work and training programs, as in Massachusetts, that provide child day care, transportation, on-the-job training in the private sector, and sophisticated systems for locating or searching for jobs are proving more successful. At least participants are apparently somewhat more likely than nonparticipants to find steady work paying decent wages. The growth economy in Massachusetts undoubtedly helps.

The changes in AFDC and related policies, instituted in 1981, had strong work disincentive implications, and yet they too had little effect on the work habits of AFDC mothers. Convinced that welfare demoralizes the poor and obviates the need to work, the Reagan Administration revived the old idea of "working off" AFDC checks (which should not be confused with the work and training programs described above), and convinced Congress to (1) reduce the duration and value of various work incentives, (2) lower welfare income ceilings for families with employed members, (3) reduce age limits for AFDC, (4) eliminate CETA, which provided about a half million poor people with steady work, including child day-care jobs, (5) cut funds for Title 20 social services, which financed a large share of existing low-cost child care, and finally (6) eliminate social security benefits to college students over eighteen years of age and to elementary students over nineteen years — altogether about 567,000 students. These policy shifts, in turn, clearly had the potential of adding up to a million relatively unskilled job seekers to the labor force — just as the economy was plummeting into recession and low-paid mothers, by virtue of working, were losing AFDC, child care, and Medicaid in one fell swoop. Rarely had such strong work disincentives or a less welcoming labor market converged on poor mothers. But they kept on working. The major consequences of the new policies were to make families poorer, to cause more children to be left unsupervised, to leave thousands of fatherless families without medical care,* and in all likelihood, to depress wages even further, which many critics believe may have been the real intent of these policy shifts. Certainly they did not save much AFDC money since mothers who worked full-time received very small AFDC grants, being essentially self-supporting.

2. The Disabled. The fear of work disincentives is equally controversial in regard to the disabled. About 12 to 14 per cent of the population between twenty and sixty-four years of age suffer work disabilities. This group, too, has been exhaustively studied. About half are totally disabled, meaning they are unable to work at all or can only work irregularly. Since disability goes hand in hand with poor education, advancing age, and poverty, it is not surprising that blacks are twice more likely than whites to be disabled, and are even more prominent among the totally disabled, or that more women than men fall in this group (47). The handicapped need more medical and hospital care than others, but are considerably less likely to have health insurance. When they do, their policies are less often comprehensive. They spend about three times more of their own money on medical care than the nondisabled. Many are dependent on others for help in moving about and for personal care (57, 61).

Nonetheless, studies generally find that most of them work full-time for part or all of the year. But whether black or white, married or single, and irrespective of education or occupation, their wages are lower than those paid the nondisabled. Many have difficulty finding jobs, and even those with excellent credentials and a fine work record before they became disabled often find the labor market very unwelcoming.

In all industrialized nations during the 1970s, public cash transfer and service programs received increased applications from the disabled.

---

*In 1984 Congress finally took corrective action by requiring states to continue Medicaid coverage for nine months (with an optional extension for another six months) when families lose AFDC because of increased earnings. But there are still many working mothers unable to afford day care for preschoolers and thousands of "latchkey" children.

Whether disabilities were more frequent, or the disabled were experiencing more difficulty finding work, or had become more aware of programs designed to assist them was not clear. In the U.S., the phenomenon caused great consternation, especially after the General Accounting Office (GAO), an investigative arm of Congress, estimated from a sample of cases that one fifth of the 1979 caseload was ineligible. Before long three villains were identified: lax administration (a required review was long overdue), malingering beneficiaries, and benefits that sometimes exceeded predisability earnings — which presumably could only be a work disincentive.* In 1980 Congress enacted a bill calling for careful review of the caseload.

When the Reagan administration took office, the review was accelerated under tightened eligibility rules with the apparent twin intent of ferreting out fraud and shrinking the caseload.† (17) Working under great pressure and relying almost solely on case records, 400,000 reviews were completed by June 1982. Almost half had resulted in negative decisions, 64,000 of which were reversed on appeal, leaving a backlog of thousands yet to be heard by 700 administrative law judges who had been hurriedly hired or transferred to cope with the crisis. Another 800,000 cases were scheduled for review during the following year.

From the beginning of the process, "horror stories" made daily headlines. Twelve suicides were reported, one with a shotgun in front of a social security office. A severely brain-damaged child was notified that benefits were cut off because she was "fit to attend school." A man in an iron lung was dropped because he was "medically improved" and able to work. To handle an impossible caseload, staff examiners shortcut the process by failing to secure proof of medical improvement and by rarely seeing anyone in person before making decisions. All over the country, lawyers were busily helping the disabled file appeals, and complaints surfaced everywhere about the abrogation of rights established by law or regulation. When appeals were filed, beneficiaries had the right to be examined by physicians of their choice, with social security paying the bill if necessary. They also had the right to receive benefits for three months after notification or until the judge made a final decision, whichever occurred earlier. But the Department of Health and Human Services (HHS) refused to pay for medical examinations during this period, and the backlog of appeals meant that well over three months elapsed before cases were heard,

---

*The wrong income concept, "covered earnings," was used in the study that led to this charge. Gross earnings could be substantially higher (5). It was also known that the wages of disabled beneficiaries did not keep pace with the rise in the allowable earnings ceiling (12). But the law was quickly amended to lower disability benefits if they exceeded 80 per cent of taxable earnings prior to qualifying for disability benefits, and to require that private pensions as well as public benefits be offset when beneficiaries received several benefits simultaneously.

†The author is indebted in the following pages to Glenn Pascall (34) for his cogent review of the "disability mess."

thereby leaving appellants in a double bind—many had no income or resources, but if they failed to submit new evidence contradicting the government's findings, appeals were summarily dismissed.

In response to rising public anger over the situation, the GAO undertook another study. Reporting in early 1983, investigators concluded that social security officials had improperly cut off benefits for many individuals with severe mental impairments and with no or little capacity to function in a competitive world. Disability examiners had confided that "unless a claimant was 'flat on his back,' 'comatose,' or 'in a catatonic state,' he or she would not meet the new criteria for eligibility" (51).

In June 1983, District Court Judge William Gray of the 9th Circuit Court ruled the government was operating "outside the law" by its failure to obtain medical evidence of improvement before cutting people from the rolls. He ordered HHS to notify everyone dropped since 1981 of their right to reapply (34). Complying in part, but still refusing to pay for medical examinations, HHS sought relief from the U.S. Supreme Court, which agreed that further remedies could be delayed until the full 9th Circuit Court handed down a decision. When it was finally forthcoming in February 1984, the Court charged the Administration with "flouting the law by terminating without proof of medical improvement." HHS responded with a "non-acquiescence" order which said, in effect, that it would not comply since it disagreed with the Court's decision, a move which many lawyers felt bordered on contempt. By that time twenty-four states had joined the fray. From the beginning of disability insurance, state vocational rehabilitation agencies handled much of the initial work in screening people in and out of the system. Now, under court orders or on their own initiative, states categorically refused to process further terminations, all of which were costing them a great deal of money since some level of government had to come to the aid of the thousands of impoverished disabled individuals and families who were cast adrift weekly by the federal government. Shortly after news spread on March 27, 1984 that the House had just enacted a bill—by a vote of 410 to 1—barring terminations if the government had not documented medical improvement, and requiring face-to-face interviews before making decisions to terminate, the Administration finally caved in, to the extent of announcing an eighteen month moratorium on reviews (40).

Two months later, after scores of similar court reversals, federal District Judge Joseph S. Lord III of Philadelphia, in reversing a decision involving a woman whose illness left her weighing only eighty-eight pounds, said it was "blatant hypocrisy" for the government to regard her as anything but totally disabled. "If the purpose of the Department of Health and Human Services is to crush defenseless human beings, as it seems to be, it would succeed unless in cases like this courts interposed a protective arm" (26). In reporting the decision, and calling attention to HHS's refusal to apply findings in one case to other similar ones in the same judicial circuit, highly regarded legal reporter Anthony Lewis commented

> These disability cases . . . are not just abstractions of legal theory. They involve human beings: mostly poor, desperate people with wasted intestines and missing limbs. Few know about their rights or have lawyers to fight for them. For a Government to say that each must litigate an issue of law again, no matter how often it has been decided, is lawless in the most profound sense. (26)

Lewis also summarized a sharp denial of his viewpoint by the distinguished Deputy Solicitor General Paul M. Bator, who pointed out that if the government had to treat every case it lost in the lower courts as binding in all like cases, there would be no chance for other federal circuits to consider the issue, for conflicts among the circuits to develop, or for reflection to deepen understanding. Instead there would be pressure to take every such case to the Supreme Court and for the court to rush to judgment.

After tumultous public hearings, on September 19, 1984 by unanimous vote Congress enacted a bill requiring medical evidence of improvement before cutting people from the rolls. Also, examiners were required to take into account the cumulative effects of multiple impairments, and to give greater weight to the significance of pain as a disabling factor (42). Five months later, broader definitions of disability were announced by HHS. They recognized, for example, that symptoms of mental illness can disappear temporarily without presaging significant improvement, and that people able to cope in a sheltered daily life can easily deteriorate under the stress of working. Anxiety neurosis and agoraphobia were accepted as disabling conditions — almost a century after they were formally described as such by Freud. But the agency still refused to take pain into consideration, having decided instead to refer the issue to the National Academy of Sciences for further study (50).

Despite the fact that half of the negative decisions since 1981 were reversed, by the end of August 1985, there were almost a million fewer disabled beneficiaries and their dependents than when the Reagan Administration took office. After losing their only means of support, some were soon found among the squatters in abandoned buildings, they were found clothed in rags in the midst of freezing storms, eating from garbage cans, sleeping in doorways and under bridges. A few froze to death in New York City and the nation's capital. Some were also working — how many, no one knows. Because many who were cut off did not appeal, the government saved a lot of money despite the cost of reviewing cases, paying administrative law judges, battling the courts, and conferring about strategy. One has visions of tense conferences of high-paid officials, meeting almost daily for three of the four years, in efforts to contain the crisis. In the meantime, many people feel irreparable harm was done to public confidence in government, not just in the social security system. But whether anything was learned about how to prevent the program from ever harboring work-shy malingerers — outside of regular, realistic, objective reviews — is still unanswered. In the spring of 1986, HHS decided to resume its reviews.

Predictability: Methods of Financing. How predictable benefits are depends remarkably on methods of financing. Many references have already been made to the problems flowing from the public assistance grants-in-aid. At this stage a closer look will be taken at four universal programs — unemployment insurance, workers' compensation, social security, and employer-provided pensions.

1. Unemployment Insurance and Workers' Compensation. For various historical reasons, state unemployment insurance and workers' compensation are financed solely by employers,* the former through payroll taxes and the latter most often through private insurance carriers. Whether the cost is actually borne by employers is another matter. It is not subject to corporation income tax, and much is passed on to consumers in higher prices or borne by workers in the form of foregone wages. But the "flypaper theory," which holds that the cost "sticks" to the party actually paying the tax collector, is often used to justify employer domination of the programs (18). Where strong unions prevail, the lack of worker participation in financing may be less crucial, but a declining share of the labor force is unionized, and the poorest programs are in the South, where unions are the weakest.

Equally important, the employer's cost in both programs essentially reflects past charges incurred for benefits from his firm, which gives employers as a group a high stake in restraining benefit levels and duration, and the coverage of programs. Workers' compensation has probably suffered most. Of sixteen standards regarded as hallmarks of sound programs, on the average, states met eight in 1972. Seventeen states met less than five. They included Kentucky, with its dangerous coal mines, which met none (31). Despite improvements since then (37), many programs still leave a good deal to be desired. Clues to one overriding problem are found in the fact that in 1978, only 57 per cent of total program costs were distributed in benefits (38), as compared with over 98 per cent in social security and 86 per cent in unemployment insurance (41). A good part of the difference reflects the inordinate amount of lengthy, expensive litigation, especially over employers' liability for permanent disability. Attempts to reform the system move ahead slowly, in good measure because of the overpowering influence of the insurance industry.† After spelling out the faults in detail, Berman (4) concludes that workers' compensation, except

---

*In three states, employees pay unemployment taxes.

†Workers' compensation is the second largest property liability insurance line, topped only by automobile insurance (60).

in a few states like Ohio where private compensation insurance companies are not allowed to operate, "represents a tremendous success for employers in transferring the cost of occupational casualties onto workers, their families, and the public."

Unemployment insurance financing has been hotly debated for years. Federal and state governments both impose payroll taxes for this purpose, but much of the former is forgiven so long as states maintain their programs. The balance pays administrative costs and helps to build reserve funds. Tax rates vary among employers, depending on some measure of their cost-benefit experience or the number of approved claims as well as on the condition of reserve funds. Employers with relatively high benefit costs pay the highest rates, but when reserves are high, tax rates for employers with good "experience ratings" have often been as low as zero. If reserves are low, as after a long period of high unemployment, tax rates typically rise (6). In 1984 one state after another had to make upward adjustments. Setting and manipulating rates in this way hurts industries that are unable to stabilize employment and has forced the federal government to bail out states so that statutory benefits can be paid. Severe, prolonged recessions always threaten the system. Such factors play a central role in explaining why working in covered employment does not necessarily mean qualifying for unemployment benefits, let alone doing so for the duration of joblessness.

2. *Social Security and Private Pensions: The Politics of Insecurity.* Social security was long accepted as the most secure and predictable of cash transfers. But when several foreseen and a few unforeseen trends collided in the late 1970s, charges of imminent bankruptcy suddenly became the news of the day. What precipitated the charges? A cash-flow problem in one part of the system, for which short-term solutions were readily at hand — leaving ample time to negotiate whatever long-term solutions were indicated. To understand the cash flow problem and why it was catapulted into such a hot political issue requires a closer look at financing arrangements and the political climate.

Social security is essentially a "pay-as-you-go" scheme in which workers and their employers pay taxes that soon go out in benefits. By law a separate account or trust fund must be maintained for Old Age and Survivors' Insurance, Disability Insurance, Hospital Insurance, and Supplementary Medical Insurance, which taken together add up to OASDHI. Funds may not be transferred from one to another except by Congress. The share of social security taxes allocated to each fund depends, in the first instance, on actuarial estimates of future demands on each part of the system. Actuaries estimate the effect of myriads of variables, using both optimistic and pessimistic assumptions. Then a line is drawn between the two sets of estimates to derive an intermediate estimate, all three are forwarded to Congress, and legislators make their best "guesstimate." It is well to keep human fallibility in mind at this stage, since neither actuaries nor Congressmen have crystal balls at their service.

Two very important long-term trends were easily taken into account: the aging of the population and the maturing of the social security system — which began by sending $22 million monthly to 140,000 retired beneficiaries and their dependents, and by 1977 sent $54 billion monthly to over 20 million retired workers and their families. Two unanticipated events in the 1970s had profound impacts on income and outgo. In 1972 benefits were indexed to inflation by an overly generous formula, only to be followed by years of stagflation, when both unemployment and inflation rose simultaneously, the latter to remarkable heights. Prolonged high unemployment cut deeply into tax revenues, more people than usual applied for benefits, and inflation increased payouts well over expected levels. In 1977 Congress responded by enacting steeper tax schedules, but the economic problems still persisted. By 1980 the social security system lost $100 million monthly for every million jobless workers, and inflation pushed benefits up by 14.3 per cent. Soon actuaries predicted a severe cash-flow problem in the Old Age and Survivors' Trust Fund by 1982, to be followed by shortages in the Disability Trust Fund.

The short-term remedies were to scale back the overly generous indexing formula and to transfer funds from one trust to another, which would ordinarily be done without fanfare. But before Congress took action, the situation was exploited for all it was worth by long-standing opponents of the system. There have always been individuals and groups who for one reason or another have wanted social security repealed, leaving citizens free to plan individually for all of their retirement income. Leading exponents of this view were increasingly prominent in Washington during the late 1970s and early 1980s; a few were close advisors to, or on the staff of, the White House. After suffering for years with a system they regarded as an assault on freedom and a savings disincentive, it was inevitable that the turn of events would seem propitious for efforts to get rid of social security. But despite herculean efforts toward that end, while they undermined the confidence of the young that the system would endure until they qualified for benefits, countless people made it clear in letters to Washington, conversations with members of Congress, and public opinion polls that they were staunch supporters — and protectors — of the system. Soon the bipartisan negotiations necessary to deal with long-term problems in social security got underway, with the President's appointment of a commission. The resulting reform blueprint was enacted by Congress, with very few changes. If the economy is reasonably well managed so that deep, prolonged recessions are avoided, the solvency of the system is protected well into the twenty-first century, when another generation, with current facts, can make the necessary adjustments. The chief danger in the meantime is the attractive surplus that will build up around the turn of the century and for several decades thereafter. Then the challenge will be to avoid raising benefits and to ward off external forays on the trust funds.

The major changes enacted by Congress were as follows:

- Coverage was expanded to include federal civilian employees.
- Cost-of-living adjustments (COLAs) were delayed six months, from July 1983 to January 1984; future COLAs are to be based on the increase in wages or prices, whichever is lower, and will be made only once yearly.
- The schedule for social security tax increases was accelerated.
- Up to 50 per cent of social security benefits are to be subject to federal income tax when income exceeds $25,000 for single persons and $32,000 for married couples; the resulting revenues will be transferred to the trust funds.
- The retirement age will be raised to sixty-six years in 2009 and sixty-seven years in 2027.
- In the meantime, credits for working beyond sixty-five years of age will be increased as an incentive to do so.

While this package will accomplish its varied purposes, it will probably take considerable time to restore citizen confidence — especially among young workers — in the system and in the federal government. One of the chief sources of anxiety now is that while the Administration may well avoid further efforts to cut back cash benefits to the elderly, similar efforts will be renewed with other more vulnerable parts of the social security package — disability insurance and Medicare.

In the meantime, while the social security system was under assault, private job-based pensions were being undermined right and left. In fact, as compared with social security, many workers began to feel their promised pensions were mere will-o'-the-wisps. From the time social security was enacted, it was regarded by most workers as simply a base on which to build whatever they viewed as an adequate retirement income (2). While some could not afford more, many others expected to accumulate savings, income from assets, and most importantly pension rights. But except for fairly large firms, few offered pension plans to their employees. As recently as 1983, just over half of American workers had such coverage; and for years complaints surfaced about plans that favored top management, excluded young workers, required unreasonably long periods for vesting,*

---

*Most require a specified number of years with the company before pension benefits become nonforfeitable — ten years is typical in the private sector as compared with five years in government plans (55). Private employer plans may also credit years toward vesting only after employees reach a specified age, like twenty-five years, which means that an eighteen-year-old would have to work until he was thirty-five years old before his benefits were vested. If employees leave earlier, the approved practice is to refund their contributions with interest. But this was not routine in the private sector until Congress passed the Retirement Equity Act of 1984.

and left survivors with no protection. The Employee Retirement Insurance Annuity Act (ERISA) of 1974 was designed to correct some of these faults. But many still persisted in 1983, when three quarters of American workers earning $20,000 or more were covered, and only one fourth earning under $10,000. Older workers were much more likely to be covered than younger ones, and widows were often overwhelmed to learn that their husbands' pensions were cancelled with their death.*

Nonetheless, covered workers had come to regard their pensions as immutable. But between 1980 and early 1984, 500 firms terminated their pension plans, and the trend was picking up steam. In May 1984, Jane Bryant Quinn (39) wrote, "You cannot count on a company pension anymore. Those are harsh words but true. Your company's employee-benefits book may explain in great detail exactly how your income will be figured at retirement. But in most cases, companies have no legal obligation to fulfill this promise."

Why are so many firms closing out pension plans? Business analysts explain that after many years of underfunding, pension funds did exceptionally well in recent years. The stock market returns were fine, interest rates were high, and employment low, a combination that adds up to temporary overfunding. "That surplus cash," Quinn noted, "is like red meat to circling tigers. Companies are generally not allowed to borrow from their pension plans. But no law bars them from terminating the plan and tucking the surplus in their pockets" — to be used however management and stockholders prefer. The companies often claim that huge pension reserves make them altogether too-enticing targets for takeovers, which have become the mania of the 1980s in the business sector. The money involved is substantial. By July 1985, the biggest "surpluses" recaptured by terminations included $362.8 million by Occidental Petroleum, $325.8 million by Celanese Corporation, $284.7 million by Firestone Tire & Rubber, $273 million by Great Atlantic & Pacific Tea, and $125 million by Reynolds Metal. United Airlines was awaiting approval of a termination which would recapture $962 million (10).

Since pension rights up to the date of termination and after retirement must be honored, how do companies make money in the process? First, since benefits of only half of all workers are typically vested in a given year, some companies assumed they owed the other half nothing.† To the lucky group, they usually paid off their obligations at pension levels *earned by the*

---

*Part of the age and income disparities was due to the fact that pension plans were very rare among small firms.

†The Retirement Equity Act of 1984 closed this loophole, as well as requiring corporations to extend coverage to all workers twenty-one years or older, to credit years of service (toward vesting) from eighteen years of age, to provide survivors' rights, to permit longer breaks in service without forfeiting pension rights, and recognized recent court decisions defining pensions as joint assets in divorce settlements.

date of termination, which are considerably lower on the average than their value at retirement. The pay-off was usually in the form of a lump sum or annuity. In estimating what was due workers, finance officers tended to be optimistic about future interest rates and returns on investments. The greater their optimism, the less the company owed to workers. A case in point was when Harper & Row terminated its pension plan in 1981. The firm estimated that sums as small as $250 would average 15 per cent interest yearly for the balance of a young employee's working life. The Pension Benefit Guarantee Corporation (PBGC), a federal body which insures some private pension plans, found this unreasonably high, and ordered an interest rate no higher than 10.75 per cent to be used. While many companies insist employees lost nothing in the process, a recent Department of Labor study estimates that at 5 per cent inflation, the average employee in a terminated plan lost 35 per cent of his real, expected retirement benefit (39).

Because employees protested with such vigor, some companies offered another pension plan. They usually shifted from an insured *defined benefit* plan to an uninsured *defined contribution* plan, which is a very different kettle of fish. The former, insured up to $1,602 monthly, guarantees pensions of defined levels at retirement age, while the latter simply agrees to make cash or stock payments into an employee's retirement account, and in the case of cash, to invest it in the employee's behalf. It has not been uncommon with such pension plans for employers to skip periodic payments, especially during an employee's early years with the firm, making them up, if ever, much later, thereby earning well below the level anticipated by workers. This type of plan is particularly hard on older employees, but as Quinn observes, even with the young, "while things may turn out well, again they may not. There is no guarantee." Workers lose in another way. If a new plan is substituted, they begin from day one, earning credits toward vesting, just as they would on a new job (25).

What corporations gain in these terminations is the difference between the cost of lifelong pensions after retirement of all vested employees and the accrued value of pensions at the time of termination, the difference in cost of the two types of pension plans if they elect this option, and whatever savings they realize with respect to retirees. In the past, if pension funds ran a surplus, they paid the money out in COLAs to retirees or invested their savings as a cushion against the day when earnings dropped. Now COLAs are increasingly a bygone luxury.

While these terminations are legal and have the blessings of the Reagan Administration, new guidelines have been issued by the Labor Department, Internal Revenue Service, and PBGC to give some protections to workers. Annuities, for instance, must be purchased for everyone, whether vested or not, and no more than one termination will be approved every fifteen years. "But how can we plan for retirement," workers ask, "if our pensions are cashed out every fifteen years, and replaced with something of less worth?" As for employers, the new laws and regulations, some insist, are so costly that they see no alternative but to terminate pension plans altogether.

The chaos among private pensions these days makes the social security system seem like the Rock of Ages.

References

1. "Average Weekly Earnings, by Industry." *Monthly Labor Review,* **108** (November 1985), pp. 83, 84.
2. Ball, Robert M. *Social Security: Today and Tomorrow.* New York: Columbia University Press, 1978, pp. 246–248, 390–420.
3. Bell, Winifred. *Aid to Dependent Children.* New York: Columbia University Press, 1965, pp. 174–198.
4. Berman, Daniel M. *Death on the Job: Occupational Health and Safety Struggle in the United States.* New York: Monthly Review Press, 1978, pp. 61–73.
5. Bernstein, Merton C. Letter to the Editor. *New York Times,* July 30, 1979.
6. Blaustein, Saul J. and Isabel Craig. *An International Review of Unemployment Insurance Schemes.* Kalamazoo: W. E. Upjohn Institute for Employment Research, 1977, pp. 110–113.
7. Burns, Eveline M. *Social Welfare in the 1980s and Beyond.* Berkeley: University of California, Institute of Governmental Studies, 1977.
8. Dickinson, Jonathan. "Labor Supply of Family Members." In James N. Morgan et al., Eds., *Five Thousand Families, Patterns of Economic Progress,* Vol. 1. Ann Arbor, Mich.: Institute for Social Research, 1974, pp. 177–250.
9. *Effects of Earnings Exemption Provisions Upon the Work Response of AFDC Recipients,* 5 Vols. Philadelphia: National Analysts, Inc., 1972.
10. English, Carey W. "As Corporate 'Raids' on Pensions Pick Up Steam." *U.S. News and World Report,* **99** (July 29, 1985), p. 65.
11. "1985 Federal Poverty Income Guidelines." *Social Security Bulletin,* **48** (July 1985), p. 48.
12. Franklin, Paula A. and John C. Hennessey. "Effect of Substantial Gainful Activity Level on Disabled Beneficiary Work Pattern." *Social Security Bulletin,* **42** (March 1979), pp. 3–17.
13. Garfinkel, Irwin. "Income Transfer Programs and Work Effort: A Review." *Studies in Public Welfare,* Paper No. 13. Prepared for the Subcommittee on Fiscal Policy, Joint Economic Committee. Washington, D.C.: U.S. Government Printing Office, February 18, 1974, pp. 1–33.
14. ———— and Larry S. Orr. "Welfare Policy and the Employment Rate of AFDC Mothers." *National Tax Journal,* **27** (June 1974), pp. 275–284.
15. ———— and Robert Plotnick. "How Much Does Unemployment Insurance Increase the Unemployment Rate and Reduce Work, Earnings, and Efficiency?" Discussion Paper No. 378–76. Mimeographed. Madison: University of Wisconsin, Institute for Research on Poverty, 1976.

16. Gil, David G. *Unravelling Social Policy.* Cambridge, Mass.: Schenkman Publishing Co., 1973, pp. 31–56.
17. "Give the Disabled a Grandfather." Editorial. *New York Times,* October 18, 1983.
18. Hamermesh, Daniel S. *Jobless Pay and the Economy.* Baltimore: Johns Hopkins University Press, 1977, pp. 31–47.
19. Handler, Joel F. and Ellen Jane Hollingsworth. *The "Deserving Poor"—A Study of Welfare Administration.* Chicago: Markham Publishing Co., 1971, pp. 153–161.
20. Hausman, Leonard J. "The Impact of Welfare on the Work Effort of AFDC Mothers." In President's Commission on Income Maintenance Programs. *Poverty Amid Plenty: The American Paradox.* Washington, D.C.: U.S. Government Printing Office, 1970. Vol. 2, *Technical Studies,* pp. 83–100.
21. "Income Support Programs." *Social Security Bulletin, Annual Statistical Supplement 1983,* p. 229.
22. *King* v. *Smith* 392 U.S. 309 (1968).
23. Klausner, Samuel Z. *The Work Incentive Program: Making Adults Economically Independent.* Philadelphia: Center for the Study of the Acts of Man, 1972.
24. Kuttner, Robert. *The Economic Illusion: False Choices Between Prosperity and Social Justice.* Boston: Houghton Mifflin Co., 1984, p. 80.
25. Lewin, Tamar. "Terminating Pension Plans." *New York Times,* July 10, 1984.
26. Lewis, Anthony. "Respect for Law?" *New York Times,* June 18, 1984.
27. MacDonald, Maurice. *Food, Stamps, and Income Maintenance.* New York: Academic Press, Inc., 1977, pp. 91–108.
28. Merton, Robert K. *Social Theory and Social Structure,* rev. ed. New York: The Free Press, 1957, pp. 19–84.
29. Morris, Robert. *Social Policy of the American Welfare State: An Introduction to Policy Analysis.* New York: Harper & Row, Publishers, 1979, pp. 15–37.
30. Munts, Raymond and Irwin Garfinkel. *The Work Disincentive Effects of Unemployment Insurance.* Kalamazoo, Mich.: The W. E. Upjohn Institute for Employment Research, 1974.
31. National Commission on State Workmen's Compensation Laws. *Report of the Commission to the President and Congress.* Washington, D.C.: U.S. Government Printing Office, 1972.
32. Opton, Edward A. *Factors Associated with Employment Among Welfare Mothers.* Berkeley: The Wright Institute, 1971.
33. Palmer, John L. and Joseph A. Pechman. Eds. *Welfare in Rural Areas: The North Carolina–Iowa Income Maintenance Experiments.* Washington, D.C.: Brookings Institution, 1978.
34. Pascall, Glenn. *The Trillion Dollar Budget: How to Stop Bankrupting America.* Seattle: University of Washington Press, 1985, pp. 212–214.
35. Pechman, Joseph A. and P. Michael Timpane. Eds. *Work Incentives and Income Guarantees: The New Jersey Negative Income Tax Experiment.* Washington, D.C.: Brookings Institution, 1975.
36. Piven, Frances Fox and Richard A. Cloward. *Regulating the Poor: The Functions of Public Welfare.* New York: Vintage Books, Inc., 1971.
37. Price, Daniel N. "Workers' Compensation Programs in the 1970s." *Social Security Bulletin,* **42** (May 1979), pp. 3–24.

38. ————. "Workers' Compensation: 1978 Program Update." *Social Security Bulletin,* **43** (October 1980), pp. 3–10.
39. Quinn, Jane Bryant. "Your Precarious Pension." *Newsweek,* **103** (May 21, 1984), p. 74.
40. Rich, Spencer. "Reviews of Disability Rolls Halted." *Washington Post,* April 14, 1984.
41. Schobel, Bruce. "Administrative Expenses Under OASDI." *Social Security Bulletin,* **44** (March 1981), pp. 21–28.
42. Shapiro, Margaret and Spencer Rich. "Hill Alters Rules for Disability." *Washington Post,* September 20, 1984.
43. Shea, John R. *Welfare Mothers: Barriers to Labor Force Entry.* Springfield, Va.: National Technical Information Services, 1974.
44. Sherman, Sally. "Reported Reasons Retired Workers Left Their Last Job: Findings from the New Beneficiary Survey." *Social Security Bulletin,* **48** (March 1985), pp. 22–30.
45. Smith, Vernon Kent. *Welfare Work Incentives.* Studies in Welfare Policy, No. 2. Lansing: Michigan Department of Social Services, 1974.
46. "Social Security in Review: OASDI and SSI Increases." *Social Security Bulletin,* **48** (January 1985), p. 5.
47. "The Threat to Social Security for Blacks." Fact Sheet no. 5. Mimeographed. New York: Study Group on Social Security, 1979.
48. Tinsley, LaVerne C. "Workers' Compensation: 1984 State Enactments." *Monthly Labor Review,* **108** (January 1985), p. 52.
49. "Unemployment Insurance Data." *Monthly Labor Review,* **108** (November 1985), p. 84.
50. United Press International. "U.S. Easing Disability Rules." *Washington Post,* February 2, 1985.
51. "U.S. Agency Calls Cuts in Disability Pay Improper." *New York Times,* April 17, 1983.
52. U.S. Bureau of the Census. *Current Population Reports, Consumer Income 1980,* Series P–60, no. 131, Table D.
53. ————. Current Population Reports, *Consumer Income 1983,* Series P–60, no. 146, Table 33.
54. ————. Current Population Reports, *Consumer Income 1983,* Series P–60, no. 148, Table A and p. 103.
55. ————. *Statistical Abstract of the United States 1985.* Washington, D.C.: U.S. Government Printing Office, 1984, p. 368.
56. U.S. Congress, Joint Economic Committee, Subcommittee on Fiscal Policy. *Studies in Public Welfare,* Papers 1–20. Washington, D.C. U.S. Government Printing Office, 1973–1975.
57. U.S. Department of Health, Education, and Welfare. *Work Disability in the United States: A Chartbook.* Washington, D.C.: U.S. Government Printing Office, 1977.
58. Universal Social Security Coverage Study Group. "Report: Executive Summary." *Social Security Bulletin,* **43** (June 1980), pp. 15–25.
59. "Welfare Checks, State by State." *U.S. News and World Report,* **99** (December 23, 1985), p. 10.
60. Williams, J. Arthur, Jr. and Peter S. Barth. *Compendium of Workmen's Com-*

pensation. Study made for National Commission on State Workmen's Compensation Laws. Washington, D.C.: U.S. Government Printing Office, 1972, Appendix A, p. 13.

61. Wolfe, Barbara L. "Impacts of Disability and Some Policy Implications." Discussion Paper no. 539–79. Mimeographed. Madison: University of Wisconsin, Institute for Research on Poverty, 1979.

62. Worcester, Dean A., Jr. "Blueprint for a Welfare State That Contributes to Economic Efficiency." *Social Service Review,* **54** (June 1980), p. 169.

CHAPTER 10

Anti-poverty Strategies: Education and Health Care

Introduction

Americans have long viewed education and good health as expressways out of poverty. Every census survey confirms this belief. Whether black or white, male or female, each significant advance along the educational route makes for a systematic increase in income. Similarly, the able-bodied are consistently more likely to work steadily and earn more than the disabled or sickly. But race and sex disparities still survive, in large part reflecting the hundreds of years in which schooling was considered irrelevant for girls or blacks, if not harmful to the social fabric.

The notion that education should be viewed as a basic human right is of fairly recent origin in the U.S., and many facts cast doubt on whether health care is yet so regarded. In both areas, our laws promise more than is delivered. In both cases, too, the national ambivalence results in a start–stop policy course reflecting in turn a societal resolve to equalize access and to protect minimum standards, and conversely the conviction that so long as schools and health care facilities exist, both individual strength of character and the economy are best served when government maintains a neutral stance. If these two perspectives had not been so highly politicized, and if our social institutions were not so rigid and so protective of their respective turfs, the goal of guaranteeing a good education and fine health care to everyone would be far less elusive.

In this chapter, the role of the federal government in efforts to equalize access to educational and health care services, the conflicts they aroused, and recent policy reversals, are examined.

Public Education in a Segregated Society

Federal Policy

In 1954, in the case of *Brown* v. *Board of Education of Topeka* (8), the U.S. Supreme Court held that separate schools for blacks and whites were inherently unequal and ordered that children be admitted to schools on a racially nondiscriminatory basis. The decision heralded a dramatic intrusion of the federal government into affairs previously controlled by local school boards. A year later, faced with the problems the ruling raised for seventeen states with laws requiring racial segregation, the court called for desegregation with "all deliberate speed." During the following years, the new policy was refined and elaborated in a succession of court decisions. One of the most controversial, *Swann* v. *Charlotte – Mecklenburg County Schools* (90), was handed down in 1971. It concerned schools in Charlotte, North Carolina, where laws required segregated public facilities. After considering a range of remedies, the school board decided that busing children was the most logical. The plan was quickly challenged, and the case was in the courts for years. Finally, the decision of Judge James B. McMillan approving busing as a solution to *de jure* segregation, was upheld by the U.S. Supreme Court.*

The policies enunciated by the courts were further shaped by Congress and six presidents, three Republicans and three Democrats. In 1957 President Eisenhower appointed the first Civil Rights Commission, with primarily fact-finding functions. The commission's research and reports in turn helped pave the way for the Civil Rights Act of 1964 and the Voting Rights Act of 1965. The reform climate of the 1960s, directed toward creating a "Great Society," also enabled Congress to pass a long series of education laws to help states make the transition. Federal funds and technical aid were provided for efforts to modernize, enrich, and upgrade the schools and to develop new educational materials.† Special assistance was provided to districts with large concentrations of minority groups and for poor and middle-income youths and adults seeking postsecondary education. Some of the laws and programs are very familiar — the Elementary and Secondary Education Act (ESEA), which through basic grants to state education agencies and a series of demonstration and experimental projects reached upwards of 6 million children in 1980, vocational and adult education programs that helped some 15 million people and over the years built the nation's network of community colleges, special programs like Upward Bound designed to encourage gifted youth to finish high school and college, and financial aids including low interest loans, grants, and subsidized work – study plans to enable youth to continue with post-

---

*In 1981 at a testimonial dinner sponsored by the National Conference of Christians and Jews given in honor of black attorney Julius L. Chambers, who argued the Swann case, and white Judge McMillan, the judge recalled that when the case reached him he knew little about Charlotte's schools, but he found the evidence of unconstitutional segregation in his home community "overwhelming." He added that he had not hesitated to order busing as a tool of desegregation since "it had been for so long used as a tool to maintain segregation" (100).

†With greater awareness of racism, it became apparent that many texts used nationally in elementary and secondary schools always depicted blacks in subservient roles to whites, and totally ignored their military, scholarly, and cultural contributions.

secondary education (52). President Carter's last budget funded Pell grants to cover an average of 46 per cent of college expenses for poor students and Guaranteed Student Loans for all income groups at levels set to assist 5 million students in fiscal 1982.

Taken together these federal initiatives enunciated a new national policy directed toward (a) equalizing and improving educational opportunities of individual citizens and (b) modernizing a central social institution, the public school system, so that it would better reflect the spirit and needs of the times. That the income of minorities and race relations would improve as a consequence was anticipated by many people.

In an abrupt policy shift in 1981, the Reagan Administration announced its opposition to busing, quotas, and affirmative action, and its support for income tax exemptions for segregated schools, tax credits for private school tuition, and vouchers to help families pay the cost of whatever schools they chose for their children.* Believing that the federal role in education should "return to its traditional minimal level," the Administration proposed to consolidate and reduce support for educational grants to the states and cities, to cut student financial aids, and to reduce or eliminate direct grants for higher education. None of these programs, it was claimed, had justified their cost, and the Administration was convinced people would make better decisions about going to college and learn more while there if they paid a higher share of the cost. Many people agreed that something was needed to motivate more students and educators to strive toward excellence in all levels of education, but there was sharp disagreement about measures that would inevitably fall heaviest on poor people and their communities.

So far the Great Society educational policies and programs have withstood attempts to dismantle them. Each year the White House has proposed sizeable cuts, and each year Congress has appropriated more than was requested. But White House opposition has had measurable impacts. Now, the combination of the huge deficits accumulated by the Administration, its refusal to raise taxes, and the enactment of the Gramm–Rudman–Hollings bill requiring a balanced budget by fiscal 1991 make federal funds for education much more vulnerable. The President's confident claim after signing the bill that his planned military build-up could be financed by deep cuts in "wasteful and unnecessary domestic programs" did nothing to allay this fear.

Policy Implementation: 1954–1985

Court desegregation decisions required states to submit plans detailing the racial balance they would try to achieve in the schools, the methods to

---

*In November 1985 vouchers of $600 were being promoted, an amount falling seriously short of private school charges and those of many public school districts for nonresidents — as educators and newspaper editors over the country were quick to point out.

be used, and their time schedule. What exactly "all deliberate speed" meant no one was quite ready to say. But clearly schools and states needed time to comply with a change of this magnitude. Responses varied widely. Some school districts desegregated immediately; far more resisted for years. In 1963, nine years after *Brown,* nine out of every ten school districts had submitted desegregation plans. But the pace of actually rearranging children had been so glacial that unless it quickened another 3,180 years would pass before an appreciable share of black and white children attended school together (54). The Civil Rights Act of 1964 helped to raise the rate of voluntary and enforced compliance. It granted authority to the Office of Education to withhold funds in case of noncompliance and to the U.S. Attorney General to initiate legal proceedings, if necessary.

The "good news," the New York Times (73) announced twenty-five years after *Brown,* was that only 15 per cent of minority group children any longer attended schools where they comprised 99 to 100 per cent of the student body. By far the greatest progress had been made in the South, small towns, and medium-sized cities. In 1979 about one in every five black southern children still attended "racially isolated" schools — the term used when 90 to 100 per cent of enrollees are of the same race. But about six out of every ten in the Midwest and three out of every ten in the Northeast and West did so.*

An intensive study of desegregation efforts in fifteen cities provided some clues to the puzzle (19). Cities made most progress where civic "elites" in the business community favored compliance — for any of a score of reasons, including the "image" community leaders wished to project to the nation — and lent their weight and prestige to the effort. This often occurred in the South. At the other extreme were cities whose "elites" either vigorously opposed desegregation or, as was more frequent in the North, remained aloof from the struggle. When political leaders also chose a hands-off stance, the deadlock could persist for years. But the most troublesome of all situations was when large ethnic groups solidly opposed to desegregation were pitted against ideologically demanding black civil rights advocates, with each group holding out for total surrender.

Investigators found school boards singularly ill-equipped for the challenge. With low levels of tolerance for ambiguity or conflict, little knowledge of the practical problems superintendents coped with daily, and long-accustomed to function with almost undue autonomy, the boards were unprepared by inclination and experience to conduct the delicate negotiations the situation required. Where school boards were elected, their political ambitions often caused them to follow, not lead, their constituents. In some cities, the only solution the courts could find was to take over admin-

---

*Nationally in 1968 two thirds of black students were in virtually all-black schools. Today the figure is down to one third.

istration of desegregation plans,* a step which often raised as many problems as it solved.

Instead of desegregating the schools, recalcitrant school boards authorized new schools in the heart of black ghettos rather than on the periphery of white–black neighborhoods. They gerrymandered teacher and student assignments to schools as well as school boundaries. They issued a flood of press releases with racist innuendoes about the "inherent" dangers of busing. Partly to convince everyone that they could not afford busing, they dwelt on their "impending bankruptcy" and refused decent salary raises to teachers — who responded with strikes that hardened community resistance to tax increases for the schools. To ease tensions, the federal government provided funds for transportation. (One of the first policy announcements by the Reagan Administration was its opposition to mandatory busing to achieve racial balance.)

While the laws that guided national education policy for twenty-six years are little changed, and hundreds of desegregation plans are still in the courts, the slowdown in civil rights enforcement and the clear and remarkably consistent message from the White House that parents, not government, should decide where their children attend school, have caused gains to fade somewhat. By 1984, one out of every three minority students in Texas, Louisiana, Mississippi, Alabama, and Tennessee was enrolled in a "racially isolated" school, and for the region as a whole the ratio had moved to 1 : 4 (37). Old funding practices for black schools had begun to reappear. In Georgia, white school boards presiding over systems with more than 70 per cent black students required 50 per cent less in property taxes than those with more than 70 per cent white students (5).

School Financing, Neighborhood Schools, and Neighborhood Segregation

Trying to desegregate schools in a segregated society committed to neighborhood schools is complicated at best. The problem is made more difficult by the heavy reliance on local property taxes for financing elementary and secondary schools. In 1960 localities provided 60 per cent of school revenues as compared with only 35 per cent from state funds. This pattern gradually shifted until by 1980, state revenues met 47 per cent of the cost, as compared with 40 per cent from local sources. While states have long had equalizing funds intended to help poorer school districts, conditions of sharing could be so filled with loopholes and exceptions that state aid often favored the favored. Lineberry and Sharkansky (49) cite a case in point. In the mid-1970s, twenty-five suburban school districts in the Detroit area

---

*Boston is a case in point. For a thoughtful, insightful, and compassionate book on the subject, none surpasses *Common Ground* by J. Anthony Lukas (50).

were able to spend an average of $500 per pupil more than the city of Detroit. In 1984, the richest New Jersey school districts spent $1,100 more than the poorest districts (35).* A series of state court decisions — in California, New Jersey, and Connecticut, among others — said the states had to equalize aid so that poor districts did not have to tax themselves more than rich districts to achieve equal levels of school opportunity. By 1981, twenty-eight states had reworked their aid formulae, generally giving more to every district but the highest increases to the poorest ones. Then the federal government consolidated many programs into block grants at reduced funding levels, and localities began raising taxes to compensate for the loss in federal aid. Desegregation efforts suffered disproportionately. Because states were uncertain if any federal aid would continue for long, they invested in single purchases, like computers, books, and the like. Also while federal funds previously favored poor school districts, as states took over this responsibility, a good number chose formulae based on enrollment, not relative need. In Mississippi only 5 per cent of the block funds were set aside for poor districts, as compared with 60 per cent in Connecticut. The large cities suffered the greatest loss. In effect, instead of $135.7 million in categorical aid, they received $50.3 million in block grants. The losses in several cities — Buffalo, Cleveland, St. Louis, and Seattle, for example — exceeded 85 per cent between 1981 and 1983 (6). In order to carry out court-ordered desegregation plans, urban schools often had to dip into other program funds or lay off teachers.

In days when 40 per cent of the nation's households — and only one quarter of the nation's voters — have children in elementary or secondary schools (87), convincing voters to support higher school budgets becomes ever more problematical. In recent years voters have tended to support tax hikes to enhance quality, but not equity. The hope is that some day the two will merge.

Because of these obstacles, some cities have chosen to abandon the neighborhood school concept. Milwaukee has earned well-deserved praise for its elaborate system of magnet schools, each specializing in particular grades, subjects, or teaching approaches. In 1981 fifty-three schools served 25,000 students, many of whom were bused daily. Families were free to choose their favorites. They commonly shopped around, asking questions about recent competency scores and the like. By creating a fine school system, free choice resulted in one of the most desegregated systems in the nation (103).

Another alternative is to desegregate neighborhoods. But "not next door" has long been a battle cry of segregationists. The isolation of blacks in the inner cities is no new phenomenon. But as better-off and better-educated blacks broke through barriers in the suburbs, the problems for

---

*Variations among states are even greater. In 1984 New York spent $4,783 per pupil while Utah spent only $2,119 (97).

those left behind and for cities have intensified. In 1954 all but one of the nation's largest cities had a white majority. By 1983 twenty-five had black or mixed majorities. Almost three fifths of all blacks live in large cities where a good many are clustered in decaying, neglected poverty areas, where four of every ten family heads in 1983 were jobless, three out of every ten had only an eighth grade education or less, and about the same proportion of families had no one working at all.

The effect on city revenues has been disastrous. Despite rising property taxes, special health and welfare levies, and new income taxes for residents and (too seldom) city-employed suburbanites, during the 1970s large cities hovered at the brink of bankruptcy. By borrowing from the private sector —which often resulted in transferring power to the city's bankers — and drastically cutting services and payrolls, the cities managed to survive (45). Then they encountered the Reagan Administration budget cuts and a prolonged recession, with the result that little could be done to make the poverty pockets in central cities more livable, safer, or more integrated. Even the mixed blessings of gentrification are losing ardent supporters in the face of continuing danger and tension — for every suburbanite who moves into the cities these days, two move out. Unless children are bused, in other words, desegregation of inner city schools is at a standstill.

As for the suburbs, while middle- and upper-income blacks have overcome obstacles and are buying homes, over 80 per cent of the population still live in essentially segregated neighborhoods. Even in the suburbs, blacks have often concentrated in particular neighborhoods, and many difficulties had to be surmounted to gain even this small toehold. As whites moved toward the periphery of cities, they organized restrictive covenants to bar blacks and other "undesirables." When this obstacle was outlawed by the courts, other more subtle blockages appeared. The practice of "redlining" by lending institutions, whereby credit is approved or rejected on the basis of neighborhood residence rather than individual credit histories, has long been a weapon invoked against minorities. Without credit, they found it impossible to buy or renovate homes. Rental agents added to the problem with countless ploys for refusing to show houses, breaking appointments, and delaying decisions until white buyers came forward. Despite fair housing legislation in 1968, one survey after another in the intervening years has revealed discriminatory practices against blacks, female-headed families, and families with children (1, 40, 53, 101).

As would be expected in a representative democracy where citizens vote their preferences and defeat representatives who go too seriously astray, federal housing laws and policies also show a high regard for the status quo — a fact that has always made for segregated neighborhoods. While the federal government was involved in public housing as early as the 1930s, the shortage of money followed by a shortage of manpower resulted in little progress until after World War II. In 1949 a new housing act was passed linking urban renewal with housing. It was a Janus-like creature, looking toward inner cities with public housing and slum clearance and toward suburbs with guaranteed low interest loans for single dwellings. Officials responsible for approving loans were cautioned against upsetting local residential patterns or approving poor credit risks (60). And so white suburbia was created.

Public housing was equally sensitive to local residential patterns, with the result that most public housing developments are located in inner cities or small towns where only one race resides and is likely to apply (89). The decision in recent decades to give priority for new units to the aged — predominantly white — at the expense of young fatherless families — predominantly black — has similar racist overtones.*

The Impact of School Desegregation

The impact of school desegregation on the access of blacks to the same educational opportunities and experiences that whites enjoy, which is what the remarkable shift in federal policy hoped to achieve, has been measured relentlessly, but rarely in useful or insightful ways. Most large-scale, widely publicized studies have been limited to numerical measurements of white–black pre- and post-*Brown* school enrollment and educational attainment, or comparative scholastic achievement as measured by various widely used tests. But no large study correlates findings with the degree of school desegregation or differences in the quality of education offered. These shortcomings have serious consequences. While comparative trends in enrollment and school attainment have intrinsic value, this is not true in a desegregation context, at least, of scholastic test results. Since they almost always show that blacks as a group trail well behind whites, unless the results are correlated with credible measures of educational quality and degree of desegregation, the results simply reinforce whatever preconceptions people (including officials) have about differences between the two races. This is born out by the flood of speculations following yearly announcements of test results. Even though the "rising tide of mediocrity" in the public schools is widely lamented, the gap between white and black scores is virtually always explained by variables external to the schools — individual motivation, family background, genes, poverty, peer pressures, neighborhood influences, too much TV, and the like, depending on the writer's liberal or conservative bias. But the interesting fact is that dozens of small studies involving one or a few schools not only flatly contradict the findings of large-scale studies, but also strongly

---

*In the private market, blacks, as compared with whites, have to pay more for less. Surveys made in 1977 are typical of others in recent years. They showed that among homeowners, the share of blacks paying 35 per cent or more of their income for housing was double that of whites. Black renters were in almost as serious a bind (96).

suggest that the quality of schooling has a great deal to do with test results. Where schools have strong, committed leadership, sound academically based curricula, high aspirations for and expectations of students (and parents), opportunities to overcome individual learning deficiencies, and teachers with a deep respect for learning and for their mission of developing literate, thoughtful, self-critical adults, whether schools are in slums or suburbs, or students are primarily black, Hispanic, or white, test results are well above average. If federal policies simply made more such schools available to minority children, it would be cause for celebration. But in the meantime, care should be taken not to confuse the comparative ability of students with the comparative quality of schools.

With these caveats in mind, let us turn to some of the findings. In 1940, only one tenth of blacks aged twenty-five to twenty-nine had graduated from high school. By 1983, eight tenths had done so, and of those twenty-five years or older just under one quarter had one or more years of college to their credit. In 1960, only three out of every 100 blacks had completed four or more years of college. By 1983, one in every ten had one or several college degrees to his or her credit. These accomplishments show up in labor force trends. In virtually all types of managerial or professional work, blacks are more heavily represented today than even as recently as 1970. While much more progress is needed before racial differences in schooling and jobs disappear, more gains were made between 1965 and 1980 than in any fifteen years since the turn of the century, and there is no reason to question that *Brown,* a vigorous civil rights movement, and the Presidential leadership that helped to enact the series of federal aids for education deserve the credit. The most serious shortfall was the failure of the economy to provide enough jobs to go around. Until this problem is addressed, education will never pay off as well for blacks and women as it does for white men.

By the mid-1970s, the issue of school desegregation had become almost hopelessly intertwined with the rise in violence and decline in quality of big-city schools — as though blacks and other minorities were responsible for the problems of society (102). Counterpoised with these problems are some remarkable success stories. In Charlotte, North Carolina, only 84 of 20,000 black children attended schools with white children in 1964. In 1970 the first court-ordered plan for systemwide busing to achieve racial balance was undertaken. Today the schools are integrated, and it has been a dozen years since anyone was elected to the Board of Education on an antibusing platform. For the past four years students have scored above average on national achievement tests, and the gap between white and black scores is narrowing. In Austin, Texas, after years of litigation, a "triethnic" desegregation plan became effective in 1980. Today about 29 per cent of the city's students are Hispanic and 19 per cent are black. They are intermixed at all levels with white students. Since this came about, there has been a reversal of a seventeen-year decline in enrollment, a rise in the school attendance rate, an improvement in test scores, and a narrowing of the gap in scores of minority and white students (59).

Back in 1954, *Brown* seemed to have little relevance for Seattle schools. Then during the 1960s and 1970s blacks moved north and west in increasing numbers. Today about half of Seattle's students are white, with the balance consisting of black, Asian, Hispanic, and American Indian children. In the fall of 1978, Seattle became the first major American city to undertake a voluntary, comprehensive desegregation plan. At first many white students left; now the rate is declining, and student achievement scores are rising. According to the National Education Association's report recounting gains in these three cities (59), school desegregation can also be credited with slowing (and in Seattle reversing) the trend toward greater residential segregation.

Shaker Heights, Ohio, is often regarded as a shining example of school and neighborhood desegregation. Considered one of the ten most integrated suburbs in the nation, its high school has also been named among the twelve finest high schools in the nation. In the early 1980s, Shaker Heights spent three times the national average per pupil (84). In Washington, D.C., where there are no longer any but a few white students, the all-black Kelly Miller Junior High School deserves mention for its scholastic achievements. When news that minority students were still lagging behind their white peers made headlines in 1985, this school, whose students come from families of modest means, including a significant number of public housing families, was among the city's leaders in achievement scores. Last reports showed Miller's 8th graders averaging 9.4 (4th month of the ninth grade) in math and 9.0 in reading. Ninth grade averages were 11.1 in math and 11.4 in reading. The school offers a humanities program for talented and gifted students: eighth graders averaged 12.9 on all test scores combined, while ninth graders averaged 13.6. After observing the school and its principal, Claude Moten, William Raspberry (72) concluded that the answer seemed to be that "Claude Moten believes his youngsters can learn, and is able to infect his staff with that belief." The school has a waiting list for its humanities program composed of "youngsters eager to prove they are just as bright."

Finally, the Upward Bound alumna who was recently awarded the prestigious Rhodes scholarship deserves mention. Barbara Harmon-Schamberger, child of an AFDC mother, in testifying before a Senate subcommittee about the importance of continued support for Upward Bound said quite simply, "Five years ago my highest aspiration was a steady paycheck from any reliable source — honorable, illegal or otherwise. My only goal: to stay off food stamps. My world views were limited to country boundaries. . . . West Virginia's last Rhodes Scholar was the son of a governor. I, their latest, am the daughter of a welfare mother." She is also West Virginia's first woman Rhodes Scholar (38).

Without doubt school desegregation also helped to precipitate a white migration to the suburbs, which left an almost all – minority group population in city schools.* But was this phenomenon due solely to desegregation? Or must responsibility also be shared by the rigidity of court desegregation plans, the failure of some ethnics to become really integrated into American mainstream society, the pervasive failure to reverse the decline and neglect of inner cities, and the failure to assure sufficient jobs to go around, thereby sparking tensions between modestly educated and relatively unskilled or redundant workers most threatened by joblessness? And how much responsibility for the failure to bring about more improvement in educational achievement among minority students — and for the "growing mediocrity" of the nation's schools — is due to the persistent emphasis in schools of education on teaching techniques rather than academic substance or on perfecting lesson plans rather than instilling a commitment to excellence?

Currently the Administration is financing a study of school desegregation focusing primarily on white flight to the suburbs. Gary Orfield, University of Chicago political scientist and widely recognized expert on school desegregation, on resigning from the study's advisory board, expressed reservations about the study, which was designed to examine not the effect of desegregation on minorities but only whether whites liked it (57). Too often, he commented, desegregation is viewed as a benefit only to minorities, and the widespread popular belief is that it harms whites academically, both suppositions unsupported by any credible evidence. In a society with increasing numbers of blacks and Hispanics, he noted, we are all enriched by knowing each other and having opportunities to form friendships and to work together in neighborhoods and communities without regard to race.

In retrospect, the sharp shifts in federal policy and the either/or mentality they signify have become as much part of the problem as the solution. Desegregating schools and investing in efforts to upgrade education never held promise of reversing educational outcomes for everyone. Nor are hands-off policies that rely chiefly on adversity to heighten motivation likely to do so. If we seriously wish to reach all children and youth effectively, or even to reduce functional illiteracy significantly, comprehensive programs, spanning at least the first two decades of life, that take into account the full range of backgrounds, aptitudes, and aspirations, will be necessary. We may not succeed in turning low achievers into high achievers, but we can at least take care that impediments of our own making are not the problem.

---

*Such migrations were most marked in the Northeast, where the share of students in predominantly minority schools rose from 67 per cent to 80 per cent during the 1970s, as blacks moved in and whites departed for the suburbs (39).

The Chronic Health Care Crisis ⸺⸺⸺⸺⸺⸺⸺⸺⸺⸺⸺

The U.S. has some of the finest doctors and hospitals in the world, and pays more per person for health care than any other nation. Yet, among industrialized countries, twelve had lower infant mortality rates in 1985, and all others have a lower percentage of low birth weight babies born each year (15, 68). In 1983 almost a quarter of our children under five years of age were not immunized against childhood diseases (58). About three tenths under seventeen had never seen a dentist (14). Only three fifths of pregnant women received any prenatal care during their first trimester (58).

The poor showing in the international community has a great deal to do with persistent poverty, racism, and our relative indifference to the health of *all* children, not just our own. But credits must also be shared with the different ways health care is defined, organized, and financed on the two sides of the Atlantic.

Federal Policy

The federal government has long assured personal health care for its own — the armed forces, veterans, and federal civilian employees. Efforts to enlist federal help in behalf of the poor date back to the mid-nineteenth century. In 1854 President Franklin Pierce, insisting the federal government could not grant aid just for humanitarian reasons, vetoed a bill, passed by comfortable majorities in both houses of Congress, that was intended to help states provide for mentally ill indigents. Years passed before anyone as passionately devoted to reform as Dorothea Dix (24, 86) who had initiated and promoted the theory of federal responsibility for mental health care tried again. But from the early 1900s almost uninterrupted efforts were made to secure federal help in compensating for the inequitable distribution of services in the private market (18, 42). Gradually, limited efforts succeeded in behalf of a handful of infants and mothers, crippled children, and disabled adults, community-based mentally ill, and public assistance recipients.*

Medicare and Medicaid. The great watershed legislation, Medicare for the aged and Medicaid for some of the poor, was approved in 1965. While widely hailed as a triumph of political negotiation, the compromises

---

*In 1947 the Hospital Survey and Construction Act — better known as Hill–Burton after its sponsors — also provided funds for hospital construction in underserviced areas. In discharging this mission, preference was given to suburbs and rural areas. Then as people moved out of central cities, and the hospital construction boom outdistanced need by about 100,000 hospital beds, urban ghettos became "medical wastelands" with neither doctors nor hospitals (55).

embodied in the laws evoked predictions of an unprecedented health care crisis fueled by rapidly inflating medical and hospital prices. The nub of the problem was the apparent reliance on faith, rather than rational controls, in shaping programs that promised to funnel billions of dollars to the private health care market in exchange for a more democratic distribution of services. To some critics it seemed naive in the extreme to move ahead without first requiring more efficient organization of services, setting limits on greed, and taking steps to correct the strong bias in the health care system toward treatment rather than prevention. The importance of these steps is underlined by the fact that in 1965 there were about 18 million aged, of whom one third were poor, and another 25 million younger poor persons. While some had qualified for earlier publicly financed health care, the enactment of Medicare and Medicaid meant that millions of new "paying" patients, many seeking long-overdue care for multiple problems, could soon be knocking at doctors' doors — a forecast of great interest on Wall Street.

Medicare consists of two insurance policies. The first, Medicare – Part A, is compulsory. It covers hospital and skilled nursing home care for disabled social security beneficiaries and virtually all people sixty-five years and older — two groups for whom private insurance was either prohibitively expensive or nonexistent at the time. Despite the frequency of chronic illness and disability among the elderly, cost-sharing arrangements are far more generous for short-term care of acute conditions. Coverage of psychiatric care is very limited, although many older people suffer with chronic depression (67). Part A is financed chiefly from social security taxes even though beneficiaries who retired before 1966 paid no share of taxes for this purpose, and many retiring since have paid very little. General revenue financing would have been more logical and more consistent with democratic values. It might also have forestalled the rising crescendo of attacks on the aged for "pushing up" health care costs, and facilitated extension of coverage to all uninsured citizens.

Medicare – Part B is voluntary insurance in which anyone covered by Part A may enroll by paying monthly premiums — $15.50 in 1986 — which in turn cover about one quarter of the cost, with most of the balance coming from general revenues. The insurance pays 80 per cent of "allowable charges" for specified medical and related services, equipment, and supplies. Unfortunately, some items commonly needed by the elderly are not covered, including eyeglasses, dentures, dental care, hearing aids and batteries, prescription drugs unless administered by health professionals, and constant attendants when other adults in the home work or become too exhausted to cope alone, as often happens when caring for victims of Alzheimer's disease, for example.

Both programs have deductibles and other cost-sharing features, which typically rise yearly. In 1986 the deductible in Part A rose to $492 for each benefit period.* To cover part or all of these costs and those for excluded items, many elderly people buy supplementary health insurance, a fact that has stimulated vast growth in supplementary insurance schemes and a proliferation of unscrupulous agents who con people into purchasing expensive, overlapping, and sometimes worthless policies out of dread of losing their independence (51).†

Medicaid, a federal grant-in-aid, helps states and localities to finance a range of health care services and supplies for individuals and families qualifying for AFDC and SSI, as well as a few "medically needy" families who except for income would qualify for these programs. Like AFDC, Medicaid programs vary considerably among the states. While intended to finance a broad range of services, the majority of Medicaid funds pay for hospitalization of the terminally ill aged and long-term nursing home care for the disabled aged. Congress also intended Medicaid to stimulate early screening, diagnosis, and treatment of poor children. But while millions have been immunized and received eye and ear examinations, more millions have not. In 1983 children constituted 44 per cent of all persons covered by Medicaid, but only 12 per cent of the funds were spent in their behalf. Tying the program to AFDC was an equally important obstacle, since this automatically excluded youngsters in most two parent families. In 1984 Congress moved to correct this problem by requiring states to extend coverage to all children under five years of age whose families met AFDC income and assets tests. But the new provision has been so little publicized that few families yet know about it.**

Administration: The Anomalous Role of Fiscal Intermediaries.

After trying for decades to persuade the federal government to enlarge its role in health care, the laws that finally emerged were filled with concessions to powerful opponents. Perhaps most important was the decision that Medicare was to be administered, not by a neutral agency, but by fiscal intermediaries — a collection of insurance firms to be selected by hospital administrators in each geographical area. Among other functions, fiscal intermediaries were charged with contracting with hospitals and nursing homes for patient care, setting maximum "allowable charges" for professional services, and processing and paying bills. "The Blues," as Blue Cross and Blue Shield are known in insurance circles, were by far the most frequent choice for this role.‡

---

*A new benefit period begins sixty days after the last hospitalization.

†The fear of catastrophic expense or loss could be considered a national phobia. Americans buy over 80 per cent of all insurance purchased in the world (41).

**The law includes a schedule for phasing-in children born after September 1983. All poor children under five are supposed to be covered by 1988.

‡In the Medicaid program, states could designate their preference. Many selected "the Blues."

"Allowable charges" — the maximum subject to federal reimbursement —were to reflect "customary" and "prevailing" professional fees and "reasonable" hospital charges. They were to be set and updated periodically. From the outset the responsible boards were dominated by the principal actors in the health care system. Hospital administrators sat on Blue Cross boards, and doctors proliferated on Blue Shield boards. Soon the sheer volume of work reinforced the natural tendency of symbiotic relationships to approach the process in a "once-over-lightly" mood. "Allowable charges" in Medicare and Medicaid often exceeded reimbursement rates in regular Blue Shield policies (10), while the expansionist tendencies of hospitals were whetted by "cost-plus" contracts. As with defense industries, they were reimbursed for actual costs, however much these exceeded estimates in yearly contracts. In short, hospitals were given a blank check to fill out as they pleased. During one term of office as Pennsylvania's Commissioner of Insurance, Dr. Herbert Denenberg saved Philadelphia residents alone over $65 million by requiring Blue Cross to void contracts with ninety hospitals and negotiate new ones with tougher cost controls (10). But he was a rare exception.

Inept administration compounded the problem. Investigations of the Blues during the 1970s found evidence of incompetent, careless administration, including failure to follow up on easily identified fraud, and approval of gross overcharges (46, 48). The problem was not limited to the Blues. In 1982 Trafford (93) reported that government auditors identified more than $70 million in overpayments for Medicaid patients in thirty states. Fraud and "abuse" accounted, they concluded, for up to 25 per cent of Medicaid payments. Intentional fraud, one Blue Cross official interviewed by Trafford insisted, was not common, but "hospital billing offices have a reputation for being notoriously sloppy and prone to mistake." Clearly this was not the quality of administration required in a program with no effective cost controls.

The Health Care System

The task of providing the best possible care to a growing population at reasonable cost is greatly complicated by the fact that health care is inherently evolutionary and inflationary. Everyone wants the best possible care, doctors have been socialized for centuries to make every effort to save lives, and every year brings new discoveries and inventions to help in the process. But our health care system has some uniquely inflationary attributes. Its strong bias toward hospitalization and high technologies has earned the U.S. the reputation for having a "sickness care system," not a health care system, while the strong preference of doctors for solo practice has caused our medical care to be derisively dubbed a "cottage industry." Finally, now that health care has become a very profitable business, increasing participants think of it as a "commodity," not a "service," and their preoccupation is with maximizing profits, not providing the best and most appropriate care. A closer examination of each side of the triangle will shed light on the cost dilemma.

The Bias Toward Hospitalization and High Technologies. The skewing of our medical care toward hospitalization (rather than home and office care or preventive services like nutrition programs for infants and nursing mothers) dates back to the Depression when hospitals were in severe financial straits because patients could not pay their bills. In this crisis, the American Hospital Association designed Blue Cross insurance to help patients and hospitals. Initiated at Baylor University Hospital in the mid-1930s, by the decade's end Blue Cross plans insured 4 million people for hospital care. By the early 1970s the number exceeded 100 million. Blue Cross officials long tried to convince the medical profession to collaborate with a plan to cover doctors' fees, but viewing "third party payments" as intrusions on the doctor–patient relationship, years passed before organized medicine yielded to Blue Shield. Even then, only treatment of sickness or injury was insured. So, many Americans became accustomed to putting off health checkups until they were sick or injured. Following this pattern, Medicare was specifically forbidden to spend a nickel on preventive care until 1982, when enrollment fees in Health Maintenance Organizations (HMOs) were finally approved for reimbursement.

With many households having only hospital insurance, it was tempting to shift treatment from doctors' offices to hospitals, just as higher financial returns on surgery were credited with the ascendance of surgery over more conservative treatment. In 1965, 6,544 operations were performed for every 100,000 elderly people. By 1975 the ratio had jumped to 15,482 per 100,000 (27). Doctors have been faulted repeatedly for overhospitalizing, overoperating, overtesting, and overmedicating. Some years back, Dr. John Bunker (9), distinguished anaesthesiologist, after studying medical care in the U.S. and England, concluded that half of the surgery performed here might be unnecessary. Some procedures were three times more prevalent than in England. After investigating coronary bypasses performed on elderly patients in 1982 — at a cost of $950 million to Medicare and the patients — the Congressional Office of Technology Assessment found at least 15 per cent to be of doubtful medical value (78). In 1984, the National Academy of Sciences reported that 19 per cent of hospital admissions and 27 per cent of patient days were unnecessary (61). Worse yet, in 1981, a study in one hospital found 30 per cent of patients suffering with iatrogenic disorders — those induced by their doctors' treatment or diagnostic procedures (13).

The tendency to duplicate expensive equipment in every hospital has been sharply criticized. A CAT* scanner may save some lives. But at a cost of $1 million each, is one essential in every hospital?† Prestige in hospital circles these days, the critics claim, is measured in terms of exotic equipment. But because of costly duplication a great deal is grossly underused.

Finally, the rise in hospital costs must to some extent reflect the fear of death that seems to burden so many people today, and the view in some quarters, including the Administration in Washington, that regardless of cost, "heroic" measures must always be made to save or prolong life. Among the heaviest costs are those incurred trying to save very low birth weight babies with multiple handicaps, trying to prolong life among the terminally ill aged, and in organ transplants and artificial heart surgery. One third of Medicare funds is spent on hospital care during the last twelve months of life, even though some patients would undoubtedly prefer to die naturally — and in greater dignity — at home (94). Until a national policy is formulated, reflecting a broad consensus and taking the range of individual and family feelings into account, consumers, doctors, and hospitals can scarcely be faulted for adding, willingly or unwillingly, to this burden on health care costs.

The Role of Doctors. In sorting out responsibility for rising costs, employers with health insurance plans, insurance companies, and medical scholars increasingly drew attention during the early 1980s to the unique role of physicians.

To paraphrase Dr. Arnold Relman, editor of the *New England Journal of Medicine* (74), in twentieth century America the medical profession has enjoyed a sovereignty unmatched by other professions. None has conducted its business with such autonomy or been so well rewarded. It has virtually unchallenged control of the health care market, where doctors' decisions account for 70 per cent of all expenditures. Once patients seek the doctor's help, he controls both demand and supply in a market socialized to follow his orders. For that matter, only his peers usually have the knowledge and competence to challenge him. But peer oversight has been notoriously weak.

It was not always this way, nor is it true worldwide. Harvard sociologist Paul Starr (88) recounts how U.S. doctors gained their autonomy and power. The decision to organize and handsomely support the American Medical Association had a great deal to do with it. The AMA functioned like a medieval guild intent on making its members larger than life and protecting their turf. For years the AMA limited the supply of doctors by

---

*Computerized axial tomography.

†A few doctors claim that patients with no problem suggesting need for a CAT scan yet insist on the procedure, even refusing to enter a hospital without such equipment. But surely doctors, like other professionals — and parents — can learn to handle unrealistic demands, and to recognize when patients require education and counseling, not indulgence.

controlling medical school admissions, by resisting federal aid for medical education, and by exploiting opportunities to denigrate and exclude osteopaths, chiropractors, podiatrists, physical therapists, and other professionals with specialized skills from licensed patient care. Even the training and education of medical technicians and nonmedical hospital and clinic administrators were perceived by the AMA as a threat to its private domain. By the same token, while doctors often acknowledged that nurses were necessary, they often treated them as handmaidens even when nursing shortages reached critical levels, rather than as partners who could improve patient care if their experience, talents, and judgment were given more scope and respect.

Eventually the surge in health insurance and the enactment of Medicare and Medicaid so enhanced the ability to afford health care that rocketing demand made it impossible for the AMA any longer to stem the increase in doctors or the hiring of other health professionals. In 1960 there were 250,000 doctors. Now the number has doubled, about 17,000 medical students graduate yearly, a surplus ranging from 50,000 to 180,000 is predicted by 1990, and there is already a "doctor glut" in large cities on the east and west coasts (47, 92).

It is too early to say what this portends for medical styles, structure, or charges. But the great majority of fourth-year medical students these days are opting for group, not solo, practice, usually for financial reasons, and young doctors in medically glutted cities are offering evening hours and making home calls (17, 95). Unlike so many older doctors who refuse to see Medicaid patients, out of financial necessity more younger doctors are doing so. As with all monopolistic markets, the laws of supply and demand have had little relevance heretofore in the health care market. Thus, studies show that more doctors and higher physician–population ratios made for higher fees, higher utilization rates, and more hospital admissions (21, 29, 36). Many experts assume that this will continue to be true. Although a few reports suggest a recent decline in doctors' incomes, between 1975 and 1983 their average income rose 36 per cent more than average family income, and the AMA claims that pretax net income of self-employed physicians averaged $115,900 in 1984. It was growing faster than expenses despite the much publicized and worrisome rise in the cost of malpractice insurance (23).* While theories explaining the upward push in medical fees abound, the fee-for-service model in U.S. medicine is most frequently blamed. Dr. George Crile (20), the renowned cancer specialist long associated with the Cleveland Clinic, claims this model keeps prices unrealistically high and inhibits the shift to new, better, but less profitable modes of treatment. He explains that although doctors may be dedicated to service,

---

*Malpractice premiums rose 80 per cent between 1975 and 1983 when five malpractice suits were filed for every 100 patients; by 1983 the ratio was 16 per 100,000. Obstetricians are by far the most frequently sued. In 1982 over $1 million was awarded in forty-five cases (2, 3).

when they become accustomed to a style of life depending on a stream of high fees — for a delicate surgical procedure, for instance — they tend to repeat it long after less costly and less traumatic therapy has proved just as or more effective. Dr. Crile would solve the problem by placing all practicing physicians on salary.

Megacorporate Health Care Services. For-profit corporations have long been part of the health care system. Barbara and John Ehrenreich (25) examined the rising fortunes of medical and hospital supply firms five years after Medicare and Medicaid were enacted. Almost one quarter of the $69 billion then spent on health care went for drugs and supplies sold to doctors, hospitals, and nursing homes. Hospital supplies alone cost $7.5 billion; by the 1980s they had become a $15 billion industry (31).

But the striking change in recent years is the rapid growth of for-profit health care *services*. Most nursing homes were always proprietary, as is still true.* But now the expectation of fine profits has lured entrepreneurs to buy or manage acute care hospitals, mental hospitals, alcohol and drug abuse centers, freestanding emergency clinics, preferred provider organizations, health maintenance organizations, and home health care services.

Of the 7,000 hospitals in the nation in 1983, 1,500 were owned or managed for profit-making purposes (83). The largest is the Hospital Corporation of America (HCA) with 360 hospitals and revenues of $4 billion in 1984. Like its competitors, Humana and American Medical International, HCA has its own health insurance plan which gives discount rates to subscribers who use HCA facilities (11, 91, 104). In addition to their U.S. holdings, the twenty-three major proprietary hospital firms own or manage sixty hospitals in other countries. The top ten chains operate over 70 per cent of all proprietary hospitals, and each has diversified into other health care areas, including nursing homes, freestanding clinics, and hospital and clinic management. Over 50 per cent of all nongovernmental mental hospitals are now owned by for-profit corporations (22, 82). Community Psychiatric Centers, Inc., headquartered in San Francisco, has seen its profits increase fourfold since 1980 (31).

The times have been propitious for these firms. As public funds dried up or were cut back, public and voluntary nonprofit hospitals closed or were in such serious financial straits that selling out seemed the best solution. In contrast with their difficulty in raising money, the commercial firms had

---

*The 21,500 now operating depend on government for over half of their income. Thomas Moore (56), writing in *Fortune,* waxes enthusiastic over the fine returns on investments in a few nursing home chains like Beverly, whose sales and earnings have grown over 50 per cent every year since 1976 (30). Unfortunately for the aged, an estimated half of the 1.4 million confined in nursing homes could be better and more happily cared for at home if there were adequate community services (99).

no trouble at all. In fact they are awaiting the next stream of cuts to pick up more good bargains.

One of the real accomplishments, among many claimed, is the range of new or more accessible alternatives to hospital care. Home health care is the most rapidly growing of this group. It has been predicted that by 1995 proprietary firms will have captured 60 per cent of the market (82, 85). Their development is a response to widely published reports that one fifth of the out-of-pocket expenses ($25 billion) of the elderly for health care yearly is spent on home health services. By early 1985, 17,000 home health care providers had responded to the challenge, and over 5,700 were already approved for Medicare reimbursement (32). The services provided are wide-ranging. Delivery of meals, different levels of nursing care, physical therapy, and instruction in the use of complex medical equipment are among the more common (44). Despite heavy start-up costs, this group of firms expected to collect $1.9 billion in revenues in 1985.

Freestanding clinics (dubbed both "doc-in-a-box" and "7 and 11 medicine") now spot the landscape. Usually sited in busy shopping centers, open virtually around the clock seven days weekly, by 1984 they numbered 1,100, were doing a booming business, and were receiving some rave notices from patients. In the fall of 1983, their average bill for emergency service was $42.39, about one third the cost for equivalent care in a hospital emergency ward (11, 22).

After a slow beginning, Health Maintenance Organizations (HMOs) are also riding the crest of what economists have dubbed "the industrial revolution in health care." Initially patterned after the model introduced by industrialist Henry Kaiser in 1942, HMOs today are usually organized by doctors intent on providing comprehensive care to enrollees who prepay annual fees. The particular virtue of HMOs is the strong incentive this payment plan provides for identifying problems early, treating them promptly, and avoiding overoperating, overdosing, and overtesting. Critics fear they may sometimes shortchange patients by refusing to approve necessary tests or hospitalization. By 1985, 350 HMOs had 16 million subscribers. Most were for-profit corporations. They have attracted primarily young families, although since Medicare payment of dues was approved, elderly people are increasingly choosing this option (11, 34, 82).

How are these health care corporations making such tidy profits? By cutting costs and raising prices. Labor costs are often reduced by "flexible" staffing (daily scheduling according to need), and wages tend to be low, except for doctors who are courted since their referrals are so vital. Heavy automation is also the rule. Regional and national firms have central computer systems that handle every possible detail. Prices are generally high, in some areas as much as 24 per cent higher than equivalent service in the nonprofit or public sectors, for hospital and nursing care. Careful credit checks also help to "cream" or screen out all but good credit risks. This is facilitated by careful siting in affluent suburbs, for instance. The firms generally prefer states in the Southwest with fewer hospital and nursing home regulations. Admirers doubt the quality of care has suffered, and are filled with praises for the centralized automated management and their success in filling genuine need. Critics fear the intrusion of the profit motive will shift the balance of medical power, and evidence already suggests that doctors are under considerable pressure in some of the for-profit corporations to keep profits in mind as they plan treatment or make referrals. Even when charges are reasonable, the fear arises that once the for-profits swallow up most of the nonprofits, prices for health care will rise dramatically. But the overriding question is whether profits, professional standards and ethics, and compassion can coexist. In the meantime the voluntary, nonprofit sector is busily aping the new arrivals by forming regional networks to facilitate centralized, automated administration, which is credited with saving as much as eighty-five cents per dollar over their earlier methods.

The Revolt Against Surging Health Care Costs

By the early 1980s the public was outraged by seemingly uncontrollable health care costs. Between 1965 and 1984 total expenditures rose from $41.5 billion to $387.4 billion, finally averaging $1,580 per person; and they were still rising faster than family income (62). During the last decade consumer prices pushed up 124 per cent, doctors' fees rose 148 per cent, and the cost of a hospital room jumped 234 per cent (61). While the debate in Washington and state capitals focused on Medicare and Medicaid, government expenditures for these programs only accounted for 23.6 per cent of the total. In 1983, of every dollar spent on personal health care, all levels of government paid forty cents, private insurance thirty-two cents, consumer out-of-pocket expenses accounted for twenty-seven cents, and private philanthropy one cent.

Leaders of the Revolt and Their Reform Initiatives. In the early 1980s, faced with the need to sell 70,000 cars in order to pay its health insurance bill, Chrysler Corporation hired Joseph Califano, Secretary of Health, Education, and Welfare under President Carter, to propose ways to cut costs. He began by asking what Chrysler's health care dollars ($530 per car) bought? No one really knew. Working with management, the union, and Blue Cross, the treatment given every employee over several years was catalogued and analyzed. The study disclosed cases of outright fraud, excessive and inappropriate hospital admissions, and exorbitant yearly price hikes. But to some extent it seemed that everyone — management, workers, health care providers and suppliers, and insurance firms — had behaved as though waste was a virtue and cost irrelevant. For no identifiable reason, average daily cost at six Detroit hospitals varied from $452 to $608, and average hospital stays from $3,208 to $6,077. Doctors' fees often bore no logical relation to either the time or skill required. The average charge for a twenty-minute cataract operation was $2,000, which meant opthamologists could make $1 million by performing three operations daily, four days weekly for forty-two weeks. But serious abdominal surgery requiring four or five hours cost an average of $1,500. Dermatologists were paid double the rate of other doctors. The Chrysler team confronted local health care providers, restructured health care benefits, and saved $58 million the following year (75).

In the meantime, corporations, unions, and insurance companies were writing new health insurance policies to set limits on extravagant doctors and expansionist hospitals (70). The new policies often required second opinions for elective surgery and advance submittal of treatment plans. Many paid the full cost only if workers went to "preferred providers" — preselected doctors and hospitals. Cost-sharing provisions increased in frequency and amount (26, 31).*

States were also cutting back programs. They had good reason to be worried. Between 1981 and 1983, the cost of employee health benefits rose by 47 per cent, while the cuts in Medicaid left states paying 46 per cent of the bill (66). In 1983 forty-six states passed 300 laws affecting health care, virtually all addressed to cost containment. Among other features, the new laws regulated hospital costs, limited funds for construction, encouraged doctors to compete by lowering prices, cut back eligibility for Medicaid, restricted and eliminated services, and introduced or increased cost-sharing arrangements. Altogether one million fewer people received Medicaid by 1984, and $3.9 billion less was spent on the program† (76).

With large and small employers, unions, insurance companies, state and local leaders, and some 20 to 30 million elderly people (12) joined in battle to constrain costs, a bill modelled after cost containment experiments tested in several northeastern states was written, passed by both houses of Congress, and signed into law within a record four months.

The Federal Response. The new law applies only to Medicare reimbursements in acute care hospitals or other short-term medical facilities.** Over a three-year period beginning October 1, 1983, the basis for Medicare reimbursement was shifted gradually from *actual cost* to a new prospective

---

*However beneficial these changes were from some perspectives, they were very difficult on modestly paid workers with young children. For many the new charges were higher than they could afford (43).

†Some federal cuts were restored in 1984 by Congress, and states also became somewhat more generous.

**Senator Edward Kennedy urged that the law be extended to nursing homes and to charges for all hospital patients in order to forestall premature hospital discharges or the shifting of unreimbursed Medicare costs to younger patients (7).

payment plan reimbursing a *fixed cost* for treating a specific medical condition. This approach is also known as the DRG plan after the approximate 450 "diagnostic-related groups" that were analyzed before the law became effective. It provides for treating only one condition at a time, with each having a preset average duration of in-hospital care. If patients remain longer, the hospital bears the additional cost; if they go home sooner, hospitals retain the profits. It was expected that hospital stays would vary, as usual, but would balance out at about the average.

In the year after the law became effective, hospital admissions dropped sharply, and the length of hospital stays for Medicare patients fell 10 per cent (71). For the first time since 1966 Medicare payments to hospitals rose by only 6 per cent, while nationwide health care costs grew by only 9.1 per cent, the lowest in many years (62). To everyone's relief, the Medicare trust fund was pronounced solvent until at least 1998 (65). Paradoxically, despite having less business, hospital profit margins on Medicare patients rose 14 per cent, about triple the average profit margin in recent years on patients of all ages (4, 79, 80).

What constituted unreserved good news in some quarters raised alarms and skepticism in others. Some economists doubted the new law had anything to do with declining hospital admissions or more modest advances in health care costs. During recessions, they pointed out, workers in fear of layoffs and loss of health insurance hasten to take care of long-standing health problems. When economic conditions improve, they are eager for steady work, and hospital admissions fall. Health care specialists credited the changes to the rapidly increasing alternatives to hospitalization. Sociologists hypothesized that shared consciousness of runaway costs and the fears of health care providers that even more severe controls might be enacted — and extended to all charges and all patients — caused everyone involved to modify expectations and demands.

But if each was partly correct, none told the whole story. During 1985 about 5,000 complaints were received by the Senate Committee on Aging, chaired by Senator John Heinz of Pennsylvania (81). In addition, consumer groups, senior citizen organizations, the AMA, and many individual doctors, patients, and families claimed that cost savings had been accomplished at the expense of good health care for elderly patients. The General Accounting Office and the inspector general of the Department of Health and Human Services in Washington publicly faulted the Health Care Finance Administration's failure to prevent abuses of the system or even to collect data or to investigate complaints so that Congress would know what needed correction. Instead it simply issued regulations reminding hospitals to notify patients of their right to protest premature discharges (33, 63).

What had gone wrong? First, instead of using the DRG length of stay as an *average,* hospitals considered it a *ceiling,* never to be exceeded. Families complained of gravely ill patients dying en route home after premature discharge, of others arriving home too sick to be cared for adequately, and of many more, especially the poor or those without supplementary insurance, being "dumped" on public hospitals.* Doctors complained of administrative pressures to send patients home early. In one hospital lists were posted in the physicians' lounge of doctors who "cost the hospital money" or "saved money for the hospital," according to how quickly they discharged Medicare patients (81). ABCs documentary, "Growing Old in America," broadcast in early 1986, told of a California hospital chain offering to share "savings" with doctors who discharged patients before the "ceiling" was reached. Pressures like this were particularly likely in hospital chains that owned nearby nursing homes — where cost-plus reimbursement was still in effect.

Geriatric specialists pointed out that the new reimbursement formulae virtually ruled out very promising, but time-consuming treatment methods. Dr. Frank Veitch, chief of vascular surgery at Montefiore Hospital in the Bronx (98), illustrated the problem. Patients with severe disabling arteriosclerosis of one or both legs once had no option but amputation. But in recent years, 90 per cent of the 2,000 patients with this condition who received vascular surgery were restored to full use of their legs and returned to their previous life style. The process well exceeds DRG time limits, but the alternative, amputation, means lifelong wheelchair confinement for most patients, usually in a nursing home at a cost up to $100,000 yearly.

Limiting the new plan to hospitals, it was found, had encouraged doctors to perform more procedures in the office, but not always at a savings. A two-year study released in late 1985 reported that fraud by opthamologists was costing the federal government $2 billion yearly and inducing thousands of elderly people to undergo unnecessary eye surgery (28). Many instances of exorbitant charges for lens implants, at hundreds, even thousands, of dollars over the limit set for this twenty-minute surgical procedure in hospitals ($2,400), were reported.†

While this study was underway, Medicare–Part B became one of the most rapidly escalating programs in the federal budget, and Congress decided to freeze doctors' fees in Medicare, simultaneously offering incentives to participate in the program and to accept Medicare ceilings as

*The Department of Health and Human Services was supposed to pay higher rates to hospitals serving large numbers of poor patients, but refused to do so until Congress and a federal judge ordered compliance. Finally in July 1985 the department agreed to *consider* special reimbursement only if hospitals could prove their higher costs were due to accepting more poor patients (64).

†Eye doctors were also offered, and many accepted, kickbacks for placing orders for lenses with particular suppliers. The "bribes" included large sums of cash, free trips to Europe, cash deposits in Caribbean banks, free stock in the company or surgical equipment, and free use of boats, cars, and resort homes.

payment in full (69). Two thirds of the doctors agreed to do so, just under half for all elderly patients, and the balance for some (77). Medicaid patients fared less well. States set limits so low — $9 for an office visit in New York, $263 for "regular delivery" of a baby in Maryland — that many doctors refused to see Medicaid patients or threatened to bow out unless fees were raised (1).

Almost 30 million Americans today have no health insurance, and at least 12 million encounter serious problems in trying to secure medical service (16). The group includes poor women pregnant with their first child who no longer qualify for AFDC, and in growing numbers receive no or very little prenatal care. In 1985 for the first time in eight years, death rates of infants between one month and one year of age increased. It was the largest increase in eighteen years, and the upward trend shows no signs of slackening. As Marian Wright Edelman (15) has asked, "How many four-pound babies will it take to balance the federal budget?"

References

1. American Civil Liberties Union, Cleveland Chapter. *ACLU Legislative Alert.* February 1980, p. 2.
2. Associated Press: Baltimore. "Obstetricians May Stop Handling Medicaid Cases." *Washington Post,* December 29, 1985.
3. Associated Press: Chicago. "Malpractice Suits Near 'Crisis' Point, AMA Says." *Washington Post,* January 18, 1985.
4. Associated Press: Washington. "Hospital Profits Climb in New Medicare Plan." *New York Times,* November 28, 1985.
5. Atkinson, Rick. "Segregation Rises Again in Many Southern Schools." *Washington Post,* April 1, 1984.
6. Barringer, Felicity. "Studies Say U.S. Desegregation Support Fell Under Block Grants." *Washington Post,* September 18, 1983.
7. Beck, Melinda. "More Red Ink for Medicare." *Newsweek,* **102** (August 1, 1983), p. 28.
8. *Brown* v. *Board of Education of Topeka.* 347 U.S. 483 (1954).
9. Bunker, John P. "Surgical Manpower." *New England Journal of Medicine,* **232** (1970), pp. 135–144.
10. Butler, Robert N. *Why Survive? Being Old in America.* New York: Harper & Row, Publishers, 1975, pp. 208–212.
11. Carey, Joseph. "Health Benefits for Employees Enter New Era." *U.S. News and World Report,* **99** (July 22, 1985), pp. 73–74.
12. Carlson, Elliot. "Hospital Horror: How Patients are Run Down by the Health Care Steamroller." *Modern Maturity,* (October/November, 1984), pp. 108–114.
13. ———. "Is Our Health Care System Killing Us?" *Modern Maturity,* (April/May 1984), pp. 30–36.
14. Children's Defense Fund. *Black and White Children in America: Key Facts.* Washington, D.C.: Children's Defense Fund, 1985, p. 83.

15. ————. *A Children's Defense Fund Budget: An Analysis of the President's FY 1986 Budget and Children.* Washington, D.C.: Children's Defense Fund, 1985, pp. 5, 80–93.
16. Cohn, Victor. "The Forgotten Patient." *Washington Post,* Health section, February 27, 1985.
17. Colburn, Don. "Doctor Increase Outstrips Population Growth." *Washington Post,* Health section, November 27, 1985.
18. Corning, Peter A. *The Evolution of Medicare.* Social Security Research Report no. 29. Washington, D.C.: U.S. Department of Health, Education, and Welfare, 1969.
19. Crain, Robert L. *The Politics of School Desegregation.* Garden City, New York: Doubleday & Co., Inc., Anchor Books, 1969, pp. 374–385.
20. Crile, George, Jr. *Surgery: Your Choices and Alternatives.* New York: Delacorte Press/Seymour Lawrence, 1978, pp. 113–140.
21. Davis, Karen and L. B. Russell. "The Substitution of Hospital Outpatient Care for Inpatient Care." *Review of Economics and Statistics,* **54** (May 1972), pp. 283–301.
22. Dentzer, Susan. "The Big Business of Medicine." *Newsweek,* **102** (October 31, 1983), pp. 62–74.
23. ————. "Taking a Scalpel to Doctors." *Newsweek,* **101** (January 14, 1983), pp. 58–59.
24. Deutsch, Albert. *The Mentally Ill in America.* Garden City, New York: Doubleday, Doran & Co., 1938, pp. 158–185.
25. Ehrenreich, Barbara and John Ehrenreich. "The Medical Industrial Complex." In David M. Gordon, Ed., *Problems in Political Economy: The Urban Perspective,* 2d ed., rev. Lexington, Mass.: D. C. Heath & Co., 1977, pp. 437–447.
26. English, Carey W. "Why Fringe Benefits are Levelling Off." *U.S. News and World Report,* **98** (January 14, 1985), p. 68.
27. Estes, Carroll L. *The Aging Enterprise: A Critical Examination of Social Policies and Services for the Aged.* San Francisco: Jossey-Bass Publishers, 1979, p. 104.
28. "Eye Doctor Fraud Victimizes Seniors." *Senior Citizen News,* **6** (September 1985), p. 2.
29. Feldstein, Martin. "An Econometric Model of the Medicare System." *Quarterly Journal of Economics,* **85** (February 1971), pp. 1–20.
30. Fisher, Anne B. "A 'Cutback' Play in Health Stocks." *Fortune,* **108** (September 5, 1983), pp. 137–138.
31. Fisher, Anne B. "The New Game in Health Care: Who Will Profit?" *Fortune,* **111** (March 4, 1985), pp. 138–143.
32. Freudenheim, Milt. "Business and Health Profit Squeeze in Home Care." *New York Times,* August 13, 1985.
33. ————. "Cost Controls Raise Concerns in Health Care." *New York Times,* July 30, 1985.
34. ————. "Surge of Prepaid Health Plans." *New York Times,* December 15, 1984.
35. Friendly, Jonathan. "Efforts Are Failing to Close Gaps Separating Rich and Poor Schools." *New York Times,* February 19, 1985.

36. Fuchs, Victor R. and Marcia J. Kramer. *Determinants of Expenditures for Physicians' Services in the United States, 1948–1968.* New York: National Bureau of Economic Research, 1972.

37. Gest, Ted. "School Desegregation Grinds to a Halt in South." *U.S. News and World Report,* **96** (May 21, 1984), pp. 49–50.

38. Gilliam, Dorothy. "Upward Bound." *Washington Post,* September 23, 1985.

39. Goodman, Walter. "Brown v. Board of Education: Uneven Results 30 Years Later." *New York Times,* May 17, 1984.

40. Greene, Jane G. and Glenda P. Blake. *How Restrictive Rental Practices Affect Families with Children.* HUD 00001624 Project. Springfield, Va.: National Technical Information Service, July 1980.

41. Guarino, Richard and Richard Trubo. *The Great American Insurance Hoax: How to Protect Yourself against Insurance Fraud.* Los Angeles: Nash Publishing Co., Inc., 1974, p. 5.

42. Hirschfield, Daniel. *The Last Reform.* Cambridge, Mass.: Harvard University Press, 1970.

43. "The Insurance Gap Widens." *CDF Reports,* **7** (December 1985), p. 6.

44. Johnson, Kathryn. "Major Surgery for Ailing Medicaid Program." *U.S. News and World Report,* **95** (October 17, 1983), pp. 91–93.

45. Judd, Dennis R. *The Politics of American Cities: Private Power and Public Policy.* Boston: Little, Brown & Co., 1970, p. 230.

46. Kass, David I. and Paul A. Pautler. *Physician Control of Blue Shield Plans.* Staff Report. Washington, D. C.: Federal Trade Commission, Bureau of Economics, November 1978, pp. 12–58.

47. Krieger, Lisa. "Too Many Doctors." *Washington Post,* Health section, February 27, 1985.

48. Law, Sylvia A. *Blue Cross: What Went Wrong?* New Haven: Yale University Press, 1976, pp. 59–114.

49. Lineberry, Robert L. and Ira Sharkansky. *Urban Politics and Public Policy,* 3rd ed. New York: Harper & Row, Publishers, 1978, pp. 312–316.

50. Lukas, J. Anthony. *Common Ground.* New York: Alfred A. Knopf, 1985.

51. Lyons, Richard D. "Elderly in the U.S. Are Sold Unneeded Health Insurance as Medicare Supplement, Congressional Staff Finds." *New York Times,* November 28, 1978.

52. Maeroff, Gene I. "After 20 Years, Education Programs Are a Solid Legacy of Great Society." *New York Times,* September 30, 1985.

53. Mariano, Ann. "Discrimination in Housing Said to Be Widespread." *Washington Post,* October 26, 1985.

54. Matthew, Donald R. and James W. Prothro. "Stateways v. Folkways Critical Factors in Southern Reactions to Brown v. Board of Education." In G. Dietze, Ed., *Essays on the American Constitution.* Englewood Cliffs, N.J.: Prentice-Hall, Inc., 1964, p. 144.

55. McKinney, Edward A. "A Health Care Crisis — for Whom?" *Health and Social Work,* (February 1976), pp. 101–106.

56. Moore, Thomas. "Way Out Front in Nursing Homes." *Fortune,* **107** (June 13, 1983), pp. 142–150.

57. Mouat, Lucia. "Politics Holds Back School Desegregation." *Christian Science Monitor,* November 29, 1985.

58. National Center for Health Statistics. *Health, United States 1984.* Washington, D.C.: U.S. Government Printing Office, 1984, pp. 10–11.

59. National Education Association. *Three Cities That Are Making Desegregation Work.* Washington, D.C.: National Education Association, 1985.

60. Orfield, Gary. "Federal Policy, Local Power, and Metropolitan Segregation." *Political Science Quarterly,* **89** (Winter 1975–76), p. 786.

61. Pascall, Glenn. *The Trillion Dollar Budget: How to Stop Bankrupting America.* Seattle, Wash.: University of Washington Press, 1985, p. 182.

62. Pear, Robert. "Growth in Spending on Health Care Slows to 9.1%." *New York Times,* August 1, 1985.

63. ————. "Medicare Extends Patients' Rights." *New York Times,* January 9, 1986.

64. ————. "Medicare Payments Raised for Hospitals Serving Poor." *New York Times,* July 2, 1985.

65. ————. "Medicare Trust Fund is Seen as Healthy Until 1998." *New York Times,* March 29, 1985.

66. ————. "States Are Moving to Control Costs for Health Care." *New York Times,* February 27, 1984.

67. President's Commission on Mental Health. *Task Panel Reports 1978.* Washington, D.C.: U.S. Government Printing Office, 1978. Vol II, pp. 454–459.

68. "Progress Against Infant Deaths Slows." *CDF Reports,* **7** (April 1985), pp. 1–2.

69. Quinn, Jane Bryant. "Medicare Patients Can Help to Enforce Law Limiting Doctors' Fees." *Washington Post,* Washington Business section, July 23, 1984.

70. ————. "A New War on Health Care Costs." *Newsweek,* **103** (April 9, 1984), p. 87.

71. Raske, Kenneth E. "Give the New Hospital Payments System a Try." *New York Times,* January 4, 1986.

72. Raspberry, William. "The Mystery of Kelly Miller." *Washington Post,* September 20, 1985.

73. Reinhold, Richard. "25 Years After Desegregation, North's Schools Lag." *New York Times,* May 17, 1979.

74. Relman, Arnold S. "The Power of the Doctors." *The New York Review,* March 29, 1984, pp. 29–33.

75. Rich, Spencer. "Chrysler Saves $58 Million in Battle Against Health Care Waste." *Washington Post,* Washington Business section, April 19, 1985.

76. ————. "Medicaid Facing New Cutbacks." *Washington Post,* December 23, 1984.

77. ————. "Medicare Fee Curb Accepted in Record Number of Cases." *Washington Post,* January 25, 1985.

78. ————. "Medicare Study Blames Costs on Advances." *Washington Post,* July 27, 1984.

79. ————. "Shorter Stays Help to Cut Costs of Health Policy." *Washington Post,* May 22, 1985.

80. ————. "Study Finds Hospitals Profit Despite Limits on Medicare." *Washington Post,* November 26, 1985.

81. Rovner, Sandy. "Medicare: The Cost of Cost-Cutting." *Washington Post,* Health section, January 15, 1986.

82. Salmon, J. Warren. "Organizing Medical Care for Profit." In John B. McKinlay, Ed., *Issues in the Political Economy of Health Care.* New York: Tavistock Publications, 1984, pp. 143–187.

83. Sanoff, Alvin P. "A Conversation with Paul Starr: Medicine Has Overdrawn Its Credit in American Society." *U.S. News and World Report,* **95** (September 12, 1983), pp. 77–78.

84. Shaker Heights City School District. "The Sun Also Rises." *The School Review,* September 1981, p. 1.

85. Shenson, Douglas. "Will 'M.D.' Mean 'More Doctors'?" *New York Times,* May 23, 1985.

86. Snyder, Charles M. *The Lady and the President: The Letters of Dorothea Dix and Millard Fillmore.* Lexington, Ky.: The University Press of Kentucky, 1975.

87. Solorzano, Lucia. "Schools Open with a Lean Year Ahead." *U.S. News and World Report,* **93** (September 6, 1982), pp. 43–45.

88. Starr, Paul. *The Social Transformation of Medicine.* New York: Basic Books, Inc., Publishers, 1983.

89. Steiner, Gilbert Y. *The State of Welfare.* Washington, D.C.: Brookings Institution, 1971, p. 158.

90. *Swann v. Charlotte-Mecklenburg County Schools* 402 US 1 (1971).

91. Tolchin, Martin. "Private Hospitals Are Now Offering Health Insurance." *New York Times,* July 5, 1985.

92. Trafford, Abigail. "For Doctors, Too, It's a Surplus." *U.S. News and World Report,* **95** (December 19, 1983), pp. 62–64.

93. ———. "Those High Hospital Bills Aren't Always Right." *U.S. News and World Report,* **92** (May 17, 1982), unpaginated.

94. ——— and Clemens P. Work. "Soaring Hospital Costs." *U.S. News and World Report,* **95** (August 22, 1983), pp. 39–42.

95. Tracy, Eleanor Johnson. "Physician, Sell Thyself." *Fortune,* **111** (April 1, 1985), pp. 109–110.

96. U.S. Bureau of the Census. *Current Housing Reports,* Series H–150–77, Annual Housing Survey 1977, Pt. E, Table A–1.

97. ———. *Statistical Abstract of the United States 1985.* Washington, D.C.: U.S. Government Printing Office, 1984, p. 143.

98. Veith, Frank J. "No Way to Lower Health Care Costs." *New York Times,* September 16, 1985.

99. Vladeck, Bruce C. *Unloving Care: The Nursing Home Tragedy.* New York: Basic Books, Inc., Publishers, 1980, pp. 3–4.

100. Wicker, Tom. "Busing After a Decade." *New York Times,* August 26, 1981.

101. Wienk, Ronald E. et al. *Measuring Racial Discrimination in American Housing Markets, The Housing Market Practice Survey.* Washington, D.C.: U.S. Government Printing Office, April 1979.

102. Williams, Dennis A. "Why Public Schools Fail." *Newsweek,* **97** (April 20, 1981), pp. 62–65.

103. ——— and Eric Gelman. "Hope for the Schools." *Newsweek,* **97** (May 4, 1981), pp. 66–72.

104. Worthy, Ford S. "A Health Care Merger That Pains Hospitals." *Fortune,* **111** (June 24, 1985), pp. 106–109.

CHAPTER 11

Anti-poverty Strategies: Social Services

Introduction

During the 1960s there were vigorous debates over how to end poverty and how to improve and expand the social services. That the two issues were soon joined is in part testimony to the reluctance of Americans to undertake the basic structural and attitudinal changes required to create the Great Society that became the official goal of the decade. Even in those days when the national conscience about poverty was at times aroused to fever pitch, only half measures were seriously contemplated. The way issues were framed sounds rather simplistic today. First there was the question of which was the better anti-poverty strategy, cash transfers or services, as though moving ahead on both fronts simultaneously, let alone undertaking large-scale reforms like full employment and tax reform, was impossible to contemplate.

When services were favored, another question arose. Which was the better anti-poverty investment, "soft" or "hard" practical services? These concepts came into vogue as opponents of psychological counseling or casework began to push for "practical" services like child day care for working mothers, vocational education, on-the-job training, and the like. While the distinction helped to correct the overemphasis on personal disorders as a cause of poverty and encouraged the development of a wider range of services, the causes and consequences of poverty were too varied and complex, and the damage inflicted by childhood poverty often too extensive, to be resolved by either "soft" counseling or "hard" practical services. Experience had long confirmed that to achieve even modest goals for poor families, both were often necessary for either to succeed. But policy debates in the 1960s rarely opted for the holistic approach. One reason was the prevailing political opportunism. It was as though policy advisors and policy makers settled in advance for whatever seemed politically feasible. One result was the greatest burst of social welfare legislation since the 1930s. Another was widespread confusion in the social welfare marketplace as old and new collided and both tried to protect and enlarge their joint and respective turfs.

220

Social services are organized under public auspices, in voluntary, non-profit organizations, and in the economic market. With considerable overlap, especially between the last two, where people seek help largely depends on their income. Some services, like adoption and protective services for children or the elderly, are organized publicly as part of the protective function of the state. Increasingly in recent decades, social service professionals have combined a nine-to-five job in the voluntary, nonprofit sector with part-time private practice.*

The 1970s witnessed a mushrooming of social services. By 1975 observers were writing about the "emergence of a system of personal social services" that might some day take its place among other "freestanding" service systems like health care, education, housing, and manpower training. While the boundaries of such a system are indistinct, there is less doubt about its major functions. The model that follows is indebted to both Morris (28) and Kahn (21). See both for additional typologies.

- Individual and family counseling to help people cope better with "anxieties, ambiguities, and distresses of modern urban life" (28)
    Examples: social casework, marital counseling, family therapy
- Concrete services to facilitate role performance
    Examples: child day care, homemakers, meals-on-wheels, family planning services, vocational rehabilitation, transportation services
- Encouragement and strengthening of social relationships and resources
    Examples: social networking, senior citizen centers, youth centers, congregate meals, summer camps, recreation services, neighborhood settlements, neighborhood development
- Protective and rehabilitative services for abused, neglected, abandoned, exploited, wayward, and delinquent children, battered wives, and exploited or abused elderly persons
    Examples: substitute care including foster homes, runaway shelters, institutional care, and group homes; legal services, and services to reunite families or prepare people for return to community life
- Advocacy, liaison, and access
    Examples: active help to service users in securing needed services and benefits, information and referral services, efforts to improve the functioning of social service networks and to assure equal access

By the late 1970s the services listed above, and many others, reached all income and age groups. The growth in services reflected heightened demand, creative responses in the economic market, and the stimulative effect of federal leadership and federal funds. But while the poor had more

*Kahn and Kamerman's (22) excellent study of where Americans turn for personal services today includes a chapter on services provided through the economic market and the personnel involved.

services, they were still shortchanged so far as community-based preventive and supportive services were concerned, a fact of life in the U.S. that has long helped to explain their overrepresentation in grim child-custodial institutions, prisons, and juvenile reformatories. In the 1980s when the federal government cut budgets, eliminated or restricted programs, and repealed regulations that protected equity and access, the distribution of preventive and supportive services became even more concentrated. In the following pages, the evolution of social services for the poor is traced with particular attention to (a) the role of the federal government, (b) the anti-poverty impact of different service strategies, and (c) the scarcity of effective services for troubled children and youth.

Historical Overview of Major Federal Legislation _____

The Social Service Amendments of 1962

Background. For years public welfare officials insisted that because their caseloads were filled with disorganized, multiproblem families, cash grants were not enough; social services were also essential. Nothing in the public assistance grants-in-aid prohibited federal reimbursement for service costs, but several factors discouraged state officials from taking the initiative. Annoyed by federal audit exceptions, they preferred not to risk launching new, costly activities. Also, the pressured, form-ridden, social control atmosphere of public assistance and its low salaries warded off qualified social work professionals. Fewer than 1 per cent of welfare workers and only 14 per cent of their supervisors had MSW degrees in 1960 (43). Most jobs on the front line where services would be delivered were temporary way stations for unemployed teachers, college dropouts, and high school graduates with no better job in sight; and turnover rates were inordinately high. The situation differed among states. In depressed southern labor markets, most personnel had at least graduated from college; up in Massachusetts, virtually none had. Added to these barriers was the inability — and among some key public welfare leaders the adamant refusal — to consider purchasing services from the voluntary, nonprofit sector which employed most credentialed social workers. By the early 1960s the hope of public welfare leaders was for their agencies to become great umbrella organizations, attracting all income classes for a full range of social services. In part this aspiration reflected their skepticism about professional counseling whether provided by social workers, psychologists, or psychiatrists. Just "naturally warm people" could be more effective, they implied in one Congressional hearing after another. As for the poor, if welfare workers had more time to devote to families, it was argued, more welfare families would become self-supporting.

About the time of President Kennedy's election, a national welfare crisis was precipitated. A new City Manager in Newburgh, New York, insisting that recent migrants, loafers, and immoral mothers proliferated on the welfare rolls and were bankrupting the city, convinced the City Council to approve a long list of restrictions. They ranged from limiting the time a family could receive welfare, requiring able-bodied people to work, and threatening to place children of unmarried mothers in foster care to forcing welfare families to pick up checks at the police station. Since localities had no power to make unilateral policy in federal – state public assistance programs, this package was soon declared illegal. But it attracted national press coverage and provoked a ground swell of public support. National leaders heard the message: welfare reform was overdue.*

Several advisory groups, weighted with welfare officials and social work educators, were quickly assembled to advise the president. To no one's surprise, considering their membership, providing social services to welfare families was high among the recommendations. In 1962 Congress enacted social service amendments in company with other changes in the public assistance titles of the Social Security Act.

Federal Policy and Its Impact. The new amendments required states to provide services directed toward preparing people for self-support, strengthening families, enabling the aged to remain in the community as long as possible, and facilitating institutionalization if necessary. States were promised 75 per cent reimbursement — rather than the usual 50 per cent for administrative activities — for the cost of "defined" social services and related staff development activities. To introduce a modicum of prevention, people could qualify for services who had been or were likely to become dependent within one year. To make certain that services were appropriate, social studies were required on everyone designated to receive services. To provide "ample" time for workers to provide services, their caseloads were to be reduced to no more than sixty cases. In turn, supervisors were to be responsible for no more than seven service workers.

To the consternation of many professional social workers who had supported the new amendment, public welfare agencies hired very few additional professionals, and had to be pressured to recruit MSWs for even their top staff development positions. But there was no delay in reorganizing and producing social studies in order to qualify for the generous 75 per cent federal funding.

In Washington, conflict immediately developed over what the "defined services" should be. Social casework, the primary specialty of graduate schools of social work, eventually won top billing, and in time state man-

---

*For a vivid account of this crisis and its resolution, see *The Wasted Americans* by Edgar May (27).

uals dutifully spelled out what social casework was. With the exception of appointing or adding homemakers to help the aged, very few "hard" services were suggested or offered, although countless services would have been consistent with the broad mandate in the law. No reliable research regarding the content or impact of services was carried out concurrently, but in the late 1960s Hollingsworth and Handler (15) reviewed case records in Wisconsin with these questions in mind. The typical service worker, they learned, visited families once every three months (as required by federal law) and had a brief, unfocused, pleasant chat. No evidence was found even suggesting, let alone proving, that these contacts changed behavior, produced needed household or personal items, or resulted in making any new resources available to families. About the best that could be claimed was that they were probably harmless, largely because welfare workers carefully avoided sensitive or controversial issues in their effort to keep relationships with families relatively unruffled.

Demonstration Projects. The 1962 amendments also authorized a very flexible demonstration grant program to test ways of reducing dependency. Numerous projects improved the identification with and preparation for work, and helped to identify changes required in public assistance law to make it a more positive force in the lives of the poor.*

One group of projects provided school-related work for AFDC high school students and waived the federal requirement that their earnings be counted in determining eligibility. When well-directed (which was too seldom the case), the projects caused school dropout rates to plummet, grades to rise, teacher–student relationships to improve, and a heightened identification with work to develop. One far-reaching result was an amendment to the Social Security Act permitting — later requiring — student earnings to be disregarded routinely. Another project facilitated the collection of national data on grade levels, by age, of AFDC school dropouts. Over half were found to be two years behind normal grade placement when they left school, which could only increase their risk of lifelong poverty. The law was soon amended to permit school children to qualify for AFDC until their twenty-first birthday. Another many-faceted project, designed to prepare older youth and adults for work, was suggested and carried out with great skill and commitment by professionals at a community college in Oregon. While an unusual success rate, as measured by subsequent job placements, wages earned, and public assistance savings, was reported, the project also pointed to the urgent need for broad author-

*The author was the first demonstration project specialist in charge of this program. During its first four years, virtually all of the best projects were proposed by George Narensky, then a BFS regional representative. While most federal and state officials viewed the program as a simple funnel for increased federal funding, Narensky saw it as a long-awaited opportunity to test inhibiting features of federal public welfare law and regulations.

ity to purchase services from both public mental health clinics and voluntary social service agencies. In time, this idea, too, gained the support of lawmakers.*

Finally, many projects proved that services were no substitute for decent cash grants or jobs, and that public welfare agencies were not promising direct service providers. Even when project approval was eagerly sought, agency administrators never hesitated to transfer project personnel to routine assignments, to leave vacancies unfilled, and to hobble services with a welter of defeating controls. Research skills also proved to be too primitive in most departments to produce reliable measures of outcome.

The War on Poverty

Nothing could have contrasted more sharply with the Social Service Amendments than the Economic Opportunity Act of 1964. Always underfunded and cut back prematurely, it nonetheless greatly increased service options for the poor and significantly expanded their rights to public entitlement, thereby beginning a process of democratizing the service structure and equalizing access.

"Hard" Services. The main targets were poor, jobless, out-of-school youth and urban ghettos. Dozens of practical, remedial, and compensatory services were initiated in the effort to lure youth back to school or into manpower training and development programs that would prepare them for steady jobs at decent wages. The new services included high school and college work–study programs, vocational education, remedial education, on-the-job training, opportunities for intensive socialization, education, and skill development in urban or rural Job Corps centers, the chance to join volunteer corps servicing urban and rural ghettos and Indian reservations, and in time a series of programs to help gifted youth to continue their education at colleges and universities. Most programs were multifaceted, offering medical and dental services, job counseling, and whatever remedial help was indicated. Welfare mothers also received job training, which day care for their children made feasible. When Head Start for preschoolers was added, nutrition programs and parent participation were included. Eventually the aged — and children — were helped through Foster Grandparents. In addition, thousands of young people served as outreach workers, helping the homebound, making home repairs, cleaning up neighborhoods, running errands for the elderly, and informing other poor people of their right to public services.

For those who participated, the War on Poverty provided more useful,

---

*Most of the improvements in the law that were designed to reduce dependency were repealed in 1981 at the insistence of the Reagan Administration.

legitimate, civilian roles than poor out-of-school youth had known since the Depression years — and more encouragement and help to remain in school than the poor had ever known in the U.S. Unfortunately, opening up new long-term jobs was not a formal part of the package, and because so many difficulties poor black youth encounter in the labor market have relatively little to do with skills, it became painfully clear, once economic conditions worsened in the 1970s, that the shape of poverty was little changed. But according to official measurements, it declined by a third during the 1960s.

Institutional Change. There were other innovations. To quicken decision-making and increase local influence, Office of Economic Opportunity staff dealt directly with local organizations, some of which like Community Action Programs (CAPs) and neighborhood service centers were created with this in mind. Maximum feasible participation of the poor was the slogan of the War on Poverty, and so they were invited to help plan, deliver, and occasionally evaluate services.* Advocacy roles for professionals were also heavily stressed. They helped people establish eligibility and made sure they received their full share of benefits and services. At another level, poverty lawyers argued in behalf of the poor in a host of class-action suits against government agencies, winning impressive victories. In the process, they succeeded in expanding the rights of welfare recipients, migrants, women, minorities, public housing residents, and other disadvantaged groups.

Similarly, efforts to mobilize the poor led to attempts to destigmatize welfare so that more "eligibles" would apply. Eventually poor people were sufficiently aroused and involved to march against the "gatekeepers," and demonstrations and sit-ins spread from the Atlantic to the Pacific. In large northeastern states, the movement resulted in adding thousands of families to welfare rolls and securing larger grants for many more (32). In time, the noisy, vigorous, and effective activism of the poor was blamed for the backlash that developed against the War on Poverty, and it may well have played a role. But it was also true that white America was not yet willing to set aside its biases and was more than ready to find excuses for sounding a retreat.

Financing Arrangements. The War on Poverty was financed primarily from federal funds that were distributed in response to thousands of approved projects and contracts. This form of financing has very different implications from financing services through well-established grants-in-aid, as with the Social Service Amendments: even though Congress was

*The nature and amount of participation varied from one city to another. For different assessments, see Kenneth Clark and Jeannette Hopkins (8) and Daniel P. Moynihan (30).

wrathful over the failure of public welfare services to reduce dependency, those services expanded; but even if poverty projects succeeded miraculously, since they were time-limited by law, they could disappear overnight unless they found an institutional berth in permanently funded agencies.

Still another problem is inherent in a project or contract approach. Designing projects and writing approvable proposals usually requires professional skills and experience, just as organizing and overseeing projects often does. With myriad communities all seeking to participate, the demand for specialists in this area jumped by leaps and bounds. As did their salaries. One result was that there was never a shortage of critics who called attention to the anomaly of a War on Poverty that funneled so much money to middle-income professionals. This is a valid observation but scarcely a fair criticism. As political scientist Gilbert Steiner (40), observed in another connection, services require servants.

As the program drew to a close, the pressing question was whether successful programs could be institutionalized. If they were integrated with old-line federal agencies would the momentum be lost? In the end, popular projects were transferred—Head Start, for example, to HEW, employment training programs to the Department of Labor, and college work-study and other educational initiatives to the Office of Education. A small skeletal "poverty" staff continued to administer a variety of volunteer programs including Foster Grandparents. But in the end it was public welfare specialists, not poverty warriors, who were to oversee the emergence of a national system of personal social services.

Title 20 of the Social Security Act

Background. By 1967, rather than declining, AFDC caseloads had almost doubled since 1960, primarily due to activists and lawyers involved in the War on Poverty. In a desperate attempt to check the growth of welfare, Congress enacted the harshest public welfare law since the federal government created AFDC. But social services fared well. The target population was broadened to include persons who within five years had been or could reasonably be expected to become dependent. The scope of services was broadened, and in addition to continuing the 75 per cent reimbursement rate, day care was raised to 90 per cent. The law also authorized purchase of services from voluntary nonprofit and public agencies.

The law was shaped without any input from or discussion with public welfare specialists in the Bureau of Family Services (BFS), which in itself was unprecedented. Just two months prior to its enactment, there was a sweeping reorganization of welfare-related agencies in HEW, an event that, similarly, was planned in the greatest secrecy. Obviously both Congress and HEW executives had lost confidence in BFS. But the ensuing disarray paralyzed efforts to write the regulations required to implement the new law, with the result that they were not distributed until two days before President Nixon took office in January 1969.

In the meantime, having spotted a loophole in the law, California began transferring service costs incurred by public schools, mental health clinics, hospitals, and prisons over to public welfare, thereby receiving 75 per cent federal reimbursement for routine state activities, and in the process defeating the goals of the new law. News spreads quickly among states, and soon others followed suit. By July 1972 the states estimated their 1973 federal reimbursements for services would total $4.7 billion, substantially higher than Congress had anticipated.* These raids on the federal treasury were finally halted by an amendment attached to the Revenue Sharing Act of 1972, which "capped" — that is, shifted from an open-ended to a closed-ended grant — the social services for 1973 at $2.2 billion, of which 90 per cent had to be spent in behalf of public assistance applicants or recipients. The only exceptions were for child care, family planning referrals, and services for special groups like the mentally retarded, drug addicts, alcoholics, and children in foster care.†

Among Nixon's campaign promises was his intention of embarking on "creative federalism," a policy designed to turn power back to the states and to limit the scope, influence, and cost of the federal government. The new ceiling on social services appeared to be a first step toward retrenchment. To avoid this fate, a powerful national coalition of state officials and social service leaders organized to persuade Congress to enact a new title in the Social Security Act, dealing solely with social services. The new law, reflecting their recommendations, was signed on January 4, 1975.

Federal Policy. Title 20 provided for a block grant to states with a "permanent" ceiling of $2.5 billion. Permanence proved short-lived. The ceiling was raised to $2.7 billion in 1977, to $2.9 billion in 1979, and was expected to rise to $3 billion by 1982.

Funds were to be targeted toward five broad goals spelled out in the previous law: to reduce dependency, strengthen families, protect children from neglect, abuse, or exploitation, forestall avoidable institutionalization, and facilitate it when there was no other option. At least half of the federal funds had to be spent in behalf of people receiving AFDC, SSI, or

---

*Ironically, California leaders who initiated this trend were among the loudest critics of federal growth when they assumed office in Washington in 1981.

†This period, including the reorganization of welfare in HEW and the seemingly uncontrollable spurt in service costs, has been studied intensively. See Martha Derthick's (10) *Uncontrollable Spending for Social Service Grants* and Paul E. Mott's (29) *Meeting Human Needs: The Social and Political History of Title 20.* The reorganization unfortunately relied on blanket rules and formulae which swept away the good along with the mediocre and poor, and the flexible with the rigid. Former welfare experts were succeeded in regional offices by people with no knowledge of public welfare law, but with highly developed bureaucratic instincts for expanding their own domain. Instead of alerting Congress to a loophole in the law, they aided and abetted the states in exploiting it.

Medicaid. Higher-income families could qualify, but fees had to be charged if their incomes exceeded 80 per cent of median income in the state. Information and referral services, protective services, and family planning referrals were available without regard to income. Group eligibility was possible when most members of a group were demonstrably poor, as in public housing.

States had to match federal funds and could not use them to replace regular state expenditures. Generally the ratio of federal to state funds was 75 : 25, but a few services qualified for 90 : 10, and special day-care grants became available with no matching requirement. The costs of administration and staff development, including social work education, were to be covered.

The law had unusually generous provisions for purchasing services from other public agencies, voluntary nonprofit organizations, private firms, and individual service providers. Written contracts were required, and charges had to be "reasonable" and "necessary." States were to submit yearly service plans specifying the services they expected to offer, the approximate number of persons to be served, a description of their planning process (which had to involve citizens), and their evaluation and reporting plans.

The new law was a remarkable reflection of many lessons learned during the previous fifteen years. It also represented an important shift of power to the states, which had complained for years that overly tight federal controls distorted their budgets and prevented flexible responses to unique needs.

Implementation and Impact: 1975 to 1981. Title 20 greatly enlarged the range of social services for the poor and near-poor. By the late 1970s about 11 million people received Title 20 services at a cost to federal and state governments of $3.8 billion.* By far the highest expenditure was for child day care, which was primarily provided to free mothers to work or to enroll in the Work Incentive Program where they received vocational training and supervised work experience. The ability to extend day care to families above welfare levels meant that many low-paid mothers could make systematic plans for their children rather than leaving them unsupervised or with neighbors. A few state and local welfare agencies also encouraged AFDC mothers to return to school, and provided the day care that made this plan feasible.

The next largest expenditure was for homemaker services, primarily to help aged people who otherwise would have to be institutionalized. Title 20 also provided protective services for abused and neglected children and oldsters, as well as services to eligible children in foster home and residen-

*All program data in the following pages are from the 1979 *Annual Report* for Title 20 (44).

tial care. Funds were used to deliver meals to homebound people, to provide group meals for the aged, and to pay for recreational, legal, vocational rehabilitation, and home management services. They were provided to special groups like delinquent and disabled children, the mentally retarded, and addicts. They proved especially helpful as arrangements were made to return people to the community after periods of institutionalization. Home helpers of all kinds were made available for a few hours or by the day.

Patterns varied considerably among the states, which bore testimony to their claim that they needed greater latitude in shaping their own programs. Child day-care costs in 1979 ranged from almost half of all Title 20 money in Delaware and New York to less than 5 per cent in Idaho, Montana, North Dakota, and Wisconsin. Child protective services varied from a high of 65 per cent in Alaska to less than 2 per cent in Illinois, Massachusetts, and Rhode Island. Counseling was allocated less than 1 per cent in North Carolina as compared with 52 per cent in Pennsylvania.

Because families often needed more than one service simultaneously, and the service structure was highly fragmented, a "case management" role evolved. In this capacity, service workers at the Title 20 agency — public welfare or social service departments — first talked with applicants so that together they could decide what services were needed. They then met with appropriate service providers to discuss plans. The case manager was available as services progressed, to offer encouragement and support during tense or discouraging periods, and to make certain that the services promised were faithfully delivered. While federal reports on the program were remarkably sterile, providing no insight regarding the content, quality, or effect of services, at the local and state levels one fact was very clear: the "hard services" for young families were in great demand. Before long all that could be offered was a place on the waiting list.

Because of its generous purchase of service provisions, Title 20 stimulated the growth of a social service industry. Social workers flocked into private practice, organized consultant firms, and formed group practice corporations (37). This trend was reinforced by an explosive demand for marriage and family therapy, and by the access that social workers in some settings and states had to "third party" payments from Medicare, Medicaid, and private insurance firms (22).* Title 20 also brought about changes in the voluntary nonprofit social service sector. A case in point is the family agencies spotted over the nation. Usually small, hard-pressed for funds and sometimes for clientele before Title 20, by 1980 so many

*Among professionals practicing psychotherapy, social workers now outnumber psychiatrists two-to-one and psychologists by a somewhat lower ratio. In this role they may be employed by voluntary nonprofit family agencies or mental health clinics or be engaged in full- or part-time private practice. Many combine agency employment with private practice (12).

services were purchased by welfare agencies that public funds had become the primary source of support for greatly enlarged family agencies (22).

The "New Federalism" Reshapes Title 20. In the spirit of the "New Federalism," espoused by the Reagan Administration, an attempt was made in 1981 to convince Congress to consolidate ninety special purpose grants into seven block grants to be administered by the states with a minimum of federal regulation, almost no accountability standards, and over 20 per cent less in federal funds. While Congress obliged in principle, only fifty-seven programs were brought together in nine block grants, with the balance reserved for special attention at reduced funding levels. Title 20 essentially ended in the latter group, but with the remarkable consistency the Administration has shown on this score, recommendations for consolidation and grant reductions have resurfaced each year.

How much the repeal of federal requirements has changed the nature and impact of the program is not yet known, but it is widely believed that the very poor receive a smaller share of services than in 1979. States are no longer required to match federal funds or to maintain state effort. The targeting provisions, which assured AFDC and SSI recipients a hefty share of services, and the income guidelines which set upper income limits, were among those repealed. States are no longer required to involve citizens in planning or allocating funds, and reporting requirements have virtually disappeared.* The 1981 cut was followed by another almost as large. Finally in 1984 Congress rebelled and restored part of the cuts. The end result by mid-decade was a federal grant for Title 20 of about $2.7 billion, as in 1977 and 1978. But it buys much less than it did back then and covers a smaller share of the population. The consumer price index is 67 per cent higher now, there are about 14 million more people, 10 million more who are poor, and over 2 million more unemployed. So supply has plummeted as demand has surged.

After reeling with shock from the federal budget cuts for several years, and raising taxes, the states began to respond to the persistent demand for more services, especially for children. By 1983 it was clear that millions of mothers, for example, were anxious to support their families if they could only find affordable, reliable child day care (5). But the only federally assisted day-care programs that remain relatively untouched by budget cuts or restrictions, the Dependent Care Tax Credit and Head Start, are of little relevance for the working or nonworking poor. Less than 15 per cent

---

*This means that neither citizens nor service specialists have any way of knowing how taxpayer money is being spent unless they investigate the program state-by-state. The Children's Defense Fund in Washington, D.C. has become almost a clearing house for information regarding children's services, and regularly undertakes state-by-state telephone surveys in key subject areas. A few foundations have financed large-scale impact studies, but what citizens in a democratic society want and need from government is evidence of open, systematic accountability.

of Head Start programs operate for a full working day, and all Head Start programs together only cover one fifth of eligible children. As for the child care tax credit, unless it is transformed into a refundable credit, the primary beneficiaries will continue to be middle- and upper-income families.

Child day care was far from the only need states and cities had to consider. The schools, Medicaid, AFDC, neighborhood development, civic services of all kinds had suffered a long drought. In some states, well after Wall Street celebrated the economic recovery in late 1983, the homeless and hungry were still increasing in number. But it was the abused, abandoned, neglected, exploited, missing, disturbed and disturbing children, and what was happening to their scarce services, that finally stirred public compassion. Time would not wait for these groups. A more detailed look at who they are and what they need will set the issue in perspective.

Services for Troubled Children and Youth _____

High-Risk Groups and Trends

No one really knows how many seriously troubled or emotionally damaged children and adolescents we have in the U.S. But estimates reach into the millions. They include some 3 million emotionally disturbed children (23), about 1.5 million abused or neglected children, and about the same number of missing and homeless children, over 40,000 who are charged with status offenses — like incorrigibility, truancy, or running away, and another 57,000 or so adjudicated delinquents who are committed yearly to juvenile training schools, chiefly for nonviolent offenses (5). (A relatively small group of juveniles commit a disproportionate share of violent offenses.) Then there are the school dropouts (about one fifth of students who enroll in high school) and the teenagers who are already drinking heavily or regularly using illegal drugs (34). Finally the 1 million unmarried teenage girls who become pregnant each year and the boys who father their children without plans to support them must be added to these overlapping groups.

In every group the majority of members are white, even though black rates are generally higher. Similarly, while one group — runaway children — are reported to come primarily from middle- and upper-income families, poor children usually run the higher risk of falling into these troubled populations.

Except for drug usage, which after declining slightly among teenagers in the early 1980s has now levelled off, the other problems are all trending upwards. Reports of child abuse rose sharply in the recession, as was expected since distraught, jobless parents are predictably tense and irritable. As someone once said, "The real battle of recessions is fought in the homes of the jobless." Juveniles admitted to custodial facilities rose by almost 100,000 between 1979 and 1982, and the average number in custody at any given time rose by about 10 per cent (42). Youth suicides and homicides also increased.

But exactly how many young children and teenagers need help is almost irrelevant since effective services are so scarce that they reach only a small fraction. This is why it is so important to protect and nurture some relatively recent service innovations that represent a reversal of years of community neglect. A brief review of the traditional methods of "serving" children in the juvenile justice, child welfare, and mental health systems will shed light on this issue.

Traditional Services for Troubled Children

During the past decade the Children's Defense Fund (6, 7, 23) produced a series of remarkably insightful and informative reports about what happened to children who came under the supervision or care of the child welfare, juvenile justice, or mental health systems. Common themes ran through the reports. All three systems relied heavily on out-of-home care, often in large institutions sometimes at considerable distance from where families lived. The institutions were typically understaffed, underserviced, overly restrictive, demeaning in their treatment of "inmates," and too seldom offered adequate protection for children. Only rarely was much effort made to avoid removing children from their homes or to place them in nearby community-based group homes or other small residential settings. All three systems tended to keep children beyond reasonable limits, and to discharge them ill-prepared for family or community life. Similarly, all three often overlooked families — before, during, and after placement. To add to the problems, in the late 1970s an estimated 10,000 children were placed out-of-state, which made visits unlikely even for devoted parents. Little effort was made to follow up on these children to be sure they were in good hands and were regularly supervised. Some states could not even provide a count of children involved.

Finally, none of the three systems worked well or closely with the others. Children in need of psychiatric attention were rarely referred for service by child welfare or criminal justice. Nor did these two pay much heed to each other. Many children fell through the cracks, neglected and overlooked by all three service sectors (23).

Status Offenders. Children committed for status offenses — which would not be a crime if committed by adults — were among the most pathetic. Often described as "intractable," "wayward," "unmanageable," "incorrigible" when picked up by the police or turned over to them by parents, for want of appropriate services many of these children were incarcerated for indefinite terms in state training schools otherwise filled with serious offenders. In the mid-1970s experts estimated status offenders accounted for up to half of the young inmates in the U.S. On the average they served longer terms than delinquents guilty of serious offenses, including homicide. These facts help to explain the many "horror stories" splashed across front pages, about raped and beaten children, children in solitary confinement or under heavy sedation for months, children faced with days of unending boredom and nights of terror and tears (9, 17, 33, 46).

For many reasons including the shortage of juvenile facilities, at some stage between being arrested and sentenced, about 400,000 children also spent a day or two in adult jails. They were nine times more likely to attempt suicide than youngsters in secure detention homes (5).

Runaways.   Of an estimated 1.2 to 1.5 million children who run away yearly, most stay away only briefly. But between 20 to 30 per cent of the group left home after prolonged physical or sexual abuse, some having been literally pushed out and others afraid to return. The average age of those who eventually come to formal attention is fourteen. Many have long-standing mental health problems. No fewer than one third of the girls and one sixth of the boys have already attempted suicide. With too little education, no work skills, and unprepared for independent living, many end on the streets, becoming easy prey to the commercial sex industry. About 5,000 unidentified children are buried each year (20), and from time to time grisly evidence confirms that runaways are frequent victims. The parents of some of these children never report them missing, which means they are not included in official counts. Nor are the police looking for them. An increasing number have run away from the child welfare or juvenile justice system, and are ready to risk any danger to avoid returning.

Neglected, Abandoned, and Abused Children.   Neglected and abandoned children have been sent to poorhouses and other custodial institutions for centuries. The parents of some were too poor to care for them; for others, parents were too neglectful to be trusted with them. In either case, the underlying problem was usually their social situation — poverty, joblessness, alcoholic parents, deficient diets, poor education, and no hope. While the "abused child" as a category is a modern invention, it is undoubtedly an old phenomenon familiar to millions of children who were removed or ran away from their parents over the years. Spanning all age groups from infancy through seventeen years, today these children are "warehoused" until foster homes are found or, if parental rights have been severed (which can be difficult and time-consuming), adoptive homes are approved. Healthy white infants are much easier to place than older, black, and disabled youngsters, who tend to pile up in institutions until their eighteenth birthday when they are discharged, often with no jobs or even reasonable preparation for work, no home, no friends, and no idea of where to turn for help.

About 400,000 children are in foster homes, where some have found the acceptance and stability they need. But since rejected children frequently experience difficulty adjusting, about half of the children are moved from one home to another, confronting failure in each. Recent newspaper articles tell of fourteen-year-old Rickie who committed suicide after realizing his planned adoption might fall through. At the time he was in his thirty-second foster home in nine years (1).* Child welfare experts were quick to clarify that so much "churning" is rare. The average length of stay is nearer three years; but to a child aching for a home of his own, even 1,095 days could seem forever.

The foster home system is riddled with problems, some of its own making. Good foster homes are hard to find, and are always in short supply. Foster home payments are not generous, and many special needs of children must be paid out of foster parents' pockets — or not at all. In some areas, whenever foster parents become attached to a child and express interest in adoption, an immediate transfer is arranged. The reason, it has been argued, is that voluntary agencies derive a major share of income from foster home supervision. Once children are adopted, this source of revenue dries up, and a good foster home is lost.

Emotionally Disturbed Children. Only about one third of the emotionally disturbed children in the U.S. receives any professional help, and a good share of the help is inappropriate, according to some forty studies reviewed by the Children's Defense Fund in the early 1980s (23). The most readily available help is the most restrictive and costly — inpatient hospital care. At least 40 per cent of the children should never have been admitted or remained too long. Despite the demonstrated success of outpatient services, only one state was systematically trying to close down psychiatric institutions for children and replace them with more open, community-based services. In a few states, children were still placed in adult wards and received essentially the same treatment as adults. Only seven states had taken even the first, limited steps toward creating a "system of care" for children and adolescents, including a full range of mental health services to be planned and delivered in a coordinated fashion. Although child advocacy services had been strongly recommended in each state by the Joint Commission of Mental Health of Children (18), as a necessary mechanism for assuring necessary services and monitoring, the

---

*No systematic study of the impact of frequent shifts in foster homes on school achievement have been located, but the system must produce more than its share of functional illiterates.

Children's Defense Fund found little evidence of any organized voice in behalf of mentally ill children.

Troubled Families. For all of these children, the pervasive tragedy was the scarcity of preventive and supportive family-centered services. Many situations and conditions that resulted in the removal or flight of children had existed for years. Some were known to family doctors, school teachers, welfare workers, neighbors, and the policemen on the neighborhood beat. Yet families were left to deteriorate until some dreadful crisis occurred, whereupon children were whisked away or ran away, often too late to undo years of damage.

While underlying problems like joblessness, poor schooling, malnutrition, and lack of basic health care are important causative factors of family breakdown, years of experience have shown that if damaged, incompetent families are identified early and receive appropriate community-based services, many families can be helped sufficiently to prevent removal of the children; and some families make remarkable strides. A wide range of services and approaches have proved effective not only in saving lives but in reducing costs. In working with neglectful families, homemakers have helped mothers to cope with parenting, homemaking, and their own feelings (11, 31, 38, 45).* With emotionally disturbed children, community-based services including teams of special educators, social workers, psychologists, child psychiatrists, nurses, occupational therapists, or volunteers have helped to make extended hospital care unnecessary. Most such programs involve entire families, and many are carried out chiefly in the home. The Children's Defense Fund reports briefly on many different effective approaches with children ranging from infancy through adolescence, many of them severely disturbed (23). Some programs focus on helping families reunite after children have been institutionalized for some time. Instead of assuming that mothers whose children were removed are inferior or incompetent, if not irrelevant, these programs give help to the mothers, too, in their children's absence. Follow-up studies of the children show that they are far more likely to return to stable, accepting, upbeat homes if their families have access to new resources during the children's absence (2, 19, 25, 35, 36, 41). The services provided ranged from homemakers, day care, legal services, respite care, day-care treatment, vocational counseling, job training, and skilled social casework to the help of carefully trained volunteers.

One of the outstanding programs in the country is the Group Live-in Experience (GLIE) in New York City. Initially organized by Sister Lorraine Reilly, it evolved into an advocacy program for families in the city's largest low-income housing project. But this was just the beginning.

*In 1976, when the U.S. had twenty home helpers per 100,000 population, Sweden provided 923, Norway 840, and the Netherlands 500 (26).

By 1972 the organization had applied for and received money from the city to develop the first community-based, temporary home for adolescents in crisis (including runaways and homeless youth). By 1975 GLIE operated three group homes. The following year federal funds for runaway centers helped to expand the program. Although now technically classified as a mental health agency, GLIE defines its mandate broadly and strives to provide whatever is needed. By 1981 this approach had resulted in a 24-hour emergency placement center called the "Crash Pad," a counseling center that includes a Center for Decision-Making which focuses on reuniting families of the adolescents in its various programs and preventing family breakdown in the surrounding community, two short-term group homes, four long-term residences, a home for autistic boys, a school, several work and employment programs, and a recreational program. By using a mixture of private and public funds, becoming daily more difficult to secure, GLIE serves about 500 youth yearly. Shortly after arrival, they receive complete medical, social/ psychological, and educational assessment. The only eligibility requirement is the desire to work at the task of achieving their goals. The school, which serves students in the surrounding community as well as GLIE residents, is accredited by the New York Board of Education and staffed by public school teachers. Students select their own program in consultation with a teacher *each morning* from a range of remedial and career-related courses and programs in the creative arts. Classes are small (ten students); no bells ring; and no authority figures loom over students. About 200 receive stipends for part-time work in nonprofit and public agencies in the city. GLIE has developed its own labor-intensive businesses, including a thrift shop, an outdoor farm on a cleared urban lot, and greenhouses — where farmers' markets and elite gourmet shops in the city sometimes buy their produce. GLIE developed its long-term homes and supervised apartments to help older youth who have no home or cannot return home to become independent, productive adults. By the time they leave (sometimes as long as three years after arrival), they have definite vocational skills, money in the bank earned through GLIE, a job, and an already-furnished apartment. Staff members continue to be available to help in the transition to being on their own. (16)

Holistic projects of this type serve to highlight the pitfalls inherent in special purpose grants *if administrators and workers emphasize their uniqueness rather than working at relating whatever they have to offer with all other relevant services that troubled youth and families may need.* It is obvious from the foregoing material that troubled families and their children have many problems in common, even though they may result in quite different behavior.

Beyond the principal value of these innovative projects — helping people to find themselves and to live more stable, fulfilled lives — identifying problems early, preventing them from becoming seriously handicapping, and interceding with whatever community-based services are indicated is an approach that saves a great deal of money over time. In some of the mental health projects, every $1 spent saved $4 to $5 for institutional care *just for the length of time children and families received services* (23). But, of course, institutional confinement may continue for years, possibly for a lifetime. Given these savings, various explanations have been advanced to account for the difficulty in "selling" services for children and families to the public and their representatives in state legislatures and Congress. "Children don't vote" is probably the long-time favorite. Steiner (39) sees the sharp conflicts pervading family issues as the root of the problem. Grubb and Lazerson (13) advance the thesis that in our highly materialistic, competitive society, while parents usually care deeply about their own children, they have no time or thought for other peoples' children. On the other hand, when some experienced, very talented lobbyists offered their services to prevent more children's programs from being eliminated or cut in 1984, their efforts succeeded against very heavy odds. So it may be that liberals and children's advocates have simply not been very talented at selling their viewpoints or causes. Good intentions, in other words, are no substitute for expertise.

Reform and Counter-Reform

In 1974 and 1980 three pieces of legislation were enacted by Congress that had the potential for generating preventive and supportive services for children and their families, and reforming the juvenile justice system: the Juvenile Justice and Delinquency Prevention Act of 1974, the Runaway and Homeless Youth Act of 1974, and the Adoption Assistance and Child Welfare Act of 1980.

Juvenile Justice and Delinquency Prevention.   The heart of the new law was a requirement that, as a condition of receiving federal funds, states develop comprehensive plans to remove all nonoffenders (dependent, neglected, and abused children) as well as all status offenders from secure detention, correctional institutions, and adult jails, and place them in "sheltered facilities." The law provided funds for (a) development of new approaches and techniques to prevent delinquency and (b) the development and implementation of cost-effective alternatives to the traditional ways of handling delinquents.

Most states opted to participate in the program. Despite lax federal enforcement and relaxed state timetables, by 1982 forty-three states had reduced the number of nonoffenders and status offenders in detention by 75 per cent. Between 1979 and 1984, the number in secure facilities dropped by 83 per cent. But 25,000 status offenders were yet to be transferred, and while fewer juveniles were in adult jails, it was clear in 1985 that the majority of states still condoned this practice in some circumstances. In other words, while federal leadership and federal funds brought about a significant improvement, much remained to be done (4, 5).

Promising innovative programs to prevent delinquency and to provide alternatives to incarceration for adjudicated delinquents also got underway. The emphasis on diverting status offenders from the juvenile justice system led to more referrals to community-based services and contributed to a marked decline in juvenile arrests.* Of the many projects providing alternatives to incarceration, the Juvenile Resource Center of Camden, New Jersey was cited as one of the finest (3). The services included formal and informal education, individual, group, and family counseling, career guidance, job development, recreation, experience in "positive socialization," and preparation for independent living. Serving about 200 juvenile offenders yearly, the program achieved a recidivism rate of 20 per cent, well below the norm for juvenile offenders. Forty per cent of the participants earned high school general equivalence diplomas while registered with the program, and another 20 per cent completed their studies shortly after leaving. A good many received on-the-job training in the project's own income-producing ventures, which included a delicatessen and a pizza parlor. Over 80 per cent obtained jobs in the private sector before completing the program.

Since the Reagan Administration took office, it has consistently recommended zero funding for this program, but its strong bipartisan support in Congress has resulted in annual appropriations of $70 million, and in 1984 Congress reauthorized the Act for another four years. Having failed to repeal the law, the Administration is charged with having tried to undermine it administratively by substituting a punitive philosophy for the preventive philosophy in the law. Congress reacted by increasing its oversight of the federal office responsible for the program, reaffirming its original intent, and requiring an audit of state systems responsible for monitoring compliance with deinstitutionalization requirements. Nonetheless, the fear that the Administration would eventually succeed in repealing the law or slashing funding levels has a chilling effect on decisions to purchase or construct alternative facilities.

That such fears were justified became clear shortly before Christmas, 1985, when the Justice Department, using the Gramm–Rudman–Hollings law as justification, announced the immediate freezing of funds for all juvenile programs, pending a request to Congress to rescind the annual appropriation. Since the law enforcement functions of the department were viewed as "sacrosanct," most cuts are expected to fall on grant programs. The outrage of project directors over the country was reflected in Congress. Only time will tell how the issue is resolved (24).

Services for Runaway and Homeless Youth.

The Runaway and Homeless Youth Act of 1974 provided federal funds for the development of

---

*Demographic shifts also contributed to the decline.

services to be based outside the juvenile justice system for youth under eighteen years of age. By 1985 the federal government was helping to fund 265 runaway centers that served some 200,000 youth. Open around-the-clock, the centers provide crisis intervention and information and referral services, legal assistance, counseling, and shelter. Half of the youngsters are helped to reunite with their families. While shelters can only provide temporary lodging (most have only eight or fewer beds), youth who continue on their own receive follow-up services to lessen the risk of their returning to the streets. The National Runaway Switchboard also facilitates easy communication between runaways and their families. The law encourages networking among the centers, which in turn facilitates the prompt dissemination of new more effective ways of helping.

Because of funding limitations, about nine requests for money to organize new centers are rejected for every one approved. The current centers are estimated to serve no more than one in every three runaways and to shelter no more than one in every twelve. A 1983 General Accounting Office study documented the need for far more after-care service, more outreach for youth on the streets, and greater attention to developing their living and coping skills. To meet part of this need, in 1983 special grants were given to 100 shelters, only to be discontinued the following year. In particular need of more long-term services are the "pushouts," the emotionally disturbed, addicted, suicidal, and pregnant — whose problems are beyond the scope of crisis-oriented centers.

The Reagan Administration tried to meld the program into the Social Services Block Grant (Title 20), and when this failed, to reduce federal support. However, Congress withstood these efforts. In 1983 program funds were doubled (from $10.5 million to $21.5 million). They rose to $23.2 million for 1984, but the Administration used only $18 million for runaway centers. Forty new centers were funded for 1985, with total funding held to the 1984 level. As noted earlier, in December 1985 the Department of Justice announced a freeze on all funds for runaway centers in order to keep departmental expenditures below levels required by the Gramm–Rudman–Hollings bill.

Child Welfare and Mental Health. In 1980 Congress enacted the Adoption Assistance and Child Welfare Act to provide sharply increased funding for child welfare programs and to create what Gutowsky and Koshel (14) describe as a "strong federal presence guiding the nature and structure of state child welfare activities." The law had three goals: to provide the necessary services to keep troubled families together, thereby reducing out-of-home placements, to place children already in state care into permanent homes (either their own or an adoptive home), and to improve the quality of life for children in foster home care. Adoption subsidies were authorized (at long last) for hard-to-place minority, disabled, and older children. States were required to review every child who had been in foster care more than six months, to make plans for systematic reviews thereafter, and to establish statewide inventories of all such children to assist in matching them with appropriate homes. The timing of the new law could not have been less fortunate, given the outcome of the national election. The necessary federal regulations were not published until December 31, 1980 and would not be effective until after comments (due March 16, 1981) were received, reviewed, and if advisable incorporated. But the Reagan Administration promptly rescinded the regulations, and recommended the program be incorporated in the Social Services Block Grant (Title 20), to be funded at sharply reduced levels. Anxious to protect the new programs until they were firmly established, and determined to safeguard rights that would be lost with consolidation, Congress rejected the Administration's plan but agreed to cut funding for foster care services. This tug-of-war was played out every year. By 1985 both foster care services and adoption subsidies were budgeted at significantly higher levels, but offsetting these gains were some very strategic losses. The "parent" child welfare services, part of the Social Security Act since 1935, were funded below the 1981 level until 1984, when only $2 million was restored. In 1985 another $31 million was added. This program is the linchpin for the improvement in the states' foster care programs. Similarly staff development, research, child abuse grants, and the Alcohol, Drug Abuse, and Mental Health Block grant, an Administration creation approved by Congress in 1981, suffered substantial cuts. All of these programs and other small special purpose programs were vital to the success of each other as well as to the success of the services planned under the 1980 Adoption Assistance and Child Welfare Act. Their interdependence became particularly apparent as child abuse and emotional disorders among children rose drastically during the 1980s. Instead of developing new services for foster care children and concentrating on finding adoptive homes, child welfare agencies were forced to deal with emergencies involving critically endangered youngsters. Mental health coordination grants, intended to facilitate joint planning by child welfare, juvenile justice, and mental health facilities, were particularly missed — until Congress of its own initiative provided several millions of dollars for this purpose in 1984.

Despite the uncertainty and budget cuts, states succeeded in placing many foster care children in permanent homes — quite often returning them to their own families — but frequently without the needed preparatory or transitional services contemplated in the new law. Counterbalancing this outward movement was a considerable rise in the number of abused children placed in foster homes. Some states made heroic efforts to protect and serve children. Budgets were increased to compensate for the lost federal funds, and even though statewide services were beyond their reach, numerous states initiated projects offering comprehensive services in limited geographical areas and staffed by workers specially trained for their particular assignment. So, some children were helped, and in the process states learned more about what was essential for effective services.

Throughout these years the Administration has insisted that services for families and children are solely a state responsibility. This view takes us back not to Franklin Roosevelt, but to pre–Theodore Roosevelt days, before the Progressives convinced the federal government to enact a long list of social legislation, including the protection of working women and children. For an Administration that exudes confidence in America's future to be so intent on restoring the distant past—at the expense of children who are its future–seems very strange indeed.

References

1. Barron, James. "Teen-Ager's Suicide Points to Lost Generation in Foster Care." *New York Times,* March 4, 1985.
2. Burt, Marvin R. and Ralph R. Balyeat. *A Comprehensive Emergency Services System for Neglected and Abused Children.* New York: Vintage Press, 1977, passim.
3. *A Children's Defense Budget: An Analysis of the President's FY 1984 Budget and Children.* Washington, D.C.: Children's Defense Fund, 1983, pp. 173–174.
4. *A Children's Defense Budget: An Analysis of the President's FY 1985 Budget and Children.* Washington, D.C.: Children's Defense Fund, 1984, p. 150.
5. *A Children's Defense Budget: An Analysis of the President's FY 1986 Budget and Children.* Washington, D.C.: Children's Defense Fund, 1985, pp. 5, 186, 190–191, 194–196, 205.
6. *Children in Adult Jails.* Washington, D.C.: Children's Defense Fund, 1976.
7. *Children Without Homes.* Washington, D.C.: Children's Defense Fund, 1978.
8. Clark, Kenneth J. and Jeannette Hopkins. *A Relevant War Against Poverty: A Study of Community Action Programs and Observable Social Change.* New York: Harper & Row, Publishers, 1968.
9. Cole, Larry. *Our Children's Keepers.* New York: Grossman Publishers, 1972.
10. Derthick, Martha. *Uncontrollable Spending for Social Services Grants.* Washington, D.C.: Brookings Institution, 1975.
11. Goldberg, Gertrude. "Non-Professional Helpers: The Visiting Homemaker." In George A. Brager and Frances P. Purcell, Eds., *Community Action Against Poverty.* West Haven, Conn.: New Haven College and University Press, 1967, pp. 175–207.
12. Goleman, Daniel. "Social Workers Vault Into a Leading Role in Psychotherapy." *New York Times,* April 30, 1985.
13. Grubb, W. Norton and Marvin Lazerson. *Broken Promises.* New York: Basic Books, Inc., Publishers, 1982.
14. Gutowski, Michael F. and Jeffrey J. Koshel. "Social Services." In John L. Palmer and Isabel V. Sawhill. *The Reagan Experiment.* Washington, D.C.: The Urban Institute Press, 1982, pp. 307–328.

15. Handler, Joel F. and Ellen Jane Hollingsworth. *The "Deserving Poor": A Study of Welfare Administration.* Chicago: Markham Publishing Co., 1971, pp. 125–128.
16. "Homeless and Runaway Youth Find Support, Stability." *CDF Reports,* 3 (November 1981), pp. 6–7.
17. James, Howard. *Children in Trouble: A National Scandal.* New York: David McKay Company, Inc., 1969.
18. The Joint Commission on the Mental Health of Children. *Crisis in Child Mental Health: Challenge for the 1970s.* New York: Harper & Row, Publishers, 1969.
19. Jones, Mary A., Renée Neuman, and Ann W. Shyne. *A Second Chance for Families: Evaluation of a Program to Reduce Foster Care.* New York: Child Welfare League of America, 1976, p. 58.
20. Jordan, Mary. "Victims Advise Panel on Missing Child Funds." *Washington Post,* May 22, 1985.
21. Kahn, Alfred J. *Social Policy and Social Services,* 2d ed. New York: Random House, 1979, pp. 26–31.
22. Kahn, Alfred J. and Sheila B. Kamerman. *Helping America's Families.* Philadelphia: Temple University Press, 1982, pp. 35–79, 112–152.
23. Knitzer, Jane. *Unclaimed Children: The Failure of Public Responsibility to Children and Adolescents in Need of Mental Health Services.* Washington, D.C.: Children's Defense Fund, 1982, pp. ix, 17–41, 66–79.
24. Kurtz, Howard. "Justice Dept. Freezes Juvenile Programs." *Washington Post,* December 19, 1985.
25. Lahti, Janet. "A Follow-Up Study of Foster Children in Permanent Placement." *Social Service Review,* **56** (December 1982), pp. 556–571.
26. Little, Virginia. "Open Care for the Aged — Swedish Model." *Social Work,* **23** (July 1978), pp. 282–284.
27. May, Edgar. *The Wasted Americans: Cost of Our Welfare Dilemma.* New York: Harper & Row, Publishers, 1964.
28. Morris, Robert. *Social Policy of the American Welfare State: An Introduction to Policy Analysis.* New York: Harper & Row, Publishers, 1979, pp. 117–120.
29. Mott, Paul E. *Meeting Human Needs: The Social and Political History of Title 20.* Washington, D.C.: National Conference on Social Welfare, 1976.
30. Moynihan, Daniel P. *Maximum Feasible Misunderstanding.* New York: The Free Press, 1969.
31. "New York City Agency Keeps Families Together." *CDF Reports,* **2** (November 1980), pp. 6–7.
32. Piven, Frances Fox and Richard A. Cloward. *Poor Peoples' Movements: Why They Succeed, How They Fail.* New York: Vintage Books, 1979, pp. 264–362.
33. Richette, Lisa Aversa. *The Throwaway Children.* New York: Dell Publishing Co., Inc., 1969.
34. Russell, Christine. "Teen-Age Drug Use Levels Off After Decline." *Washington Post,* November 7, 1985.
35. Shames, Miriam. "Use of Homemaker Services in Families That Neglect Their Children." *Social Work,* **9** (January 1964), pp. 12–18.
36. Sherman, Edmund A., Michael H. Phillips, Barbara L. Haring, and Ann W. Shyne. *Services to Children in Their Own Homes — Its Nature and Outcomes.* New York: Child Welfare League of America, 1973.

37. Smothers, Ronald. "Social Work Growth is Reported Slowed by Cuts in Spending." *New York Times,* November 28, 1981.
38. Snyder, Ruth. "Homemaker Service — A Supportive and Protective Service for Children and Adults." Mimeographed. New York Department of Welfare, 1962.
39. Steiner, Gilbert Y. *The Futility of Family Policy.* Washington, D.C.: Brookings Institution, 1981.
40. ————. *The State of Welfare.* Washington, D.C.: Brookings Institution, 1971, pp. 35–40.
41. Torczyner, C. and Paré, Arleen. "The Influence of Environmental Factors in Foster Care." *Social Service Review,* **53** (September 1979), pp. 358–377.
42. U.S. Bureau of the Census. *Statistical Abstract of the United States 1985.* Washington, D.C.: U.S. Government Printing Office, 1984, p. 182.
43. U.S. Department of Health, Education, and Welfare. *Public Welfare Personnel, 1960.* Washington, D.C.: U.S. Government Printing Office, 1962, p. 22.
44. U.S. Department of Health and Human Services. *Annual Report to the Congress on Title 20 of the Social Security Act, Fiscal Year 1979.* Washington, D.C.: U.S. Government Printing Office, 1980.
45. Watkins, Elizabeth G. "So That Children May Remain in Their Homes: Homemaker Services Strengthen Aid to Dependent Children Program." *The Child,* **18** (October 1953), pp. 25–29.
46. Wooden, Kenneth. *Weeping in the Playtime of Others.* New York: McGraw-Hill Book Co., 1976.

CHAPTER 12

Reaganomics and Social Welfare

Theoretical and Ideological Base

During 1980 inflation soared, unemployment rose, the federal deficit followed suit, economic growth rates continued to lag behind other industrial nations, Americans smarted from the impasse with Iran over the U.S. hostages there, and many citizens were whipped into a frenzy of frustration over the presumed military superiority of the Soviet Union. By fall it seemed clear that victory would go to the presidential candidate who promised to solve all of these problems simultaneously, which was what Ronald Reagan did. In the process he promoted the Kemp–Roth version of supply-side economics, Milton Friedman's monetarism, and a significant arms buildup as solutions to the national malaise.

Reagan's Supply-Side Mix

To grasp what the President had in mind requires a few comments about economics, in general, and demand- and supply-side theories, in particular.

Economists share a belief in the importance of *expectations* in the shaping of economic behavior. That is, they believe that if investors or consumers expect prices to be stable, they behave in one way; if they expect them to rise or fall, they behave in other ways; if they conclude that financial markets are unpredictable, they shun stocks in favor of tax shelters, gold, art objects, real estate, and the like. However their prescriptions may differ, economists are virtually unanimous in their belief that unless citizens have faith in the economic system — in its growth potential, relative stability, and predictability — it spells trouble. This is why many feel that the rapid shifts in economic policy in the last fifteen years destroyed investor confidence and discouraged business firms from investing in large-scale modernization. It is also an article of faith among mainstream economists that economic markets work perfectly if left alone. If anything goes wrong, it is because something interfered with market mechanisms. The "something" is almost always "big government" — with its heavy-handed regulations, "confiscatory" taxes, and most frequently, its deficits. While there are economists who scoff at such ideas, they still play an important role in economics teaching around the country.

Turning to supply- and demand-side theories, both are methods of analyzing the economy for policy-making purposes. Both lead to economic prescriptions. Supply-siders begin with the assumption that the dominant actor in the economy is the producer, not the consumer and his pocketbook, as demand-siders hold. "Pure" supply-side theory is the old classical economic theory taught in virtually all universities before John Maynard Keynes came along to rescue a depression-ridden world with his demand-side theory.* Both groups of theorists use the same tools — like tightening or easing the money supply, raising or lowering government spending, or raising, lowering, eliminating, or creating certain types of taxes — but they do so for different theoretical reasons and often at different stages in the business cycle. Each school of thought has many versions and attracts a mix of conservatives and liberals. Thus, conservative Milton Friedman and liberal Walter Heller are both demand-siders. Similarly, supply-siders include purists like Jude Wanniski, whose most urgent reform proposal, return to the gold standard, is rejected by many supply-siders, while he, in turn, discounts the importance of the federal deficit as a cause of inflation, which in 1981 was tantamount to heresy among the President's men. The argument, in other words, is not between two theories or philosophies, but many versions of both, so many in fact as to raise questions about whether economics yet qualifies as a science.†

While Reaganomics was touted as supply-side economics, it borrowed from both, possibly because the Administration had several inherently contradictory missions. On the one hand, reversing the long decline in productivity rates was perceived to require the transformation of the nation from a society grounded in personal consumption to one grounded in savings and business investment (52). At the same time, uppermost to many people was the urgency of curbing inflation; and the Administration was also intent on investing heavily in notoriously inflationary military hardware. Since by definition to the economists advising the President, government is the root of all evil, it was assumed that overbearing federal tax, social welfare, and regulatory policies were responsible for inhibiting savings and investment, thereby causing the lag in productivity and capital formation. So, the Administration prescribed three supply-side remedies. The large three-year cut in marginal tax rates and tax indexing were intended to increase the take-home pay of workers and employers, which would give them the incentive to work harder and the wherewithal to save more and to invest more; indexing taxes to the rate of inflation had the additional virtue of preventing the government from growing by the

---

*Ronald Reagan studied economics at Eureka College in Illinois between 1928 and 1932.

†Lester Thurow's recent book, *Dangerous Currents* (52) and Robert Lekachman's book, *Economists at Bay* (27) present insiders' perspectives on this issue.

"bracket creep" sleight-of-hand. Social welfare cuts were intended to encourage low- and middle-income citizens to work harder and more steadily, and to take individual responsibility for planning and saving for their own future needs. As for the government regulations that hobbled industry and "wasted" so much time and money, they were to be eliminated or modified. For good measure, virtually all requirements in federal grants-in-aid to the states would be dropped. As for inflation, its persistence, White House advisors concluded, was due to overly accommodating monetary policies. To cure the problem, they turned to a demand-side solution: "tight" money, permitting only a slow rate of growth of the money supply.

Taken separately, there is nothing new about these prescriptions. But juxtaposing them was unusual. Referring to John Kenneth Galbraith, with whose theories he rarely agreed, Wanniski observed that

> . . . he has it exactly correct. He said that Reagan policies are like trying to walk uphill and downhill at the same time. Supply-siders are trying to encourage production and demand-siders are trying to induce recessions to bring down interest rates and inflation. (59)

It is well to remember, Wanniski added, that the reason for increased government spending over the past dozen years was that "we've been squeezing the economy by inducing recessions to fight inflation." To continue that policy was to court ever-larger deficits even without the stimulus of new defense hikes.

But the President's men disagreed. According to David Stockman, then Reagan's Director of the Office of Management and Budget, the policy package would

> signal investors that a new era was dawning, that the growth in government would be displaced by the robust growth of the private sector, thus reversing the gloomy assumptions in the disordered financial markets. (18)

Furthermore, this "robust growth" would begin at once, expectations having skyrocketed as a result of the President's upbeat program. Jobs would open up, everyone would work harder, longer, and strive toward excellence, business investments would surge, and taxes would pour in,* swelling federal coffers sufficiently, with the help of social welfare savings, to pay for the arms race and put the budget in balance by 1984. Possibly, said the skeptics, but would it not be wiser to postpone the defense hikes until the new revenues are in hand? In the real world, months can elapse before all key actors receive, understand, and believe the signals, let alone act on them. As it turned out, irrespective of merits or demerits in the White

---

*It is reported the White House even expected tax evaders in the "underground economy" to surface because of its tax cuts (52).

House package, the misperception of response time was a costly flaw. While Stockman confidently anticipated celebrating a bull market of "historic proportions" in the spring — and then anticipated it in the summer —and then the fall (18),* the economy plunged into recession, a fact reluctantly acknowledged by the President only after a million workers were laid off within a few months. Overly tight control of the money supply was the villain, according to most economists. But the President's belief in his program and in the power of optimistic expectations was so strong that despite a series of economic reversals, storm warnings from Wall Street, and the departure from Washington of most supply-side advisors, every new quarter of the fiscal year was heralded by contradictory headlines like those that appeared on the front page of the *New York Times* on September 20, 1982: "Business, Reacting to Slump, Cuts Spending Plans Further"; "President Contends Economic Recovery 'Has Been Sighted.'" Then just before the fall elections, the Federal Reserve Board shifted from targeting the money supply to targeting interest rates (20, 39) as was done in Carter's last years — whereupon financial writers proclaimed "Reaganomics is Dead." But not quite: the President's major tax and spending cuts and defense buildup remained intact, as did his unquenchable optimism.

The Role of the Federal Deficit

During months of discussion it became clear that while most of Wall Street heartily approved tax and social welfare cuts, many doubted the federal deficit could be reduced by the President's package. Between recession and sharp tax cuts, government revenues were declining while expenditures were rising, chiefly because of the President's determination to increase the defense budget by $1.6 trillion within a five-year period. Even members of his team worried about this large hike. They questioned his initial embargo on searching for "fat" in the defense budget. Some doubted the Pentagon could spend such windfalls wisely or even keep expenditures under reasonable control. Others took exception to the arbitrary, off-the-cuff estimates of what was required to "restore" America's military supremacy, insisting that careful planning toward precise objectives was the only rational approach. Many people had reservations about directing the preponderance of federal research and development resources toward military objectives. If the "best and the brightest" were lured by the ready cash at the defense department, who and what resources would be left to solve scientific, organizational, and social problems in the domestic scene? How could the U.S. ever expect to compete with Japan where the opposite priorities prevailed? But these "details" were brushed aside in the haste to push the budget through Congress (12).

*For more details, see David A. Stockman, *The Triumph of Politics*. New York: Harper & Row, Publishers, 1986, pp. 17–134.

Once it was enacted, both supply- and demand-siders found fault with the new package (33). In addition to its internal inconsistencies, Wanniski held, the emphasis on the federal deficit and the implication that it was too high were both misplaced. So long as the deficit represented approximately the same share of GNP, as was the case from 1971 through 1980, its actual size was irrelevant. Heilbroner and Thurow (19) reinforced this view from another perspective. With the high degree of integration between local, state, and federal budgets as a consequence of the growth in grants-in-aid, the size of federal deficits or surpluses is relatively meaningless, they insisted. What mattered was the combined deficit or surplus of all government — state, local, and federal. When this more appropriate concept is used, there was no deficit to eliminate until 1980, when it grew to a little over 1 per cent of GNP, which the authors dismissed as irrelevant. "Would such a feather tilt the inflation scale?"

Other economists pointed to the lack of evidence that inflation was caused by high or increasing deficits during the 1970s, as the Administration claimed. Despite the public outrage when the Carter deficit reached $59.6 billion in 1980, Alperovitz and Faux (3) found that when properly measured — in relative rather than absolute terms — deficit spending as a percentage of GNP and changes in price levels moved in opposite directions during eight of the eleven years from 1971 through 1981. Furthermore, if, as some economists assume, inflation *follows* an increase in deficit spending, the evidence still fell short: in only one of the eleven years did inflation accelerate during the year following a rise in the deficit. Focusing so exclusively on the deficit, these economists charged, simply diverted attention from far more relevant issues. What the U.S. and other nations around the world experienced in the 1970s was not simple inflation, but stagflation — the simultaneous rise in prices and joblessness — stemming from a sluggish economy and declining productivity. An economy, furthermore, that was suddenly and severely jolted by enormous price increases in energy costs (thanks to OPEC) and health care costs, especially. In very short order the jolts rocketed throughout the economy, pushing up prices, wages, and interest rates. It was the fact that the most inflationary sectors —energy, health care, food, and housing— were all *basic necessities,* not mink coats or even postponable durables like refrigerators, freezers, TVs, or automobiles, that defeated so many attempts to reverse it. What was needed was a serious effort to understand and prescribe for *sectoral* inflation and how to restructure the economy so that it could function at full employment without endangering price stability.

Other critics agreed federal deficits were only a small part of the problem. It was their accumulation in the national debt and high interest rates that should worry people. The higher interest payments rose as a share of the federal budget, the less flexible and useful it became as an economic tool to fight inflation. As the largest economy in the world, we had an obligation to other nations, as well as to ourselves, to protect options that could make the difference between reasonable stability and uncontrollable volatility (43).

But even as the discussion continued, the economy was sinking into recession, and soon the President's supporters were predicting a 1982 deficit of $100 to $200 billion. At the same time, vociferous complaints were registered from all sides that high interest rates were "strangling" the economy. Chrysler engineers and auto workers might perform miracles and produce the best cars in the world but their company might yet be forced into bankruptcy with the killing interest due on public and private loans. As for small businesses and private households with no government assistance, the rate of bankruptcies was mushrooming. But optimists still found reason for hope when inflationary pressures dropped below double digit levels, and interest rates began to decline. Others with more far-sighted vision worried about the impending collision of declining tax revenues and steeply accelerating defense hikes.

Their worst fears were realized when the Administration's next budget was unveiled in early 1982. By then federal revenues had fallen far behind White House forecasts. Yet the Administration was still intent on an 18 per cent increase for defense. Even with a $40 billion cut in other federal expenditures, primarily from social programs, this meant, White House spokesmen conceded, a deficit of $91.5 billion. Less politicized estimates ran from $100 to $150 billion — and as high as $725 billion over the next three years.

In the face of these predictions, the Administration first tried to disclaim its belief in the importance of federal deficits. But the outcry from its more consistent followers evoked a quick denial, and soon citizens were confronted with the paradox of an Administration overseeing astronomic peacetime deficits and its chief spokesman endorsing a Constitutional amendment requiring a balanced budget. While such an amendment had wide popular support, many Constitutional lawyers and economists experienced in the ways of government had serious reservations. Economic fads should not be enshrined, they held, in the basic law of the land. Furthermore, forcing a balance every year could disastrously restrict the flexibility of the President and Congress in economic policy making. If, as proposed, Congress could only make appropriations in excess of income by securing a three-fifths majority, this could prove to be difficult for even a small deficit in the worst of times. While the attempt to force a balanced budget failed —by a vote or two year after year—the issue could only grow in importance, fed as it was by daily reports of $250 billion and higher federal deficits and the startling fact that the U.S. had become the world's largest debtor nation—drawing nearly $400 billion from abroad to underwrite what one columnist described as "imprudent military increases and misconceived tax cuts" (17).

When Senators Philip Gramm (R–Texas), Warren Rudman (R–NH), and Ernest Hollings (D–SC) began talking about a method of forcing a balanced budget within a few years, few people expected much to come of the idea. But with modifications to protect some programs for the poor and elderly, it eventually sailed through Congress with comfortable majorities in both houses. Known formally as the Balanced Budget and Emergency Control Act (P.L. 99–177), it became law on December 12, 1985. Promptly challenged in the courts, one enforcement procedure was declared unconstitutional within weeks. Appeals were then filed with the Supreme Court. In the meantime the law remained intact, and its implementation was not stayed by the court.

The law requires a balanced budget by 1991. Each year deficit reduction targets are to be set by the Office of Management and Budget (OMB) and the Congressional Budget Office (CBO). If they disagree, the targets will be set half way between their estimates. On the first round in the budget process, the President, as usual, submits his budget to Congress, and if they wish, either or both houses prepare alternative budgets. But all such budget proposals must meet the specified spending reduction targets. During a greatly accelerated budget process, the President and Congress are to make every effort to reach agreement. If they fail to do so, an across-the-board spending reduction process, known as *sequestration* goes into effect. OMB and CBO at once calculate the necessary reduction rates for defense and nondefense programs, and work out the exact budget cuts to be made in each *nonexempt* program. Their fully documented report is forwarded to the General Accounting Office and, after review and approval, to the President, who then submits it as a bill to Congress to approve or disapprove. If approved, it goes back for the President's signature or veto, like any other bill.

The law spells out rules that must be followed during *sequestration:*

- Half of all cuts must be made in defense.
- Spending reduction rates apply across-the-board.
- No program may be eliminated.
- Some programs may be cut by only a small, specified percentage.*
- Some programs are exempt from any cuts at this stage.

The exempt programs include social security, veterans' compensation and pensions, AFDC, SSI, food stamps, child nutrition, WIC, Medicaid, the earned income tax credit, and interest on the national debt. Without some of these concessions, the bill would probably not have become law.

Despite relief in some quarters that the federal government had — at long last — taken steps to "get its house in order," reservations about the

---

*This group includes community mental health care centers, migrant health care centers, veterans' health programs, Indian health programs, and Medicare.

law abound. The idea of depriving any modern economy of one of its basic stabilizing tools alarms many economists. Interviewed by Hobart Rowen (44), former Economic Council chairman Walter Heller commented,

> Like any mandated and rigid formula, it would undermine, perhaps even pervert, the role of the federal budget as an economic balance wheel in the economy. Rigid reductions of the deficit through thick and thin — through recovery and recession — could wreak havoc on the economy.

Members of Congress who voted for the law despite their reservations are accused of pandering to ill-advised popular preference for a balanced budget or of taking refuge behind automatic cuts rather than withstanding special interest pressures and voting as their own conscience dictates. Some lawmakers, it was held, afraid the label of "big spender" would stick, voted for the bill knowing it was bad law and bad economics. Social welfare advocates found other faults: the accelerated budget process will leave no time for public input or discussion, which is the essence of democracy, and no program is protected from cuts — or elimination — in the initial stage; furthermore, they see no reason why all social welfare programs, having taken the brunt of budget slashing since 1981, should not be at least partially exempt. But critics counter that a stepped-up decision-making pace will free time for other important business, while focusing on deficit reduction today will lighten the burden on future generations. Also, the rules guiding the automatic process are more consonant with national values than those reflected in recent budgets (35, 48, 51).

But perhaps what is most important is the paralysis in decision making in the federal government that Gramm – Rudman – Hollings has come to symbolize. People are elected to high office to make decisions, not to delegate this function to a mindless robot programmed to slash everything in sight. At this stage the fate of the law is uncertain. Not unexpectedly, in the summer of 1986 the Supreme Court held the procedure for sequestration to be unconstitutional. How Congress will resolve the issue or even if it will choose to do so probably depends on the outcome of the fall election.

The Impact of Reaganomics

Redistribution to the Rich

During the 1980 campaign, Reagan promised very welcome tax relief. As the message came across, everyone would gain something and no one would lose. But when his plan to cut marginal tax rates over the next three years was unveiled in 1981, it was clear that while it was generous to the rich and their corporations, when combined with scheduled social security tax increases, low-income households would be worse off. When the new tax law emerged from Congress, cuts affecting average taxpayers had been slightly modified, and a long list of special "giveaways" to powerful, well-off interest groups and corporations had been added.

What was less expected was a tax package so blatantly crammed with perverse supply-side features. For instance, while changes in corporate income taxes would virtually wipe out this source of revenue by 1986, they also served to divert industrial investment from equipment to structures and conferred huge tax benefits on big utilities, manufacturing companies, and the oil and gas industry. But they offered little to high technology companies or to small business and service industries with low capital requirements, which create the preponderance of new jobs every year (21). The schedule for accelerated depreciation provided incentives to *postpone* investments for several years, while liberalization of estate and gift taxes assured further concentration of family wealth and failed to include any incentive to encourage productive investment.

But the bauble of the year was so-called "safe harbor" leasing — which Alexander Stuart (47), writing in *Fortune* several years later, explained is something akin to "food stamps for corporations, prosperous as well as pinched" — which permitted profitless companies to sell their otherwise unusable tax benefits to profitable companies in almost "riskless paper shuffles." In less than two years, this provision would finance $40 billion worth of assets, saving thriving companies billions of dollars, and wiping out the entire tax liability of some.*

Similarly, changes in individual income taxes were designed to cut taxes for the rich but no step was taken to close unproductive tax loopholes. While incentives to save were increased, incentives to spend were left intact. Among new provisions, top marginal tax rates were cut from 70 to 50 per cent, and capital gains taxes were lowered to a maximum of 20 per cent. Citizens working abroad were excused from paying taxes on the first $75,000 of earned income. When Budget Director David Stockman tried to persuade his colleagues to end some offensive and egregiously unproductive tax shelters, he was reminded that Reagan was elected to lower, not raise, taxes. All together, new loopholes and exemptions alone were expected to lower taxes of special interest groups by $28 billion between 1981 and 1986; and this was on top of a hefty collection of long-standing "tax expenditures" for the affluent.

Perverse supply-side subsidies were also created or increased as the President's men wheeled and dealed his program through Congress. Stockman was stunned by the experience. "Do you realize the greed that came to the forefront?" he asked his interviewer (18). The "hogs really came feeding. The greed level, the level of opportunism, just got out of

---

*Zero tax liability was a familiar phenomenon during previous administrations, too, but not on the level condoned in 1981.

control." After almost wiping out corporate income taxes, what Lewis (28) described as "grotesque increases" were made in sugar, tobacco,* and peanut price supports. The sugar subsidies, "finally" killed by Congress in 1979, were revived at an estimated cost to consumers of from $2 to $5 billion yearly. User fees, pressed on Reagan by Stockman apparently, for owners of private airplanes and boats, lost out in the Congressional free-for-all. One result, as Bethel (6) pointed out, was a multimillion dollar subsidy to private pilots with an average income of $44,000.† Stockman also proposed cutting government funds for the Export–Import Bank by $752 million, but collided with some of the nation's major manufacturers, who typically receive about two thirds of the benefits. Not surprisingly, they successfully negotiated for $250 million more than planned.

So, life has been good since 1981 for the nation's rich corporations, their owners, and other very well-off people. Between 1980 and 1982, alone, the number of millionaires doubled—from 4,414 to 8,408. Their effective tax rates having resulted in pleasantly large windfalls, they enjoyed tax savings averaging $122,812 in 1982 (25). They suffered a slight setback that year when daily reports of flagrant inequities became political dynamite and a frightened Congress facing fall elections defied the President by raising taxes — without repealing his major tax cut — and removed or modified a few of the more offensive 1981 handouts. In the process some long overdue procedural reforms were made, like withholding a share of taxes on interest and dividends, but by 1989 tax revenues would still fall $239 billion short of what would have been collected under the 1980 law (43).

Impact of Cuts in Marginal Tax Rates. Between 1981 and 1984, the yearly worth of Reagan tax cuts averaged

- $20 to taxpayers with incomes under $10,000
- $330 to those with incomes between $10,000 and $20,000
- $1,200 to those with incomes between $20,000 and $40,000
- $3,080 to those with incomes between $40,000 and $80,000
- $8,390 to the fortunate ones whose incomes were $80,000 or more (32).

In 1985 Joseph Pechman (37), the great tax expert long associated with the Brookings Institution, reported on tax trends over the past two decades. Taking all federal, state, and local taxes into account, in 1966 the poorest one tenth of households spent 16.8 per cent of their income on taxes; by 1985 their share had increased to 21.9 per cent. Despite a presum-

*In 1986 it was reported that the federal government pays subsidies amounting to $137 daily to each tobacco grower (8).

†Airline tickets in 1981 covered about 80 per cent of the cost of government services received by commercial airlines. Private aviation paid for less than 25 per cent of its government services.

ably progressive income tax system, back in 1966 the richest tenth of taxpayers spent only 30.1 per cent on taxes; by 1985 the share had dropped to 25.3 per cent (49). In the process, for a variety of reasons including tax policy, income distribution in the U.S. had become more concentrated than in any year since 1947.

How did the rich respond to their good fortune? Did they justify their President's faith that they would invest their windfalls productively — as was required for his program to succeed? Two years after he took office, productive investments had still not rebounded. Instead, merger mania had seized the corporate world, while bulging inventories and high interest rates convinced financial institutions and industrial leaders that the time was not yet ripe to invest in the U.S. on any significant scale. As Edward Boyer (7) wrote in *Fortune* in the fall of 1983,

> Sorting out the year's winners and losers yields a picture of an economy grounded even more than before on personal consumption and even less on business investment. That, of course, is exactly opposite of what the Reagan Administration policies were designed to produce. Liberalized depreciation write-offs were supposed to stimulate business investment, while cuts in personal income tax rates were expected to promote the added savings to finance the extra plant and equipment. Instead, the savings rate has fallen and business shows no taste for adding capacity. Says Firestone chairman John J. Nevin, "Tax incentives haven't helped us one damn bit."

Furthermore, Boyer added, deregulation "clobbered" several industries, including the airlines and railroad equipment companies.

Modest progress was chalked up so far as productivity was concerned, but this was not due to increased work effort but to the drag that record unemployment exerted on wages, especially those of nonunion workers who dominate the labor force today (30). As one financial writer observed, the two years following Reagan's inauguration were filled with contrasts: while Wall Street "blossomed like an exotic plant," millions of workers lost their jobs and the poverty roster "burgeoned" (9). Nor did savings or investments pick up later (46). Despite high interest rates, stable prices, and "federal incentives to encourage thrift," another financial writer lamented, "Americans are saving a smaller share of their incomes than at any time since the 1940s" (24). While economists differ in their assessment of the way such measurements are to be made, they agree that the rate of personal savings in the U.S. falls substantially below the level in other nations (2). As for gross business investment in new plants and equipment, no change occurred between 1979 and 1985, when corrected for the drop in inventory investment (5). Ironically, the bankers who had invested so heavily abroad and often, critics held, so unwisely, were tottering among threatened defaults partially brought on by our high interest rates, while the overvalued dollar caused foreign markets for U.S.-produced goods to shrink, especially among some of our close neighbors in South America who had been our largest trading partners. So, our workers lost jobs, our trade deficit surged to its highest peak, and cries for and against internationally divisive protective legislation agonized an already fractured society.

Redistribution From the Poor

Budget-Cutting Principles and Reality. While President Reagan promised during his campaign to get the "federal government off our backs," he said little about budget cuts per se. Instead, like President Carter four years earlier, he implied they would largely result from ferreting out waste, fraud, and duplication and reducing the federal work force. But these never prove to be promising sources for huge budget cuts. A reminder of how the federal dollar was spent in 1980 suggests still other obstacles in his path. About forty-eight cents of each federal dollar was spent for social welfare, most of it for programs like social security, Medicare, veterans' benefits, and SSI. But candidate Reagan had promised oldsters and veterans to leave their benefits untouched and as a result had attracted many votes. Another twenty-eight cents was scheduled for defense, but he hoped to raise this to at least thirty-three cents. Interest on the national debt, chiefly to pay for past and future wars, took another ten cents. Without the new defense increment, this left only fourteen cents, which was about equally divided between all other government operations and grants-in-aid to states and localities. If the last item was left intact, just to pay for the arms buildup would require that government operations be cut by more than half, and not even the most paranoid critic of government seriously proposed that savings of this magnitude were possible.

For all practical purposes, this left grants-in-aid, entitlements with less numerous and powerful protectors than the aged and veterans, educational loans and grants, research grants, and housing programs as prime targets for the first round of budget slashing. This meant that low-income families and children, and the inner cities where many of them lived would bear the chief brunt of the new "fiscal constraints" — pegged at $41 billion in 1981. Despite this obvious fact, when the *Program for Economic Recovery* was unveiled, it abounded with assurances that "all members of society, except for the *truly needy,* will be asked to sacrifice in the effort to control spending." To this end, the Administration had developed objective principles to guide the process:

- preserve "social safety net programs"
- revise entitlements to eliminate "unintended benefits"
- reduce middle- and upper-income benefits
- recover clearly allocable costs from users of government services
- apply "sound criteria" to economic subsidy programs

- stretch out and retarget public sector capital improvement programs
- impose fiscal constraints on other programs of national interest
- consolidate categorical programs into block programs
- reduce overhead and personnel costs of the federal government (34)

To the extent that targets can be identified in terms of households, detailed review of the President's program suggests that only one of these principles clearly applied to affluent households — the intent to recover user fees from such groups as private pilots and yacht owners. Their quick success in changing the Administration's mind has been discussed. Two other groups, the "truly needy" — by which the Administration seemed to mean the nonworking poor — and the working poor were not so fortunate. Despite protestations of compassion for the former and shared sacrifices from all citizens, the bulk of contemplated budget cuts, program elimination, and policy shifts fell on these two groups. Or to put it differently, financing the arms buildup and salary hikes for military personnel became largely their responsibility.

Nor were "social safety net" programs immune from cuts. After pointing out that "not every program defended in the name of the disadvantaged can or should be considered part of the essential social safety net," the Administration identified those programs that merited the highest priority — social insurance benefits for the elderly, basic unemployment benefits, cash benefits to dependent families and individuals, and "social obligations" to veterans. "Only modest revisions," it was explained, "are proposed for these programs" (34). While it was true that no direct cuts were made in welfare grants or unemployment benefits (since both were set by the states, not the federal government), between new policy and procedural restrictions and the elimination or reduced funding of closely related programs, both groups could only end much worse off if the President's program was approved. To cast further doubts on the "social safety net" concept, before long a convenient "leak" from the White House revealed plans to cut back social security benefits, an idea that was promptly denied in the face of nationwide outrage.

The Democratic Study Group of the House of Representatives listed some impacts on the poor of the President's proposals as initially submitted to Congress (58).

- AFDC benefits would be terminated or reduced for 1.2 million children and their parents.
- About a million people would lose food stamps.
- Nutrition assistance (WIC) would be eliminated for about 700,000 low-income infants, young children, and their pregnant or lactating mothers.
- Health care would be cut for innumerable poor people by a "cap" on federal Medicaid funds and the elimination or relaxation of rules relating to eq-

uity, types and range of medical services, standards, and payment formulae.

- Over 300,000 CETA public service jobs would end at once, with all CETA jobs disappearing by September 30, 1981.
- Legal assistance would be denied hundreds of thousands of poor people unable to afford private lawyers.
- Housing assistance would be reduced for some 140,000 low-income families and individuals.

The litany can be continued almost indefinitely. Of the proposed cutbacks, most were approved — or even increased — by Congress. A few child nutrition programs were saved in part, and some programs slated for elimination survived with less money — and quite often, as with legal services for the poor, under new administration whose mission was to phase out the program. Many families were placed in double, even treble, jeopardy. Oldsters who owned their homes received less heating assistance and home weatherization benefits although fuel costs rose due to oil decontrol and gas deregulation. The jobless had less access to retraining programs, emergency relief, food stamps, and trade adjustment assistance. The working poor could easily lose AFDC, Medicaid, child day care, and low-cost mass transit at one fell swoop. Undernourished women pregnant with their first child could be denied AFDC, Medicaid, and access to supplemental nutrition programs.

In other words, rather than sharing sacrifices, they were dumped unceremoniously on the most vulnerable, poorest, and least powerful. It was this gap between stated principles and reality that soon earned the Administration the reputation for being social Darwinists at heart. The consistent targeting of cutbacks on programs for the poor, it was held, must reflect a determination to leave parents with no option but to work — at any cost to their children and at any wage or under any conditions employers chose to impose.

Subversion of the Legislative Process. The haste with which the President's program was pressured through Congress in 1981 was one of the more disheartening and alarming experiences of the year. Forced through within weeks, with no opportunity for public hearings, many legislators complained they had no precise notion of what they voted on until the new laws were published. Few had ever witnessed such a maelstrom of White House "wheeling and dealing" to win support for its program. Bypassing traditional opportunities for public input and limiting time too sharply for reasonable in-house discussion were justified by the White House and its Congressional supporters as the only way to guarantee the quick economic turnabout necessary for the President's package to succeed. Pervading everything was the President's claim to an "overwhelming mandate" from the voters. But both public opinion polls and direct word from constituents left many members of Congress in doubt, and of course many questioned that such a close election could accurately be described as an "overwhelming mandate." Notwithstanding such reservations, the practical effect of the White House style was to permit the President's men virtually a free hand to reverse forty-five years of social legislation within weeks and to force Congress to rubberstamp their decisions. To some close observers it seemed like a giant stride toward fascism. To others, it was just one more dispiriting example of our frequent impetuous, uncritical, ad hoc response to crises.

During his years in office, the President has been remarkably consistent in his approach to social welfare and to Congress. What cuts were not approved one year were demanded the next — and the next. If anyone was uncertain about his priorities, his barrage of telephone calls, penalties for dissidents, and rewards for supporters easily settled the issue. In 1982 Congress insisted on a more leisurely pace, and in the process saved a few social programs the Administration hoped to kill or severely cut back. But not until 1984, with the fall elections looming over everyone, was any notable reversal of the downward trend in federal support achieved — by skilled public interest lobbyists in conjunction with a sophisticated, determined, well-organized coalition of women's groups and the Children's Defense Fund. But while children's programs fared better, the primary burden of government savings still fell on the poor and near-poor.

Impacts of Budget Cuts, Recession, and Taxes. Sorting out the multiple misfortunes that befell the poor in recent years is not easy. Each year during Reagan's first term in office, the poverty rate was higher than it had been since the 1960s. Between 1980 and 1983 alone, the poverty count rose by 6 million people. Even though the number dropped modestly in 1984 — after two years of strong economic recovery — the poverty rate still remained stubbornly high, and actually rose for Hispanic children. Of the 5 million new poor during the first two years, the government-induced recession was held responsible for adding 1.5 million, while budget cuts added another 557,000. Researchers concluded that the poverty roster was 2.2 million higher than it would have been without the tight money policy and budget cuts of Reaganomics. The former was hardest on two parent families; the latter on families headed by women (10, 36).

After studying four major programs serving low-income households — food stamps, AFDC, Medicaid, and SSI — the Southern Regional Council reported that Administration cutbacks had forced 4 million people off the rolls by 1984 (41). This group included 3.2 million who lost food stamps, 330,000 dropped from AFDC, 300,000 from Medicaid, and 108,000 from SSI. Southern states, female-headed families, blacks, and children fared the worst. Despite the sharp rise in poverty, 680,000 fewer Southern children received federal assistance of some type than in 1980 (45).

With impact studies so often based on discontinued grants, welfare historians speculated that the actual count could be far higher. Whenever in the past harsh policies were imposed, and the poor were treated accordingly, many refused to apply however great their need. Also, denials of aid were only part of the problem. Countless thousands of families suffered cash or service reductions (40).

The losses would have been far greater had Congress in 1982 and thereafter not modified Administration proposals. As it was, social welfare programs targeted toward low-income Americans were cut from 15 per cent of the federal budget to 10 per cent between 1980 and 1985 (1). In real value, the programs serving children and their families suffered a loss of $10 billion yearly in federal funds alone and hard-pressed states could often not meet their former level of support (8).

Not unexpectedly, the poor became poorer during Reagan's first term. Each year the share of poor families with incomes below one half of the poverty threshold ranged from 32.2 to 34.7 per cent, the highest since poverty has been measured. Each year, too, found exceptionally high childhood poverty rates — higher than in any year since the mid-1960s. As Senator Moynihan of New York wrote in his new book, *Family and Nation* (31), "The United States in the 1980s may be the first society in history in which children are worse off than adults." At least, as Peter Edelman (13) commented, we should now realize that making the rich richer does not mean that something will trickle down to the poor, and that economic recovery is not a sufficient solution for poverty.

The Administration also planned huge cuts in educational and housing programs and benefits. Strong opposition nationwide and in Congress protected education to some extent. After the long series of reports showing the superior achievements of children in other modern nations, it was hoped the White House would relax its budget-cutting stance. But while the President urged higher standards, more skillful teachers, greater striving toward excellence, and replacement of routine yearly wage increments by merit raises, no additional financial help was forthcoming. Between 1981 and 1985, the federal share of the total national commitment for education fell from 9.2 per cent to 6.2 per cent. Although forty-three states raised their academic requirements, over a half million fewer children received federally assisted compensatory or remedial educational services by 1985 (8). While the average cost of higher education rose 49 per cent in private colleges and universities, and 43 per cent in their public counterparts, an average Pell grant for low-income students rose by only 29 per cent, and the maximum grant by just 9 per cent. Adjusted for inflation, total expenditures for Pell grants fell 5.7 per cent from 1981 to 1986 (8). Overall, student aid declined by 13 per cent (1).

Despite the epidemic of homelessness and a critical shortage of low-cost dwellings, federal housing budgets were slashed. Over the years the federal government invested heavily in homeownership, as it still does for Americans who have good credit and can afford to purchase homes. In 1986 homeowners' income tax deductions for mortgage interest payments alone cost the federal government an estimated $28.6 billion, up from $8.2 billion in 1979. The tax break on state and local property taxes cost another $10.8 billion in foregone federal taxes. Yet another multibillion dollar loss to the treasury results from tax-exempt revenue bonds which enable states to subsidize mortgage payments. Finally the government spends some millions insuring home mortgages so that banks will charge lower interest rates. But only 3 per cent of federal tax breaks for owner-occupied housing goes to households with incomes below $15,000 and, according to the National Association of Home Builders, the tax-exempt revenue bonds which financed almost 400,000 homes in 1984 are rarely available to either poor or moderate-income families (8). Because they are disproportionately poor, blacks and Hispanics profit much less from these subsidies than whites.

In 1983, the Congressional Research Service reported, three fifths of households with incomes below half of the national median income lived in physically inadequate, overcrowded, or exorbitantly priced housing. Low-cost housing is virtually nonexistent in the nation these days. Nonetheless, new housing starts for multifamily dwellings (which the poor are most apt to afford) fell from 456,000 in 1978 to 283,000 in 1983, and continue to decline. At present an estimated 2.5 million families are displaced from their homes yearly by either government or private action, including demolition, abandonment, arson, and conversion to condominiums or nonresidential use.

Even before budget cutting swept Washington, only about one-quarter of low-income renter households received any federal assistance. But from the outset the Reagan Administration wanted the federal government out of the housing market. Between 1981 and 1985, the appropriated budget authority* for low-income housing assistance was slashed 60 per cent, while funding for low-income homeownership loans and rental assistance was cut by 50 per cent. For fiscal 1986, the Administration urged a moratorium on all new commitments for "assisted" housing; Congress rejected the idea but lowered the budget considerably. Then, as part of its "privatization" policy, the Administration proposed selling off a number of U.S. assets, including the government's public housing stock. This news left the widespread impression that ideology had blinded political leadership to both the nature and extent of the low-income housing crisis.

Rising taxes constituted still another pitfall for poor households during the 1980s. If they heard or read about tax cuts in 1981, they must have been

---

*This concept includes funds for current expenditures plus the amount that can be obligated yearly for the construction of new units. This means that the immediate impact of budget cuts is far less than the long-term impact.

very confused to learn how much they owed at the end of the year. Although the cut in marginal tax rates saved households with incomes under $10,000 about $20 yearly between 1981 and 1984, this gain was overwhelmed by tax increases due to the fact that personal exemptions, standard deductions (zero bracket amount), and the low wage earners' tax credit were not indexed to rise with inflation. All three items help to determine the income tax threshold — the level at which households become liable for federal income taxes. Over the years, as part of the nation's antipoverty policy, federal lawmakers kept the tax threshold above the poverty threshold so that most low-income households would owe no federal income taxes. The need to raise these three items was overlooked in the late 1970s and rejected in 1981 when marginal tax rates were lowered. The result is shown on Table 12–1. Soaring inflation resulted in narrowing the gap from 16.4 per cent to 2.5 per cent between 1979 and 1980. Then the relationship shifted. In 1981 the poverty threshold exceeded the income threshold by 7 per cent; by 1984 the gap grew to 17.2 per cent. In that year Congress made small adjustments in the three crucial items, and the gap narrowed somewhat. But considerably larger adjustments are needed to shift the federal income tax from a pro-poverty to an anti-poverty instrument or even to neutralize it in this regard. A recent study by the Center on Budget and Policy Priorities concluded that 696,000 members of families with children were pushed into poverty by federal tax policies in 1979; by 1984 the

TABLE 12–1. Relationship Between Poverty Level and Income Tax Threshold for a Family of Four, 1975–1985

Year	Poverty Level for Family of Four	Income Tax Threshold	Percentage by Which Tax Threshold Falls Below or Exceeds Poverty Level
1975	5,500	6,692	21.7
1976	5,815	6,892	18.5
1977	6,191	7,533	22.0
1978	6,662	7,533	13.1
1979	7,412	8,626	16.4
1980	8,414	8,626	2.5
1981	9,287	8,634	− 7.0
1982	9,862	8,727	−11.5
1983	10,178	8,783	−13.7
1984	10,612	8,783	−17.2[a]
1985	11,003	9,437	−14.2[a]

[a]Estimated.

Source: "Federal Tax Treatment of Individuals Below the Poverty Level." Hearings, U.S. Congress, Joint Committee on Taxation, June 1985. Reproduced in *A Children's Defense Budget: An Analysis of the FY 1987 Federal Budget and Children.* Washington, D.C.: Children's Defense Fund, 1986, p. 162.

number had tripled — 2,147,000 (50). By failing to adjust personal exemptions, standard deductions, and the low earners' tax credit, the tax base — the number of people owing taxes — was broadened at the bottom of the income scale and the size of the tax bill owed by the poor increased fivefold as the rich basked in huge tax cuts and most of their loopholes remained intact. Anomalies of this order explain the widespread insistence on comprehensive reform to assure a fair tax system. Fortunately this goal was accepted by both the Senate and House of Representatives as Congress shaped its tax reform bill in 1986, which means that the federal income tax system will again become a powerful anti-poverty instrument.

Impact of Reaganomics on Blacks. Of all the groups victimized by Reaganomics, none has fared worse than blacks. The firm stance of the Administration in favor of tax-exempt status for blatantly racist colleges sent out an early warning of more trouble to come. Soon it was apparent that virtually all programs planned for the greatest cuts were those that serve blacks disproportionately (14). Black youth unemployment rates, always too high, were over 50 per cent during the spring of 1983. Long-term joblessness rose by over 70 per cent during the first few years of Reagan's first term. The Equal Employment Opportunity Commission cut by half the number of discrimination suits brought against employers, and the Administration proposed that small companies no longer be required to file written affirmative action plans, although they were often the worst offenders. Affirmative action, some observers insisted, was virtually gutted (16). Blacks soon learned that they could expect no support for tougher fair housing laws, despite continued evidence of lax enforcement. In the first two years of the Reagan Administration, only two minor suits were filed against landlords, as contrasted with an average of thirty-two yearly in each of the previous administrations. Fewer than 5 per cent of the first 3,231 presidential appointees were black, and not unexpectedly, considering the views of Washington leadership, greater tolerance for discrimination was soon spreading across the nation (14, 60).*

Balance Sheet for Tax Savings and Budget Cuts

While no study of the net impact of all budget cuts and the changing incidence of federal taxes has been made to date, in 1984 the Congressional Budget Office calculated the net impact of the cut in marginal tax rates and the loss or reduction of benefits in cash and four major noncash programs — Medicare, Medicaid, food stamps, and housing subsidies. Table 12–2 shows the results for various income groups. It should be noted first that

---

*This trend may be somewhat checked by a group of decisions handed down by the U.S. Supreme Court in June 1986. In essence, the court approved affirmative action plans intended to correct documented past discrimination.

TABLE 12–2. Tax and Budget Cuts: The Impact on Household Incomes[a]

	All households	$10,000 or less	$10,000– 20,000	$20,000– 40,000	$40,000– 80,000	$80,000 or more
Gain from tax cuts	$1,090	$ 20	$330	$1,200	$3,080	$8,390
Loss in cash benefits	−170	−250	−210	−130	−90	−90
Loss in noncash benefits	−100	−160	−90	−60	−80	−40
Net Gain or Loss	$ 820	$−390	$30	$1,010	$2,900	$8,270

[a]Projections for the 1984 calendar year. Numbers have been rounded.

Source: Congressional Budget Office. Reprinted in *New York Times*, April 4, 1984, p. A17. In article by Robert Pear. "Budget Study Finds Cuts Cost the Poor as the Rich Gained."

the loss in tax revenues far outweighs the savings to the treasury from budget cuts — $1,090 as compared with $270 for a net loss of $820 per household. As for the impact on different income groups, despite the protestations about protecting "social safety net programs," the poorest group of households was the only one that ended in the red — by an average of $390. The richest, on the other hand, enjoyed an average net gain of $8,270.

While the tax cuts were egregiously inequitable in their impact, it should be kept in mind that despite the political hyperbole about everyone sharing sacrifices and gains, the goals and political philosophy of the Administration inevitably resulted in the distribution shown in the table. The only error was in assuming that well-off people, given an incentive windfall by government, would rally behind their president and invest their gains productively — and that most other families would at least save rather than spend their smaller increments.

A few reminders may clarify some anomalies in the distribution of benefits in Table 12–2. First, poverty thresholds for four person families hovered near or above $10,000 during these years and rose above $19,000 for eight person households. So the poverty population spills well over into the group with incomes between $10,000 and $20,000. As for the noncash benefits — all of which are selective — received by upper income households, until very recently this was possible and perfectly legal. AFDC families, for instance, might be asked to share someone's home, including their close relatives', but the family would be treated as a separate unit for welfare purposes unless the relatives involved were liable for support under state law. Now that virtually everyone in the household is so regarded, many grants have been discontinued. Another anomaly about census data, on which this table is based, should also be noted. Information about household income is collected in March of each year for all current members of the household; but they each report their income for the preceding year, irrespective of where they lived. Given the mobility of families — as young couples move in or out of parental homes, parents divorce or reunite, and children move back and forth among grandparents, parents, or other relatives — it is often true that someone who qualified for food stamps in the preceding year had moved in with her parents by the time income data were collected. About the only safe generalization, in other words, is that a new policy or a better-paying job or a reduction in benefits caused someone in the household to lose some transfer income.

Still another approach to measuring the impact of Reaganomics was used by the Urban Institute. By calculating changes between 1980 and 1984 in real disposable family income, they found that the poorest 40 per cent of families suffered a loss while the upper 60 per cent enjoyed a gain. When each quintile's share of aggregate income was compared over time, it turned out that the lowest three quintiles each received a lower share of the total in 1984, and their loss was all offset by the increased share of the richest quintile — further evidence that income distribution became more concentrated in Reagan's first term. Detailed investigation resulted in a conclusion that a "substantial part" of the shift resulted from Reagan budget cutting and tax reduction policies. Moreover, the report added, "there is little room for the agenda to shift back," since the deficits will exert constant pressure for more retrenchment in benefits for poor and middle-income families (42).

Many analysts have noted the increased concentration of income during recent years, but in early 1986 two reports, one by Sheldon Danziger and Peter Gottschalk and the other by Frank Levy and Richard Michel, suggested that the focus should be broader than the impact of Reaganomics. Both studies emphasized a long-standing and disturbing trend: the fundamental deterioration of wages in the economy. Looking at the income of families with children between 1973 and 1984, the first study reported that the real median income of the poorest fifth of families declined by a third during this period, of the next poorest quintile by a fifth, and of the middle quintile by a tenth, while the median of the richest quintile held essentially constant. The poorest fifth started with just under 6 per cent of aggregate income and ended with slightly more than 4 per cent. The richest, on the other hand, started with 38 per cent and ended with over 42 per cent. While the increased percentage of families headed by women, accompanied by a decline in the value of government benefits to families under sixty-five years of age, contributed to the problem, the decline in the value of wages which make up the bulk of family income was far more important. Real average weekly earnings fell by an eighth between 1973 and 1984. Back in 1973, 21.5 per cent of family heads with children made too little to sustain a family of four at the poverty level even with full-time, year-round jobs. By 1984 that figure rose to 29.9 per cent. The wage loss experienced by family heads was somewhat offset by the increased number of working wives, but their wages fell far short of filling the gap (15).

Why did wages falter? One important reason is the decline in manufacturing, especially of durable goods, where high-paid union workers congregated. As jobs were lost, new ones were found primarily and increasingly in the service sector where wages are considerably lower on the average and unions relatively scarce. Part of the explanation is in the rise of foreign competition, which frightens even unions into wage concessions, which they may never recoup. Another reason is the advent of baby boomers in the labor force, which usually means younger workers earning lower wages. Then there is the pressure exerted by high unemployment rates, especially in recent years. Unemployment during the 1980s, labor economists point out, is a different phenomenon from that in the 1970s. It has been much higher, of considerably longer duration, and has not declined with economic recovery at nearly the pace experienced after previous recessions. Nor was there such stubbornly high unemployment among young workers —blacks and Hispanics especially — as in the past five years. Combined with the Administration's refusal to raise the minimum wage since 1980, the budget cuts — which not only lowered income but dumped service workers into the jobless ranks, lower AFDC income ceilings for families with an employed adult, new penalties for AFDC mothers who give up jobs, and an exceedingly clear signal at the expense of air traffic controllers — and the public — that strikers could expect no sympathy in Washington resulted in intense pressure on wages. The only cheerful note is that demographic changes are beginning to push wages up for young service workers, notably in the fast food chains. But this is little comfort to prime age jobless factory workers.

No one yet knows which of these factors weighed most heavily in the downward trend in wages. But as a *Washington Post* editor wrote, "some fundamental and fearsome things have happened to the economy" since the recessions began in the 1970s that "bode no good for the future." The fear among some economists is that the Administration is oblivious to the gravity of the problem, being preoccupied with its own ideology and its optimistic assumption that permanent prosperity is here at last, thanks to Reaganomics. "But the recovery is cyclical," Thurow (53) observes, "not permanent," and nothing has been learned about inflation that was not already known: if the economy is sufficiently strangled and voters are willing to condone joblessness for as many as 12 million workers at one time, and countless more over a year, the strongest inflation can be stopped in its tracks.

Impact on the States

In 1981 the Reagan Administration recommended a significant devolution of responsibility for social welfare services to the states. Toward this end, the plan was to consolidate a long list of special purpose grants into a few block grants and to reduce funding by about a fifth. Then old laws would be supplanted with new ones shorn of requirements that protected equity, access, state matching levels, accountability, and service priorities; and responsibility for allocating funds and administering block grants would be the states' prerogative. While Congress approved this package in principle, the consolidation process fell far short of the Administration's goals, primarily because members of Congress feared that some relatively small, new, but important children's services might lose out in the scramble for funds. In 1982 the Administration persisted with its plan, this time in the form of a "SWAP" package whereby the states would take over full responsibility for food stamps and AFDC in exchange for the federal government assuming full charge of Medicaid. After governors pointed to inequities in the exchange and resisted the idea of taking over programs they had long felt should be sole federal responsibilities, "SWAP" was soon tabled. Since then budget cutting has been the major approach.

At the state level the loss of federal funds to both cities and states, accomplished as it was with precious little warning, forced every manner of adjustment simply to remain solvent. By early 1983 twenty-two states had deficits topping $5.7 billion (57). Thirty-three had trimmed budgets, imposed hiring freezes, laid off workers, or deferred paying bills. Sixteen others had balanced their budgets by using all of these approaches.

The decline of federal funding and the removal of legal protections for current and potential service consumers threatened to widen the gap between rich and poor states, and between inner cities and affluent suburbs. To make matters worse, the severely ailing economy caused state outlays for welfare and other human services to soar, while revenues from income, business, sales, and excise taxes dropped sharply. Almost two thirds of the nation's largest cities expected to be in the red by the end of 1983.

Both the states and cities were soon in a flurry of activity, searching for new funds, new methods of cutting costs without sacrificing services, and new partnerships with the private sector. Over the next few years various types of taxes went up and down like teeter-totters as state and city budgets lunged between surplus and deficit. User fees became common for municipal services ranging from library service to tree trimming. Cities leased public property, like golf courses, tennis courts, parking lots, and various other recreational facilities to private operators, who then charged sufficiently high fees to pay the city and still reap a profit. Financial stringency encouraged consolidation of cities and suburbs. Special purpose districts and authorities were created to provide all types of services, including fire protection, parks, health care, libraries, water and sewage disposal, garbage collection, and street maintenance. Within three years after Reagan took office, 29,000 such special districts were spotted across the nation, and they spent over $25 billion yearly (4). Some had been formed in earlier years, but most sprang up during the 1980s. By 1985 numerous cities had turned to private firms to manage their adult jails, and seventy-five communities had turned fire fighting over to the private sector (22, 56).

Views regarding the respective quality and cost of private and public services varied. While private business enthusiasts pointed to lower costs under private management, critics complained of thinner services, slower response time, overreliance on low-paid, essentially untrained, hourly help or volunteers, as in some private fire-fighting firms, and the harsh consequences for people who forgot to pay their bills or could not afford to do so. With the decline in wages and the rise in poverty, many people believed the trend toward privatization presaged further polarization of income classes, neighborhoods, and races, and a dangerous decline in community. The mere act of shifting public services to the private sector was held by some to reduce job opportunities and/or wages for blacks who had increasingly held civil service jobs which paid relatively well, and now found themselves fighting job discrimination and lower wages in the small business sector (29, 55).

But by the mid-decade it was apparent that something remarkable had happened at the state level. A new brand of leaders — vital, sophisticated, highly competent, and often socially progressive — had emerged in state capitals. The improvement was not credited to Reaganomics directly or indirectly, but was viewed as a long-awaited consequence of the shift to one man – one vote. As predicted, giving due weight to the urban vote had produced better educated, more far-seeing, less parochial, and far more competent legislators and governors. Legislatures were more likely than in the past to meet annually; lawmakers were better paid and better serviced; women and blacks were much more numerous. While the federal government had become awash in red ink and showed little sign of resolving the paralysis in decision making, state governors and legislators had turned historically high deficits into surpluses. They had won elections *after* raising taxes even in recession years. The schools had been strengthened, and while funding for social services and health care still lagged behind the 1979 level when inflation was taken into account, state leadership was increasingly giving top priority to children in the hope, as Haynes Johnson (23) put it, "that the next generation of Americans will be better able to compete in the tougher global economy of the 1980s and beyond." Some traditionally laggard states updated child protective statutes, initiated comprehensive children's services, and provided far more generous funding. Many raised AFDC grants. Overall, in personnel and government performance, it was clear that the quality of our statehouses and state legislatures had notably improved (11).

So whatever motivated the effort to rid the federal government of its long-standing obligation for social welfare, the timing was our good fortune. To date state leadership has proved to be more than a match for the most determined effort to undermine and dismantle social welfare services.

Looking Toward the Future _____

There is no *intrinsic* reason for anyone in America who is willing and able to work to be out of a job. There is no intrinsic reason why every American should not have access to the basic necessities of life. In the face of this nation's enormous wealth, any economic ideology that cannot produce employment at a decent minimum standard of living for all Americans willing to participate in the work of our society is a failure by the simple test of common sense.

Gar Alperovitz and Jeff Faux (3)

The future scope and size of social welfare depends in good measure on the future of the political economy. Elizabeth Drew's brilliant reporting on how money infects the political process gives more than ample warning of the crisis confronting our democracy. For years now, unable to resist the spigots of money turned on for a favorable vote on measures that exacerbate inflation and further the decline in economic productivity, politicians have turned aside criticism by blaming the poor and jobless. If Americans enjoyed a higher level of economic literacy, this self-serving, cruelly divisive search for villains would promptly be repudiated. As it is, between our economic naiveté, the disarray among our economic mentors, and the strain of managing when real earnings rarely rise, voters are easy prey for the most outworn and self-serving nostrums.

Today the major impediment to full production and full employment *with* stable prices, according to a growing group of thoughtful economists, is not the lack of viable proposals but the widespread misperceptions about the nature of our political economy and how it works. As Alperovitz and Faux (3) put it, "the problem is the lack of fit between the way the world actually is" and the way it is *perceived* to be. The consequence of this "poor fit" is that we tend to accept as inevitable and necessary what is simply the result of poor management of the economy. A case in point is the apparent conviction of many people that high rates of unemployment are an essential check on inflation. So, rather than demanding better performance by leadership, the lucky ones let the jobless pay the price. Yet there is no hard evidence proving the alleged causal trade-off between unemployment and inflation rates, and all over the industrial world during the 1970s both rates rose simultaneously.

Similarly, we have heard for years that government involvement in the economy is intrinsically damaging. Yet one of the major success stories of our economy — its fabulous food production — is the result of decades of deliberate, consistent government investment in agricultural research and ubiquitous consultative services to farmers. In other words it is not an "invisible hand," averse to any mortal interference, that determines our economic destiny, but rather the ideologies, decisions, oversights, and greed of fallible human beings.

We all have a great stake in helping to correct such misperceptions. The price that our failure to accept reality exacts from all of us — the distortion of democratic values, the fracturing of the sense of community, the hardening of hearts against the jobless and poor, the predictable decline of our standard of living — may still not equal in severity the price paid by millions of jobless people who see no future for themselves nor any way to protect their children from the same fate. It is well to remember, as we read about still another study of the breakdown of the black family, that when unemployment experience is held constant for blacks and whites, the difference between their divorce and separation rates virtually disappears.

Also since Americans have condoned progressively higher unemployment rates following each recession since World War II, unless we change our course, the day will surely come when any of us could be among the long-term jobless.

The new breed of economists insist that a full production economy with full employment and stable prices is within our reach. Fine blueprints for achieving this goal have been developed, one by Alperovitz and Faux in their recent book, *Revitalizing America* (3), and another, dwelling on similar themes, *The Second Industrial Divide: Possibilities for Prosperity,* by Piore and Sabel (38).* They make no pretence that the task ahead will be easy. But neither was putting a man on the moon. We first need, they tell us, a new political ethic in Washington. The federal government, as the only institution with the scope and resources to provide leadership in managing the economy, will have to forego its pattern of backscene, hidden payoffs in the form of expensive subsidies, tax loopholes, extravagantly overpriced defense contracts, indiscriminate loans to failing corporations, and other products of wheeling and dealing with powerful interest groups eager to claim a share of the largest flow of funds in the nation. Instead, what is needed is open, informed, principled, steady planning and resource allocation, based on explicit and widely shared values. If we can find the moral strength to accept such an ethic for ourselves and for government, and to hold leaders accountable, we can move ahead with the reform agenda.

Alperovitz and Faux ground their proposals in the widely shared values of fairness and decentralization, with open democratic economic planning to be carried out routinely at the local, possibly regional, and federal levels, but always directed toward enhancing freedom and strengthening local communities. Thus they speak of both national full production and community full production, of national full employment and community full employment. The greatest problems of the economy, they have concluded, are the long indifference to the economic health of communities and the absence of a feeling of *community* — the spontaneous sharing of people bonded by similar traditions and experiences that move them beyond their private preoccupations to a concern for the greater good. It is small and medium-sized firms that have been part of the community for years where workers and management make the special effort during hard times that makes the difference between success and failure. It is determined neighbors pulling together that result in clean, safe, and attractive neighborhoods. Years of high labor mobility have exacerbated our rootlessness. They have also left countless "throw-away" cities, houses, and unem-

---

*Two other fine books in which the authors examine very similar issues are Robert Kuttner's *The Economic Illusion* (26) and Shirley Williams' *Politics is for People* (61). Williams, founder of the new Social Democratic Party in the United Kingdom, gives many insights about problems in her own country as well as the United States.

ployed workers behind. The rebonding of Americans and the strengthening of local economies are major objectives of the reform proposals. Investment capital would be deliberately targeted toward areas with surplus labor and surplus housing, thereby preventing waste and decay while enabling jobless workers to remain in their home communities, knowing that new jobs would soon be available. The goals, in other words, are sustained full production and sustained full employment at both community and national levels.

In working out plans to control inflation, Alperovitz and Faux stress the need for a "conserving ethic" on the part of everyone. They focus specific proposals on the sectors that have been most inflationary in recent decades: the basic necessities — energy, food, health, and housing. Here, too, their perspective is both national and local. In the food sector, for instance, they not only recommend different national policies and different formulae for restraining the price-setting power of food oligopolies, but they also stress ways we can all save on food: growing and processing food in every region of the country rather than concentrating it in a few states and organizing far more farmers' markets and consumer cooperatives are just a few of their many ideas. In the housing area, the authors point to very successful local housing developments sponsored by unions and nonprofit organizations, and to the valuable experience gained by local housing authorities during years of collaboration with the federal government in providing housing for low-income families. In each sector, in other words, they search for local resources and local initiatives, and stress the development of local planning skills. What Alperovitz and Faux see as most promising is not vertical but horizontal planning and economic development.

As Tobin of Yale (54) urged years back, Alperovitz and Faux drew up their guidelines on the assumption that the basic necessities would be guaranteed to everyone — for the vast majority through steady work at decent wages. In supporting the "right to work," they clarify that this does not mean the right to get drunk on the job, to give less than an honest day's work, to be uncooperative or unproductive. It simply means that if freedom means anything, it means that everyone able and willing to work should have realistic opportunities to do so in jobs that pay at least enough to cover the basic necessities. The freedom of employers, too, would be enhanced by the assurance of consistent, predictable economic policy that makes long-range planning possible.

Comprehensive health care coverage for everyone is another essential. They doubt, as many others do, that health care costs can be sufficiently controlled so long as the "fee for service" payment pattern continues, and they see many areas where reasonable constraints on greed are needed. In this sector, too, they believe decentralized administration is the preferred model.

This brief sketch merely gives the flavor of numerous proposals for solving the political and economic problems that have brought about the long decline in economic productivity and threaten much greater inroads on our standard of living. Nothing that is proposed is beyond our capabilities, once we reach consensus on what we want to achieve and the values we wish to reaffirm.

If we decide to move in this direction, some major social welfare programs could become much smaller and more manageable or, as with food stamps, unnecessary. The role of the schools in educating and reeducating will take on heightened significance, as will personal and social services. But before the goals are achieved, a good case can be made for transferring *all* income maintenance programs to the federal government and leaving states and communities responsible for the services. Our hodgepodge of income strategies could be more readily rationalized if brought together. Also, it is logical to give to that level of government chiefly responsible for economic policy the obligation of paying the cost of inefficient management of the economy. Standardized, uniform benefits in programs like unemployment insurance and AFDC could also help in the long run to equalize wage structures over the country.

The vitality of the social services, on the other hand, is better assured by state–local financing and organization. Responsive, creative services require intimate awareness of the traditions, expectations, norms, and networks of the various groups in a given community, and effective services need to be flexible, to reflect a realistic grasp of the qualities needed in paid personnel and volunteers, and to be accountable to the people they serve. By its very size and distance and the degree of bureaucratization necessary to discharge its major functions, the federal government has rarely been well attuned to the needs or potentials of community social services. Even though income and service programs are separated, the two could routinely come together in behalf of individuals or groups that could benefit from both. Eligibility for AFDC, for instance, could automatically trigger referrals to community-based information and referral services.

Underlying and pervading every plan to restore and sustain a healthy economy and to rid ourselves of the plague of periodic inflation is the need to come together again and to learn to share both the sacrifices and the benefits. "A meaningful vision of community," Alperovitz and Faux write,

> is the only way to unite those who are now isolated and bring us all back into citizenship. The metamorphosis of the American economy continues. It is bringing us face to face with our responsibility for the country's future. The market does not choose. *We* choose. (3)

References

1. Adams, Gordon. "Changed Priorities and Our National Security — or Spare Parts and Spare People." Mimeographed. Speech given at the National Women's Democratic Club, Washington, D.C., October 23, 1984.

2. Alm, Richard. "The American Savings Slump — A Fluke or a Real Threat?" *U.S. News & World Report,* **99** (November 25, 1985), pp. 64–65.

3. Alperovitz, Gar and Jeff Faux. *Rebuilding America.* New York: Pantheon Books, 1984, pp. 72, 157, 281, passim.

4. Barnett, David L. "States, Cities Struggle to Make Ends Meet." *U.S. News & World Report,* **94** (February 14, 1983), pp. 87–89.

5. Berry, John. "Deficits, Slow Growth Taint Success of Reaganomics." *Washington Post,* June 23, 1985.

6. Bethel, Thomas N. "The Tax-Cut 'Revolution': Money Will Run to the Same Old Shelters." *Washington Monthly,* **13** (July/August 1981), pp. 37–43.

7. Boyer, Edward. "The Recovery is Reshaping the Economy." *Fortune,* **108** (October 3, 1983), pp. 60–65.

8. *A Children's Defense Budget: An Analysis of the FY 1987 Federal Budget and Children.* Washington, D.C.: Children's Defense Fund, 1986, pp. 60–71, 106–118, 158–167, 193–205, Appendix A.

9. Clemente, Lila. "World Economy Remains Weak: Debt and Stagnation Abound." *Investment News,* February 1983, p. 1.

10. "Congress Study Finds Reagan Budget Curbs Put 557,000 People in Poverty." *New York Times,* July 26, 1984.

11. Doyle, Dennis P. and Terry W. Hartle. "The States Are Leading as Washington Follows." *Washington Post,* September 8, 1985.

12. Drew, Elizabeth. "A Reporter in Washington: Sketchbook." *The New Yorker,* **57** (June 8, 1981), p. 141.

13. Edelman, Peter B. "The Headlines Mask Some Very Bad Numbers." *Washington Post,* September 2, 1985.

14. *Falling Behind: A Report on How Blacks Have Fared Under the Reagan Policies.* Washington, D.C.: Center on Budget and Policy Priorities, 1984.

15. "From Poor to Poorer." Editorial. *Washington Post,* February 1, 1986.

16. Gest, Ted. "Civil Rights Drive Shifts to Low Gear." *U.S. News & World Report,* **97** (July 2, 1984), pp. 27–30.

17. Gillies, Archibald. "Start Planning for Post-Reagan America." *New York Times,* March 5, 1986.

18. Greider, William. "The Education of David Stockman." *The Atlantic Monthly,* **29** (December 1981), pp. 27–54.

19. Heilbroner, Robert and Lester Thurow. *Five Economic Challenges.* Englewood Cliffs, N.J.: Prentice-Hall, Inc., 1981, pp. 13–14.

20. Heinemann, H. Erich. "Reagan's Shift in Emphasis." *New York Times,* January 7, 1983.

21. Heller, Walter W. "Supply-Side Follies of 1981." *Wall Street Journal,* June 12, 1981.

22. Herbers, John. "Larger Governments Assuming Services from Cities." *New York Times,* February 20, 1984.

23. Johnson, Haynes. "Gambling with the Nation's Future." *Washington Post,* December 8, 1985.

24. ———. "The 134-Mile-High Stack." *Washington Post,* September 22, 1985.

25. Kilborn, Peter T. "Reagan Economics Record Called Good but Mixed." *New York Times,* October 24, 1984.

26. Kuttner, Robert. *The Economic Illusion: False Choices Between Prosperity and Social Justice.* Boston: Houghton Mifflin Co., 1984.

27. Lekachman, Robert. *Economists at Bay: Why the Experts Will Never Solve Your Problems.* New York: McGraw-Hill Book Co., 1976.
28. Lewis, Anthony. "If It Squeals, It's Pork." *New York Times,* December 3, 1981.
29. Main, Jeremy. "When Public Services Go Private." *Fortune,* **111** (May 27, 1985), pp. 92–102.
30. May, Todd, Jr. and Vivian Browstein. "Fortune Forecasts: Business Clamps Down on Costs." *Fortune,* **106** (September 6, 1982), pp. 29–30.
31. Moynihan, Daniel Patrick. *Family and Nation.* New York: Harcourt, Brace, Jovanovich, 1986.
32. New York Times News Service: Washington. "Federal Study Says Poor Get Poorer, Rich Get Richer." *Baltimore Sun,* April 4, 1984.
33. Nordhaus, William. "Forum: Economic Affairs: Reagan's Dubious Tax Revolution." *New York Times,* August 9, 1981.
34. Office of Management and Budget. *A Program for Economic Recovery.* Washington, D.C.: U.S. Government Printing Office, February 18, 1981, passim.
35. Pear, Robert. "Automatic Spending Cuts Set Today." *New York Times,* March 1, 1986.
36. ―――. "Budget Study Finds Cuts Cost the Poor as the Rich Gained." *New York Times,* April 4, 1984.
37. Pechman, Joseph A. *Who Paid the Taxes, 1966–1985?* Washington, D.C.: Brookings Institution, 1985.
38. Piore, Michael J. and Charles F. Sabel. *The Second Industrial Divide: Possibilities for Prosperity.* New York: Basic Books, Inc., Publishers, 1984.
39. "Requiem for Reaganomics." Editorial. *New York Times,* November 19, 1982.
40. Rich, Spencer. "Food-Stamp, Welfare Benefits Down." *Washington Post,* March 24, 1985.
41. ―――. "4 Million Reported Cut From Welfare." *Washington Post,* March 24, 1985.
42. ―――. "Report Says President Aided Rich." *Washington Post,* August 16, 1984.
43. Rivlin, Alice M. Ed. *Economic Choices 1984.* Washington, D.C.: Brookings Institution, 1984, p. 30.
44. Rowen, Hobart. "Gramm/Rudman Is Pure Mischief." *Washington Post,* October 17, 1985.
45. Schmidt, William E. "Study Says Reagan's Cuts in Aid to Poor Affected South the Most." *New York Times,* March 15, 1985.
46. Seligman, Daniel. "Why Americans Won't Save Enough." *Fortune,* **109** (April 2, 1984), pp. 26–36.
47. Stuart, Alexander. "Leasing Leaves the Harbor." *Fortune,* **107** (January 24, 1983), pp. 91–94.
48. Sundquist, James L. "Has America Lost Its Social Conscience — and How Will It Get It Back?" Mimeographed. Paper Delivered at Florence Heller Graduate School for Advanced Studies in Social Welfare, Brandeis University, November 21, 1985.
49. Swardson, Anne. "Rich Pay Less Tax, Poor Pay More; Study Says System Is Less Progressive." *Washington Post,* January 24, 1985.
50. *Taxing the Poor.* Washington, D.C.: Center on Budget and Policy Priorities, 1984.

51. Taylor, Paul. "Most Americans Oppose Reagan Budget Priorities." *Washington Post,* February 14, 1986.
52. Thurow, Lester C. *Dangerous Currents.* New York: Random House, 1983, pp. 124–141.
53. ————. "How to Get Out of the Economic Rut." *New York Review,* February 14, 1985, pp. 9–12.
54. Tobin, James. "On Limiting the Domain of Inequality." *Journal of Law and Economics,* **13** (October 1970), pp. 263–277.
55. Tolchin, Martin. "Localities Shift to Private Firefighters." *New York Times,* July 28, 1985.
56. ————. "More Cities Paying Industry to Provide Public Services." *New York Times,* May 28, 1985.
57. "Tomorrow: A Look Ahead From the Nation's Capital." *U.S. News & World Report,* **94** (February 14, 1983), pp. 87–89.
58. U.S. House of Representatives, Democratic Study Group. "The War on Poverty." Special Report No. 97–15, April 8, 1981, p. 3.
59. "Wall Street Week" Transcript, "Hey Jude!" November 13, 1981, pp. 9–16.
60. Wiessler, David A. and Jeannye Thornton. "Minorities' Drive Thrown in Reverse?" *U.S. News & World Report,* **93** (September 27, 1982), pp. 40–42.
61. Williams, Shirley. *Politics is for People.* Cambridge, Mass.: Harvard University Press, 1981.

Index